Questioning Collapse

Human Resilience, Ecological Vulnerability, and the Aftermath of Empire

Questioning Collapse challenges scholars and popular writers who advance the thesis that societies – past and present – collapse because of behavior that destroyed their environments or because of overpopulation. In a series of highly accessible and closely argued essays, a team of internationally recognized scholars brings history and context to bear in their radically different analyses of iconic events, such as the deforestation of Easter Island, the cessation of the Norse colony in Greenland, the faltering of nineteenth-century China, the migration of ancestral peoples away from Chaco Canyon in the American Southwest, the crisis of Lowland Maya kingship, and other societies that purportedly "collapsed." Collectively, these essays demonstrate that resilience in the face of societal crises, rather than collapse, is the leitmotif of the human story from the earliest civilizations to the present. Scrutinizing the notion that Euro-American colonial triumphs were an accident of geography, *Questioning Collapse* also critically examines the complex historical relationship between race and political labels of societal "success" and "failure."

Patricia A. McAnany is Kenan Eminent Professor in the Department of Anthropology at the University of North Carolina, Chapel Hill. A member of the editorial board of the *Journal of Anthropological Archaeology*, she has received fellowships from the National Endowment for the Humanities, Dumbarton Oaks, and the Radcliffe Institute for Advanced Study at Harvard University. She is the principal investigator of the Xibun Archaeological Research Project in Belize (www.bu.edu/tricia) and of the Maya Area Cultural Heritage Initiative (www.machiproject.org), which works with descendant Maya communities. She has authored *Living with the Ancestors: Kinship and Kingship in Ancient Maya Society*; edited *K'axob: Ritual, Work and Family in an Ancient Maya Village*; and recently co-edited *Dimensions of Ritual Economy*.

Norman Yoffee is a scholar of ancient Mesopotamia and social evolutionary and anthropological theory. He teaches in the Departments of Near Eastern Studies and Anthropology at the University of Michigan, Ann Arbor. He is the author and editor of eleven books, including *Myths of the Archaic State: Evolution of the Earliest Cities, States, and Civilizations; Excavating Asian History: Interdisciplinary Studies in History and Archaeology;* and *Negotiating the Past in the Past: Identity, Memory, and Landscape in Archaeological Research*, as well as the editor of the *Cambridge World Archaeology* series.

Questioning Collapse

Human Resilience, Ecological Vulnerability, and the Aftermath of Empire

Edited by

PATRICIA A. McANANY
University of North Carolina, Chapel Hill

NORMAN YOFFEE
University of Michigan, Ann Arbor

CAMBRIDGE
UNIVERSITY PRESS

CAMBRIDGE UNIVERSITY PRESS
Cambridge, New York, Melbourne, Madrid, Cape Town,
Singapore, São Paulo, Delhi, Mexico City

Cambridge University Press
32 Avenue of the Americas, New York, NY 10013-2473, USA

www.cambridge.org
Information on this title: www.cambridge.org/9780521733663

© Cambridge University Press 2010

First published 2010
Reprinted 2010 (twice), 2011, 2012

A catalog record for this publication is available from the British Library.

Library of Congress Cataloging in Publication Data

Questioning collapse : human resilience, ecological vulnerability, and the
aftermath of empire / edited by Patricia A. McAnany and Norman Yoffee.
    p. cm.
Includes bibliographical references and index.
ISBN 978-0-521-51572-6 (hardback) – ISBN 978-0-521-73366-3 (pbk.)
1. Social archaeology.   2. Archaeology and history.   3. Civilization –
History.   4. Regression (Civilization)   5. Resilience (Personality trait) –
History.   6. Human ecology – History.   7. Imperialism – History.   8. Race
relations – Political aspects – History.   I. McAnany, Patricia Ann.   II. Yoffee,
Norman.   III. Title.
CC72.4.Q44   2009
930.1–dc22   2008044128

ISBN 978-0-521-51572-6 Hardback
ISBN 978-0-521-73366-3 Paperback

Contents

List of Figures

Contributors

For additional information about contributors, see short autobiographies placed at the end of each chapter.

Joel Berglund
Retired Vice-Director, Greenland National Museum and Archives,
    Nuuk, Greenland, now living in Gothenburg, Sweden
berglund.joel@telia.com
cv at sitemaker.umich.edu/nyoffee

David Cahill
Professor, Department of History, University of New South Wales,
    Sydney, Australia
d.cahill@unsw.edu.au
http://hist-phil.arts.unsw.edu.au/staff/staff.php?first=David&
    last=Cahill

Frederick Errington
Distinguished Professor, Department of Anthropology, Trinity
    College, Hartford, CT
Frederick.Errington@trincoll.edu
http://internet2.trincoll.edu/facProfiles/Default.aspx?fid=1000731

Tomás Gallareta Negrón
Investigador, Sección de Arqueología, Centro Yucatán del Instituto
    Nacional de Antropología y Historia, Mérida, Mexico
tomasgn@sureste.com
http://www.kiuic.org/english_f/staff.htm#negron

Deborah Gewertz

G. Henry Whitcomb Professor, Department of Anthropology,
  Amherst College, Amherst, MA
dbgewertz@amherst.edu
https://cms.amherst.edu/people/facstaff/dbgewertz

Terry L. Hunt

Professor, Department of Anthropology, University of Hawai'i,
  Manoa
thunt@hawaii.edu
http://www.anthropology.hawaii.edu/faculty/hunt

Carl P. Lipo

Associate Professor, California State University, Long Beach
clipo@csulb.edu
http://www.csulb.edu/~clipo

Patricia A. McAnany

Kenan Eminent Professor, Department of Anthropology, University
  of North Carolina, Chapel Hill
mcanany@email.unc.edu
http://anthropology.unc.edu/people/faculty/mcanany

J. R. McNeill

University Professor, School of Foreign Service and Department of
  History, Georgetown University, Washington, DC
mcneillj@georgetown.edu
http://explore.georgetown.edu/people/mcneillj/?action=viewgeneral
  &PageTemplateID=125

Tim Murray

Professor, Department of Archaeology, La Trobe University,
  Melbourne, Australia
t.murray@latrobe.edu.au
http://www.latrobe.edu.au/archaeology/Staff_directory/
  murray.htm

Kenneth Pomeranz

Chancellors Professor, Department of History, University of
  California, Irvine
klpomera@uci.edu
http://www.hnet.uci.edu/history/faculty/pomeranz/

Christopher C. Taylor
Professor, Department of Anthropology, University of Alabama,
   Birmingham
ctaylor@uab.edu
http://www.sbs.uab.edu/Depts/Anthro/Anthropology/facstaff/
   CTaylor/CTaylor.html

Michael Wilcox
Assistant Professor, Department of Anthropology, Stanford
   University, Palo Alto, CA
mwilcox@stanford.edu
https://www.stanford.edu/dept/anthropology/cgi-bin/web/?q=
   node/95

Drexel G. Woodson
Associate Research Anthropologist, Bureau of Applied Research in
   Anthropology, University of Arizona, Tucson
dwoodson@u.arizona.edu
http://bara.arizona.edu/faculty/cv/cv-dwoodson.pdf

Norman Yoffee
Professor, Department of Near Eastern Studies and Department of
   Anthropology, University of Michigan, Ann Arbor
nyoffee@umich.edu
sitemaker.umich.edu/nyoffee

Preface and Acknowledgments

The intellectual stimulus and rationale for this book are presented in some detail within the pages of Chapter 1 and need not be repeated here. The niche within which the contributions of this book fit comfortably is one overlooked by many contemporary scientists and historians but not laypersons or students. This book came about in response to the hunger within the latter two audiences for readable and accessible narratives that deal with the manner in which people across space and time have sustained themselves and reproduced or transformed their societies, particularly in reference to environmental circumstances. We hope that the collective wisdom assembled within the pages of this book will help to inform and guide the thinking of those who contemplate where we have been and where we are heading.

Many people provided encouragement and shared their expertise in ways that helped to bring this book to completion. First came the members and audience of the symposium held at the 2006 meetings of the American Anthropological Association in San Jose, California. We were surprised by the intensity of the audience and their desire to see the papers published in a manner that would be accessible to students and laypersons – to break the cycle of purely internal dialogue and critique within the discipline of anthropology. Next, John Ware and his able staff at the Amerind Foundation in Dragoon, Arizona, hosted a week-long seminar in October 2007 for those of us engaged with this project. This opportunity allowed participants not only to exchange views but also to reinforce our commitment to write a book in which primary data about human resilience, ecological vulnerability, social regeneration, and the long-term repercussions of colonialism would be presented in plain language. Present at the Amerind seminar was Beatrice Rehl, Publishing Director for Humanities and Archaeology at Cambridge University Press. Her support and enthusiasm for this project have never wavered. Her assistant Tracy Steel and production editor Holly Johnson provided technical support at many stages of the publication production process, as did David Anderson at the technical editing stage. Satoru Murata and Pablo Robles made time to work on the many images that serve as illustrative materials and teaching aids in this book. We extend a special thank you to Adam Kaeding for compiling the index.

Our global society has now reached the point at which we can change – perhaps irrevocably – the face of the planet on which we live. As a social species, we never before have been so powerful, but we also never before have been so aware of what came before, of challenges faced, and of crises averted. The chapters of this book provide perspective and richly textured information about both the past and present. By doing so, we hope to shed light on the way forward.

Patricia A. McAnany
Norman Yoffee
Summer 2008

1

Why We Question Collapse and Study Human Resilience, Ecological Vulnerability, and the Aftermath of Empire

Patricia A. McAnany and Norman Yoffee

Scholars – especially historians, archaeologists, and social anthropologists, the authors of these chapters – are strange animals. Historians spend lots of time toiling in dusty archives, and archaeologists excavate in the ground to discover clues to what happened in the past. Sociocultural anthropologists often live among peoples whose languages, food, houses, clothes, and beliefs are very different from our own. Wouldn't it be easier and much more lucrative to become a doctor or lawyer?

Although we are not psychologists, it seems that one reason why we dedicate ourselves to figuring out how societies got along in the past, or how such a rich diversity of peoples continues to exist today despite the homogenizing forces of globalization, is that we like to tell stories. We also like puzzles, how one finds pieces of information (data) and from the pieces constructs a picture (in prose) that will convince other puzzle players that our story has "hit the nail on the head." This is an ancient and distinctly human desire, to tell a story and to tell it well. As scholars, we also want our stories to make a larger point about how our fellow humans lived in the past and about the variety of human experiences in reference to environmental interaction. We believe optimistically that an examination of the lives of others may lead to better understanding of how we might live today.

But along the way we face the fact that our stories are not easy to construct and even harder to narrate to a public that is interested in what we do. Information collected may even (and often does) lead scholars to conflicting conclusions. Scholars' prose can become tortured – full of scholarly references to other researchers' efforts and couched in conditional phrases such as "could have" or "possibly" in order to express the uncertainty in understanding peoples and cultures remote in time or space – or perhaps both – from us. Also, the best scholars, who excel in the practice of research and writing, tend to write for a small peer group of similar researchers. Specialization may advance a field of study, but it creates distance from interested laypersons and inquisitive students. This book is an effort to shorten that distance.

HOW THIS BOOK CAME TO BE

We begin by telling the story about how this book came about. One of us, Patricia McAnany, who is a Maya archaeologist, was approached by the Archaeology Division of the American Anthropological Association (AAA) to organize a panel at the annual meeting of the AAA that would address the issues swirling around the popular writings of Jared Diamond, especially the 2005 publication of *Collapse: How Societies Choose to Fail or Succeed* and his earlier *Guns, Germs, and Steel: The Fates of Human Societies*. Tricia asked Norman Yoffee, a historian and archaeologist of Mesopotamia, to co-organize the session and lend his expertise on the subject of societal change. In this way the organizers could represent the Americas as well as the ancient Near East and could cast a wider net in identifying appropriate examples and scholars who know a great deal about them.

The panel took place in San Jose, California, in November 2006. Before the first paper was to be read, at 8 A.M., as we were setting up our computers and PowerPoint presentations, we were approached by representatives of the Anthropology and Education section of the AAA. They asked whether they could record the papers and make them available on the Web for high school teachers. Because Diamond's books are used by high school teachers and many college and university professors, the AAA representatives wanted to provide additional source materials that would balance Diamond's perspective. Surprised by this request, we hurriedly polled our participants, all of whom agreed to be recorded. After the session numerous colleagues came forward and urged us to revise and publish the papers

FIGURE 1.1 Areas of the world, past and present, discussed in the chapters of this book. (Map prepared by Satoru Murata)

because they wanted to use the research we had presented in their classes. Over a long lunch we decided not just to publish most of the existing papers, but also to add other case studies. We realized that we also needed to gather participants together one more time to figure out how each study could form part of a larger narrative. John Ware, the executive director of the Amerind Foundation, agreed to host our group at the foundation's headquarters in Dragoon, Arizona – one of the most beautiful places imaginable. The Amerind Foundation is a nonprofit organization dedicated to furthering anthropological research and public outreach education. And so we gathered in the high Sonoran desert of southern Arizona in October 2007 for an advanced seminar.

Each of the fifteen scholars who contribute to this book is a world-renowned specialist on the society, topic, or time period about which he or she writes and thus provides an insider's point of view. (Brief, personalized autobiographies for each author can be found in the notes for each of the following chapters.) Each is deeply concerned about the inaccuracies of popular portrayals and feels that students and laypersons alike deserve to read a better story – one that is more deeply contextualized and perhaps more complicated but in the end more interesting. Participants committed themselves to setting aside abstruse academic prose and cumbersome in-text references in favor of a more user-friendly text. Also attending the seminar were representatives of the *New York Times, Archaeology* magazine,[1] and Cambridge University Press. The first two later told their own stories about the seminar, and the third agreed to publish the papers, further revised after our discussions. You see the final results before you.

WHAT'S THE BEEF BETWEEN SCHOLARS AND POPULAR WRITERS?

Among the issues we wanted to explore in our AAA symposium and in our subsequent seminar were the reasons for the incredible success of Jared Diamond's books. After all, Diamond is a Professor of Geography at UCLA, not an anthropologist, archaeologist, or historian. He obviously reads prolifically the obscure (to most laypersons and students) publications of historians, archaeologists, and sociocultural anthropologists and can present their research with verve and clarity and as important knowledge for a larger public. In *Guns, Germs, and Steel,* Diamond confronts racist views of the past that claim that Western superiority is due to the genes and genius of Westerners. In *Collapse* he warns of real and potential environmental destruction in the present by arguing that past societies and cultures collapsed because they damaged their environments. His successful writing style of distilling simple points from complex issues is a remarkable gift; it is no wonder that his books win prizes and are used in classrooms.

Diamond's *Collapse* has found resonance in many recent books, some almost as popular as his: Elizabeth Kolbert's *Field Notes from a Catastrophe,* Tim Flannery's *The Weather Makers: How Man Is Changing the Climate and What It Means for Life on Earth,* and Eugene Linden's *The Winds of Change: Climate, Weather and the Destruction of Civilizations.*[2] Al Gore shared a Nobel Prize for his work on the perils of mismanaging our environment. Diamond is probably the best-known writer of anthropology even though he is not an anthropologist!

In this book most of the chapters are critical of Diamond's stories. This is why the AAA session was organized in the first place. Whereas we are indebted to Diamond for drawing together so much material from our own fields of research and for emphasizing how important anthropological and historical knowledge is for the modern world, as scholars we want to get things right. We also want to write in such a way that the public can grasp not only the significance of research findings but also how we do research and why we think that some stories are right, whereas others are not as right or incomplete and still others are dead wrong.

Thanks to Diamond's provoking inquiries and more generally those of the popular media, we focus this book on several questions: (1) Why do we portray ancient societies – especially those with indigenous descendants – as successes or failures, both in scholarship and in the popular media? We want to get the stories of social change right, and descendants of the ancient societies we study demand it. (2) How do we characterize people who live today in the aftermath of empires? Today's world is the product of past worlds, and the consequences of the past cannot be ignored. (3) How are urgent climatic and environmental issues today similar to those faced by our ancestors? Can we learn from the past?

As a point of departure, we start with the question of societal collapse and then discuss the notion of choice. We consider the concept of resilience and its usefulness for understanding change both past and present, and how different ecologies are more or less vulnerable to profound perturbation. Finally, we ponder why and how history and context matter in our rapidly changing postcolonial time.

THE QUESTION OF SOCIETAL COLLAPSE

Over two decades ago the sociologist Shmuel Eisenstadt wrote that societal collapse seldom occurs if collapse is taken to mean "the complete end of those political systems and their accompanying civilizational framework."[3] Indeed, studying collapse is like viewing a low-resolution digital photograph: it's fine when small, compact, and viewed at a distance but dissolves into disconnected parts when examined up close. More recently Joseph Tainter, after a search for archaeological evidence of societal "overshoot" and collapse, arrived at a conclusion similar to Eisenstadt's: there wasn't any.[4] When closely examined, the overriding human story is one of survival and regeneration. Certainly crises existed, political forms changed, and landscapes were altered, but rarely did societies collapse in an absolute and apocalyptic sense. Even the examples of societal collapse often touted in the media – Rapa Nui (Easter Island), Norse Greenland, Puebloan U.S. Southwest, and the Maya Lowlands – are also cases of societal resilience when examined carefully, as authors do in the chapters in this book. Popular writers' tendency to approach the past in terms of a series of societal failures or collapses – while understandable in terms of providing drama and mystery – falls apart in light of the information and fresh perspectives presented in this book.

Abandoned ruins – the words themselves evoke a romantic sense of failure and loss to which even archaeologists – most of whom are reared in the Western tradition – are not immune. But why is it that when we visit Stonehenge we don't feel a twinge of cultural loss, but simply a sense that things were very different 5,000 years ago? Is it because Stonehenge is somehow part of *our* civilization? On the other hand, the Great Houses of Chaco Canyon, the soaring pyramids of ancestral Maya cities, and the fallen colossal heads of Rapa Nui tend to invoke a sense of mysterious loss and cultural failure, and a notion that something must have gone terribly wrong environmentally. For many of us these places and people are not part of the Western experience. Moreover, descendant communities – in all three cases – live marginalized on the edge of nation-states without the resources and connections to worldwide media that are needed to tell their own story, at least to an English-speaking public. Might these abandoned places, in many cases, be just as accurately viewed as part of a successful strategy of survival, part of human resilience? Michael Wilcox makes this point in Chapter 5 about the abandonment of Chaco Canyon by the ancestors of contemporary U.S. Puebloan peoples. Joel Berglund in Chapter 3 does too, in discussing the Norse colony on Greenland, which lasted for 500 years. Abandonment also can be read as indicative of opportunity elsewhere and of the societal flexibility to seize that opportunity; Patricia McAnany and Tomás Gallareta Negrón stress this in Chapter 6 in their discussion of eighth-to-ninth-century Maya society, during which time parts of the Maya region were dramatically depopulated while others became much more densely peopled.

Although it would be wonderful to feel that scholarly understanding of abandonment stood outside contemporary societal concerns, it is pretty clear that today's worries about the future make their way into our explanations of the past. Times of political turmoil and chronic warfare beget interest in turmoil of the past, and times of environmental woes beget theories of past environmental troubles. Historians and archaeologists, who are not immune to seeing the past through modern lenses, try to test the relevance of their ideas by looking for multiple lines of evidence that point to the same conclusion.

In our chapters we hold interpretations of past environmental abuse up to critical scrutiny for two reasons. First, because the fit between ideas and evidence is never straightforward. Methods and measures are constantly under refinement, and innovations in scientific method often change interpretations dramatically. To give an archaeological example, if a column of sediment from a lake bed contains evidence of a decrease in tree pollen from the bottom to the top, does that mean that – over time – the region around the lake was deforested, replaced with trees that yielded fewer grains of pollen, or that a mosaic of forest and fields was created with none of the forested areas located near the lake? All might be plausible, but one might be more plausible if another line of supporting evidence – such as an increase in plant remains of a food crop such as corn – can be mustered in favor of one interpretation. Scholars are and must be cautious: a good story is not necessarily the one that incorporates all of the data at hand. Some "good stories" are simply wrong.

Second (and for better or worse), humans have a long history of both interacting assertively with their environments as well as coalescing into fragile political groups that fission easily. Archaeologists such as Sander van der Leeuw have shown that landscape alteration has occurred in human societies since the end of the Pleistocene (Ice Age), 10,000 years ago.[5] It is not difficult to find evidence of pre-industrial landscape alteration – particularly in heavily populated environments such as the Maya Lowlands – but it is another matter altogether to link that evidence in a convincing and rigorous fashion to site abandonment or changes in political forms. The notion that the present recapitulates the past is not necessarily true. We ask how long human societies have possessed the technological ability to profoundly change and destroy their environment and bring down their societies.

In concluding comments to this book and elsewhere, J. R. McNeill amasses a formidable body of evidence suggesting that the human ability to impact environment on a global scale is newfound and cannot be pushed back beyond the Industrial Revolution of the 1800s.[6] So, in the apocalyptic sense that appeals to fatality in the human imagination – and writers such as Arnold Toynbee and Oswald Spengler preceded Diamond in this – the end may be in sight, but it hasn't been for very long. Understanding what happened in the past – both politically and environmentally – is not irrelevant to contemporary and future societal challenges, particularly environmental ones, as we discuss later in this chapter and throughout the book. Adopting a well-informed long view of how humans have lived on this biosphere we call Earth can promote decision making and policy development that results in human survival and resilience rather than the reverse.

CHOICE AND GEOGRAPHIC DETERMINISM

In his book on societal collapse, Jared Diamond proposes that societies choose to succeed or fail. On the other hand, in *Guns, Germs, and Steel* there was no choice: today's inequalities among modern nation-states are argued to be the result of geographic determinism.[7] In the first scenario, societies (or power brokers within societies) make the decisions that result in long-term success or failure. In societies that fail, leaders are selfish and advance schemes that endanger the ecological well-being of their community, polity, or island. At the root of this thesis is the modern neoliberal theory of self-interested motivation as well as the assumption of unconstrained and rational choice. A scalar sleight of hand occurs when methodological individualism – an economic theory designed explicitly to model individual behavior and motivation – is applied wholesale to "societies" – past and present – in which many conflicting agendas and contra-motivations tend to be negotiated before any decision or action. Many economists view the motivational assumptions of self-interest and rational choice theory as lacking explanatory power, even when applied to Western societies.[8] When applied globally and into deep time, this theory has particular difficulties, as revealed by case studies in this book. For example, Frederick Errington and Deborah Gewertz, who work in Papua New Guinea, argue that Papuan worldviews are not grounded in Western ideas of rational self-interest.[9] Furthermore, there is no necessary linkage between a selfish decision made in the short term and adverse long-term consequences. Kenneth Pomeranz observes that the much-cherished wooded glens of England are the result, for the most part, of the selfish desires of a postmedieval aristocracy to maintain fox-hunting preserves. About the same time in China – where horse culture and fox hunting were not part of aristocratic behavior – the transformation of forest to farmland was tolerated and even encouraged to provide a livelihood for an expanding population.[10] So today people of China are surrounded by fields rather than forest, while environmentalists in England chain themselves to old-growth trees to protest road construction projects. But this difference is not due to selfless long-sightedness in the one case and lack of it in the other.

If we are to understand global events today, we must perceive that the basis of intentionality and motivation can differ profoundly across the globe. This is the message of Christopher Taylor (Chapter 9), who objects to a Malthusian explanation (too many people on too little land) for the tragedy of the Rwandan genocide, and Drexel Woodson (Chapter 10), who writes of the struggles of Haitian people against the backdrop of the legacies of French colonial and post-independence policies (not a ruthless geography), and Errington and Gewertz (Chapter 12), who discuss the troublesome ease with which Indonesian (and other) logging firms secure permits to despoil the hardwood forests of Papua New Guinea.

For those of us studying early states, archaeologists and historians alike, it isn't easy to discern intentions and their effects in the remote past. Nevertheless, both Norman Yoffee, in the case of ancient Assyrians of the first millennium B.C.E., and Kenneth Pomeranz, who studies China in the eighteenth and nineteenth centuries, argue that decision makers, however powerful – and they certainly were – were not so powerful as to engineer their own environmental ruin.

Many current global inequalities indisputably are the product of historical colonialism and their enduring legacy. This is not simply an academic issue, as Tim Murray notes in Chapter 11. Australians are engaged in making a new Australia where Aborigines have not only rights but a history as well, which should be the history of all Australians. Discussing the persistent fragility of empires, David Cahill (Chapter 8) points out that the Inca empire that stretched across the South American Andean mountain chain did not simply fall to the gun- and germ-bearing Spaniards but was vulnerable because of the presence of internal factions that inevitably exist within empires that tend to be held together by force of arms. Spaniards found and adroitly used willing allies among indigenous groups – such as the Cañaris people – who already were resisting Inca domination. In general, considerable variation took place in the "encounters" between Europeans and peoples of the Americas, South and East Asia, Africa, and Oceania; neither guns nor germs nor steel played a prominent role *initially* in colonial incursions in the Americas. In the long run, Europeans succeeded because of the persistent inflow of immigrants along with new disease vectors and weaponry.[11]

If one takes a long view, as archaeologists and historians are wont to do, then the situation in the year 2009 seems less the manifestation of a geographic destiny than it is a temporary state of affairs. Can anyone say that the present balance of economic and political power will be the same in 2500 as it is today? For example, in the year 1500 some of the most powerful and largest cities in the world existed in China, India, and Turkey. In the year 1000, many of the mightiest cities were located in Peru, Iraq, and Central Asia. In the year 500 they could be found in central Mexico, Italy, and China. In 2500 B.C.E. the most formidable rulers lived in Iraq, Egypt, and Pakistan. What geographic determinism can account for this? Is history a report card of success or failure?

RESILIENCE AND SOCIAL CHANGE

An important part of the "science of the long view"[12] is the concept of resilience, or "the ability of a system to absorb disturbance and still retain its basic function and structure," albeit in altered form.[13] This statement is not very different from that of Eisenstadt quoted above regarding the rarity of civilizational collapse. Yes, things change and they change profoundly, but more often elements of a society (including belief systems and ways of making a living) retain their basic structure and function within longer cycles of change. Resilience means that some kinds of change, especially political change, can be quick and episodic, whereas other kinds of change, for example, changes in kinship structures and belief systems, can be slower moving. Also, both kinds and different paces of change can coexist.[14]

The notion of resilience, instead of collapse, is relevant to the chapters of this book because, on close inspection of archaeological evidence, documentary records, or both, it becomes clear that human resilience is the rule rather than the exception. For instance, Rapa Nui society – before European incursions – remained populous and vital despite deforestation of their island from the introduction of exotic species (in this case, the Polynesian rat) and land clearance for farming (Hunt and Lipo, Chapter 2). Medieval Norse colonists (who originally came from Iceland) migrated to other parts of their world when climatic conditions worsened and no bishop could be persuaded to come to Greenland (Berglund, Chapter 3). Chinese farmers and bureaucrats alike weathered the economic and political crises of the nineteenth to mid-twentieth centuries to live in one of the most dynamic economies on the planet today and perhaps also one of the most polluted environments (Pomeranz, Chapter 4). Native Americans of the Southwest abandoned settlements and founded others in a successful long-cycle strategy of coping with a harsh environment and hostile neighbors (Wilcox, Chapter 5). Although the term "Maya collapse" is ingrained in both popular and scholarly literature, Maya people lived on after the supposed collapse and into Postclassic times in populous cities and kingdoms. Today seven million people still speak a Mayan language and struggle to make a living in southern Mexico and northern Central America (McAnany and Gallareta Negrón, Chapter 6). Norman Yoffee (Chapter 7) shows how Mesopotamia presents a classic case of resilience, as structures of authority and identity endured through several cycles of change.

Although change is inevitable, and living through some kinds of change is difficult, painful, or even catastrophic, "collapse" – in the sense of the *end* of a social order and its people – is a rare occurrence. Resilience is a more accurate term to describe the human response to extreme problems. As archaeologists, anthropologists, and historians, we are not fortune tellers or prophets, but the historical lessons of resilience may help us chart a course for the future.

ECOLOGICAL VULNERABILITIES

Environmental challenges (and crises) have posed risks to societies since humans began to domesticate their landscape shortly after the close of the last Ice Age about 10,000 years ago, and perhaps even earlier. Today we are profoundly concerned about the fragility of our ecosystem and wonder whether we are poised on the brink of an ecological calamity on a global scale. How can information from the past guide us through these perilous times?

The human footprint on the earth is a deep one, and it has been that way since humans domesticated plants and animals and began actively to transform the surface of this planet into fields, pastures, and managed forests.[15] The concentration of humans into villages and then into urban settlements has clearly accelerated this environmental transformation because cities are insatiable consumers of food and energy.[16] Our case studies in this book show that societies modify their practices in response to perceived crises. But it is possible that investments made in response to recurrent crises of short duration may leave us vulnerable to unknown longer-term cycles of risk that ultimately bring into play a cascade of unwelcome changes.[17] The resilience of the larger social collective – be it a modern nation or a ninth-century Maya polity – is endangered by such crises, which can originate from a host of sources, including climate change and political decision making. In any case, understanding ecological vulnerabilities – past and present – leads us to ask the right questions and take needed actions. Here we are very much in agreement with Jared Diamond, but not because we suspect that rulers of the past – alleged to have been shortsighted – ruined their environments and failed. Rather, it is because we know that past societies (and their leaders as well as the opponents of leaders) experienced a variety of crises and responded to circumstances as best they could.

Prominent among past societies that have been labeled ecocidal failures are the ancestors of the contemporary people of Rapa Nui (Easter Island). For reasons of scale and historical isolation, islands are particularly vulnerable to rapid and profound ecological transformation with the arrival of humans. As Terry Hunt and Carl Lipo (Chapter 2) narrate, the island of Rapa Nui is no exception. The island ecosystem, having evolved in isolation with a limited set of tree species and no co-evolution between tree-seed reproduction and rodent predation, was dramatically altered by the introduction of Polynesian rats. Rats arrived on Rapa Nui as a transported food source or as stowaways in the large, ocean-going outrigger canoes used to colonize the Pacific. The rats, which multiplied quickly into the millions, found an accessible and protein-rich food source in the soft-shelled nuts of palm trees. The consequent loss of tree species on Rapa Nui certainly was not a good thing, but there was little population fall-off on Rapa Nui until Europeans landed on the island. The grasslands of today's Rapa Nui are the result of a historical sequence that included the introduction of a rat species by Polynesians, introduction of European diseases, population reduction from colonial slave raiding, and colonial transformation of an agricultural landscape into pastureland.

Of course, we tend to see transformations that are closer to home more benignly than those in distant locations. After pilgrims landed at Plymouth Rock on the coast of what today is called Massachusetts, they proceeded to reduce dramatically the hardwood forests of New England to transform the landscape into an agricultural and stock-grazing one. Although biodiversity was lost and drainage features permanently altered,[18] no one has labeled this behavior as ecocidal, as far as we know, although the term genocidal has been employed in reference to the catastrophic Colonial Era reduction in indigenous peoples of the Americas. Under colonization, indigenous societies had limited choices in reference to environmental management and limited opportunities to tell their side of the story. T-shirts, sold at the Mashantucket Pequot Museum located next door to the successful Foxwoods Casino in southern Connecticut, allude to the colonial process and subsequent nonrecognition of the first colonizers of the Americas by the U.S. Bureau of Indian Affairs with the logo "Piquot Nation – first to greet, last to be recognized." In Chapter 5 of this volume, Michael Wilcox, of Yuman and Choctaw ancestry, writes of the survival of Native Americans as a success story of those who against all odds survived near-holocaust policies, a resilient people who look to the triumphs of their history so as to plan a brighter future.

THE AFTERMATH OF EMPIRE: WHY HISTORY AND CONTEXT MATTER

The term "postcolonial" has become popular in academic prose, an acknowledgment of the fact that the far-flung empires of the late nineteenth and early twentieth centuries – choreographed from European capitals – largely have been dismantled. Currently the United Nations seats 192 autonomous countries in its assembly hall, and the number is growing. Although some are the product of expedient political decisions by colonial powers, others formed from resistance to those very decisions, and still others represent ethnic amalgams of considerable antiquity. In February 2008 the prime minister of Australia formally apologized to indigenous Australian peoples for the harsh antifamily and anticultural survival policies imposed by the state and only rescinded beginning in the 1970s. It would appear that we are entering a new era, living in the aftermath of empire. On the other hand, the legacy of colonialism does not fade so quickly. There are gross inequities in the distribution of resources in the world, access to education, and opportunities to make a livelihood. Some of these inequities are the result of historical realities within a nation, such as the era of slavery within the United States, which still haunts and frustrates both black and white populations.

How is this relevant to understanding the abandonment of Chaco Canyon in the American Southwest? As our authors repeatedly state, history is not a win–lose game for the subjects of colonialism; victors have reason to be cautious when assigning labels such as "success" or "failure." As Wilcox (Chapter 5) and Errington and Gewertz (Chapter 12) point out, the inequities of colonialism are an ongoing process played out internally in terms of access to education and political voice as well as internationally in the arenas of resource distribution and political clout. For Wilcox, the notion that the great architectural achievements of Chaco Canyon can be labeled a societal failure constitutes an example of "reverse engineering," meaning the assignation of past failure to contemporary people who have been economically and politically disenfranchised as a direct result of colonial expansion of a European-derived population.

The experience of many indigenous peoples and inheritors of the colonial legacy has been one of dispossession and cultural survival, rather than collapse. When viewed in this historical context, are the people of Haiti, for example, free to choose success or failure? Woodson (Chapter 10) explores the historical circumstances behind the label of "failed state" and considers now what must be done. In Chapter 9 Taylor discusses why the Rwandan genocide cannot be analyzed as an environmental or demographic problem. Errington and Gewertz (Chapter 12) refuse to "blame the have-nots." Only by understanding history and culture can something like genocide and economic underdevelopment be understood.

FINAL THOUGHT

In 1990 – nearly two decades ago – a group of scholars met at the School of American Research for an advanced seminar on historical ecology and ended by drafting the "Santa Fe Accord" to express their alarm over the current peril to humanity and the biosphere.[19] Since that time there has been a general awakening to the perilous situation that confronts our biosphere and humanity. This book does not seek to minimize this peril but to understand it more deeply, more historically, and more contextually. We leave the reader with a closing thought that is further developed in the case studies in this book.

Our past and the resilience of human populations form the basis on which twenty-first-century humans attempt to understand life. We have inherited daunting environmental and social challenges and added more of our own making, but we also can appreciate the long centuries of humans who have solved problems in the past and thus still survive today. But, to use our knowledge of the past, we must see how the past was both similar to as well as different from today. For example, we suggest that the choices of past rulers, elites, and power brokers were constrained by limitations of technology and communication that generally do not exist today. The challenges ahead are profound and require inspired problem solving and human resilience. Fortunately, these are attributes that human societies have long displayed.

Notes

1. George Johnson, "A Question of Blame When Societies Fall," *New York Times*, December 25, 2007, http://www.nytimes.com/2007/12/25/science/25diam.html; Eric Powell, "Do Civilizations Really Collapse?" *Archaeology* (March/April 2008): 18, 20, 56.
2. Kolbert 2006; Flannery 2005; Linden 2006.
3. Eisenstadt 1988: 242.
4. Tainter 2006: 71–72.
5. van der Leeuw and the ARCHAEOMEDES Team 2000; van der Leeuw and Redman 2002.
6. McNeill 2000, 2005.
7. Diamond 2005 and 1999, respectively.
8. Levitt and Dubner 2005 explore these limitations in their popular book *Freakonomics*.
9. For another example of the interlacing of ritual practice and economic process, see Wells and McAnany 2008.

10. Ken Pomeranz, personal communication, October 2008; see also Pomeranz, Chapter 4 in this volume.
11. Raudenz 2001.
12. Gunderson and Folke 2003.
13. Walker and Salt 2006 is a highly accessible presentation of "*resilience thinking.*" A series of case studies that employ resilience thinking are presented in *Panarchy* (2002), which is edited by conservation ecologists Lance Gunderson and C. S. Holling. Also see Redman (2005) for application of resilience thinking to archaeology.
14. Walker and Salt 2006.
15. Although highly controversial, Shepard Krech (1999) presents a convincing case that even in North America – where many conceive of the pre-European landscape as pristine – significant landscape engineering had occurred via burning and planting.
16. See Montoya et al. 2006: 262.
17. Dearing et al. 2007: 64.
18. See Cronon 2003 on the impact of Europeans on New England landscapes and how it differed from Native American landscape engineering.
19. This Accord is printed in the front matter of Crumley 1994.

Bibliography

Crumley, C. L. Editor. 1994. *Historical Ecology: Cultural Knowledge and Changing Landscapes.* Santa Fe, NM: School of American Research Press.

Dearing, J. A., L. J. Graumlich, R. Grove, A. Grübler, H. Haberl, F. Hole, C. Pfister, and S. E. van der Leeuw. 2007. "Group Report: Integrating Socio-environmental Interactions over Centennial Timescales," in *Sustainability or Collapse? Integrated History and Future of People on Earth.* Edited by R. Costanza, L. J. Graumlich, and W. Steffen, pp. 37–69. Cambridge, MA: MIT Press.

Diamond, J. 1999. *Guns, Germs, and Steel: The Fates of Human Societies.* New York: W. W. Norton.

Diamond, J. 2005. *Collapse: How Societies Choose to Fail or Succeed.* New York: Viking.

Eisenstadt, S. N. 1988. "Beyond Collapse," in *The Collapse of Ancient States and Civilizations.* Edited by N. Yoffee and G. L. Cowgill, pp. 236–243. Tucson: University of Arizona Press.

Flannery, T. 2005 *The Weather Makers: How Man Is Changing the Climate and What It Means for Life on Earth.* New York: Atlantic Monthly Press.

Gunderson, L., and C. Folke. 2003. "Toward a 'Science of the Long View.'" *Conservation Ecology* 7:15. Available at http://www.consecol.org/vol7/iss1/art15.

Gunderson, L., and C. S. Holling. 2002. *Panarchy: Understanding Transformations in Human and Natural Systems.* Washington, DC: Island Press.

Kolbert, E. 2006. *Field Notes from a Catastrophe.* New York: Bloomsbury.

Krech, S. 1999. *The Ecological Indian: Myth and History*. New York: W. W. Norton.

Levitt, S. D., and S. J. Dubner. 2005. *Freakonomics: A Rogue Economist Explores the Hidden Side of Everything*. New York: William Morrow.

Linden, E. 2006. *The Winds of Change: Climate, Weather and the Destruction of Civilizations*. New York: Simon & Schuster.

McNeill, J. R. 2000. *Something New under the Sun: An Environmental History of the Twentieth-Century World*. New York: W. W. Norton.

McNeill, J. R. 2005. "Diamond in the Rough: Is There a Genuine Environmental Threat to Security?" *International Security* 30:178–195.

Montoya, J. M., S. L. Pimm, and R. V. Solé. 2006. "Ecological Networks and Their Fragility." *Nature* 442(July 20):259–264.

Raudzens, G. Editor. 2001. *Technology, Disease, and Colonial Conquests, Sixteenth to Eighteenth Centuries: Essays Reappraising the Guns and Germs Theories*. Leiden, the Netherlands: Brill.

Redman, C. L. 2005. "Resilience Theory in Archaeology." *American Anthropologist* 107:70–77.

Tainter, J. A. 2006. "Archaeology of Overshoot and Collapse." *Annual Review of Anthropology* 35:59–74.

van der Leeuw, S. E., and the ARCHAEOMEDES Team. 2000. "Land Degradation as a Socionatural Process," in *The Way the Wind Blows: Climate, History, and Human Action*. Edited by R. J. McIntosh, J. A. Tainter, and S. K. McIntosh, pp. 357–383. New York: Columbia University Press.

van der Leeuw, S. E., and C. L. Redman. 2002. "Placing Archaeology in the Center of Socio-natural Studies." *American Antiquity* 67:597–605.

Walker, B., and D. Salt. 2006. *Resilience Thinking: Sustaining Ecosystems and People in a Changing World*. Washington, DC: Island Press.

Wells, E. C., and P. A. McAnany. Editors. 2008. *Dimensions of Ritual Economy. Research in Economic Anthropology* 27. Bingley, U.K.: JAI Press.

PART I

HUMAN RESILIENCE AND ECOLOGICAL VULNERABILITY

2

Ecological Catastrophe, Collapse, and the Myth of "Ecocide" on Rapa Nui (Easter Island)

Terry L. Hunt and Carl P. Lipo[*]

Easter Island! The name is synonymous with mystery and the intrigue of archaeology. The hundreds of giant statues – *moai* – located on a remote windswept and treeless landscape practically demand that archaeologists answer the question of what happened there. Easter Island, or Rapa Nui as it is known to the island's native Polynesians, has also become the "poster child" for what happens when societies squander their resources and destroy their environment. In his book *Collapse,* Jared Diamond describes an ecological catastrophe brought on by the island's inhabitants that led to their own destruction.[1] Diamond calls it "ecocide": the choice to construct giant statues led to the island's ecological devastation and the collapse of the ancient civilization. He and other researchers offer the ecocide story as a parable for our own potential destruction of the global environment. But is the story told for Easter's human-induced environmental change correct, particularly what's been said about the causes and consequences? We consider new evidence from Rapa Nui in light of recent discoveries from the Hawaiian Islands and offer some perspectives for the island's ecological transformation and the consequences.

From our own archaeological research on Rapa Nui we show that a much later settlement for the island than has been previously recognized calls into question important aspects of its ecological history.[2] When we take a closer look at the palaeo-environmental and archaeological evidence we find a complex history of ecological

FIGURE 2.1 Giant stone statues (*moai*) at Ahu Tongariki, Rapa Nui. (Photo by Terry Hunt)

change for the island, not a single cause but a variety of impacts that occurred in combination with one another. This history is quite different from the notion of ecocide in which reckless Polynesians overexploited their environment. It is essential to disentangle environmental changes in Rapa Nui from a population collapse that resulted from European contact. Such contact brought Old World diseases and slave trading. Contrary to today's popular narratives, ancient deforestation was *not* the cause of population collapse. If we are to apply a modern term to the tragedy of Rapa Nui, it is not ecocide, but genocide.

Rapa Nui is small (164 square kilometers) and isolated in the remote southeastern Pacific. Except for the Polynesian islands of Pitcairn, Ducie, and Henderson, themselves small, remote, and relatively impoverished, Rapa Nui's nearest neighbors are more than 3,000 kilometers away. Voyaging from the central islands of eastern Polynesia would have normally gone against the prevailing trade winds, with the island forming only a small target, although westerly winds associated with periodic El Niño conditions may have carried Polynesian colonists on a downwind voyage to the island.

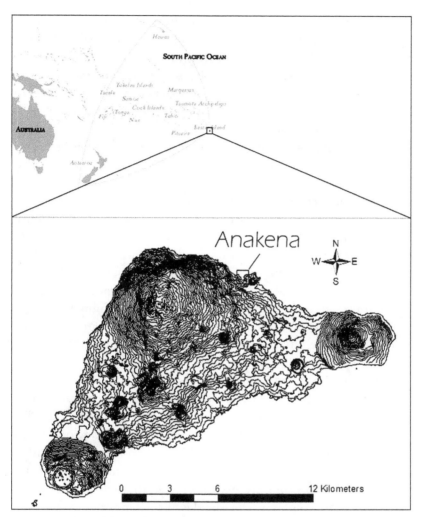

FIGURE 2.2 Rapa Nui and southeastern Pacific.

Rapa Nui also has a limited number of native plants and animals reflecting its young geological age, small size, and great isolation – quite apart from its losses in recent ecological history. Concerning the island's biology C. Skottsberg wrote that "there is in the Pacific Ocean no island of the size, geology and altitude of Easter Island with such an extremely poor flora ... nor is there an island as isolated as this ... [T]he conclusion [is] that poverty is a result of isolation –

even if man is responsible for disappearance of part of the flora, [Rapa Nui] cannot have been rich."³ Today biologists count only forty-eight "native" plants. Fourteen of these, including sweet potato and the other cultigens, were ancient Polynesian introductions. However, studies of pollen found in lake-floor sediments and identifications of wood charcoal from ancient cooking ovens suggest many other woody plants once covered Rapa Nui.

The island has few, if any, indigenous terrestrial vertebrates. Two lizard species may be native to the island, but biologists are not certain. The only land birds found on the island today are recent introductions, but archaeological discoveries show that the island once supported twenty-five species of seabirds and on present evidence perhaps about six land bird species. A few seabirds survive today, but the original land birds became extinct. Since there is a lack of extensive reefs, the number of fish is small when compared to other islands of the Pacific. Sea mammals and turtles are known from Rapa Nui. On present archaeological evidence, the only animals brought in the canoes of the ancient Polynesians were rats (*Rattus exulans*) and chicken. The introduction of the former decisively affected life on Rapa Nui.

Unlike the luxuriant islands typical of Polynesia, Rapa Nui does not enjoy abundant regular rainfall and a tropical climate. There are no permanent streams. At twenty-seven degrees south, Rapa Nui is just outside the tropics, where important Polynesian food crops such as coconut and breadfruit would not have survived. Rainfall (only about 1,250 millimeters annually) can fluctuate dramatically. Most of the island's soils are excessively well drained, and devastating droughts are common. The island is also often plagued by strong winds with salt spray that damage – sometimes even destroy – the food crops that Polynesians cultivated. Rapa Nui was not a Polynesian Paradise. Droughts, winds, poor soil, and no permanent streams certainly meant problems for the ancient farmers on this isolated speck at the farthest reaches of Polynesia.

THE ECOLOGICAL PARABLE

Speculations of ecological ruin on Rapa Nui began with one of the island's early European visitors. From a single day's visit in April 1786,

French explorer La Pérouse speculated that at some time in the past Rapa Nui's inhabitants had thoughtlessly cut down all the trees. He wrote that loss of the forest

has exposed their soil to the burning ardor of the sun, and has deprived them of ravines, brooks, and springs. They were ignorant that in these small islands, in the midst of an immense ocean, the coolness of the earth covered with trees can alone detain and condense the clouds, and by that means keep up an almost continual rain upon the mountains, which descends in springs and brooks to the different quarters. The islands which are deprived of this advantage, are reduced to the most dreadful aridity, which, gradually destroying the plants and scrubs, renders them almost uninhabitable. Mr. de Langle as well as myself had no doubt that this people were indebted to the imprudence of their ancestors for their present unfortunate situation.[4]

Today the idea of the "imprudence of their ancestors" is taken up by Jared Diamond as a moral for our time: "In just a few centuries, the people of Easter Island wiped out their forest, drove their plants and animals to extinction, and saw their complex society spiral into chaos and cannibalism. Are we about to follow their lead?" Diamond continues:

Eventually Easter's growing population was cutting the forest more rapidly than the forest was regenerating. The people used land for gardens and wood for fuel, canoes, and houses – and of course, for lugging statues. As forest disappeared, the islanders ran out of timber and rope to transport and erect their statues. Life became more uncomfortable – springs and streams dried up, and wood was no longer available for fires. … As we try to imagine the decline of Easter's civilization, we ask ourselves, "Why didn't they look around, realize what they were doing, and stop before it was too late? What were they thinking when they cut down the last palm tree?"[5]

Diamond believes Rapa Nui is "the clearest example of a society that destroyed itself by overexploiting its own resources" and that the consequences of deforestation "start with starvation, a population crash, and a descent into cannibalism."[6]

Some archaeologists have argued that on Rapa Nui the efforts required to carve and transport the giant statues eventually led the population to deplete their own natural resources and plunge into a downward spiral induced by overpopulation and environmental destruction. In other words, people willingly destroyed the island and, in turn, destroyed themselves. Ecocide!

Did human recklessness, overexploitation, and overpopulation lead to deforestation and ecological catastrophe? Did a collapse of ancient population and culture result from an ecological catastrophe before European contact in 1722 C.E.?

THE ECOLOGICAL EVIDENCE

Early Observations

The earliest European visitors did not leave us with many details about Rapa Nui's environment, and the earliest accounts are contradictory. For example, the Dutch expedition led by Jacob Roggeveen in 1722, expecting to relocate a "low and sandy island" sighted earlier by Captain William Dampier, reported:

The reason why, at first, when at a farther distance off, we had regarded the said Easter Island as being of a sandy nature is that we mistook the parched-up grass, and hay or other scorched and charred brushwood for a soil of that arid nature, because from its outward appearance it suggested no other idea than that of an extraordinarily sparse and meager vegetation.

But following their stay on the island, the Dutchman wrote:

We found it not only not sandy but to the contrary exceedingly fruitful, producing bananas, potatoes, sugar-cane of remarkable thickness, and many other kinds of the fruits of the earth, although destitute of large trees and domestic animals, except poultry. This place, as far as its rich soil and good climate are concerned, is such that it might be made into an earthly Paradise, if it were properly worked and cultivated; which is now only done in so far as the Inhabitants are obliged to for the maintenance of life.[7]

Deforestation

The first clear evidence for deforestation on Rapa Nui came from pollen studies by John Flenley and his colleagues.[8] Sediments of the lake floor of Rano Kao contained microscopic pollen grains from a giant palm tree similar in size and form to the native of mainland Chile, *Jubaea chiliensis,* that once dominated the island's forest. The pollen evidence shows that the forest disappeared and was replaced by the grassland we see today. Dating just when the dramatic vegetation

FIGURE 2.3 Mature *Jubaea chiliensis* palms at La Campaña National Park (32°51′S), mainland Chile. (Photo by Terry Hunt)

FIGURE 2.4 Grasslands of Rapa Nui today. (Photo by Terry Hunt)

changes occurred, and even how fast deforestation proceeded, has
not been easy. But careful field work by Daniel Mann[9] and his colleagues, Andreas Mieth[10] and his team from Germany, and French
researchers led by Catherine Orliac[11] and our own excavations[12]
have shown that the forest disappeared over a period of about 400
years, from around 1250 to 1650 C.E. The palm trees in particular
left behind nuts that were burnt or gnawed by the rats that people
brought with them in their migration in about 1200 C.E. This clear
association of radiocarbon-dated palm nuts with people and rats
tells us when the forest grew and disappeared. From accounts of what
early visitors reported, some native forest may have survived until the
late eighteenth and nineteenth centuries.

Until recent discoveries came to light,[13] most archaeologists
believed that Rapa Nui was first settled circa 400 C.E. or a few centuries later, about 800 C.E. With the first signs of human impacts on
the forest only *after* 1250 C.E., researchers were forced to imagine an
early, largely invisible, human presence on the island with farmers
who practiced undetectable farming. In this scenario a small found-
ing population with a remarkably slow population growth had few,
if any, visible ecological impacts. Indeed, Polynesian colonizers on
Rapa Nui, in this story, would have remained archaeologically and
environmentally invisible for many centuries. Thus, it was not surprising that some scholars imagined, first, a period when people
were ecologically aware, and, then, a period when they decided to
ruin their paradise. But now, because we know that the early dates
of migration are suspect, the early period of supposed low-impact
ecological management probably didn't exist.

Multiple lines of evidence from archaeological and palaeo-
environmental research on Rapa Nui show that from the first time
that migrants landed on Rapa Nui, their presence meant impacts to
the environment. These events are easily visible to archaeologists.
Our excavations in the deep, stratified sand dune at Anakena Beach,
with more than a dozen radiocarbon dates, provide a chronology
beginning about 1200 C.E. Our oldest radiocarbon samples from the
deepest layers of our excavation contain the first artifacts, charcoal,
and bones found directly above the undisturbed clay deposits that
are riddled with the root molds of primeval palms. The oldest layers in our Anakena excavations also reveal the bones from the first

FIGURE 2.5 Excavations at Anakena Dune, Rapa Nui, University of Hawai'i archaeological field school, 2005. (Photo by Terry Hunt)

introduction of the Polynesian rat, as well as the remains of the earliest human meals, which included sea mammals, birds, and fish.[14]

The relatively late dates for first colonization came as a surprise. We, like our colleagues, had believed in a longer chronology. In questioning our own findings, we returned to the radiocarbon dates published from previous studies on Rapa Nui and found that those falling before 1200 C.E. were unreliable. Some of these dates appeared to predate that year, but when corrected by modern standards, their true age turned out to be centuries younger. The large body of dates for the island fell completely within a range that begins after 1200.[15]

Our discovery fits perfectly with the chronology for initial human impacts and deforestation after 1200 C.E. If people arrived well before the first signs of regular fires and changes in the vegetation, then we would have to assume that human and rat population growth was incredibly slow and had no visible impact for 400 to 800 years. This would be unlikely from what we know from many other Pacific Islands. Perhaps people could have survived with exceedingly small populations with low growth rates, but it is difficult to argue that rats feeding on palm nuts from an estimated 16 million trees would limit their numbers and leave the island's vegetation untouched. We will return to this issue below.

Like Rapa Nui, the careful scrutiny of existing radiocarbon chronologies and "redating" of the oldest deposits on other islands across Polynesia have consistently shifted island colonization centuries later than researchers had originally thought. The mistakenly long chronologies in places such as Hawai'i, the Marquesas, Cook Islands, and New Zealand have now been corrected with better research and more advanced technological methods. Today the earliest dates for the eastern Pacific show that archipelagos such as the Cooks, Societies, Marquesas, and Hawai'i were first colonized between 800 C.E. and 1000. Colonization of the islands of the southeastern margins of Polynesia as well as New Zealand occurred a few centuries later, about 1100–1200 C.E.[16] So a date of 1200 C.E. for Rapa Nui fits well within the broad pattern for the settlement of Polynesia.

HAWAIIAN RESEARCH

Recent archaeological and palaeo-environmental field research from the 'Ewa Plain on the southwestern corner of the island of O'ahu, in the Hawaiian Islands, provides findings that are relevant for our understanding of Rapa Nui. From extensive archaeological excavations and analysis of lake-core sediments, Steve Athens and his colleagues discovered that before arrival of Polynesians, the lowlands of O'ahu (and other Hawaiian islands) were covered in a forest of native palm trees (*Pritchardia* spp.).[17] Then, around 1000 C.E., the Hawaiian palm forests began to disappear rapidly. Within just 100 to 200 years, the forest had crashed precipitously. Whereas many archaeologists had blamed Polynesians for recklessly using fire to clear land for agriculture, new evidence from the 'Ewa Plain showed that the palms on this portion of the island vanished, but without any trace of local fires. In the same area excavations in dozens of limestone sinkholes, excellent sediment traps that capture local environmental changes over time, showed that also around 1000 the introduced Polynesian rat was exploding in numbers. At the same time native birds as well as the forest suffered dramatic decline, with some species lost to extinction. In the local lake-core sediments from nearby Ordy Pond,

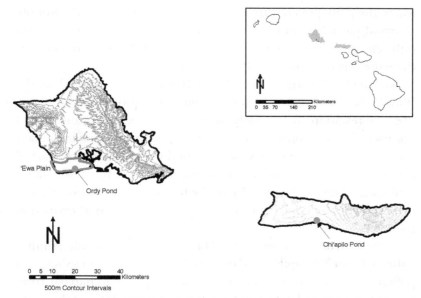

FIGURE 2.6 Hawaiian Islands showing the 'Ewa Plain on O'ahu Island and Ohi'apilo Pond on Moloka'i Island.

FIGURE 2.7 *Pritchardia* palms, National Tropical Botanical Garden, Kaua'i, Hawaiian Islands. (Photo by Terry Hunt)

where the palm pollen witnesses the fate of the native forest, minute charcoal particles from local fires make their first appearance, but only *after* the native forest had all but vanished. Fires did not destroy the palm forest on the 'Ewa Plain on O'ahu.

Archaeological studies reveal that Hawaiians first settled on the 'Ewa Plain, a dry region with poor soil, some 400 years *after* extensive deforestation had already occurred. Polynesian colonists had not used fire or chopped down the palms with stone tools to plant their crops. By the time Hawaiians settled this less-desirable part of the island, it had already lost its native forest and witnessed major ecological changes. The demise of the forest had meant loss of habitat for many birds and other native species. Their rapid extinction followed.

Evidence from elsewhere in the Hawaiian Islands records a similar pattern. From 'Ohi'apilo Pond on Moloka'i, sediment cores show that pollen from the native palms declined sharply, but charcoal from local fires appears later. The timing was the same; the palms vanished around a thousand years ago, but fire was not to blame. What happened to the lowland forests of the Hawaiian Islands?

Athens hypothesized that the introduced Pacific rat, *Rattus exulans*, was an immediate and serious destructive agent that played a huge role in the rapid loss of the native lowland forest. Rats arrived on the first canoes of colonizers in the Hawaiian Islands and encountered few, if any, predators or competition from native birds for plant foods. The Pacific rat is an agile climber sometimes described as arboreal. Field ecologists report thousands of rats living in the coconut tree canopies of Pacific atolls where they move on palm frond runways from tree to tree. Some rats, opportunistic omnivores, are content never even to visit the ground. Unlike birds, rats can consume hard, thick seed cases (even coconuts!), and they destroy the reproductive potential of nearly all the seeds they consume. As rats devoured the seeds of the next generation of native plants, forest regeneration was stopped in its tracks. Old trees died and fewer young ones replaced them. Rats were the first invasive species in the fragile islands of the remote Pacific, and their impact was (and is) devastating.

If rats played a major role in deforestation in the Hawaiian Islands, we can predict patterns in today's vegetation: First, in islands free of rats both now and in the past, native forest should survive. This is the

FIGURE 2.8 *Pritchardia remota* palms still growing on Nihoa Island, northwest Hawaiian Islands. Nihoa Island has not sustained impact from introduced rats. (Photo by Terry Hunt)

case for Nihoa Island in the northwestern Hawaiian chain. This small island has no rats and never did. Dense stands of the endemic palm, *Pritchardia remota,* persist on Nihoa despite intensive Hawaiian occupation in prehistoric times, the use of fire, and sweet potato gardens that were cultivated over much of the island.

We see a second expectation in the Hawaiian Islands where native vegetation is more common at higher elevations (above about 1,500 meters). This coincides with the range for the Pacific rat, which is limited by the absence of fruit-producing trees at higher elevations. The native forests we find today in the mountains of Hawai'i may owe their survival to the lowland habitat of the Pacific rat. The relationship between rats and changes in vegetation is not a simple one. Islands vary by biogeography, ecology, and history, and so will the impacts of invasive species like rats.

The palaeo-environmental record for Rapa Nui reveals ancient vegetation once dominated by millions of *Jubaea* palm trees. The pollen record shows that the palms have been established on the island for tens of thousands of years (going back at least 37,000 years), and they survived and adapted to significant climate changes and natural catastrophes such as droughts. Other woody plants now extinct or present only in small numbers on Rapa Nui were similar to the kinds of vegetation found on Pacific islands to the west. Rapa Nui's native biota reflects a classic case of island biogeography where the forces of evolution in isolation result in a simple community, a small number of plants and animals, unique adaptations, and few if any predators. Together these features make island ecosystems especially vulnerable to alien invasions, as ecologists working in the region know all too well.

Around 1200 C.E. Polynesian voyaging canoes arrived on Rapa Nui, perhaps from the southern islands of eastern Polynesia, such as the Australs or Mangareva-Pitcairn group. Rats were almost certainly on board. Introduced accidentally or on purpose, the consequences would be the same: rats reached an island with no native predators and an essentially unlimited high-quality food supply provided by millions of palm trees, each producing more than a hundred kilograms of nuts every year. Under these ideal conditions rats could and did reproduce at staggering rates, capable of doubling their numbers every forty-seven days. For example, as laboratory studies suggest, a single mating pair of rats with these kinds of unlimited resources can become a population of nearly 17 million in about 1,128 days, or just over three years!

We routinely see these kinds of explosions – biologists refer to them as irruptions – when rats enjoy an abundance of resources. At a latitude similar to Rapa Nui, but with a lower abundance of food resources, Kure Atoll (28°24′N) in the northwest Hawaiian Islands supports Polynesian rat densities averaging forty-five per acre, with

FIGURE 2.9 Prehistoric rat-gnawed *Jubaea* nuts from Rapa Nui (from collections at the P. Sebastian Englert Anthropological Museum, Rapa Nui). (Photo by Terry Hunt)

FIGURE 2.10 Close-up view of prehistoric rat-gnawed *Jubaea* nuts from Rapa Nui (from collections at the P. Sebastian Englert Anthropological Museum, Rapa Nui). (Photo by Terry Hunt)

maximum recorded densities reaching seventy-five. At only forty-five rats per acre, Rapa Nui would have had a rat population over 1.9 million. At seventy-five per acre, a reasonable density given the palm nuts and other forest resources, the rat population of Rapa Nui could have reached more than 3.1 million. Such documented population growth rates and rat densities on Pacific Islands suggest that Rapa Nui could have easily supported a huge number of rats soon after people first arrived. An initial peak rat population would be sustained until resources diminished and rat numbers fell.

If rats alone decimated the *Pritchardia* palm forest on the 'Ewa Plain of O'ahu, as we have described, then this provides a likely ecological parallel for Rapa Nui. The Hawaiian research demonstrates that rats were capable, on their own, of deforesting large lowland coastal areas in about 200 years or less. Rats, once introduced to Rapa Nui, would certainly have had a profound and immediate impact on the island's forest that was dominated by the nut-bearing *Jubaea* palms. Similar to the impacts on *Pritchardia* palms of Hawai'i, rats consumed *Jubaea* palm nuts and seedlings, greatly inhibiting forest regeneration. In fact, hundreds of palm nuts preserved in caves around the island show the telltale signs of rat gnawing and seed destruction. The older established palms and other forest plants provided plenty of food for rats, but few new seedlings would sprout and survive. Eventually the oldest trees died, and a strong force in deforestation followed as younger trees could not replace them. The giant palms were also undoubtedly lost to fire as people cleared land for agriculture.[18] Importantly, rats and people's use of fire must have both taken their tolls in deforestation, but there is no evidence for massive, reckless felling of trees.[19]

The idea that rats may have played a significant role in Rapa Nui's deforestation is not new. John Flenley and his colleagues hypothesized:

The effects of introduced rodents on the biota of oceanic islands are known frequently to have been disastrous, and it seems that Easter Island may have been no exception. Whether the extinction of the palm owes more to the prevention of regeneration by rodents, or to the eating of the fruits by man, or to the felling of the mature trees, *remains an open question.*[20]

RETHINKING RAPA NUI'S ECOLOGICAL CATASTROPHE

By the late eighteenth century, when European visits to the island increased, it seems the deforestation of Rapa Nui was complete, or nearly complete. A forest of an estimated 16 million palm trees and more than twenty other woody trees and shrubs had all but disappeared.

Perhaps six species of land birds, several seabirds, and an unknown number of other native species had become extinct. Much of this loss occurred before the final devastating blow of the European introduction of thousands of grazing sheep in the late nineteenth century. Certainly from an ecological and biodiversity perspective, Rapa Nui has experienced an environmental catastrophe.

Once rats arrived on Rapa Nui their numbers exploded and reached a population of millions within just a few years. At this historic instance, rat consumption of palm nuts, other seeds, and seedlings more or less halted forest regeneration. Nearly all the plants lost to extinction on Rapa Nui were on the menu as the favorite foods of rats.[21] The exception proves the rule. *Sophora toromiro*, a native woody shrub, was one of the few plants that survived into historic times. Field studies of related plants from New Zealand show that rats damage the seed casings, but in this instance such damage appears to encourage seed germination.[22] Rats inadvertently help disperse the plant, rather than destroy its chances for reproduction.

Polynesians succeeded in settling the vast Pacific in a remarkably short time. Like the *Bounty* mutineers who escaped to Pitcairn Island, small groups of people colonizing unpopulated islands can sustain growth rates of more than 3 percent, at least for short periods of time. Rapid population growth indeed would be essential to successful colonization of remote islands. Even small numbers of initial colonizers, say, about fifty, with a 3 percent growth rate, would result in populations that would rise dramatically and reach more than 2,000 (already a density of over ten people per square kilometer on Rapa Nui) in just over a century after people set foot on the island. People using fire, particularly as the population grew, had an impact on the island, and this must be added to the continuing impacts of rats.

The evidence for Rapa Nui shows that deforestation took at least 400 years (from about 1250 to 1650 C.E.). This means that the number of people grew while forest resources declined over 400 to 500 years. A maximum population for Rapa Nui, growing from an initial colonization of about fifty individuals, was perhaps 3,000 to 5,000 by about 1350–1370 C.E. This maximum population would fluctuate slightly, but probably remained in close balance with the island's resources and the inevitable uncertainties, given the hardships of periodic droughts or salt-laden winds.

As the forest disappeared, soil erosion brought problems as well. Deforestation would make drought, wind, and soil worse as the cover of trees declined over 400–500 years. Recent studies show that Rapa Nui soils were probably never very fertile,[23] and poor soil explains why early Rapa Nui agriculturalists resorted to using stone mulch and creating thousands of stone enclosures for the cultivation of crops.

There is no reliable evidence that Rapa Nui population ever grew to a large, unsustainable maximum such as 15,000 or more[24] and then crashed from deforestation and resource loss. The large population numbers, 15,000 or even 30,000, often cited for prehistoric Rapa Nui are baseless. They have been posited mainly to dramatize the putative "ecocide" in which populations plummeted. In a short essay,[25] Diamond cites a recent archaeological study that reports hundreds (922 to be precise) of habitation structures on Rapa Nui,[26] and these are dated by a technique known as obsidian hydration. These habitations provide a kind of indirect census of population, not so much in real numbers, but as an index for the rise and fall of population. Diamond argues that the population grew and then collapsed *before* Europeans arrived. However, during the period of deforestation (about 1280 to 1650 C.E., based on many radiocarbon dates), the island's population grew even though the forest declined. The first and only sign of sustained decline in the population, so vital to the "ecocide" thesis, came from 1750 to 1800 C.E., after the arrival of the first European visitors. On Rapa Nui, like so many other places in the New World and the Pacific, European germs decimated the native population that had only limited immunity to Old World diseases. Ironically, this is exactly what Diamond says happened in the New World in his celebrated *Guns, Germs, and Steel.*[27]

Whereas Rapa Nui suffered an ecological catastrophe, there is no evidence that the island represents a case of "ecocide" where a large population crashed from environmental ruin before Europeans arrived. Instead, the real and documented population collapse for Rapa Nui began on Easter Sunday, 1722, when Dutch explorers inaugurated the real tragedy of Rapa Nui. As the ethnographer Alfred Metraux described it long ago, what happened on Rapa Nui was "one of the most hideous atrocities committed by white men in the

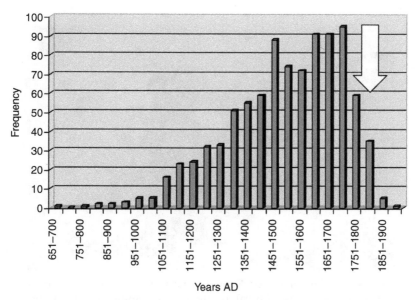

FIGURE 2.11 Distribution of habitation sites dated (in intervals) by the technique of obsidian hydration. The first sustained decline in habitations occurs only after European contact.

South Seas" and it was "the catastrophe that wiped out Easter Island's civilization."[28] As the idea of "ecocide" has gained currency, the victims of cultural and physical extermination have been turned into the perpetrators of their own demise!

The ecological catastrophe of Rapa Nui had a complex history that cannot be reduced to psychological speculations about the motivations of people who cut down the last tree. Indeed, the "last tree" may simply have died, and rats may have simply eaten the last seeds. What were the rats thinking?

The lessons of Rapa Nui plainly are of the effects of invasive species and the impact of people and their portable economies on fragile ecosystems in the remote islands of the Pacific.

On this unlikely island, Polynesian civilization thrived in isolation for more than 500 years. Despite extremely limited resources, a few thousand islanders carved and transported more than 8,000 tons of massive stone sculpture across a rugged landscape. These enormous monoliths embodied the spirits of powerful ancestors who, from their

FIGURE 2.12 Contemporary Rapanui (native Polynesians who live on the island today) take a break on their horse. Despite common misconceptions, descendants of the ancestral people thrive on Rapa Nui today.

PEOPLE OF RAPANUI TODAY

Native Rapanui Islanders, Enrique Pate Encina and his wife Francisca Haoa Hey, were born and raised on Easter Island. Enrique, who is known by his nickname Pota, works at the Padre Sebastian Englert Museum of Anthropology helping with a variety of things. He has worked with our archaeological team doing fieldwork on the island, but Pota spends most of his spare time taking care of his horses, raising their three children, Vaiaratea, Enerike Oroi, and Tehitumana, and playing music with other local musicians in his band Ohiro Reka. Asked about his cultural heritage as a native Rapanui, Pota says, "It is something that we carry in the blood; our connection to our heritage is immediate, direct, all around us on the island, always there. Our heritage comes to us from the past, but we will pass it along to our children in Rapanui language and culture. First we are Rapanui; second, we are Chilean."

venerated platforms, watched over the islanders' fragile existence in isolation. The real story here is one of human ingenuity and success that lasted more than 500 years on one of the world's most remote human outposts.

Notes

* *Terry L. Hunt:* My interest in anthropology and archaeology in particular began when I was fifteen. I had an intense interest in ancient life in Hawai'i, but I found the history books were slanted toward a culture already greatly changed by European contact. When I first picked up a technical report in archaeology showing ancient house foundations, artifacts, and details of what people had eaten, I realized I was headed for a career in archaeology. I completed my B.A. degree at the University of Hawai'i–Hilo, then went to New Zealand to learn more about Pacific Island anthropology and prehistory at the University of Auckland, where I earned my M.A. degree. From New Zealand I returned to the United States and did my Ph.D. work at the University of Washington. I joined the faculty of the University of Hawai'i at Manoa, where I have taught since 1988.

   Over the past thirty-five years I have been fortunate to do archaeological field research in the Hawaiian Islands, New Zealand, Fiji, Samoa, Papua New Guinea, and Rapa Nui (Easter Island). My interest in Rapa Nui grew from the question of how and why people invested in such great monumentality in statues, architecture, and other artistic expressions on this remote and resource-impoverished island. In 2000 I visited Rapa Nui and met a friend and former student, Sergio Rapu Haoa, who had become the first native Rapanui governor of the island. Sergio and Claudio Gomez, then the director of the local museum (Padre Sebastian Englert Museum of Anthropology), suggested I come to the island to do research.

   In 2001 I began field research as part of an archaeological field school. Our team has completed seven field seasons, including extensive surveys, excavations, and analysis of museum collections. Our work integrates student training, diverse lines of research, and native community-based archaeology and heritage preservation. Our research on Rapa Nui has brought some surprises and a realization that the island's prehistory was not as well known as many of us had assumed.

   Carl P. Lipo: My interest in archaeology stems from my schoolboy fascination with the prehistoric effigy mounds (mounds in the shape of animals) that are scattered in and around my hometown of Madison, Wisconsin. This interest resulted in my studies in archaeology as an undergraduate and graduate student at the University of Wisconsin. I expanded my horizons from Wisconsin and did archaeological research in Greece, India, and Pakistan. Subsequently I received my Ph.D. from the University of

Washington; my dissertation, completed in 2000, focused on the emergence of social complexity among late prehistoric populations in the
central Mississippi River valley. My enduring interests lie in the study of cultural transmission and the process of natural selection in cultural systems.

I started teaching at California State University Long Beach in 2002
and began working in an area famous for its record of vast historical
change, Rapa Nui. In collaboration with Terry Hunt of the University of
Hawai'i, we have been documenting the unique series of cultural events
on this remarkable island that we report in this chapter.

1. Diamond 2005.
2. Hunt 2006; Hunt 2007; Hunt and Lipo 2006.
3. Skottsberg 1956.
4. La Pérouse 1799: 318–319.
5. Diamond 1995: 63, 68.
6. Diamond 2005: 118.
7. Ruiz-Tagle 2005: 23–24.
8. Flenley et al. 1991; Dransfield et al. 1984.
9. Mann et al. 2008.
10. Mieth and Bork 2004, 2005.
11. Orliac 2000.
12. Hunt and Lipo 2006; Hunt 2007.
13. Hunt and Lipo 2006, 2008.
14. Hunt 2007.
15. Hunt and Lipo 2006, 2008.
16. Wilmshurst et al. 2008.
17. Athens et al. 2002; Athens in press.
18. Mieth and Bork 2004; 2005.
19. Some trees were certainly chopped down by people. However, despite wide-
    spread claims, there is no evidence that the palms trees were used as rollers
    or other devices to transport multi-ton statues (*moai*). Also, our archaeo-
    logical surveys on several areas of Rapa Nui show that stone tools suitable
    for cutting down palm trees, particularly in great numbers, are lacking; nor
    do we find any abundance of fragments of stone tools from such activities.
20. Flenley et al. 1991: 104 (emphasis added).
21. Hunt 2007: table 1.
22. Cambell and Atkinson 2002.
23. Louwagie et al. 2006.
24. Diamond 2005: 90–91.
25. Diamond 2007.
26. Vargas et al. 2006.
27. Diamond 1997.
28. Metraux 1957: 38.

Bibliography

Athens, J.S. In press. "*Rattus exulans* and the Catastrophic Disappearance of
    Hawai'i's Native Lowland Forest." *Biological Invasions.*

Athens, J.S., H.D. Tuggle, J.V. Ward, and D.J. Welch. 2002. "Avifaunal Extinctions, Vegetation Change, and Polynesian Impacts in Prehistoric Hawai'i." *Archaeology in Oceania* **37**:57–78.

Campbell, D.J. and I.A.E. Atkinson. 2002. "Depression of Tree Recruitment by the Pacific Rat (*Rattus exulans* Peale) on New Zealand's Northern Offshore Islands." *Biological Conservation* **107**(1):19–35.

Diamond, J. 1995. "Easter's End." *Discover* **9**:62–69.

Diamond, J. 1997. *Guns, Germs, and Steel: The Fates of Human Societies.* New York: W.W. Norton.

Diamond, J. 2005. *Collapse: How Societies Choose to Fail or Succeed.* New York: Viking.

Diamond, J. 2007. "Revisiting Easter Island." *Science* **317**:1692–1694.

Dransfield, J., J.R. Flenley, S.M. King, D.D. Harkness, and S. Rapu. 1984. "A Recently Extinct Palm from Easter Island." *Nature* **312**(5996):750–752.

Flenley, J.R., S. King, J. Jackson, C. Chew, J. Teller, and M. Prentice. 1991. "The Late Quaternary Vegetational and Climatic History of Easter Island." *Journal of Quaternary Science* **6**:85–115.

Hunt, T.L. 2006. "Rethinking the Fall of Easter Island: New Evidence Points to an Alternative Explanation for a Civilization's Collapse." *American Scientist* **94**:412–419.

Hunt, T.L. 2007. "Rethinking Easter Island's Ecological Catastrophe." *Journal of Archeological Science* **34**:485–502.

Hunt, T.L. and C.P. Lipo. 2006. "Late Colonization of Easter Island." *Science* **311**:1603–1606.

Hunt, T.L. and C.P. Lipo. 2007. "Chronology, Deforestation, and "Collapse:" Evidence vs. Faith in Rapa Nui Prehistory." *Rapa Nui Journal* **21**(2):85–97.

Hunt, T.L. and C.P. Lipo. 2008. "Evidence for a Shorter Chronology on Rapa Nui (Easter Island)." *Journal of Island and Coastal Archaeology* **3**:140–148.

La Pérouse, J.F.G. de. 1798. *A Voyage Round the World Performed in the Years 1785, 1786, and 1788.* London: J. Johnson.

Louwagie, G., C.M. Stevenson, and R. Langohr. 2006. "The Impact of Moderate to Marginal Land Suitability on Prehistoric Agricultural Production and Models of Adaptive Strategies for Easter Island (Rapa Nui, Chile)." *Journal of Anthropological Archaeology* **25**:290–317.

Mann, D., J. Edwards, J. Chase, W. Beck, R. Reanier, M. Mass, B. Finney, and J. Loret. 2008. "Drought, Vegetation Change, and Human History on Rapa Nui (Isla de Pascua, Easter Island)." *Quaternary Research* **69**:16–28.

Metraux, A. 1957. *Easter Island: A Stone-Age Civilization of the Pacific.* London: Andre Deutsch.

Mieth, A. and H.-R. Bork. 2004. *Easter Island – Rapa Nui: Scientific Pathways to Secrets of the Past.* Man and Environment 1. Department of Ecotechnology and Ecosystem Development, Ecology Center, Christian-Albrechts-Universität zu Kiel, Kiel, Germany.

Mieth, A. and H.-R. Bork. 2005. "Traces in the Soils: Interaction between Environmental Change, Land Use and Culture in the (Pre)History of Rapa Nui (Easter Island)," in *The Renaca Papers: VI International Conference on Rapa Nui and the Pacific.* Edited by C. Stevenson, J.M. Ramirez, F.J. Morin, and N. Barbacci, pp. 55–65. Los Osos, Chile: Easter Island Foundation and University of Valparaiso.

Orliac, C. 2000. "The Woody Vegetation of Easter Island between the Early 14th and the Mid-17th Centuries A.D.," in *Easter Island Archaeology: Research on Early Rapanui Culture.* Edited by C. Stevenson and W. Ayres, pp. 211–220. Los Osos, Chile: Easter Island Foundation.

Ruiz-Tagle, E. 2005. *Easter Island: The First Three Expeditions.* Rapa Nui: Museum Store, Rapanui Press.

Skottsberg, C. 1956. *The Natural History of Juan Fernandez and Easter Island* 1. Uppsala, Sweden: Almqvist & Wiksells Boktryckeri.

Vargas, P., C. Cristino, and R. Izaurieta. 2006. *1000 Años en Rapa Nui. Arqueología del Asentamiento.* Santiago, Chile: Editorial Universitaria.

Wilmshurst, J.M., A.J. Anderson, T.F.G. Higham, and T.H. Worthy. 2008. "Dating the Late Prehistoric Dispersal of Polynesians to New Zealand Using the Commensal Pacific Rat." *Proceedings of the National Academy of Sciences USA* **105**(22):7676–7680.

3

Did the Medieval Norse Society in Greenland Really Fail?

Joel Berglund[*]

The most famous "archaeologist" of our time, Indiana Jones, said it succinctly: "If you are searching for truth, you must consult the Department of Philosophy; in Archaeology we deal in facts." Probably unintentionally, the film's script writer singled out the central issue in all research. Realities are manifest in archaeological digs, for example, but responsible interpretations of these discoveries depend on the filters they must pass through. One such filter is the knowledge at the archaeologist's current disposal, not the least of which are the scientific tools available. It must be clearly understood that archaeology and history are continuous processes, constantly revised as new information comes in. Except for the fact that we shall all die sometime, there are few ultimate certainties in the world, including in archaeology and history.

COLLAPSE IN THE PAST AND PRESENT

This essay will focus on archaeology and history, on finding a grand design in details, on the relevance of using the past to draw conclusions intended for our own time, on human responses to environmental challenges, and on the possibility that these responses may lead to environmental and social change. In considering these questions, we need to keep in mind that major contours or themes are made up of many small factors, and that oversimplifying those connections and factors will inevitably produce results that at best are inadequate and at worst wrong and misleading.

45

FIGURE 3.1 A simple trowel in the hand of an archaeologist is used to discover facts and conditions of long-forgotten human lives. (Photo by J. Berglund)

Throughout history, from antiquity until the present, numerous writers have tried to fit past events into easily understood narratives. However, the past differs from the present in that learned people of the past had limited knowledge of the world; the world known at the time was only a small part of the globe. Imagination filled in the gaps. When venturing beyond the known world, a traveler might encounter monsters with two heads, a one-legged creature with a foot so large it protected its owner from the sun, cyclops, and other monstrous beings. In the words of the Swedish historian Dick Harrison, such stories were the equivalent of today's comic strips and science fiction about creatures in outer space. The perspective has changed, but the lack of knowledge involved is the same.

For examples from the twentieth century, one may point to works such as the German philosopher Oswald Spengler's *Untergang des Abendlandes* (Decline of the West), published right after World War I and notable for a cultural pessimism that predicted the western world's decay.[1] After thoroughly analyzing the various great cultures in world history, Spengler reached the conclusion that all cultures go through cycles of rise, flowering, and decay. Such a philosophy of history had already been heralded by the eighteenth-century historian Edward Gibbon in *The Decline and Fall of the Roman Empire*.[2] In six volumes, which constituted his life's work, Gibbon covered thirteen centuries of history.

FIGURE 3.2 "Odd persons." (Cosmographiae Universalis 1544; courtesy of Skapelsens Geografi)

Inspired by Spengler, the English historian Arnold Toynbee wrote *A Study of History* in twelve volumes, published between 1934 and 1961.[3] His work points out that the dynamics at work in any kind of change are determined by the nature of the environmental challenge and by the human cultural response to it.

These works have subsequently been joined by others, with popular histories in particular published practically on an assembly line, which in some respects is a welcome development because it reflects a broad public interest in history and in the past. Among recently published books in this genre one might mention Mark Kurlansky's *Salt,* which seeks to understand world history by focusing on one of the smallest of macroscopic molecules, namely, sodium chloride.[4] It is a splendid example of using a tiny component as a window on a large picture. Another example of this approach is Jared Diamond's *Collapse,* his grand attempt to explain why civilizations have disappeared and why conditions here on earth developed as they did.[5]

However, as professional historians and archaeologists, we must insist that, at a minimum, our labors in the field, in archives, and in laboratories be respected and the results of our work correctly rendered. Certain works that fail to meet these criteria must be consigned to the twilight zone between fiction and science. Discovering factual mistakes in one's own subject of professional expertise is a major problem, because it produces distrust of statements made about other topics outside one's own area of expertise.

Returning to Spengler and Toynbee, we may recall that Spengler's analysis ends with his conviction that ruin is the inevitable outcome of a civilization's cyclical movement, while Toynbee believed that finding the right belief system might maintain the proper balance between environmental challenges and culture.

We all know the expression that trees do not grow to heaven, and scholars must certainly take care that "something" does not become "too much." If we go to the Old Testament, the story about the Tower of Babel may be understood as saying that "something became too much." The writer of Ecclesiastes cautions that "there is a time for everything." In short, the ancient cultures of the Near East already had an eye for the problems that Spengler and Toynbee encountered in their work.

Why do we occupy ourselves with historical research, and what drives our interest in past events? In his book *Collapse*, Diamond repeatedly claims that archaeological research has value today, and to some degree this is true. For instance, a Danish archaeological work about Islamic water-lifting wheels had a decisive influence on the present ability to supply water within a developing country in Africa. I might also mention that studies of the Medieval vegetation in southern Greenland have singled out problems that one would want to avoid in modern farming – a topic to which I'll return later in this chapter.

By focusing on many concrete practicalities, however, Diamond overlooks an important detail, namely, that archaeological research offers more than demonstrable utility. All people have an urge to know about the past, where one comes from and what sort of events have brought us to the present. How did people think in the past, what made Paleolithic humans paint representations of their world in inaccessible caves in France, Spain, and central Europe? As *Homo sapiens* we are related to them, and although the message they painted has been lost to us, we share their yearning for explanations, for understanding. The human memory is short; it does not take many generations to forget even major events unless these have been anchored in pictures or texts. An archaeological excavation is both a picture and a text, but it is only a part of the "past present" that we attempt to approach and to understand.

Archaeologists primarily uncover objects that depend on appropriate conditions for their preservation, but our most important concern is usually with the context in which the objects are found. One might say that an excavation always has both a contents side and an interpretive side, which may be roughly divided into a quantitative part and a qualitative one. One could also distinguish that which can be measured and weighed and that which may "only" be interpreted. However, there is good reason to be aware of the danger that as soon as something may be expressed numerically, it becomes truth – what one might call conjuring with numbers. The oversimplification that is apt to follow is often what is most offensive about popular writing. One example of this is the attempt in Diamond's *Guns, Germs, and Steel* to quantify food production in terms of the number of kilometers of farmland added per year.[6] It is important to bear in mind that numbers, too, must be interpreted. Humans are fickle creatures, and the world in which their actions take place is equally unpredictable. One of our duties as archaeologists and historians is nevertheless to try to explain change, cause, and effect. Some people claim that there is no such thing as history and future, that strictly speaking there is only an eternal present. As investigators, we bring the former present into our own present, and the question is whether we can understand the former present without basing too much of our interpretation on our own present.

If archaeology is regarded as having practical value today, the implication is that the past to a large extent resembles the present. However, a number of circumstances tell us that this is not the case. For instance, it might be pointed out that the world's demography has changed and that we now face climate changes that, probably for the first time in history, are partly the result of human activity. We have it in our power to destroy life here on earth several times over by means of nuclear weapons, but it is also in our power to alter this situation – if the will is there. But do we have that will?

FIGURE 3.3 Salt sprinkler. (Photo by J. Berglund)

A SHORT ARCHAEOLOGY AND HISTORY OF GREENLAND

I have almost thirty years of experience with archaeology in
Greenland and have, as the former associate head of Greenland's
National Museum and Archives, worked for a number of years to
promote the preservation of open-air historical monuments. My spe-
cialty is the study of Norse Greenland, which applies to the period
between 982 c.e. and the last part of the fifteenth century, when
southern Greenland was populated by Nordic people, primarily from
Iceland. This new society consisted of two settlements: the northerly
and smaller Western Settlement, located in the area that today constitutes Nuuk Municipality, and the Eastern Settlement, which was the
largest and most southerly community. Both settlements were posi-
tioned between 60 and 65 degrees north latitude and were separated
by a distance of more than 600 kilometers.

With many ruins from an almost intact Medieval society, Greenland
has from the eighteenth century to the present been a focus of
archaeologists, particularly by Danish investigators, but lately including researchers from other nations as well. Together with Norway
and Iceland, Greenland came under Danish hegemony in 1387. The
Norse community lay deserted by the end of the fifteenth century.
There was no contact with either Norway or Denmark from then until

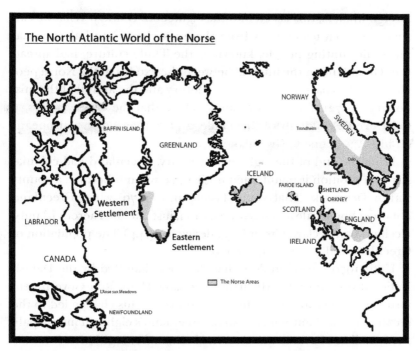

FIGURE 3.4 The Norse sphere of interest in the North Atlantic covered an area from Scandinavia through England, Ireland, Orkney, the Hebrides, the Faroy Isles, Iceland, Greenland, and the areas around Newfoundland. This is the western world of the Vikings within which they traveled and dominated. (Prepared by Pablo Robles)

1721, when the Danish-Norwegian missionary Hans Egede stepped ashore on Greenland's west coast, in the island-studded region just outside the present capital of Nuuk. He came to convert the Catholic Norse he expected to find there, but as they had long since vanished, he turned his attention to the Inuit.

Faint as it appears to have been, the memory of Norse Greenland never vanished completely. During the sixteenth and seventeenth centuries a number of expeditions were sent to the waters off Greenland, especially from Denmark, England, and Holland. Those who succeeded in getting ashore met only Inuit people. In the seventeenth and eighteenth centuries the hunt for whales switched from the waters around Spitsbergen to Greenland, and lively contact and barter ensued between Greenland's Inuit people and the foreign whalers; this lasted into the eighteenth century. What we can conclude from testimonies from these travelers and whalers is that the Inuit hunting people, known as the Thule culture, had spread over Greenland in the interval between the exodus of the Norse people in the last part of the fifteenth century and the arrival of the missionary in 1721. Further, we can conclude that the Greenlanders of today are descendants of the Thule culture that in the (European) Middle Ages came to Greenland.

From the end of the eighteenth century, Greenland had colonial status, a position it maintained until 1953, when it became a county within Denmark. That status lasted until 1979, when Greenland obtained home rule as a separate nation, just like the Faeroes Islands. (Iceland had declared its independence in 1944.) The population of Greenland today is around 57,000.

Until 1979 Greenland's archaeology was handled by the Danish National Museum, after which the Greenland Home Rule Government assumed responsibility for historic resources. This change led to the creation of local museums in all of Greenland's eighteen municipalities as well as of a main museum in Nuuk, and to legislation for monument protection and museums. This was of considerable benefit to archaeological work and also meant that the Greenlanders began to take an active part in these efforts. A milestone in Danish-Greenland museum cooperation was reached with the repatriation of museum objects from the Danish National Museum to its Greenland counterpart. This work was completed in 2001, when the last object was transferred. By that time more than 35,000 pieces had made the return trip across the Atlantic to Greenland.

WHAT HAPPENED TO GREENLAND'S NORSE?

As I said before, the Norse settlement of southern Greenland has been the subject of intensive research. The chief questions occupying scholars and others from far and near are what happened toward the end of the community's existence and what ultimately became of its inhabitants. Attempted answers have involved speculations as diverse as degeneration, pirate attacks and subsequent abductions (e.g., to the Canary Islands to serve as slaves), emigration to America, extermination by the Inuit, intermarriage with and

FIGURE 3.5 Inuit attack on the church of Hvalsey, woodcut by the Greenlandic artist Aron from Kangeq, 1822–1869. (Courtesy of the Greenland National Museum & Archives)

absorption by the Inuit population, reduced contact with the rest of the Norse world, and emigration as a response to climatic changes. This last hypothesis is the one that most scholars are currently addressing.

Other important questions have been raised concerning the settlers' adjustment to their new environment and, last but not least, about their ability to influence their physical surroundings in the long run, including whether environmental events may have been beyond their control. Current research also concentrates on the society's structure, its possible trading contacts with the Inuit, its relationship with the Church, and its apparent conservatism as reflected in archaeological finds and in the ruins themselves.

It is possible to gain a comprehensive view of both the size and reach of this Norse society established in a small part of the world's biggest island. The literary sources about the colonists are sparse, but in comparison with other immigrant populations in Greenland, such as the people from the Saqqaq, Dorset, and Thule cultures who arrived from Canada, the Norse are not anonymous – we are practically on a first-name basis with many of them. Norse Greenland society is a tangible phenomenon beginning and ending within a period of about 500 years. While Toynbee called it "an abortive Scandinavian civilization,"[7] it has frequently been pointed out that it lasted longer than the United States has existed as a polity, to give an example. It is not correct to regard the Norse society in Greenland as a failure, because it endured for as long as its inhabitants could manage the conditions they were given.

INUIT-NORSE RELATIONS

It is a recurring theme in several popular works that hostile Inuit contributed in a major way to the depopulation of the Norse settlements. The Western Settlement closed down first, toward the end of the fourteenth century, and the Eastern Settlement about a century later. Sources from the time telling about hostile Inuit are few; the most famous conflict with native peoples is the altercation with the inhabitants, probably Beothuk, in the new lands to the west (namely, North America) – Markland, Helluland, and Vinland – as reported in *Flateyarbók,* composed around 1200 and thus penned more than 200 years after the events themselves took place. These lands are also described in the "Saga of Erik the Red." Despite those conflicts, the Norse maintained contact with the lands to the west. Although we don't know for how long, they even built a base camp – scarcely a dismissive gesture – at L'Anse aux Meadows on the tip of Newfoundland's northern peninsula.

One may wonder if the resources at the disposal of the Norse simply did not suffice for yet another colonizing venture. Continuing contact with the New World is indicated by archaeological finds, such as the discovery of hair from bison and brown bear during the excavation of "The Farm beneath the Sand" at the heart of the Western Settlement. It is likely that people from Greenland sailed to Canada for lumber and other products for as long as they possessed ships that could negotiate the Davis Strait. One might add that these voyages to the other side of the Davis Strait, as well as hunting expeditions to North Greenland, emphasize a dynamic that was driven by the wish to improve their society's economy and probably also by a good degree of curiosity.

Another description appears in the report about the situation in Greenland that the Norwegian priest Ivar Bardarson gave to the Bishop of Bergen around the middle of the fourteenth century. According to this story, the Western Settlement was now deserted, and the Inuit occupied the entire area. The original document is lost, but, judging from the surviving accounts, Bardarson had told his story to someone who then wrote it down, perhaps a long time later. This leaves room for possible misunderstandings. An Icelandic annal from 1379 notes that the Inuit had been attacking the Norse, killing eighteen men and capturing two boys.

Greenland myths and tales collected in the nineteenth century also tell about conflicts between the two peoples. In this case, however, we are dealing with an oral tradition in which those who passed the stories down through time may have added a little here and subtracted a little there. For example, there is a story about how the Inuit overran the farm at Hvalsey and burned the Norse alive in their houses. When the farm was excavated in 1935, however, there was no carbonized layer or any other indication of a fierce fire, from which one must conclude that in this case the story or myth was not tied to actual events.

A different and rather more fanciful tale of violence appears in *1421: The Year China Discovered the World* by Gavin Menzies.[8] Among other accounts, Menzies tells about a visit by a large Chinese fleet to the Hvalsey Fjord, where the Chinese not only distributed their DNA among the local population, but threatened it with cannons. That story takes us far into the aforementioned twilight zone.

We are, so to speak, faced with two different ways of reconstructing an event: from parchment and from memory and storytelling. While we cannot say that the Inuit story is mistaken, it probably ought not to be interpreted literally. A similar event may have taken place that, for the benefit of later generations, was then associated with a well-recognized location where Norse people were known to have lived. The story's metamorphosis may come from a storyteller's device we also know from the Icelandic sagas about Greenland, in which the story's setting might be merely a product of the mind, but garnished with familiar place names to make listeners feel at home.

FIGURE 3.6 Ruin of the church of Hvalsey seen from the west through the entrance of the festival hall that belonged to the surrounding farm complex. The church probably was erected at the beginning of the fourteenth century and is the best-preserved medieval building in the Norse North Atlantic area. (Photo by J. Berglund)

The long and the short of it is that we must take the few sparse reports to be evidence of contact between the two groups of people. The problems are with interpreting the stories, which give rise to a number of unanswered questions. Accepting the stories at face value means accepting that encounters between the two peoples were invariably hostile. The Norse name for the Inuit, *skrælings* (a sick, weak person), also seems to suggest a somewhat arrogant, condescending attitude. Contact need not always have been confrontational, however; a look at the dissemination of news in our own time shows a parallel in that it is most often the dramatic events that make the headlines, rarely or never a story about peaceful coexistence. The Norse attitude toward the Inuit probably had its root in the difference between Christians and non-Christians, but that circumstance would not necessarily lead to conflict.

Normally contact between two parties is manifested archaeologically by finds of objects from both sides of a relationship. Such objects are extremely scarce in material from the Norse ruins in both the Western and Eastern settlements, while, conversely, they are somewhat more numerous in Thule Inuit ruins. In both cases the artifacts give the impression of having served as a kind of souvenir. Norse items have been found in Thule culture ruins in High Arctic Greenland and Canada, which reflects a meeting of some kind, at least an encounter with objects from an alien culture. These artifacts may, of course, have come from an actual encounter, but they may just as well have been obtained by trade or by plundering abandoned Norse home sites. Until new archaeological or historical discoveries shed further light on this question, the answer must remain open.

We do see that the Thule culture Inuit spread down along Greenland's west coast during the fourteenth century, possibly reaching the mouth of the Nuuk Fjord – the Western Settlement's outer limit toward the Davis Strait – as early as the beginning of that century. If seen in conjunction with an ongoing Norse exodus, the Thule people's advance could be interpreted as possibly having contributed to a decision by the Norse to abandon their farms and go elsewhere.

ADAPTATION AND SUBSISTENCE IN GREENLAND'S MEDIEVAL PERIOD

It is interesting that in recent popular works concerning the Greenland Norse, their society is often described as being at the point of collapse, as if their resources were fully consumed every year. If the situation had been that terrible, they would surely not have hesitated to reemigrate. Descriptions of that kind most likely reflect modern preoccupations. Social and material collapse is dramatic and can be made to serve as a parallel to worries of everything in our own day. It is far more rewarding, however, to examine how the Norse adjusted to the conditions in their new land. Were there great differences between Greenland and their homeland? Did they gain anything by moving to Greenland? The immediate answer must be both Yes and No.

Back home in Iceland, land had been growing scarce, and a shortage of farm property and a growing population must be considered a powerful incentive to seek new land in the west. Although that may seem like a momentous decision, if we view the Norse North Atlantic region as a whole – from the entire Norwegian coast to the Faeroes, Shetland,

FIGURE 3.7 Sheep grazing on a mountain pasture in the Qollortoq Valley in the core area of what was once the Eastern Settlement. (Photo by J. Berglund)

the Orkneys, and Iceland – it takes on the character of a large "fjord system" where people moved around freely, and where Greenland simply represented a westward expansion. With this image in mind, it is not difficult to comprehend a moving away from Greenland again, because that, too, would have taken place within the "local region."

One of the immediate advantages the settlers found was an unoccupied country with plentiful resources. Fine pastures could be exploited up to 600 meters above sea level, and there was game of every sort from ptarmigans (a medium-sized game bird in the grouse family) to reindeer, fish, and seal, as well as prestige game such as polar bear and walrus. At first, the climate was relatively mild, but it was to cool down beginning in the mid-thirteenth century until the Norse population left at the end of the fifteenth century.

The settlers brought with them a mental and physical farming culture that they now needed to repot in new soil. For the first time, domestic animals were imposed on Greenland; for the first time, Greenland's environment was indirectly exploited by farm animals such as cows, sheep, and goats. So far, so good. In time, it turned out that cows required too many resources, and to counteract this situation, the cow population was reduced in favor of smaller animals like sheep and goats. It is likely that only the large and medium-sized farms continued to keep a few cows.

If we look at the buildings, we see that large common rooms reflecting the concepts settlers had brought with them from Iceland eventually become smaller, and one may suppose that this development was a response to gradually cooling conditions. Next, we may turn to the pastures that provided the basis for keeping domestic animals. Near the farms we find fenced-in home fields, while areas farther away provided mountain pastures for summer farming. An example is known from the Western Settlement of soil improvement done by spreading mixed farm waste. The Norse also developed a unique watering system based on adjustable canals, laced across their home fields and connected to water reservoirs at higher elevations. Similar arrangements are not known from Iceland in the same period, and it may well be that the theoretical background for these engineering works came from educated men in the service of the Greenland Church.

Of lesser magnitude are the examples we have of the inhabitants' skill in replacing metal with bone and horn in a number of everyday objects. From both of the settlements we have examples such as arrows made from reindeer antlers, a lock and an axe blade made from whale bone, and belt buckles and sewing needles made of bone. Rather than regard these articles as a sign of want, one might consider them proof of imaginative use of the raw materials at hand.

It has long been a mystery why so few fish bones have been found in Greenland archaeological excavations. Some authors have suggested that there was a taboo about eating fish, an explanation that naturally offers an immediate solution to the problem. However, fish remains have always been present in excavated material, only in small quantities. Of course the Norse Greenlanders ate fish. The fjords and the ocean constituted a limitless resource, and eating fish was a tradition all over the Norse world. A recent excavation in the Western Settlement uncovered parts of a net made of baleen (whalebone), which may well have been the remains of a fishing net. Radio-isotope analyses performed in the last few years on human bones from Norse graveyards, in both settlements, tell a clear story about what people ate and in what quantities. Here there is no possible doubt: they ate

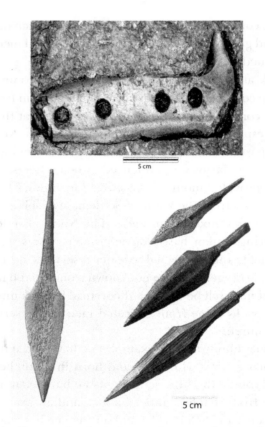

5 cm

5 cm

FIGURE 3.8 Artifacts made of reindeer antlers as a substitute for or a supplement to iron: (top) a door hinge and (bottom) a collection of arrows for hunting.

fish. These analyses also show that, as time progressed, a greater proportion of the food consumed was marine, especially fish and seal. This can only mean that supplies of food caught or grown on land decreased and were compensated for by increasing the proportion of food from the sea.

In connection with the mystery of the missing fish bones, I might add a story about an older Norwegian biologist I encountered during the excavation of the well-known "Farm beneath the Sand." We had just finished digging out a quite large vessel made of steatite, and when the biologist saw it, he said that he was familiar with that type of vessel from his childhood in northern Norway. His grandparents had collected the scraps from fish dinners in just such a vessel, and when it was filled, they boiled the fish bones into a nutritious mass that they fed to their handful of cows during the winter. Perhaps the explanation for the missing Norse Greenland fish bones is that the animals were fed the scraps, which had been rendered completely unrecognizable to archaeologists and osteologists.

CONSIDERING SUCCESS AND FAILURE OF THE GREENLAND NORSE

Even this brief overview should demonstrate that the Norse Greenlanders without a doubt were competent farmers who knew how to adjust to changing circumstances in their subsistence, to the extent that it was within their power to do so. Diamond claims in *Guns, Germs, and Steel* that the Norse community was unable to maintain a food-producing society, and that the society itself was too small and too impoverished to survive in the long run. However, this must be regarded as a "truth" in need of strong modifications. As noted earlier, the Norse Greenlanders had no problem with changing from a mainly terrestrial diet to a predominantly marine one. Their society survived for precisely as long as that was possible without sinking below what was considered an acceptable status. The Norse left the Western Settlement toward the end of the fourteenth century, while the Eastern Settlement was abandoned at the end of the fifteenth century, having outlasted the Western Settlement by a century. That is a long time, long enough to produce up to four additional generations, and longer than several twentieth-century European states have lasted. With regard to food production, it is a matter of record that during the five years that Greenland was cut off from Danish supplies as a result of World War II, sheep farming in Greenland, combined with hunting and trapping, to a high degree sustained the population.

Greenland's population in 1945 numbered 21,412 – more than four times that of the maximum population estimate for the Norse period. Moreover, neither stories nor archaeological excavations indicate any panic or social unrest of the sort Diamond imagines drove the Eastern Settlement toward collapse. On the contrary, everything points to a gradual and leisurely depopulation, a situation that also seems to apply to the Western Settlement. Archaeological

FIGURE 3.9 Ruin of the church "Undir Höfdi" built around 1300 C.E. The facing gable was a wooden construction that has now disappeared. During the centuries following abandonment, the ruin was buried under drift sand that still covers the surrounding area. The creek to the left is now hardly navigable because of drifting sand; the buildings in the background belong to a modern sheep farmer. (Photo by J. Berglund)

investigations of several Norse farm sites in the Western Settlement have uncovered nothing to suggest that the last inhabitants starved or froze to death, which is the interpretation Diamond has chosen to read into the archaeological reports. It is also impossible that Ivar Bardarson traveled from farm to farm to gather corpses in different stages of decomposition and carry them many miles to the nearest churchyard.

It is quite telling that during our Greenland Norse excavations we mostly come upon deliberately discarded objects. Furthermore, as already noted, there is no great wealth of Norse objects in Thule house ruins. The Norse took with them whatever they could carry when they left. Nor have archaeological discoveries included anything suggesting conflict, such as fires or bodies left in the Norse ruins. In one instance only was a body found at a farm in the Eastern Settlement, and the circumstances surrounding that find are unclear.

FIGURE 3.10 Ruin of the church of Herjolfsnæs situated at the southernmost part of the Eastern Settlement; the first port of call when arriving from the east. The church probably was erected in the thirteenth century as one of the biggest in the Eastern Settlement. Today only the foundation is left and parts of the collapsed surrounding wall. Around the church was the burial ground, excavated in 1921. Because of the permanently frozen ground, the largest known collection of medieval clothing was discovered here. By 1921 a large part of the churchyard had disappeared into the sea. To the right, the sea is continuously eroding the shore, a process that began in the Middle Ages and now has reached the church itself. (Photo by J. Berglund)

Survival in Greenland's communities was naturally contingent upon self-sufficiency in food production. It has already been noted that a two-pronged economic approach was used, relying on hunting and fishing on the one hand and on domestic animal products on the other. Flesh-based protein came mostly from hunting and fishing, while farm animals such as cows, sheep, and goats primarily supplied fresh milk for various dairy products. In addition, sheep and goats yielded wool for the cloth production that took place on all the farms. Briefly stated, each farm was a production unit, and its products were both exchanged among the farms and used as payment in kind for church taxes.

All this activity naturally depended on the availability of enough land and water to permit domestic animals as well as to supply all the wild game and fish the population needed. It was quite a different matter to make sure that the farm animals had sufficient fodder to see them through a winter, and that a farm was properly situated to provide a good hay harvest from fields surrounding farms and to give the animals an opportunity to graze somewhat farther away, as late into the year as possible. That takes us to a different discussion, namely, about whether the farmers contributed to a deterioration of their physical environment with their activities.

SLOUCHING TOWARD "COLLAPSE"

Particularly in the Eastern Settlement's central region, a number of investigations of soil and sedimentary conditions have been made, with core samples taken from lakes, wetlands, and areas near farm houses. The results of these analyses show that soil erosion speeded up after settlement began in 985. Additional analyses of teeth from domestic animals demonstrate increased wear from the presence of sand in their food. One may draw two possible conclusions from this: either the pasture areas had become so worn down that the animals' food inevitably became mixed with grains of sand, or else strong winds had carried in sand from other areas in the region. The destruction of vegetation meant that scrub, which normally acted as windbreaks, no longer prevented the upper soil layers from becoming exposed to wind and to subsequent erosion, which accelerated as an increasing number of plants were removed by grazing.

This scenario may have been initiated by the farmers' burning off the scrub vegetation, followed by trampling and grazing by domestic animals, but such an interpretation is not without ambiguities. Recent climate research suggests that strong winds characterized the warm period before the cooling trend that culminated in the Little Ice Age, about 1430–1850, and that this windy period peaked just before the cooling began in the fifteenth century. That means that the conditions for erosion were present during the entire period of Norse tenure, from which we might conclude that there were two different contributory causes, both pointing in the same unfortunate direction. Examples of erosion and increasing sand deposits are known from many locations in the Eastern Settlement, including from the vicinity of a big farm and a church constructed around 1300. The

FIGURE 3.11 Historical climate changes from 600 to 1900 C.E. The Norse period in Greenland, roughly 1000 to 1400 C.E., took place during a relatively warm period, while the retraction of settlement occurred a cold period. The predominating cold in the fourteenth century can be seen as a factor contributing to the abandonment of Norse settlements. (Courtesy of *Grønlands Forhistorie*, Copenhagen, 2004)

implication is that growing deposits of wind-blown sand began in this part of the community sometime in the fourteenth century, because it is unlikely that anyone would have established a farm with a church in an area that was already plagued by sand deposits.

The next inevitable question must address the number of domestic animals that may have been roaming the outdoors. Although there is evidence of stables and folds with room for quite a number of animals, it is difficult to know how many at any time were actually out grazing and contributing to the ongoing erosion. Modern sheep farmers in southern Greenland have learned to alternate between resting and active pasturage, but we have no way of knowing if the Norse farmers used the same approach. However, the number of sheep in southern Greenland today is far greater than it ever was during the Middle Ages, in 1991 about 40,000, and that brings with it a much greater threat of erosion. The likeliest explanation for the Medieval situation is probably that it was chiefly caused by burned-off vegetation cover followed by the effects of wind and weather. However that may be, blowing sand and erosion must have been detrimental to farming.

One factor over which humans had absolutely no control was the rising sea level. This development is seen most markedly at the southernmost Norse Greenland church, Herjolfsnæs, where the ocean today reaches all the way to the actual ruin, and most of the churchyard has been eroded by the sea. Another example is Sandnes church in the Western Settlement, where both church and churchyard today are entirely covered by water and sand. The situation was not that dire in the Middle Ages, although it has nevertheless been estimated that

FIGURE 3.12 A fight scene between two fighters equipped with swords and shields and therefore unlikely to have been a Norse fighting with an Inuk. The scene is carved into a weaver's sword of bone. (Courtesy of Meddelelser om Gronland)

the sea level rose at least one meter while the two Norse settlements were still viable. In fact, sedimentation cores obtained from the two main fjords in the Eastern Settlement show "submerged land," in the sense that shoreline farms innermost in the fjords may have lost as much as 250 hectares (about 618 acres) of pasture. Humans could do nothing to stop it.

It is thus possible to identify two direct threats against the Norse farming society's subsistence: one that the farmers themselves may have increased, the other one completely beyond their control. Apart from those developments, there is the unspecified menace of the advancing Thule people. It has been suggested that the Norse were powerless against this menace because they lacked military training and weapons. No weapons have been found, however; it is surely obvious that the Norse would have taken such belongings with them when they left the country. They were nevertheless no strangers to armed conflict. A battle scene was carved on a small piece of bone, but, significantly, the scene does not depict a Norseman against an Inuk.

GREENLAND IN THE NORSE WORLD

I have not yet touched on another important aspect of Norse Greenland society, namely, its connection with the rest of the North Atlantic world and with Europe. We know that at least for the first centuries the settlers maintained a lively contact with the east, not the least after the establishment of the Greenland bishopric in 1124. Their clothing styles, tools, runic inscriptions, and religion also show clearly that they remained a part of the wider Norse cultural orbit. Objects found during archaeological excavations do not indicate any effort to learn new ways from the Thule people they may have encountered, nor did any Eskimo words find their way into the Old Norse vocabulary.

The Norse preferred the familiar, and their orientation was exclusively to the Nordic world. Their society was strongly hierarchical, with powerful farmers or chieftains as its decision makers and with their Church as part of the power structure. Stories and archaeological finds alike show that this was a community with distinct social strata, and the impression is confirmed by radio-isotope analyses demonstrating that those in the top stratum were better fed than the rest. Finds of keys and locks on several farms further underline social stratification on a microplane – some people had the power to exclude others. From its top to its bottom, this society was essentially constructed like those elsewhere in the Norse world.

Relations with Europe were connected to the Church and to trade, and the most valuable Greenland product was ivory from the tusks of the walrus caught farther north in western Greenland – a commodity seen as a particularly weighty argument for maintaining a trade connection with Europe. This trade appears to have ceased in the fourteenth century. There are two differing views on why this happened. One says that, by the fourteenth century, Europeans had easier access to African ivory, which meant dwindling interest in fetching ivory in Greenland by means of a long and dangerous voyage. The other view holds that although Arab merchants and middlemen had never been able to satisfy the European demand for ivory, interest in Greenland trade and contact eventually diminished. So on top of internal difficulties we might add external problems.

The Greenland Church province had never been a particularly desirable one; the bishops were often absent from the country for years, and once appointed, bishops might take a long time to show up. In 1370 the last resident bishop died and was not replaced, although bishops for Greenland continued to be appointed for some time.

We may add yet another danger to the several already discussed as threats to the Norse Greenlanders, and that is the problem of maintaining status and an acceptable lifestyle. While they had successfully managed the switch from terrestrial to a marine diet, they might have had some difficulty with accepting a lifestyle that was not primarily based on traditional farming, if it came to that. This was not a problem for the Inuit people because their lifestyle was solely based upon hunting, and the consequences of the changing climatic conditions did not disturb that.

It is probable that emigration went on for some time, but we don't know exactly where the settlers went. As the conditions for their continued existence were altered, however, leaving their farms became the only alternative. One may therefore with some justification claim that their emigration was a rational response to a challenge with unacceptable alternatives.

Nobody deliberately chooses to fail, and neither did the Norse Greenlanders. Their choice was the right one for several hundred years. What happened later could not have been foreseen, and is not the consequence of choosing to fail.

Translated from Danish into English by Kirsten Seaver.

Notes

* I was born in Copenhagen in 1938 and graduated from the University of Copenhagen in 1976 with an M.A. in European prehistoric archaeology. As a student I joined archaeological expeditions in the Middle East, Denmark, Sweden, and Greenland. After participating in several expeditions to Greenland for the Danish National Museum, I accepted a position as head of a provincial museum in southern Greenland in 1981.

   Eleven years later I moved to Nuuk, the capital of Greenland, and was employed as an archaeologist at the Greenland National Museum and Archives. In 1998 I became vice-director of the institution, a position I held until my retirement in 2004. Apart from fieldwork, my main occupation was to administer the law of protection of monuments in the open landscape: that is, ruins or remnants from the Inuit and Norse past. I also took part in museum exhibitions and public outreach.

   My own research is focused on Norse culture and landscape. Throughout my years in Nuuk I gave courses on these subjects at the

University of Greenland, Ilisimatusarfik. For me the relation between culture and landscape is one of the most fascinating areas in archaeology. In the field it is a matter of looking and listening and having the patience to let the landscape open up.

1. Spengler 1991/1926.
2. Gibbon 2005.
3. Toynbee 1987/1947.
4. Kurlansky 2005.
5. Diamond 2005.
6. Diamond 1997.
7. Toynbee 1987/1947: vol. 1, 177.
8. Menzies 2003.

Bibliography

Diamond, Jared. 1997. *Guns, Germs, and Steel, The Fates of Human Societies.* New York: W. W. Norton.

Diamond, Jared. 2005. *Collapse: How Societies Choose to Fail or Succeed.* New York: Viking.

Gibbon, Edward. 2005. *The Decline and Fall of the Roman Empire.* London: Penguin Classics.

Kurlansky, Mark. 2005. *Salt: A World History.* New York: Walker.

Menzies, Gavin. 2003. *1421: The Year China Discovered the World.* London: Bantam Books.

Spengler, Oswald. 1991/1926. *The Decline of The West.* Oxford: Oxford University Press.

Toynbee, Arnold. 1987/1947. *A Study of History.* Volume 1. Oxford: Oxford University Press.

A Reader's Guide to Medieval Norse Society in Greenland

For a comprehensive and general view of the Norse period in Greenland good choices are the following:

H. C. Gulløv (ed.), *Grønlands Forhistorie* (Copenhagen, 2004), and Seaver A. Kirsten, *The Frozen Echo, Greenland and the Exploration of North America ca. A.D. 1000–1500* (Stanford, CA, 1996). For background on demography, archaeology, the connections between Greenland and Europe, the relations between Inuit and Norse, and the Norse legacy from the point of view of a modern Greenlander, see the Smithsonian Institution catalog *Vikings: The North Atlantic Saga* (Washington, DC, 2000). An investigation on the use of land can be read in Svend E. Albrethsen and Christian Keller, "The Use of Saeter in Medieval Norse Farming," *Arctic Anthropology* (1986): 91–107. The sagas of the journeys to North America are told in *The Sagas of the Icelanders* (New York, 2000), pp. 626–674. The first positive find of Norse presence in North America is related by the

Norwegian archaeologist Anne Stine Ingstad in "The Norse Settlement at L'Anse Aux Meadows, Newfoundland," *Acta Archaeologica* (1970): 109–154.

The question of the destiny of the Norse population is discussed in Joel Berglund, "The Decline of the Norse Settlements in Greenland," *Arctic Anthropology* (1986): 109–135; Andrew J. Dugmore, Christian Keller, and Thomas H. McGovern, "Norse Greenland Settlement: Reflections on Climate Change, Trade, and the Contrasting Fates of Human Settlements in the North Atlantic Islands," *Arctic Anthropology* (2007): 12–36; and Naja Mikkelsen and others, "The Norse in Greenland and Late Holocene Sea-Level Change," *Polar Record* (2008): 45–50. The ongoing discussion of what happened to the ivory trade is presented by Else Roesdahl in "Walrus and Ivory," in *Select Papers from the Proceedings of the 14th Viking Congress* (Tórshavn, 2001), pp. 182–191, and Kirsten Seaver, *Maps, Myths and Men: The Story of the Vinland Map* (Stanford, CA, 2004).

4

Calamities without Collapse

Environment, Economy, and Society in China,
ca. 1800–1949

Kenneth Pomeranz[*]

PROLOGUE: WHAT CHINESE COLLAPSE?

China raises problems for anyone trying to divide societies into "winners" and "losers." For most of history, it would have to be considered an unusually "successful" society if we use either the criterion of power or that of average material living standards. But during much of the nineteenth and early twentieth centuries – a blip in human history, but a critical formative moment for Western social science – China was in turmoil, and the assumption that China had "ultimately" "failed" became commonplace in Western histories. Today any such failure looks much less "ultimate": although China remains much less prosperous than most of Europe and North America, it has caught up considerably in living standards (especially life expectancy), and it is certainly among the world's great political powers. Consequently we have a series of narratives about Chinese "failure," which are products of a very particular moment.

Jared Diamond, who certainly takes the long view, avoids treating China as simply a "loser" – for the most part, it figures as part of the agricultural, literate, state-building "Eurasia" that emerges as the winner over the first 90 percent of *Guns, Germs, and Steel*.[1] But in his final chapter Diamond does use China as a foil for European success – and does so by adopting an outdated and largely discredited variety of conventional wisdom. His argument takes a fifteenth-century incident that was actually of limited significance and makes it emblematic of an

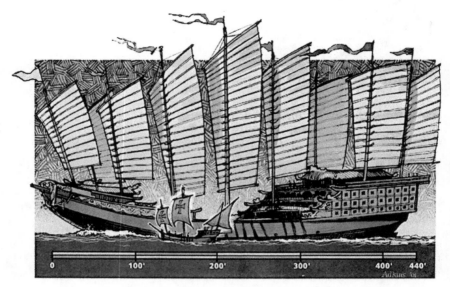

FIGURE 4.1 Comparison of Zheng He's flagship with Columbus' fleet, the latter in the foreground is utterly dwarfed.

enduring condition that he traces, as he often does, to geography. It is worth discussing this case briefly before turning to the more complex and important crises of the nineteenth century.

Between 1405 and 1433 the Ming court mounted a series of huge naval expeditions into the Indian Ocean, reaching as far as the east coast of Africa. The individual ships dwarfed any European ships of the time as did the overall fleet, with 28,000 men. But the fleet did not colonize the places it visited, much less "proceed around Africa's Southern cape westward and colonize Europe," and Diamond wonders why.[2] Moreover, after a political shift in 1433 the court stopped these expeditions, dismantled the boats and the state-run shipyard that built them, and, for a time, attempted to ban all ocean-going ships.

Diamond sees this event as significant in itself, having deprived China of gains from colonization ("the wealth flowing into Spain") that ultimately fell to Europeans.[3] This in itself is interesting, since it suggests that those gains were significant to Europe, and elsewhere Diamond tends to ignore the importance of gains from preying on other societies in explaining today's differences between rich and poor. But his more basic point is that China had a single government, so that once Beijing stopped sponsoring these expeditions, they had no alternative source of support; by contrast, Columbus sought support from various European princes before finally getting a "yes" from Ferdinand and Isabella. Diamond claims that this represents a pattern: he lists other cases in which one or another European state rejected an idea that actually proved quite successful elsewhere, and was eventually adopted back in the place that had initially rejected it. By contrast, he argues, because China was a single state for most of the time after 221 B.C.E. – a situation he attributes to geography – a single decision could, and often did, kill a promising line of technological development. Thus China's unity, which had been an advantage for technological development in earlier eras, became a disadvantage "in the very long run."[4]

There are many problems with this argument; let us focus on three. First, it explains a variable result by means of a supposed constant. Isn't 221 B.C.E. to 1433 already "the very long run"? Why should unity have been an advantage for many centuries, and then a disadvantage? Second, and more important, there is very little evidence that the Chinese government played a significant role in stifling technological change. After 1433, for instance, China's navy disappeared from the Indian Ocean, but within a few decades Chinese merchant shipping again dominated the sea lanes as far as present-day Singapore.[5] They did not "fail" to go farther because they couldn't, but because it made no sense for profit-seeking merchants to go farther. This was about as far as one could go in a single monsoon season, and once the winds shifted, it would have been foolish for any merchant to spend months in port, paying his sailors and not turning over his capital while he waited to go farther. What made sense was to trade in Southeast Asia – often meeting Indians, Arabs, or others who came as far east as they could in one monsoon season, so that goods from all over Eurasia could be exchanged without having to sail all around Eurasia – and then return home to sell one's cargo and realize one's profits. Sailing farther made sense only if one had noneconomic, "irrational" goals, such as conquest or religious proselytizing (which, of course, the Europeans did). In other words, this line of innovation was not halted, but perhaps delayed a few decades – quite like what Diamond admits happened in many European cases. And although Diamond mentions other technologies that the Chinese court stopped actively supporting at various times,[6] it did not ban any of them. Since the economy was overwhelmingly private, not state-run, it is not clear how much this withdrawal of state support mattered. We certainly lack the evidence to say that any such costs outweighed, in net terms, the benefits of unity (e.g., much less war or easier diffusion of technologies). In fact, even if the Chinese state had tried to crush technological development, it is very doubtful that it had the ability to do so: like other premodern states, Chinese dynasties simply did not have anything like the surveillance and repressive capacities that this would have required.

Third, and perhaps most important, China does not seem to have "fallen behind" at this point, but much later. In a book written several years ago, I estimated that Chinese living standards in the late eighteenth century were roughly equal to those in Europe, while living standards in the Yangzi Delta, China's richest region, roughly matched those in England and Holland (Europe's richest areas). A recent study by Jan Luiten van Zanden, using very different methods, comes to roughly similar conclusions: he has Chinese per capita income lagging Europe's by 10 percent in 1750 and the Yangzi Delta's lagging England's by the same 10 percent. (By contrast, contemporary per capita income in Canada, Germany, Japan, the Netherlands, and the United Kingdom are all more than 20 percent behind the U.S. level, while the United States lags behind Luxembourg by 25 percent.)[7] There is no room here to go into all the details, but "the great divergence" between China and the West clearly came later than Diamond thinks, and did not come from an excessively powerful state blocking innovation (or, in the language of Diamond's *Collapse,* "choosing to fail").[8] It came when technology, fossil fuels, and access to overseas resources produced an unprecedented boom in Europe, while China – for reasons we are about to explore – ran into trouble.

THE LATE IMPERIAL/EARLY MODERN CRISIS, CA. 1800–1949

The phrase "the collapse of Chinese society/civilization" is usually assumed to refer to a series of *nineteenth*-century crises, which led to a period of political instability and social misery that lasted until at least 1949. By certain "objective" criteria – deaths as a percentage of population, extent of territory lost to invaders (and length of time before it was recovered), etc. – this period was no worse than some others. A civil war in the eighth century may have killed one-fifth of the population, or perhaps even one-third;[9] population may have fallen by one-quarter amid plague, civil war, and Manchu invasion in the seventeenth century. Yet the nineteenth century stands out in our minds for at least three reasons. First, it is relatively recent and well documented. Second, because it roughly coincided with an unprecedented surge in Western political and economic power, it is often said to represent Chinese society "failing" and "falling behind" in ways that are irrelevant to earlier crises. Third, because many of the strategies by which Chinese ultimately coped with these crises came from the West, their non-Chineseness is more evident to Westerners than that of (for instance) Central Asian military institutions adopted after earlier crises.

Other large contiguous empires also broke up in the late nineteenth and early twentieth centuries – Romanov, Hapsburg, and Ottoman – and the major transoceanic empires followed after 1945. By strictly political criteria, China is actually something of a success story, since today's People's Republic takes in almost all the territory of the old Qing empire (missing only Taiwan, outer Mongolia, and parts of Siberia), while these other states fractured much more. If we treat the whole period from 1914 to 1945 (or even 1989) as a long period of disorder flowing from the collapse of multiple European monarchies, that crisis was bloodier than China's, at least in percentage terms.[10]

But it seems likely that China's social, economic, and ecological crises were deeper. Chinese living standards and life expectancy were probably no higher in 1950 than in 1750, and quite likely lower. In relative terms Chinese per capita incomes in 1750 were close to European ones, and those of the Yangzi Delta, China's richest region, close to England's; by 1900 both of those ratios were at least 5:1, and probably higher.[11] (The empire's population grew by roughly 75 percent from 1800 to 1953, although this was much slower than ca. 1680–1800.) Meanwhile, the incidence of catastrophes soared. Xia Mingfang estimates 42 million famine deaths between 1368 and 1937; over 35 million of them came after 1875.[12] Deaths from political violence also soared, including 35 million killed in Japan's 1937–1945 invasion. So although China clearly does not meet most of

Diamond's criteria for collapse – lasting population decline, reversion to "simpler" organizational forms, and so on – it could be argued that some areas temporarily met the criterion of a serious decline in "fortune," that is, living standards.[13] One can certainly ask "What went wrong?" – and many scholars have.

The unfavorable trends discussed above do not add up to "collapse," but they do suggest something much more than just *dynastic* decline or a failure to keep pace with developments in nineteenth-century Western Europe. At bottom lay a series of regional environmental crises, which were partly caused by eighteenth-century population growth, and various institutions and policies that managed these stresses well in the medium term but proved hard to modify when new circumstances made some of them dysfunctional. In some regions these problems were evident by the 1790s, and in many others by the 1830s; the Opium War (1839–1842) and its aftermath then added new and serious complications.

The often indirect effects of population on China's environment differed radically from place to place. Moreover, institutions that *restrained* population growth also contributed to nineteenth-century problems. And whatever else it may have been, state policy was not rigid: many innovations were tried to cope with novel situations, often using regional successes as models for national policy. Nothing worked to stabilize all the interlocking pieces of the Chinese empire, but some policies did lay the basis for a relatively rapid recovery in particular areas (mostly south of the Yangzi) after 1860, and even for "modern" types of development. In the long run, moreover, "China" was surprisingly successful in maintaining its sovereignty against aggressive foreigners – albeit partly thanks to world wars among the foreigners.

The rest of this essay argues the following points:

1. The idea of "collapse" is inapplicable, despite the depth of China's nineteenth- and early-twentieth-century problems.
2. Much of the crisis itself must be seen as reflecting environmental problems not solvable by any available choices; Western societies of the same era managed some similar stresses "successfully" in part by exporting them overseas.
3. Although the state (the closest thing to a unitary actor that was trying to manage the overall crisis) made choices that

deepened these crises (thus "choosing to fail" in Diamond's terms), it also made several that were well designed for limiting their immediate impact, and some (not always the same ones) that eventually contributed to overcoming them.

WHERE WERE THE VULNERABILITIES? A GEOGRAPHIC AND INSTITUTIONAL OVERVIEW

As noted above, East and South China included some of the richest places on earth before the Industrial Revolution. In particular, living standards in the Yangzi Delta (population over 31,000,000) were probably comparable to England's (the highest in Europe) around 1770. Its agriculture was exceptionally productive – not only per acre, but per labor day; people making textiles (the largest industry) earned incomes comparable to textile workers anywhere; and many of its markets were remarkably efficient. It had little heavy industry, however, largely because it lacked energy sources – wood, coal, peat, or even water power (due to flat terrain) – and mineral deposits.

The Delta traded extensively with other Chinese regions, exchanging manufactures (above all cloth) for raw cotton, rice, timber, and other primary products from North China, the Middle and Upper Yangzi, and elsewhere. Most of these hinterlands were poorer and more ecologically fragile than the Lower Yangzi and the Southeast.[14] In particular, northern China had a shorter growing season, ruling out the double cropping that was widespread in the South. Water was not as accessible, which forced most of its farmers to rely on inadequate rainfall; and that rainfall often came in sudden, uncontrollable downpours. The North's light soils (especially loess) were fertile, but easily eroded, so that river beds rose steadily despite conscientious dredging efforts. Agricultural yields and per capita incomes probably averaged about 60 percent of Yangzi Delta levels and fluctuated more. Droughts and floods were more common; most farms had only one harvest per year; and poorer transport made it harder to offset local problems by trading with unaffected areas. Moreover people without secure land use rights were more common in the North than the South; such people were especially vulnerable to disasters, and probably more likely than others to turn to banditry or rebellion.

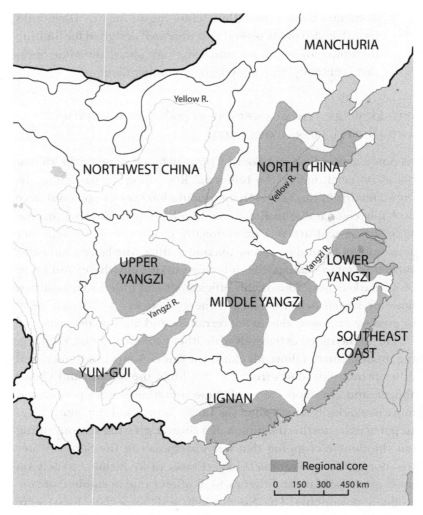

FIGURE 4.2 China divided into the "macroregions," adapted from Skinner 1977: 214–215.

Two other geographic gradients are also noteworthy. First, areas near the coast were generally richer than the interior, although such differences are much larger now than then. Second, highland areas were generally poorer than lowland ones, despite intermittent booms when demand for tea, timber, and other highland products rose. Highland populations grew sharply during the eighteenth century, partly because of the spread of corn, potatoes, and other altitude-tolerant American

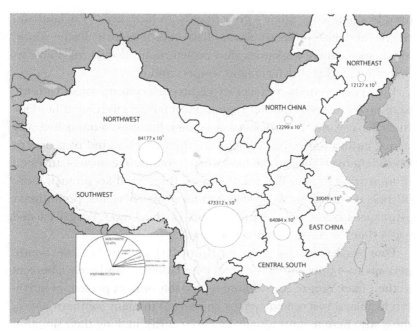

FIGURE 4.3 Distribution of water resources in China today, adapted from Pan Jiazheng 1987, unpaginated map.

crops; in some cases, serious environmental degradation followed. Highland population growth also fueled ethnic conflict, as Han immigrants clashed with indigenous people over land rights, court-ship practices, and other issues. Environmental and ethnic problems sometimes overlapped but did not map neatly onto each other. In fact, the most severe environmental problems often emerged, not where the Han pushed against other ethnicities, but on hillsides so steep (and thus easily eroded) that nobody had tried to clear them until timber prices soared and altitude-tolerant corn eliminated much of the cost of moving grain uphill to loggers. As we shall see, civil strife beginning in highland areas figured prominently in China's nineteenth-century problems; it is thus noteworthy that environmental stress, although real enough, was only loosely correlated with this violence.

The poorer parts of China also had more people in highly vulnerable economic niches. In rapidly commercializing early modern Europe, the share of the population who were proletarians – people who were legally free, but owned no land or other means of production, and lived by doing wage labor – grew rapidly. In "advanced" England and the Netherlands, proletarians may have been a majority by the 1600s. Much social theory assumes that proletarianization is inevitable as increased market activity creates winners and losers.[15]

But fewer than 10 percent of eighteenth-century rural Chinese were proletarians. In poorer regions most farmers were smallholders. In richer regions tenancy was widespread, but most tenants had very strong cultivation rights, which were themselves a kind of property. Confident of staying on the land, these tenants, like owners, invested in improving it. Also like smallholders, they could keep much more of their output than those who had no property rights: preliminary estimates suggest that secure tenants in the Lower Yangzi earned 2.5–3 times as much as landless laborers.

Poor North China had more rural proletarians than the richer South: perhaps 10–15 percent of the rural population, versus barely 5 percent in the Lower Yangzi. And although probably only 15 percent of northern farmland was rented (versus 50 percent in many southern areas), those who were tenants usually had no security, making their situation much more like that of landless laborers.[16] Finally, commercialized parts of the hill country often had unusually large concentrations of proletarians: loggers, miners, and so on. As we will shortly learn, those who were proletarianized in China faced especially dire conditions – and, unlike in Europe, they were most common in "backward" areas.

The Qing regime (1644–1912) wanted independent peasants it could get access to without going through local magnates; they generally supported security for tenants, despite a countervailing interest in keeping land rights simple. They certainly supported smallholders against attempts to consolidate large estates. A low reproduction rate among proletarians further reinforced the centrality of small farmers.

Few male proletarians married. Birth control through sex-selective infanticide (not limited to poor families) produced a shortage of marriageable women; some elite males had wives and concubines, exacerbating it. So although in each generation some luckless smallholders and tenants became laborers, most existing proletarians died childless, and the group did not grow.

Having fewer marginal men may have enhanced stability, but such extreme exclusion was probably destabilizing. Lacking the benefits of families, facing afterlives as "hungry ghosts" without offerings from descendants, and often unattached to any particular village, landless laborers were seen as having nothing to lose, and thus dangerous. We know little about how these men actually understood their plight, but they were wildly overrepresented among bandits, gangsters, smugglers, and rebels.

But before getting to that, we must see how the institutions described here responded to the unprecedented growth of ca. 1680–1800, successfully maintaining relatively high living standards while China's population roughly tripled, without major technological breakthroughs. Then we need to look at how this social system shaped the state – especially its finances – and how the state in turn intervened to try to keep the system stable.

Some population growth can be accommodated by using more labor to raise per acre yields – especially with paddy rice. An average Yangzi Delta family's farm shrank by about one-third between 1620 and 1750 (stabilizing thereafter), but more double cropping, more fertilization, and other increased labor and capital inputs raised yields enough to compensate.[17] Similar events probably happened in other paddy rice areas, although the evidence is thin. But intensification cannot sustainably raise per acre yields (and maintain per capita ones) forever; had Delta population not stopped growing, those limits might have been reached. In North China's very different ecologies, labor intensification became ineffective much sooner. This left four alternatives:

1. Deliberate population control
2. Increased rural nonagricultural employment
3. Urbanization and
4. Increasing cultivated area, either through conquest or by reclaiming unfarmed land within current borders.

Options 2 and 3, it should be noted, require that the nonfarmers (whether rural or urban) produce something that can be traded for agricultural and forest products from elsewhere; otherwise, they still press upon the local supply of land.

Late imperial China used all these expedients, but to varying degrees. To summarize:

1. The total impact of deliberate fertility control remains largely unmeasured. It must have mattered where it was heavily

used: Yangzi Delta population barely rose between 1770 and 1850, for instance. But it clearly slowed rather than stopped empire-wide population growth.

2. Rural handicraft industries, especially textiles, grew first and foremost in rich regions. Later they also increased elsewhere, particularly for *local* markets. But only a few regions – above all the Yangzi Delta – traded enough handicrafts for imported primary products for this to significantly raise their region's carrying capacity.

3. In absolute terms, China's urban population was huge, but in percentage terms it remained small for a relatively prosperous, commercialized society. As late as 1843, even the Lower Yangzi was probably under 10 percent urban (although the Delta figure was higher), and North China under 5 percent.

4. Consequently, clearing new lands loomed very large in China's eighteenth-century development. Millions of people moved to frontiers in the Southwest, on Taiwan, and in highland areas throughout the country: while we lack precise data, long-distance migration within China must have easily exceeded 10,000,000 people during the late seventeenth and eighteenth centuries, and millions more moved shorter distances. China's cultivated land roughly doubled between 1650 and 1850, with most of that probably occurring in the eighteenth century. Government generally encouraged these movements, and often even subsidized them, but it also tried to restrain migration where it feared it would lead to violence or loosen government control. The most important restrictions were a ban on migration into most of Manchuria and on permanent migration overseas. Both lasted until the late nineteenth century.

Government policy aside, the socioeconomic system described above generated migration to frontiers. First, it inhibited rapid urbanization.[18] Nobody would pay unskilled urban workers wages much above those of nearby agricultural laborers; thus they earned much less than secure tenants or smallholders. Consequently most people had little reason to move to cities, unless the job awaiting them was far above average. Instead, agricultural surplus fed handicraft workers who remained members of farm households. Individuals often

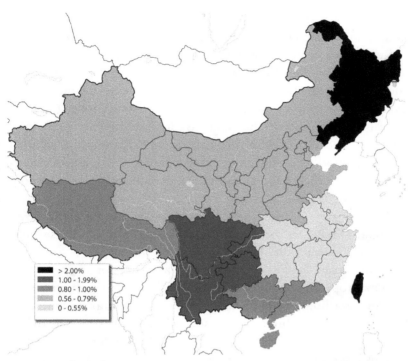

FIGURE 4.4 Population growth map, 1776–1990, based on Lee and Wang 1999: 117.

specialized (in theory, men plowed and women wove), but households combined diverse occupations. Confucian elites approved: multiple income streams reduced tax defaults, home-based handicrafts made earning money consistent with female modesty, and farm life was the kind most consistent with both social and cosmic harmony.[19] Officials often helped poorer areas imitate the combination of farming and rural industry (especially weaving) epitomized by the Yangzi Delta.

Similar forces shaped migration patterns. Although tenants and smallholders earned much more in rich regions, wages varied little. So poor Northerners, unable to put down substantial rent deposits, would gain little by heading for the Yangzi or Pearl River deltas. For the very poor of all regions, the frontier offered better opportunities: average incomes were low, but laboring to clear land usually yielded ownership or at least secure tenancy. This explains the otherwise puzzling fact that net migration moved consistently away from China's richest regions. That, in turn, reinforced income gaps among regions, while net migration toward rich regions might have reduced them.

Richer areas paid higher taxes. The Yangzi Delta paid by far the highest rates, but local elites, not the state, provided most of its public goods. Government officials provided loose supervision, encouragement, and symbolic rewards, but rarely went beyond a token financial contribution.[20] Although the Delta was the polar case, both in its land tax rates – possibly reaching 15 percent of yields versus a national average around 4 percent – and in the extent to which it provided its own services, other rich regions in the East and South also paid more than average, and received less.

Surplus revenues from these areas helped underpin family farming (and Confucian society) on more fragile terrain. These measures included subsidies for well digging in the semiarid North and Northwest, placing most emergency granaries in poor areas, promoting new crops suitable for marginal soils, providing start-up capital to people settling certain frontier regions, and not taxing new land. Even small expenditures of this sort often made a crucial difference in poor areas. The areas thus subsidized included both frontier regions (especially northwestern areas where promoting agriculture was part of keeping Mongol pastoralists out) and long-settled, environmentally degraded, areas.

The North China plain got top priority, for both humanitarian and security reasons.[21] The capital in Beijing could not be secure if the surrounding countryside was unstable. Nor could the countryside – with annual rainfall of perhaps 25 inches – be stable if its rather meager grain surpluses had to feed over 800,000 Beijing residents.

Part of the solution was an elaborate system of publicly supported granaries, which provided emergency supplies in bad years and loans to help poorer farmers through the lean season in ordinary years. For current purposes, four aspects of it merit emphasis. First, the state did the most to support granaries in areas that were too poor to rely on private donations and/or lacked good market access. Second, although this was a huge "welfare" commitment for an eighteenth-century state, it did not extend to everyone. The state was especially concerned with keeping farmers on their land after crop failures, and ensuring that they could plant their next crop; thus, the poorest of the poor – landless laborers – were often denied help. Third, the system was remarkably effective in its mid-eighteenth-century heyday. Even the horrendous 1742 drought did not cause mass starvation, and Chinese food prices usually rose much less after a bad harvest than did European ones. Fourth, by the 1790s the system was getting less government attention, and working less efficiently.

More sustained – and far more expensive – state efforts focused on North China water control: to allow smooth passage of grain tribute from the Yangzi Valley (which provided perhaps a third of Beijing's grain, as well as emergency supplies for other northern areas in years of poor harvests), to allow irrigation in a few strategic places, and to prevent massive flooding.[22] (Rich areas paid for their own water control – except in the very early Qing period, when government helped jumpstart rebuilding after devastating civil wars.) Work focused on two locations.

One was Zhili, the province surrounding Beijing, which was both drought and flood prone. Droughts would reduce the local crops Beijing could buy; floods could also block grain boats from the South. Three major hydraulic overhauls (supplemented by expensive annual maintenance) were tried during the eighteenth century; each worked for a few decades but eventually fell victim to rapid erosion in the Taihang mountains, the slow current and thus high sedimentation rates on Zhili's very flat plains, sudden violent storms, and population growth that placed ever-more people close to riverbanks. After horrendous floods in 1801 (during a rebellion elsewhere that made money scarce), the Qing stopped seeking a permanent hydraulic fix and adopted more modest goals: limiting the flooding, reducing maintenance costs, and having money available for relief when necessary.

The Yellow River/Grand Canal intersection near the southern edge of the North China plain posed even greater challenges. For centuries various versions of a roughly 1,000 mile canal had carried grain from South China to northern capitals. The Ming/Qing Canal crossed the Yellow River at right angles and borrowed water from it; major flooding upstream from the intersection would thus make it impassable. So feeding Beijing required controlling a Yellow River that carried thirty-four times as much silt per cubic meter as the Nile and mostly flowed through poor areas. Silt kept raising the river bed, and without modern dredging equipment, the only "solution" was building higher walls. In some places the bed reached 15 meters above the land outside the dikes, making a major dike break ever-more unacceptable.

During the eighteenth century the Yellow River Administration largely prevented major floods; and although costs kept rising, they remained manageable. At any rate, most Canal and Yellow River maintenance costs were folded into what Southerners paid to have their grain tribute delivered to Beijing: shipping costs per boat rose by over 500 percent between 1732 and 1821 (mostly after 1800). Most of the tribute came from the Yangzi Delta – 33 percent from just its three hardest-hit prefectures, which had under 3 percent of China's farmland.

By the Jiaqing period (1796–1820) costs were rising faster, and flooding was the worst it had been in at least 200 years. But settling for less effective flood control on the Yellow River system was less accept-able than on Zhili's smaller rivers; so during the Daoguang reign (1820–1850) even more resources were devoted to it. This redoubled effort greatly reduced flooding, and in most years the Grand Canal functioned properly. This "declining" state could still complete big projects.

But this environmental respite grew ever more expensive. Yellow River maintenance consumed between 10 and 20 percent of total Qing spending in the period between 1820 and 1850, plus consid-erable corvée labor. By comparison all nonmilitary expenses other than debt repayment totaled only 20 percent of British central gov-ernment spending between 1688 and 1815.

In sum, Qing state and society allowed a large and growing population to live relatively well by eighteenth-century standards. Economically the system relied on wealthy regions in East and South China, particularly the Yangzi Delta. Its population growth was slow, its intensively managed environment fairly stable, and it could pay dis-proportionate taxes that helped stabilize other regions. But maintain-ing these conditions also required that the crowded Delta continue trading its handicraft manufactures for rice, wheat, bean-cake fertil-izer, timber, raw cotton, and other land-intensive imports from else-where in China. It probably also required that coastal regions more generally continue being net exporters of migrants. (One could even argue that exporting tax money that stabilized other areas spared the

Lower Yangzi from having to import people.) And it required that the state use the South's fiscal surpluses efficiently. None of this could be guaranteed.

THINGS FALL APART

The system unraveled in the nineteenth century. Population growth in interior regions decreased their exportable supplies of grain, timber, and other commodities; they also developed their own handicrafts, and so imported fewer manufactures. This hurt the Yangzi Delta: by 1840 an average piece of cloth it exported bought half as much rice as in 1750, and the volume of trade shrank too.[23] The Delta did find some new markets (especially upscale and outside China proper) to offset this, but not enough. Its economy did not decline sharply, but it stagnated.

This made subsidizing other regions increasingly burdensome. We should not exaggerate this: the Delta's tax burdens were not unbearable, and although political changes made it easier for them to advocate changes, they could not demand them. But the situation certainly militated against raising direct taxes, which the Qing were disinclined to do anyway. Instead they muddled through to 1850 with assorted expedients – customs revenue from growing foreign trade, increased "contributions" from wealthy merchants to meet emergencies, a salt monopoly reform – that increased annual revenues, but slowly.[24]

Meanwhile fiscal needs were growing. Population growth in poorer regions made ecological stabilization increasingly challenging: Yellow River control, discussed above, is just one particularly expensive example. A series of rebellions revealed surprising military weaknesses and wiped out government surpluses accumulated over decades. Three of these rebellions – including by far the biggest one – originated in highland areas where Han Chinese settlers clashed with ethnic minorities: in Taiwan (1787–1788), Hunan and Guizhou (1793–1794), and Sichuan, Hubei, Henan, and Shaanxi (1796–1805). Millenarians on the North China plain led two uprisings (1770, 1813); Chinese pirates off the Guangdong coast, allied with a resurgent Vietnamese state, led the other, lasting from roughly 1790 to 1810.

Under these circumstances, opportunities for people to open new land on China's internal frontiers were also shrinking, although they did not disappear completely. Increasing encroachment on lake-beds and riverbanks yielded marginal returns and worsened flood dangers;[25] the same was true for much hillside reclamation (even with careful terracing), which also sometimes risked provoking violence from minorities living at higher elevations. If there were significant frontiers that remained unexploited, they were in Manchuria and overseas, where Qing policies did discourage settlement. But as we shall see later, it is unlikely that different policies would have done anything more than delay the problems a bit – except perhaps a radically different approach to overseas expansion, instituted many decades before anyone could have reasonably foreseen its utility.

To these strains were added the effects of increasing Western incursions and opium dealing.[26] Before 1820 these were small annoyances, the costs of which may have been offset by the additional customs revenues and employment that increased trade generated. But then things worsened rapidly. Opium imports soared – largely for supply-side reasons – from enough to supply 125,000 addicts in the mid-eighteenth century, to enough for perhaps one million 1815, to enough to supply 10 million by 1839. The Opium War (1839–1842) allowed in even more opium, imposed very unpopular treaty obligations and a significant cash indemnity, and rearranged trade in ways that, although not necessarily bad overall, sent unemployment in the Canton area soaring. Those displaced included many single young men from the crowded and ethnically tense Guangxi highlands who, lacking opportunities at home, had become laborers in Canton. It was primarily people from the Guangxi highlands – led by a self-styled messiah inspired by Protestant missionaries – who launched the Taiping Rebellion (1851–1864).

The Taiping Rebellion, one of history's biggest civil wars, killed perhaps 20 million people. With Qing armies preoccupied, what might otherwise have been manageable conflicts elsewhere became long-lasting rebellions. The Nian Rebellion (1853–1868) in North China began with clashes between local bandits and militia, but escalated when Taiping forces marched through, further unsettling the region; the Qing lacked reliable forces to intervene. When fighting made key Yellow River dikes inaccessible, maintenance slipped, triggering the long-dreaded mega-flood. The river's mouth shifted roughly 300

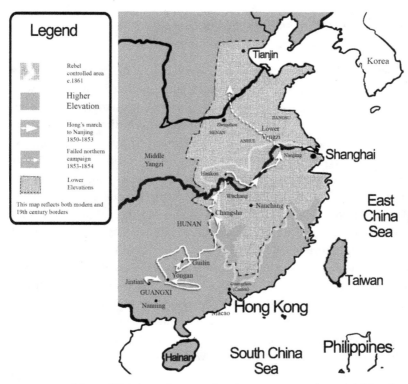

FIGURE 4.5 Map of Taiping advance, showing movement from highland to lowland areas. (Map by Ev Stanton)

miles; over 7,000,000 people suffered severe losses, the Grand Canal was wrecked, and environmental conditions were permanently worsened over thousands of square miles. Muslim rebellions in southwestern (1855–1873) and northwestern (1862–1878) frontier zones also escalated from small events while the Qing state was paralyzed; an Anglo-French assault (1856–1860) on Beijing added further woes.

Like the earlier rebellions, these uprisings largely emerged in poor, environmentally fragile areas. Migration and ethnic conflict were important background in three; the fourth, the Nian Rebellion, sprang from the most flood-prone part of the North China plain. But backwoods rebels also ravaged richer areas; the Taiping in particular followed the rivers from the Guangxi highlands to the Xiang and Yangzi valleys, bringing a decade of intense fighting to China's economic heartland.

SUSTAINABILITY, POLICY DECISIONS, AND IMPENDING
CRISES: DID ANYONE "CHOOSE TO FAIL"?

Many people, including officials, were aware of most the factors
discussed here, although no one put them together in quite this way.
Certainly the relationships among population growth, land reclamation, environmental degradation, and ethnic conflict were often discussed, and policies debated. Officials in the Anhui hill country, for
instance, were well aware that hillside deforestation caused floods
in the valleys below, and that the immigrants clearing the hillsides
could not all be deported; instead they tried (unsuccessfully) to get
them to switch from corn to crops (such as indigo) that would hold
the soil better.[27] At least by 1800 government leaders also understood
that no engineering scheme could offer permanent control of North
China's rivers; they began to make choices between places where they
would accept some flooding and others where they would pay almost
anything to avoid it. And despite the near doubling of Qing territory
from 1683 to 1759, many officials understood the dangers of imperial overstretch. Territorial acquisition ceased after 1759, and Han
settlers were often discouraged or even banned when the state feared
that they would need troops to protect them. (Leaders seem to have
been less aware that frequent changes in frontier policies would lead
both Han and indigenes to distrust the state and arm themselves.)

The danger to social stability posed by large numbers of propertyless laborers and by displaced disaster victims was also well understood. Some precautions resulted that were punitive, stigmatizing,
and probably counterproductive. On the other hand, it is impressive
to see how much was done to buffer the risks to farmers of both natural and market fluctuations, thus limiting the numbers who wound up
without productive assets. Many of these protections, which I have no
room to discuss here, were matters of local custom rather than government policy; and some measures that kept these numbers down,
such as female infanticide, were grim expedients indeed.[28] But clearly
both state and subjects were aware of limits, tried to plan, and were
often willing to override narrower interests for the sake of stability.

Qing economic policy focused on agriculture. They would have
rejected the idea that a society could benefit in the long run by moving more of its workforce out of agriculture, and a formulation often

heard today – that given its unusually high people to land ratio, China should specialize in other goods, and import food – would have struck them as perverse.

However, Qing officials did favor expanding light industry within a basic framework defined by peasant households. They noted the advantages that the Lower Yangzi, in particular, reaped from having farm women produce textiles for sale, and actively promoted imitation of that model elsewhere. Home-based commercial textile production did spread to more regions during the Qing, although how much difference official efforts made is unclear.

Nor is it clear whether officials fully understood how creating new textile regions would affect existing ones. Although the Lower Yangzi's dependence on long-distance trade was common knowledge, officials in other regions were not expected to worry about that, any more than most officials today worry about how promoting growth in their jurisdictions might affect economies elsewhere. I have not seen any Qing text connect economic change in other regions and the Delta's difficulties as we have here, much less draw further connections to the Delta's contributions of funds needed for environmental stabilization elsewhere. As R. Bin Wong has noted, Qing officials generally worked with two mental models of economic geography.[29] One envisioned the empire as many largely autarkic regional cells, while the other imagined a set of interdependent trading partners. The former model required less state supervision, which counted in its favor, especially when – as in the early nineteenth century – many felt that the state was already overextended.

With the benefit of hindsight, we can see that the latter perspective might have been better. China's regions were sufficiently interconnected by flows of people, goods, and funds that, as Mark Elvin has put it, the only possible long-term environmental equilibrium was an empire-wide one; acknowledging that might have improved policy making. For instance, the Qing might have ameliorated North China's crowding and reinvigorated the Lower Yangzi's slumping trade, had it begun permitting Manchurian and overseas settlement sooner.

The one remaining internal frontier that could have handled a massive influx of settlers was in Manchuria,[30] which the Qing had tried to keep off-limits in order to preserve a retreat for themselves that would remain suitable for hunting and nomadic lifestyles. These restrictions eased after 1860 – as the failure of ethnic Manchu troops to suppress the Taiping raised doubts about the value of a reserve for martial lifestyles, while Russian expansion in Siberia provoked fears that unoccupied lands would be lost – and disappeared entirely after 1895, when Japanese claims to Manchuria intensified those fears. Since perhaps twelve million people moved to Manchuria permanently once these curbs eased and then disappeared – and many more sojourned there for shorter periods – the ecological relief foregone during the early nineteenth century because of this ban was not trivial; but the loss was also temporary, as China did ultimately hold on to and settle this region.

Overseas colonization presents a more complex story. Much of Southeast Asia was quite sparsely populated until the nineteenth century, so it is not hard to imagine circumstances under which Chinese could have conquered parts of this territory (although they would not have had the epidemiological advantages of Europeans colonizing the Americas) and made it an outlet for people seeking land.[31] But there was no compelling need for them to do so until the late 1700s, at the earliest – and by that time European navies would have posed an additional, perhaps insuperable, barrier to claiming sovereignty in many of the most desirable areas. In the absence of formal colonization, Chinese merchants, miners, and others did go to Southeast Asia, but very few settled as farmers there. Among other restrictions, they were barred from owning land in the Dutch and Spanish colonies (present-day Indonesia and the Philippines), and the urban Chinese there were victims of repeated race riots tolerated (or even encouraged) by the colonial governments. Under the circumstances well-to-do Chinese merchants had every incentive to keep their assets in a liquid form – if they wanted land, it was better to buy some back in China, where relatives could manage it and the government could be counted on not to seize it. In many ways Chinese settlement in pre-1800 Southeast Asia was an impressive success story – Manila and Batavia both had more Chinese in 1770 than Boston, New York, or Philadelphia had people, and they occupied a strong position in the region's trade – but it did not become an important supplement to domestic supplies of land for cultivation. Then again – as with the cessation of voyages to East Africa after 1433 – there was no particular reason to see this as a valuable opportunity except through a very long retrospective glance that takes in the astonishing gains that Europeans (with considerable assistance from microbes) realized through "New World" colonization.

Once internal frontiers were largely closed (and European colonial authorities came to favor immigration), Chinese did move to Southeast Asia in much larger numbers. At least two to three million settled there permanently between the 1870s and 1930s,[32] and four to six times as many found work there for part of their lives. To be sure, this is nowhere near the over 50,000,000 Europeans who went to the Americas and Australia (from which Chinese were largely excluded by law until the late twentieth century) and the absence of a population outlet on that scale had significant consequences. But it would be hard to call this a "failure" – much less a consciously chosen one – unless one assumes that all states at all times should be looking to grab even remote territories whenever they can. And why should that have seemed a better guide to policy than "avoid unnecessary military adventures far from home" – especially at a point when China still had some open lands?

It is hard, then, to see how different Qing attitudes toward colonization in either Manchuria or Southeast Asia would (much less "should") have eliminated the fundamental predicaments of Qing political economy and ecology. The combination of transformations by which some other societies escaped from similar early modern dilemmas – dramatic technological changes, a massive turn to fossil fuels, and access to two "new" rich continents – was not in the cards for Qing China. Barring such immense changes, we can imagine ways to ameliorate China's crises, but not to completely avoid them.

That some realistic palliatives were not adopted probably had less to do with a failure to imagine useful measures than with the state's limited capacity to implement them. Despite its many achievements, the Qing state was thin on the ground, even by early modern standards. By 1840 there was only one magistrate for each 300,000 people; the state took less than 3 percent of GDP in taxes.[33] In emergencies it could raise considerably more by granting decorations and privileges in return for "contributions," but these were temporary increases. By working with non-office-holding elites who generally shared its ideology and agenda, the state could do a great deal. But departing from that agenda and building a much larger, more costly state in order to be ready for possible future emergencies would have been extraordinarily difficult, even if some eighteenth-century prophet had convincingly foretold environmental crises, rebellions, and foreign invaders with new weapons. Instead, more aggressive state making commenced *after* the crises for which a stronger state was needed had already become quite evident – which also meant after millions of people had become poorer, making increased state extraction all the more unpopular and difficult.

LONG-TERM PERSPECTIVES

No one doubts that the period 1850–1949 was extraordinarily difficult in China. But there were also constructive developments, particularly in coastal regions, and by various criteria "China" ultimately did recover.

Most obviously, by simple biological criteria, there was no collapse: the people who occupy China today are the descendants of those who lived there in 1850, and there are roughly 1.4 billion of them (more than any other country, although India is catching up fast); their life expectancies slightly exceed the global average. Tens of millions of other Chinese descendants live in Southeast Asia (from which European colonists have largely departed) and elsewhere around the globe. Indeed, from the kind of biogeographical perspective that Diamond emphasizes, one might say that China is an almost unique success.[34] Out of roughly 200 countries in the world today, six – Russia, Canada, the United States, China, Brazil, and Australia – occupy over 40 percent of the world's land area. Of these, only China represents the product of a process of expansion that was *not* greatly aided by germs: the non-Han peoples eventually incorporated into China all had the same immunities that the Han did. This has made things slower and bumpier for the conquerors, with some of those bumps playing a role in the rebellions and ecological problems discussed in this chapter; and as other chapters of this volume have shown, conquests have often not been as lopsided as Diamond suggests, even where guns, germs, and steel did all favor the same side. But for better or worse, it does not mean those conquerors have failed.

Nor can much of a case be made for Diamond's other criteria of collapse. There was no reversion to "simpler" organizational forms, and the loss of Chinese political sovereignty and stability, although dramatic, was temporary. Thus, any "collapse" would have to be of a different nature – a collapse of Chinese "civilization" represented by the alleged need to replace indigenous ways with new social patterns that were fundamentally alien; in this view today's Chinese may be biological heirs of those who lived under the Qing, but their society owes more to models from the West.

Whether one sees a "collapse" in even this limited sense thus depends partly on how one assesses the degree and timing of recovery from mid-nineteenth-century crises, and partly on how much continuity one sees between the China of 1800 and today. If one finds significant continuities between old institutions and those of a society that again has (in global terms) relatively high life expectancies, literacy rates, and most recently, incomes, one might conclude that the nineteenth-century crises, however painful, were less of a "collapse," and less ineptly handled, than many textbook treatments suggest. If one sees few continuities, this would suggest a narrative in which China did "fall apart" completely, and a viable society for the modern world had to be built from scratch with imported blueprints.

Recovery, like the crises themselves, differed dramatically among regions. The soldiers that suppressed the Taiping in the Middle and Lower Yangzi were mostly peasants (both tenants and smallholders) with something to return to; the core of the rebels had invaded from Guangxi, as we saw.[35] Demobilization went fairly smoothly, and the most economically advanced areas remained relatively peaceful most of the time until 1937. Meanwhile, determined to revive key areas quickly, the state authorized massive tax cuts for the Lower Yangzi in particular. This area (and the coast generally) also benefited from rapidly growing foreign trade; coastal Guangdong and Fujian also benefited from new opportunities for overseas settlement, facilitated by changes in Qing policy and colonial development projects in Southeast Asia.[36] In many ways, strengthened overseas links substituted for earlier intra-Chinese trade links that had contracted as interior regions filled up in the late eighteenth and nineteenth centuries: the coast's new overseas trading partners took emigrants and light industrial exports (both traditional ones like cloth and modern ones like cigarettes and patent medicines) and sent grain, timber, and other resources back to densely populated coastal China.

Economic growth resumed, without deepening ecological crisis. By one estimate the Yangzi Delta economy grew almost as fast as Japan's between 1914 and 1937; some (although not all) regional indicators of basic health and nutrition also improved significantly.

Government revenues grew much faster – perhaps as much as 900 percent (counting all levels of government) in real terms from 1850 to 1937.[37] And in rich areas, private charities – which combined traditional elite management of needed services with new organizational forms (e.g., nonprofit corporations, hospitals) and techniques (e.g., fund drives organized through newspapers) made significant contributions.

Even the richest parts of China remained poor compared to the West throughout this period; social misery was widespread, life expectancy probably stagnant (as it often is during early industrialization), government often corrupt and unstable. Foreign powers imposed themselves on many of China's more accessible – and richest – areas. Nonetheless, it is clear in retrospect that "traditional" society in this region first recovered and then gradually incubated hybrid institutions for a modern world.

Elsewhere, the situation was much bleaker. The local issues underlying the Muslim revolts and the Nian Rebellion were never really addressed.[38] The "pacifying" forces were mostly conscripts and mercenary forces from elsewhere, including many propertyless men with no other prospects. Such forces were harder to discipline and harder to demobilize: banditry, often involving ex-soldiers, remained a chronic problem. Nor did these regions receive a postwar stimulus package like the land tax cuts the Lower Yangzi received. On the contrary, phasing out Lower Yangzi grain tribute devastated Grand Canal and Yellow River control. (Beijing was increasingly fed by rail and sea shipments, allowing the state to abandon inland water transport.) Taxes rose in these regions too, and here they had to come out of economies that grew very little, or even shrank, between 1850 and 1950. The national government was increasingly focused on defending its threatened (and valuable) coastal areas, paying off war indemnities, and so on; thus despite growing revenues, it did not resume an active role in stabilizing poorer regions.[39] In some cases local elites stepped into the breach, like their peers in richer areas; during the horrible North China drought of 1920, for instance, local relief was surprisingly effective. But more often, elites in poorer regions could not or would not provide even traditional services in the way that a "Lower Yangzi model" required, much less provide modern services like mass education. Most of the floods, banditry, warlordism, and other ills that earned China the label "land of famine" during the early twentieth century were concentrated in northern and western regions.

Today's China is very different. Its population has more than doubled since the Communist victory of 1949 ended twelve years of invasion and civil war, but so has life expectancy. It has been almost fifty years since the last major famine. There is universal public education; the government is stable, if not necessarily much loved; and for the last thirty years the economy has grown faster than any other in history except much smaller South Korea.

Thus there may be some basis for a "collapse followed by rebirth" story – but only in the North and Northwest, only briefly, and with many qualifications. More generally, historians are increasingly highlighting ways in which post-1949 developments built on older patterns, rather than simply replacing them. These continuities are strongest in southern and eastern regions, which remain China's most successful. (In fact, that gap may be greater than ever.[40] The Human Development Index – the U.N.'s basic standard of material welfare – in the Yangzi Delta is roughly that of Portugal; for the southwestern province of Guizhou, it matches that of Namibia.) This suggests that, despite great hardships, these regions certainly never had even a loosely defined "collapse," in which the old society was thoroughly swept away to be replaced by an all-new modernity. Even for the North and West, continuity has been far stronger than any "collapse."

Another continuity is more worrisome. China's post-1949 economic gains have come with huge environmental costs, with the North and West again being hit the hardest. These impacts show every sign of growing rather than abating in the near future and are increasingly felt by more people than "just" the Chinese.

Collapse provides a reasonable overview of these problems but embeds it in a rather odd framework.[41] On the one hand, Diamond points to various ways in which Chinese industries use resources inefficiently, using more water, energy, and other resources to make a particular product than are used elsewhere. He does not, however, mention the

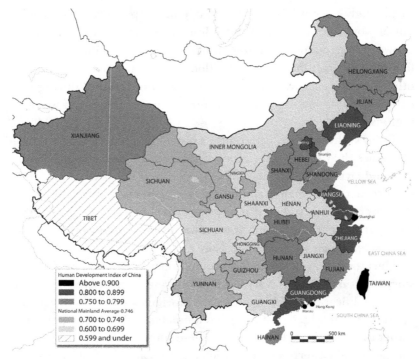

FIGURE 4.6 Human Development Index for China from Wikipedia, "List of administrative divisions of the People's Republic of China by Human Development Index," http://en.wikipedia.org/wiki/List_of_China_administrative_divisions_by_HDI.

fact that these industries are sometimes wasteful of one thing because they economize on something else that is more expensive for them than for others (e.g., certain kinds of capital equipment), or that these efficiency ratios are improving, in some cases quite rapidly. Meanwhile, he calls his China chapter "lurching giant," and says that although he does not intend this label to be pejorative, it is meant to refer to "what seems to me the most distinctive feature of Chinese history," namely, its political unification. He then rehearses briefly the argument from *Guns, Germs, and Steel* about the fifteenth-century cessation of Zheng He's voyages and the supposed failure to pursue an "incipient industrial revolution."[42] As we saw above, this argument is quite weak as an explanation of Chinese history; the imperial Chinese state did rule a vast territory, but not in anything like the centralized fashion Diamond imagines, and it is hard to find evidence that the degree

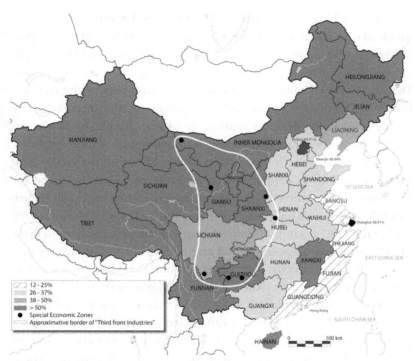

FIGURE 4.7 Percentage of public ownership, adapted from Gipoloux 1998: 8.

of centralization that did exist impeded economic development. For the second half of the twentieth century, a much more centralized and intrusive state has indeed existed, and, as Diamond notes, that has enabled both some environmentally disastrous policies and some that, whatever their other costs, have been environmentally beneficial (above all, a very intrusive birth control program); but even in the post-1949 period (and especially in the more recent period of market-oriented reform) it would be a mistake to overemphasize centralization. Provincial and local governments, a booming private sector, and millions of households make many key decisions and control many resources. Even the population policy to which the government gave top priority has had to be modified considerably in deference to various sorts of opposition; and it would be unthinkable for the government to put that much energy (including some very brutal energies) behind more than a very few initiatives at once.

Indeed, China's environmental problems today often have just as much to do with decentralization, particularly the way that local governments, which have strong pro-growth incentives, often block application of national environmental standards; again, this is something Diamond himself notes.[43] In the last three sentences of the chapter, however, Diamond returns to his emphasis on the importance of highly centralized decision making in China, placing his hopes on the national government choosing "environmental policies as bold, and as effectively carried out, as its family planning policies."[44] The complex realities of central and local power in China, the need for individual cooperation if comprehensive environmental policies are to work, and the moral preference Diamond expresses elsewhere for "talk, talk, talk" bottom-up initiatives are all swept aside here in favor of deference to a supposedly unchanging fact of Chinese history that is actually quite dubious, even in recent times, and has even less relevance in the distant past from which he claims to derive it. It would be hard not to share Diamond's anxiety about the environmental future, or his sense of urgency about China's role in it; but by reverting to a focus on centralization to frame this dilemma, he gives us an impoverished and somewhat paralyzing sense of where palliatives may come from, narrowly focused on a few top decision makers in Beijing.

Moreover, Diamond's focus on wastefulness in some Chinese industries and on the "lurching" tendencies of a supposedly hypercentralized society would seem, in the end, diversions from a more basic dilemma that he himself identifies. He quite accurately notes that if China achieved First World living standards without finding vastly more environmentally friendly ways to generate wealth than the current rich countries, the results would be environmentally disastrous.[45] (The point would apply all the more strongly if we generalized it to the poor countries of the world as a whole.) In other words, barring spectacular improvements in "clean" technologies, whatever improvements in efficiency one might imagine from changes in Chinese institutions cannot solve the basic problem. The countries that grew rich first provide no magic formula for sustained growth without environmental degradation; instead, as China tries to catch up to those countries in consumption levels, it has now joined them in diffusing some of the environmental impact of its growth far beyond its borders. (This is, in another sense, just an extension overseas of a much longer pattern in Chinese history: relieving environmental and social stresses in more developed areas by shifting them to others.) Indonesian timber fuels China's construction boom; aluminum smelters are being built along the Amazon to meet Chinese demand; Chinese carbon emissions warm the entire earth. By late imperial times the only possible environmental equilibrium in China was already an empire-wide one; today the only possible equilibrium is a global one. The pieces to be balanced are even more numerous and varied, and the potential consequences of disequilibria are staggering. But some issues still resemble those that trade, population growth, and economic development have raised for centuries, issues that have everywhere been deferred rather than "solved." Had China industrialized earlier (while importing primary products), or colonized overseas areas as well as contiguous ones, its own environment might be further from "collapse," but that of the world would not be. The "normal path" of first world environmental history – get rich first, clean up later – simply has not left enough space for everyone else to do the same.

Notes

* I started my senior year (at Cornell) thinking I would go to grad school in modern European history – then I wandered into a terrific China class and got hooked. Fortunately I went to a graduate school (Yale) that was strong in both. The bad news was that this meant starting Chinese and Japanese later than I should have – but the good news is I had a background that has helped in doing comparative and "world" history. For much of my career, I have been trying to write histories of China that would be convincing to specialists in that area, but would also shed some light on other parts of the world. Most of my work falls under the headings of social, economic, or environmental history, though I have also worked on the history of politics, religion, and gender.

   I have spent almost my entire career at UC Irvine. I also run the UC Multi-Campus Research Program in World History, a collaborative effort of scholars from several campuses interested in reorienting both teaching and research in history to be less heavily focused on stories of national development, and more on processes that cross those boundaries: environmental change, imperialism, science and technology, transnational social and religious movements, and others. My books include *The Making of a Hinterland: State Society and Economy in Inland North China* (1993), *The Great Divergence: China, Europe, and the Making of a Modern World Economy* (2000), and (with Steven Topik) *The World That Trade Created* (1999).

1. Diamond 1997.
2. Ibid.: 412.
3. Ibid.: 413.
4. Ibid.: 416.
5. Chinese shipping in Southeast Asia after 1450: Ng 1987; Blussé 1986; Wheeler 2001; Wang and Ng 2004. Wind patterns and entrepôt trade in South China Sea and Indian Ocean: Chaudhuri 1985: 34–62, esp. map on p. 41.
6. Diamond 1997: 416.
7. China and Europe comparably prosperous in 1750: Pomeranz 2000: 31–43, 2005; Allen 2004, 2005; Ma 2004: 6; Van Zanden 2004: 22–23. Contemporary income comparisons: see Penn world tables: http://www. bized.co.uk/dataserv/penndata/pennhome.htm.
8. Diamond 2005.
9. The death toll in the eighth century (An Lushan) civil war is largely guess-work. The census totals (complicated by the disappearance of people who fled but had not died, and by the collapse of the central government's census machinery) fell by two-thirds or 36,000,000 (see Fairbank et al. 1973: 120), but deaths were presumably much lower. Hansen 2000: 242 suggests the population was over 60,000,000 (versus a census figure of 52,000,000 on the eve of the rebellion) by 845, which would be inconsistent with the more extreme casualty estimates. Population losses in the mid-seventeenth century: Ho 1959: 138–139, 236; Spence 1990: 22–23, 93–94.
10. Death toll from European wars of 1914–1945: http://users.erols.com/ mwhite28/warstat1.htm (accessed February 7, 2008) provides a useful range of estimates and sources.
11. Chinese per capita GDP in 1950 no higher than in 1750, and twentieth-century Europe-China comparisons: Maddison 2007: 44. Life expectancy probably no higher: Lee and Wang 1999: 54–55; Lavely and Wong 1998.
12. Disaster deaths in late nineteenth and early twentieth centuries: Xia Mingfang 2000: 78–79, 400–402.
13. See Diamond 2005: 3 for these criteria.
14. Yangzi Delta living standards and trade patterns: Li 1998: 108; 2000: 343–390, 2005: 66–68; Pomeranz 2000: 36–43; 2002, 2005; Allen 2005; Ma 2004. Regional comparisons within China: Pomeranz 2006; Ma 2004: 6. Greater numbers of marginal people in the North: Li and Jiang 2005: 303, 310. More tenants with security in the South: Yang 1988: 91–133. Highland populations and environmental problems: Osborne 1994. Ethnic problems on the frontier: Kuhn and Mann-Jones 1978: 132–133. Sutton 2000: 450–500 shows the uneasy relationships in frontier area reflected in the myth making of both Han and Miao, with the central government coming off poorly in both versions.
15. High rates of proletarianization in Europe: Tilly 1984: 36. Low rates in China and strong land rights: Pomeranz 2006, 2008a, 2008b.
16. Fifty percent rented land in South, much less in North: Buck 1964. Esherick 1981 finds many problems with Buck, but does not change the general

pattern of high rates of freehold farming in the North and much more tenancy in the South. For specific regions see Marks 1984: 44 and Chen 1936: 19, on the far South; Huang 1990: 103 on the Lower Yangzi; Jing and Luo 1986: 34–35 and Huang 1985: 103 on the North China plain.

17. Decline in Yangzi Delta farm size, growing productivity per acre: Li Bozhong 2005: 55–66.

18. Urbanization rates: Skinner 1977: 226, revised slightly upward by Skinner 1987: 72–79. Arable land doubling ca. 1650–1850: Wang Yeh-chien 1973: 7. Long distance migrations in general: Ho 1959: 136–169; Lee and Wong 1991: 52–55; Sun 1997: 30–34. Migration to Taiwan: Shepherd 1993. Earnings comparisons of urban and rural people: Allen et al. 2006: 53, showing no significant difference between wages in agriculture and other (mostly urban) occupations; Pomeranz 2005, 2006.

19. Handicraft and female virtue: Mann 1992.

20. Yangzi Delta tax rates: Bernhardt 1992: 44–46. National tax rates: Wang Yeh-chien 1973: 127; Perkins 1967: 487. Cross-regional subsidies: Wong 1997: 113–116, 138–139, 143, 148. Pomeranz 2001: 333, 339; Wang 1973: 84–109.

21. North China ecological and economic stabilization as state priority: see, e.g., Pomeranz 1993: 128–132, 154–156; Lillian Li 2007: 38–73; Wong 1997: 113–118; Naquin and Rawski 1989: 24. Granary system: Will and Wong 1991. Efficient relief in 1742–1743 famine: Will 1990.

22. North China water control efforts in high Qing: Lillian Li 2007: 38–73; Dodgen 2001; Huang he shuili weiyuanhu 1982: 298–347.

23. Rise of rice prices relative to cloth prices: Pomeranz 2000: 323–326.

24. Growing foreign trade revenues: Van Dyke 2005: 113. Salt monopoly reform: Metzger 1973: 53–54, 57–61, 127–128, 292–293. Merchant "contributions": Ho 1962: 34, 46–50. Evelyn Rawski 2004: 213–218 makes even larger claims for the scale and significance of increasing Qing fiscal capacity; I would not go quite as far as she does.

25. Settlements crowding lakebeds increasing flooding: Perdue 1987: 196, 202, 219–233; Schoppa 2002: 137–139, 155–160.

26. Soaring opium imports: Chang 1970: 19–23, 34–36, 40. Taiping Rebellion: Jen Yu-wen 1973; Spence 1990: 170–179. Nian Rebellion: Perry 1980; Teng Ssu-yu 1961. Yellow River flood: Huang He shuili wieyuanhu 1982: 348–355. Muslim rebellions: Spence 1990: 183–193. Arrow War with Britain and France: Spence 1990: 179–180.

27. Anhui officials understanding environmental problems: Osborne 1994: 14–36. Officials realizing they can't completely prevent North China flooding: Lillian Li 2007: 61–62, 65–68.

28. Female infanticide: Lee and Wang 1999: 47–53, 107. Qing support for handicraft industry: Mann 1992; Wong 1997: 138–139.

29. Two models of economic geography: Wong 1997: 138–139. Only possible equilibrium an empire-wide one: Elvin 1998: 753.

30. Qing reluctance to have people move to Manchuria: Lee 1970; for the beginnings of a more open policy see 116–137. Eight million permanent

migrants plus 17 million temporary migrants from 1890 to 1937: Gottschang and Lary 2000: 2. Figures for the preceding forty years, in which migration increased gradually, are very hard to come by, but the annual rate was almost certainly lower than after 1890. Migration during the war and civil war years from 1937 to 1949 is likewise hard to measure, but possibly more substantial.

31. Noncolonization of Southeast Asia, despite lots of settlement and trade: Wang Gungwu 1990: 400–421; Pomeranz 2000: 201–206.

32. Migration to Southeast Asia after 1870: Sugihara 2005: 244–274. Higher figures in McKeown 2004: 156–158.

33. Number of magistrates: Ch'u 1962: 2. State building at the expense of elites not on the agenda before the twentieth century: Wong 1997: 110–126, 154–177.

34. Chinese life expectancy and global average today: https://www.cia.gov/library/publications/the-world-factbook/rankorder/2102rank.html, accessed 12 February 2008. Land areas of countries today: one of many interchangeable lists is available from World Atlas.com at http://www.worldatlas.com/aatlas/populations/ctyareal.htm, accessed 12 February 2008.

35. Peasant participation in suppression of Taiping: Kuhn 1970: 105–188. Restoration and tax cuts in Lower Yangzi: Wright 1957: 1263–1267; Polachek 1975, esp. 226–227, 253–254.

36. Coastal regions benefit from trade growth: Faure 1989. Economic growth in Lower Yangzi: Ma 2006; Ma Junya 2002. Health indicators improving in Lower Yangzi: Morgan 2004.

37. Government revenues growing 1850–1937: Hamashita 1989: 68, 72; Wei 1986: 227; Young 1971: 71; Duara 1987.

38. Nian suppressed without key socioeconomic issues being addressed, troops mostly outsiders and nonpeasants: Perry 1980: 152–156; Teng Ssu-yu 1961: 195–217, 229–232; Liu 1978: 456–460, 468–477.

39. Reorientation of national government, neglect of hinterlands: Pomeranz 1993: 120–265. Tax increases in North China: Duara 1987. Some effective famine relief in 1920–1921 famine: Fuller, no date. North China as "land of famine": Lillian Li 2007: 283–309. General gains in life expectancy and welfare since 1949: Lee and Wang 1999: 54–55; United Nations Development Programme 2000: 17–38 (pre-1978) and 39–106 (since 1978).

40. Gap in Human Development Index between coast and interior: United Nations Development Programme 2000: 62. (The gap has grown even larger since then.) Environmental costs of Chinese growth: Smil 1994, UN Development Programme, 70–75.

41. Diamond 2005: 358–377.

42. Diamond 1997: 374.

43. Ibid.: 375.

44. Ibid.: 377.

45. Ibid.: 373.

Bibliography

Allen, Robert. 2004. "Mr. Lockyer Meets the Index Number Problem: the Standard of Living in Canton and London in 1704." Available at http://www.economics.ox.ac.uk/Members/robert.allen/default.htm.

Allen, Robert. 2005. "Agricultural Productivity and Rural Incomes in England and the Yangzi Delta, ca. 1620–1820." Available at http://www.economics.ox.ac.uk/Members/robert.allen/default.htm.

Allen, Robert, Robert Allen, Jean-Pascal Bassino, Debin Ma, Christine Moll-Murata, and Jan Luiten van Zanden. 2006. "Wages, Prices and Living Standards in China, Japan, and Europe, 1738–1925." Available at www.econ.yale.edu/seminars/echist/eho6–07/Mao40407.pdf.

Bernhardt, Kathryn. 1992. *Rents, Taxes, and Peasant Resistance: the Lower Yangzi Region, 1840 – 1950*. Stanford, CA: Stanford University Press.

Blussé, Leonard. 1986. *Strange Company: Chinese Settlers, Mestizo Women, and the Dutch in VOC Batavia, 1619–1740*. Dordrecht, the Netherlands: Foris.

Buck, John L. 1964 (1937). *Land Utilization in China*. New York: Paragon Book Reprint.

Chaudhuri, K. N. 1985. *Trade and Civilization in the Indian Ocean: An Economic History from the Rise of Islam to 1750*. Cambridge: Cambridge University Press.

Chang Hsin-pao. 1970. *Commissioner Lin and the Opium War*. New York W. W. Norton.

Chen Hanseng. 1936. *Landlord and Peasant in China*. New York: International Publishers.

Ch'u T'ung-tsu. 1962. *Local Government in China under the Ch'ing*. Cambridge, MA: Harvard University Press.

Diamond, Jared M. 1997. *Guns, Germs, and Steel: The Fates of Human Societies*. New York: W. W. Norton.

Diamond, Jared M. 2005 *Collapse: How Societies Choose to Fail or Succeed*. New York: Viking.

Dodgen, Randall. 2001. *Controlling the Dragon: Confucian Engineers and the Yellow River in Late Imperial China*. Honolulu: University of Hawaii Press.

Duara, Prasenjit. 1987. "State Involution: A Study of Local Finances in Rural North China, 1911–1935." *Comparative Studies in Society and History* **29**(January):132–161.

Elvin, Mark. 1998. "The Environmental Legacy of Imperial China." *China Quarterly* 156(December):733–756.

Esherick, Joseph. 1981. "Number Games: A Note on Land Distribution in Pre-Revolutionary China." *Modern China* **7**(4):387–412.

Fairbank, John K., et al. 1973. *East Asia: Tradition and Transformation*. Boston: Houghton Mifflin.

Faure, David. 1989. *The Rural Economy of Pre-Liberation China*. Hong Kong: Oxford University Press.

Fuller, Pierre. No date. "Politics, Local Society and Relief in the 1920–21 North China Famine." Ph.D. dissertation in progress, University of California, Irvine.

Gipoloux, François. 1998. "Integration or Disintegration? The Spatial Effects of Foreign Direct Investment in China." *China Perspectives* **17**(May/June):6–14.

Gottschang, Thomas and Diana Lary. 2000. *Swallows and Settlers: The Great Migration from North China to Manchuria*. Ann Arbor: Center for Chinese Studies, University of Michigan.

Hamashita Takeshi. 1989.*Ch/goku kindai keizashi kenky/* (Research in Modern Chinese Economic History). Tokyo: University of Tokyo Institute of Oriental Culture.

Hansen, Valerie. 2000. *The Open Empire: A History of China to 1600*. New York: W. W. Norton.

Ho Ping-ti. 1959. *Studies on the Population of China, 1368–1953*. Cambridge, MA: Harvard University Press.

Ho Ping-ti. 1962. *The Ladder of Success in Imperial China*. New York: Columbia University Press.

Huang he shuili weiyuanhu, Shuilibu. 1982. *Huang he shuili shi shuyao (General History of Yellow River Water Conservancy)*. Beijing: Shuli dianli chubanshe.

Huang, Philip. 1985. *The Peasant Economy and Social Change in North China*. Stanford, CA: Stanford University Press.

Huang, Philip. 1990. *The Peasant Family and Rural Development in the Lower Yangzi Region, 1350–1988*. Stanford, CA: Stanford University Press.

Jen Yu-wen. 1973. *The Taiping Revolutionary Movement*. New Haven, CT: Yale University Press.

Jing Su and Luo Lun 1986 (1958). *Qing dai Shandong jingying dizhu jingnji yanjiu*. Jinan, China: Qilu shushe. Revised edition of 1958 text; abridged and revised translation of 1958 text published in 1978 as Endymion Wilkinson, ed., *Landlord and Labor in Late Imperial China*. Cambridge, MA: Harvard University Press.

Kuhn, Philip. 1970. *Rebellion and Its Enemies in Late Imperial China: Militarization and Social Structure, 1796–1864*. Cambridge, MA: Harvard University Press.

Kuhn, Philip and Susan Mann Jones. 1978. "Dynastic Decline and the Roots of Rebellion," in *The Cambridge History of China*. Edited by John K. Fairbank, vol. 10, pt. 1, pp. 107–116. Cambridge: Cambridge University Press.

Lavely, William and R. Bin Wong. 1998. "Revising the Malthusian Narrative: The Comparative Study of Population Dynamics in Late Imperial China." *Journal of Asian Studies* **57**(3):714–748.

Lee, James and Cameron Campbell. 1997. *Fate and Fortune in Rural China*. Cambridge: Cambridge University Press.

Lee, James and Wang Feng. 1999. *One Quarter of Humanity: Malthusian Mythologies and Chinese Realities*. Cambridge, MA: Harvard University Press.

Lee, James and R. Bin Wong. 1991. "Population Movements in Qing China and Their Linguistic Legacy." In *Languages and Dialects of China*. Edited by William S.-Y. Wang, pp. 52–77. Berkeley, CA: Journal of Chinese Linguistics Monograph Series.

Lee, Robert H. G. 1970. *The Manchurian Frontier in Ch'ing History.* Cambridge, MA: Harvard University Press.

Li Bozhong. 1998. *Agricultural Development in Jiangnan, 1620–1850.* New York: St. Martin's Press.

Li Bozhong. 2000. *Jiangnan de zaoqi gongyehua.* (The Early Industrialization of Jiangnan.) Beijing: Shehui Kexue Wenxian Chubanshe.

Li Bozhong. 2005. "Farm Labor Productivity in Jiangnan, 1620–1850," in *Living Standards in the Past.* Edited by Robert C. Allen, Tommy Bengtsson, and Martin Dribe, pp. 55–76. Oxford: Oxford University Press.

Li, Lillian. 2007. *Fighting Famine in North China: State, Market, and Environmental Decline, 1690s – 1990s.* Stanford, CA: Stanford University Press.

Li Wenzhi and Jiang Taixin. 2005. *Zhongguo dizhu zhi jingji lun.* Beijing: Shehui Kexue Chubanshe.

Liu, K. C. 1978. "The Ch'ing Restoration," in *The Cambridge History of China.* Edited by John K. Fairbank, vol. 10, pt. 2, pp. 409–490. Cambridge: Cambridge University Press.

Ma, Debin. 2004. "Modern Economic Growth in the Lower Yangzi in 1911–1937: A Quantitative, Historical, and Institutional Analysis." Discussion paper 2004–06–002, Foundation for Advanced Studies on International Development, Tokyo.

Ma, Debin. 2006. "Shanghai-Based Industrialization the Early 20th Century: A Quantitative and Institutional Analysis." Working Papers of the Global Economic History Network (GEHN), 18/06. London: School of Economics.

Ma Junya. 2002. *Hunhe yu fazhan: Jiangnan diqu chuantong shehui jingji de xiandai yanbian (1900–1950).* (Mixture and Development: The Modern Evolution of Traditional Society and Economy in the Jiangnan District, 1900–1950.) Beijing: Shehui Kexue Wenxian Chubanshe.

Maddison, Angus. 2007 *Chinese Economic Performance in the Long Run.* 2nd ed. Paris: OECD.

Mann, Susan. 1992. "Household Handicrafts and State Policy in Qing Times," in *To Achieve Security and Wealth: The Qing State and the Economy.* Edited by Jane Kate Leonard and John Watt, pp. 75–96. Ithaca, NY: Cornell University Press.

Marks, Robert. 1984. *Rural Revolution in South China: Peasants and the Making of History in Haifeng County, 1570–1930.* Madison: University of Wisconsin Press.

McKeown, Adam. 2004. "Global Migration, 1846–1940." *Journal of World History* **15**(2):155–190.

Metzger, Thomas. 1973. *The Internal Organization of the Chinese Bureaucracy: Legal, Normative, and Communications Aspects.* Cambridge. MA: Harvard University Press.

Morgan, Stephen. 2004. "Economic Growth and the Biological Standard of Living in China 1880–1930." *Economic and Human Biology* **2**(2):197–218.

Naquin, Susan and Evelyn Rawski. 1987. *Chinese Society in the Eighteenth Century.* New Haven, CT: Yale University Press.

Ng, Chin-keong. 1983. *Trade and Society: The Amoy Network on the China Coast, 1683–1735*. Singapore: Singapore University Press.

Osborne, Anne. 1994. "The Local Politics of Land Reclamation in the Lower Yangzi Highlands." *Late Imperial China* 15(1):1–46.

Pan Jiazheng (Chinese National Committee on Large Dams). Editors. 1987. *Large Dams in China: History, Achievement, Prospect*. Beijing: China Water Resources and Electric Power Press.

Perdue, Peter. 1987. *Exhausting the Earth: State and Peasant in Hunan 1500–1850*. Cambridge, MA: Harvard University Press.

Perkins, Dwight. 1967. "Government as an Obstacle to Industrialization: The Case of Nineteenth Century China." *Journal of Economic History* 27(4):478–492.

Perry, Elizabeth. 1980. *Rebels and Revolutionaries in North China, 1845–1945*. Stanford, CA: Stanford University Press.

Polachek, James. 1975. "Gentry Hegemony in Soochow," in *Conflict and Control in Late Imperial China*. Edited by Frederic Wakeman and Carolyn Grant, pp. 211–256. Berkeley: University of California Press.

Pomeranz, Kenneth. 1993. *The Making of a Hinterland: State, Society, and Economy in Inland North China, 1853–1937*. Berkeley: University of California Press.

Pomeranz, Kenneth. 2000. *The Great Divergence: China, Europe, and the Making of the Modern World Economy*. Princeton, NJ: Princeton University Press.

Pomeranz, Kenneth. 2001. "Is There an East Asian Development Path? Long-Term Comparisons, Constraints, and Continuities." *Journal of the Economic and Social History of the Orient* 44(3):3–41.

Pomeranz, Kenneth. 2002. "Beyond the East-West Binary: Resituating Development Paths in the Eighteenth Century World." *Journal of Asian Studies* 61(2):539–590.

Pomeranz, Kenneth. 2005. "Standards of Living in Eighteenth Century China: Regional Differences, Temporal Trends, and Incomplete Evidence," in *Living Standards in the Past*. Edited by Robert C. Allen, Tommy Bengtsson and Martin Dribe, pp. 23–54. Oxford: Oxford University Press.

Pomeranz, Kenneth. 2006. "Standards of Living in Rural and Urban China: Preliminary Estimates for the Mid 18th and Early 20th Centuries." Paper for Panel 77 of International Economic History Association Conference, Helsinki, Finland.

Pomeranz, Kenneth. 2008a. "Land Markets in Late Imperial and Republican China." *Continuity and Change* 22(4):1–50.

Pomeranz, Kenneth. 2008b. "Chinese Development in Long-Run Perspective." *Proceedings of the American Philosophical Society* 152(1):83–100.

Rawski, Evelyn. 2004. "Was the Qing 'Early Modern'?" in *The Qing Formation in World Historical Time*. Edited by Lynn Struve, pp. 207–241. Cambridge, MA: Harvard University East Asia Center.

Rawski, Thomas. 1989. *Economic Growth in Prewar China*. Berkeley: University of California Press.

Schoppa, R. Keith. 2002. *Song Full of Tears: Nine Centuries of Life at Xiang Lake*. Boulder: Westview Press, 2002.

Shepherd, John. 1993. *Statecraft and Political Economy on the Taiwan Frontier, 1600–1800.* Stanford, CA: Stanford University Press.

Skinner, G. William. 1977. "Regional Urbanization in Nineteenth-Century China," in *The City in Late Imperial China.* Edited by G. William Skinner, pp. 211–249. Stanford, CA: Stanford University Press.

Skinner, G. William. 1987. "Sichuan's Population in the 19th Century: Lessons from Disaggregated Data." *Late Imperial China* 8(1):1–79.

Smil, Vaclav. 1994. *China's Environmental Crisis: An Inquiry into the Limits of National Development.* Armonk, NY: M. E. Sharpe.

Spence, Jonathan. 1990. *The Search for Modern China.* New York: W. W. Norton.

Sugihara, Kaoru. 2005a. "Introduction," in *Japan, China, and the Growth of the Asian International Economy, 1850–1949.* Edited by Kaoru Sugihara, pp. 1–19. Oxford: Oxford University Press.

Sugihara, Kaoru. 2005b. "Patterns of Chinese Emigration to Southeast Asia, 1869–1939," in *Japan, China, and the Growth of the Asian International Economy, 1850–1949.* Edited by Kaoru Sugihara, pp. 244–274. Oxford: Oxford University Press.

Sun Xiaofen. 1997. *Qingdai qianqi de yimin zhen Sichuan* (Immigration to Sichuan in the Early Qing dynasty). Chengdu: Sichuan Daxue chubanshe.

Sutton, Donald. 2000. "Myth-Making on an Ethnic Frontier: The Cult of the Heavenly Kings of West Hunan, 1715–1996." *Modern China* 26(4):448–500.

Teng Ssu-yu. 1961. *The Nien Army and their Guerrilla Warfare 1851–1868.* Westport, CT: Greenwood Press.

Tignor, Robert et al. 2008. *Worlds Together, Worlds Apart.* Volume 2. 2nd ed. New York: W. W. Norton.

Tilly, Charles. 1984. "Demographic Origins of the European Proletariat," in *Proletarianization and Family History.* Edited by David Levine, pp. 1–85. Orlando, FL: Academic Press.

United Nations Development Programme. 2000. *China: Human Development Report 1999.* Oxford: Oxford University Press.

Van Dyke, Paul. 2005. *The Canton Trade: Life and Enterprise on the China Coast, 1700–1845.* Hong Kong: Hong Kong University Press.

Van Zanden, Jan Luiten. 2004. "Estimating Early Modern Economic Growth." Working Paper, International Institute of Social History, University of Utrecht. Available at http://www.iisg.nl/research/jvz-estimating.pdf.

Wang Gungwu. 1990. "Merchants without Empire," in *The Rise of Merchant Empires.* Edited by James Tracy, pp. 400–421. Cambridge: Cambridge University Press.

Wang Gungwu, and Ng Chin-keong. Editors. 2004. *Maritime China in Transition 1750–1850.* Wiesbaden: Harrassowitz.

Wang Xiaoqiang and Bai Nanfeng. 1991. *The Poverty of Plenty.* New York: St. Martin's Press.

Wang Yeh-chien. 1973. *Land Taxation in Imperial China, 1750–1911.* Cambridge, MA: Harvard University Press.

Wei Guangqi. 1986. "Qingdai houqi zhongyang jiquan caizheng tizhi de wajie" (The collapse of the central authority over the fiscal system in the late qing period). *Jindai shi yanjiu* **1:207**–230.

Wheeler, Charles. 2001. "Cross-Cultural Trade and Trans-Regional Networks in the Port of Hoi An: Maritime Vietnam in the Early Modern Era." Ph.D. dissertation, Yale University.

Will, Pierre-Étienne. 1990. *Bureaucracy and Famine in 18th Century China.* Stanford, CA: Stanford University Press.

Will, Pierre-Étienne, and R. Bin Wong. 1991. *Nourish the People: The State Civilian Granary System in China, 1650–1850.* Ann Arbor: University of Michigan Press.

Wong, R. Bin. 1997. *China Transformed: Historical Change and the Limits of European Experience.* Ithaca, NY: Cornell University Press.

Wright, Mary. 1957. *The Last Stand of Chinese Conservatism.* Stanford, CA: Stanford University Press.

Yang Guozhen. 1988. *Ming Qing tudi qiyue wenshu yanjiu* (Documentary Research on Land Contracts in the Ming and Qing Periods). Beijing: Renmin chubanshe, 1988

Xia Mingfang. 2000. *Minguo shiqi ziran hai yu xiangcun shehui* (Natural Disasters and Village Society in the Republican Era). Beijing: Zhonghua Shuju.

Young, Arthur N. 1971. *China's Nation-building Effort, 1927–1937: The Financial and Economic Record.* Stanford, CA: Hoover Institution Press.

PART II

SURVIVING COLLAPSE

Studies of Societal Regeneration

5

Marketing Conquest and the Vanishing Indian

An Indigenous Response to Jared Diamond's Archaeology of the American Southwest

Michael Wilcox*

INTRODUCTION

For many Native Americans archaeology has long been viewed in negative terms. For much of the late nineteenth and twentieth centuries, archaeologists enjoyed unrestricted access to the material culture, artifacts, sites, and human remains of my ancestors. There were no efforts on the part of archaeologists to consult with Native Peoples before conducting excavations, and museums collected artifacts largely because of their rarity and aesthetic beauty. Later, materials would be collected to expand the knowledge of Westerners about the evolution of human societies. Unfortunately, very little of this work involved interaction with descendent communities of Native Americans or any discussion of their more recent histories. As a child growing up in California, the only time that Native Americans were ever discussed in the fourth grade was in the context of Mission studies. I recall that each student was asked to create a model of mission life in colonial California and that most of the discussion of Native Peoples focused on the impact of conquest and disease among California Indian populations. One student even glued plastic Indians lying on the ground to demonstrate the impact of European pathogens. Once the Indians had all "died" in the missions, they disappeared from our textbooks and classroom discussions for much of the next eight years. This experience had a profound effect on my academic life and career.

My father's family are Yuman or Quechan from the lower Colorado River. From our family history, I learned that they controlled access to an important passage between Arizona and California and had kept Spanish colonists out of California until the late 1700s. I also knew that the last battle fought between tribes in the United States was between the Pima and the Yuma in 1849. Over the years many Yuma were forced off their farmlands and moved onto reservations or to nearby cities. Like many Native Americans, my grandfather fought in the South Pacific during World War II. He knew where he came from. He had been a part of history. And yet there was no story that explained what either he or I were doing living in the twenty-first century.

As I came to learn as a university student, the study of Native Americans has largely been confined to the fields of archaeology and anthropology. If I wanted to tell a different kind of story about Native Americans, to expose the mythology I encountered in classrooms, films, and textbooks, I would need formal training as an archaeologist and ethnographer. When I entered graduate school there were no Native American archaeologists working as university professors. Today there are three. As the result of changes within the discipline, many more Native People are entering the profession and are struggling to assert a voice in the scholarship of our ancestors. This essay explores the same questions that led me into the field – both literally and figuratively. Some of my first fieldwork took place near Zuni, New Mexico, at what is called a "Chacoan outlier." These are large buildings or "Great Houses" that were an important part of the Chacoan system. Shortly after this I worked for the O'Odham or Pima Nation on a large archaeological project in the heartland of Hohokam archaeology. In both cases I was struck by the degree of separation that existed in the literature and in the field between living Native Peoples and archaeologists. How had this rupture happened? Do Indigenous societies simply collapse and vanish? Or is the mythology of conquest and disappearance grounded in a scholarship that has until very recently simply ignored Indigenous histories?

This chapter helps to answer these questions. The first section explains how the Pima lost not only their economic power but also their past in the late nineteenth and early twentieth centuries. The second part reveals the ideological basis (and popular appeal) of

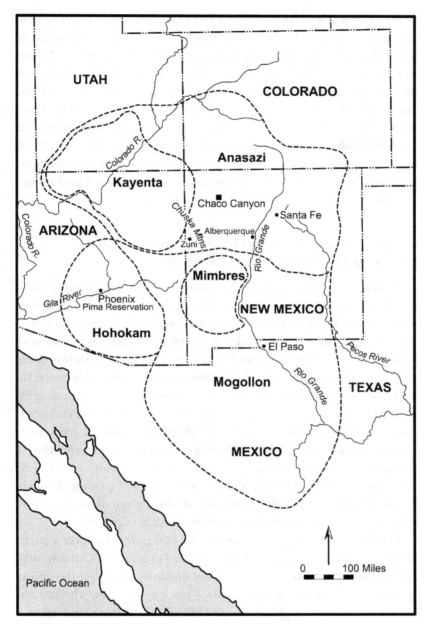

FIGURE 5.1 Regions of ancestral Southwestern peoples, including Pueblo dwellers (Anasazi, especially at Chaco Canyon) and O'Odham (Pima) and earlier Hohokam.

Jared Diamond's account of European ascendancy. I explain how archaeological scholarship (and discussions of abandonments in particular) has played an important part in the portrayal of Native Americans as "failed" stewards of the environment. The third segment exposes Diamond's thesis of overpopulation, deforestation, and collapse at Chaco using archaeological evidence. The final section deals with the survival of Pueblo communities during the Pueblo Revolt of 1680. Here I provide a counternarrative to both of Diamond's works through a discussion of "abandonments" and demonstrate the important role that narratives and ideology play in any account of European ascendancy and conquest.

AN OPENING FABLE: HOW THE PIMA LOST THEIR PAST AND THE HOHOKAM WERE BORN

Most people visiting Arizona are unaware that a major river once ran from the mountains of New Mexico, through Phoenix, across the northern Sonoran Desert, and into the Gulf of California. Fewer realize that, contrary to popular imagery, most Indians in the arid Southwest were agriculturalists. In the years leading up to the Mexican American War (1846–1848), U.S. Cavalry expeditions, exhausted by heat and lacking provisions, were shocked to find a large community of Indian farmers diverting water from the Gila River into an elaborate system of canals that fed expansive fields of wheat, cotton, corn, melons, and squash. Throughout the 1800s, Pima farmers freely offered thousands of pounds of emergency provisions and water to the U.S. Army. By the 1870s, the tribe had provided both safe passage through the desert and up to 6 million pounds of wheat annually to gold rush dreamers, military parties, and transcontinental migrants.[1]

The Pima never called themselves by that name. In 1692 a party of Spanish soldiers happened upon a small group of O'Odham men and asked them who they were. They dutifully recorded the reply, "pimas," as the name of the people – not knowing that the phrase *pimaas* translates roughly from O'Odham as "I don't understand what you are saying" or "huh?" It is not surprising that incomprehension and ignorance would come literally to define a people. What is surprising is the degree to which their history has been ignored by archaeologists and historians and replaced with other more fantastic tales of disappearance or invisibility. The act of "ignoring," of deciding which stories to tell and how to tell them, is an essential instrument of conquest. The power to articulate some stories and to disregard others, to name a people the "Huh?" and to deny their own self-definitions, has helped give rise to an American mythology few people acknowledge, but that is marketed and sold to us on television and the internet and in academic and popular print media. It is a mythology filled with tales of mysterious disappearances of Indian civilizations such as the *Hohokam* or *Anasazi* – ancient and remote peoples who apparently left no descendents and whose "failures," as interpreted by Diamond and others, provide us with cautionary tales of societal collapse.

But just like these imagined groups (no Native person ever referred to themselves as Anasazi or Hohokam), the popular narratives of conquest and disappearance are just that – a mythology. And any consumer of that mythology, concerned with the destruction of the planet or searching for an account of European dominance, need look no further than our own more recent past for fables just as fantastic and unbelievable as those articulated by popular authors such as Diamond. The stories of how the Hohokam along the Gila River or the Anasazi at Chaco Canyon self-destructed and vanished through environmental mismanagement are, as we shall see, largely fictional. So too is the notion that colonization and conquest were accidents of geography or biology. The descendents of these groups, the Pima, their neighbors, and the Pueblos, still live in the lands of their ancestors. And one could argue that the most damaging "collapses" and "failures" they have endured have been at the hands of scholars who have ignored their presence in a modern world or failed to tell the tell the stories that explain that presence.

The real question we should be concerned with is why these fictions exist. I would argue that the stories of Indigenous disappearance and the fables of conquest and European ascendancy articulated by Jared Diamond in *Guns, Germs, and Steel: The Fates of Human Societies*, as well as his subsequent work *Collapse: How Human Societies Choose to Fail or Succeed*,[2] are not only factually incorrect but also exemplify a powerful impulse to reshape and reconfigure colonial histories to suit the needs of a changing audience. Diamond's accounts of poverty and failure market a new version of conquest and Indigenous failure in which human agency and ideology are ignored. The narratives we choose to believe, how we construct the winners and losers, how we locate our own society in a continuum of "failure" and "success," are born of universal human impulses to make sense out of the social and cultural worlds in which we live. But this mythology, rarely challenged publicly by archaeologists and historians, often obscures other more immediate causes of Indigenous "failures." It provides us with a set of more palatable, self-serving narratives – narratives that remove the reader (as a consumer of information) from a position of critical reflection, participation, and responsibility. But the consumer is an active agent in this exchange. And the story of how the O'Odham became the Pima and how the "Hohokam" were invented demonstrates the powerful consequences associated with the marketing of success and wealth for the victors, and failure and poverty to the victims.

Race and citizenship, not *indigenous environmental mismanagement* as Diamond states in *Collapse,* is at the center of the story of the Pima and the invention of the Hohokam. Having cornered the agricultural market and secured contracts and treaties with the U.S. government in the 1850s, the Gila River Pima, much like their Hohokam ancestors, were arguably the most powerful economic group in the entire Southwest. But within a decade of American settlement, Anglo farmers would divert so much water upstream that the Gila would run dry before it reached Pima farms. For white farmers citizenship had its privileges. Recognizing the economic power wielded by the Pima and eager to populate western territories with yeoman farmers and ranchers, the United States government passed the Desert Land Act (1887), offering 640 acres to any Euro-American willing to cultivate farmland along the desert waterways of the Southwest.

Understanding the mechanisms of plant reproduction, the Pima (hereafter referred to as the O'Odham, as they call themselves) knew from centuries of practice to segregate fields in order to prevent bees from cross-pollinating the wrong flowers.[3] They had a year-round crop cycle alternating fallow and active fields in order to not exhaust the fragile desert soils and drained irrigated fields to prevent salinization of the soil. They engineered hundreds of miles of canals with precise slope and elevation calculations (without writing) and coordinated the opening of gates and barriers to direct water flow

a

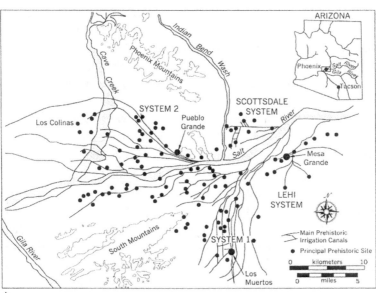

b

FIGURE 5.2 Ancestral O'Odham agricultural features: (a) canal at archaeological site called Snaketown with Emil Haury standing at the top of the massive canal and (b) irrigation system in Phoenix area. (Source: Fish and Fish 2008: 10, 83; courtesy of the Arizona State Museum, Figure 5.2a is Cat. No. C-1043; reproduction of Figure 5.2b with permission from David Doyel, map prepared by Jean Baker)

at proper intervals. These were technologies they had developed for over a thousand years. Incredibly, in *Collapse* Diamond completely ignores the history of the O'Odham and cites the presence of abandoned fields in the O'Odham homeland as evidence of willful environmental mismanagement, fed by "overextension," a euphemism for greed. Greed, willful environmental mismanagement, and ignorance *did* in fact lead to the abandonment of O'Odham fields and farms. But if Diamond had bothered to glance at the history of the region, he might have cast a very different set of characters into the roles of enlightened heroes and ignorant villains.

Because rain provided all the water needed for farms east of the Mississippi, Anglo-American settlers had no experience with irrigation agriculture. The massive tracts of land (40 acres per household was the norm) were far too large for any single family to operate. They overwatered their fields and did not understand the importance of drainage.[4] Minerals built up through evaporation and salinization ruined both crop and soil. Individual farmers, unfamiliar with the scale of communal coordination required to practice this kind of farming, could not manage the canals, and millions of gallons of water were wasted. Within a few years of passage of the Desert Land Act, Anglo-American farmers had diverted so much water upstream that the Gila River was dry by the time it reached the O'Odham farms.[5] Cattle compounded the problem by overgrazing. Erosion followed and flash floods cut arroyos into the dry earth, lowering the water table. The river was dying, and so were the O'Odham.[6]

In 1873 a delegation of O'Odham officials, led by General Antonio Azul, traveled to Washington, DC, to plead with the government to stop the theft of water by Anglo farmers. His pleas fell upon deaf ears. Indians, lacking rights of U.S. citizens until 1924, were unable to defend themselves or their water rights in the U.S. legal system. The democratic process insured that the rights of voters would be affirmed and defended by elected representatives. But in this version of democracy, full citizenship was restricted to white males. No politician could justify the protection of Indian interests when in conflict with their constituents; by 1878 the 45th Congress recommended that the issue be settled by *removal of the Pima* (as well as every other tribe in the Southwest) to Oklahoma. In a few short years the O'Odham were reduced to dependence upon the federal government. To make matters worse, the Bureau of Indian Affairs followed a practice of sending teachers, clerks, and Indian Agents infected with tuberculosis to work in the dry environment of Arizona. By 1893 half of all O'Odham children and adults succumbed to the disease. Starvation and disease among the Pima were no accidents.[7]

When the first groups of American archaeologists and anthropologists came to investigate reports of a massive irrigation system, large abandoned village complexes, and massive adobe "Great Houses" in 1880, they simply could not fathom that any connection existed between this advanced civilization and the starving and impoverished O'Odham.[8] Rather than documenting the tragic consequences of American agricultural policies and the recent collapse of the O'Odham economy (which was happening right before their eyes), they chose instead to invent an imaginary ethnic group based upon the O'Odham word *hohokam*, roughly translated as "things which are all used up." And so the Hohokam were invented, and the Pima lost their past.[9] Unfortunately this is a common story, and it is only in recent years that archaeologists have bothered to explore the historical bridges between the Hohokam and contemporary Native Americans.[10]

Ignorance of history (and for that matter archaeology) is at the heart of the fables of poverty and environmental mismanagement rendered in the popular works of Jared Diamond. Fables in which Native Americans and other Indigenous Peoples are both blamed for their own poverty and misfortune through "accidental conquests" in *Guns, Germs, and Steel: The Fates of Human Societies* and used as examples of environmental mismanagement in *Collapse: How Societies Choose to Fail or Succeed*.

The lack of scholarly response to these works continues to confound me nearly a decade after their publication. First, I suppose it is because so many intelligent people have read and now accept the grand narrative of conquest and Western domination as gospel. Second, I must take responsibility because I know that an alternate tale, written from the perspectives of Indigenous peoples, is far more interesting.

How is it that five hundred years after Columbus we still read about the perpetually vanishing primitive or the mythical *Hohokam* or the *Anasazi?* How does Diamond's biocultural Armageddon, fueled by

Old World diseases or environmental mismanagement, explain the presence of the O'Odham, myself, or my children? Is it all geography and biology? Or have archaeologists and historians simply chosen to ignore the presence of Indigenous peoples and their histories? As a response to the questions raised by Diamond's texts (hereafter referred to as *Guns* and *Collapse*), I'd like to explore the appealing nature of these works and raise questions about Diamond's notion that conquests are accidents of biology, geography, and technology. I'll demonstrate how Diamond's discussion of deforestation and environmental catastrophe at Chaco Canyon relies upon a selective view of archaeological and historical evidence. As is the case with the O'Odham, archaeologists have contributed to the mythology of the vanishing Anasazi and generated a pervasive narrative of environmental mismanagement by Native Americans. While few would agree totally with Diamond's work, North American archaeologists bear significant responsibility for many of his conclusions. Archaeological interpretations of abandonments, and a failure to integrate indigenous histories, have helped support a national mythology in which conquests are accidents and Indigenous peoples are to blame for their own problems.

A CONVENIENT DIALOGUE: CONQUEST (AND PROSPERITY) AS ACCIDENT

Disguised as an attack on racial determinism, Diamond's *Guns, Germs, and Steel* lays out the most palatable of narratives of Western global domination. For Diamond, the disparities between the "haves" and "have-nots" (as depicted in Diamond's introductory conversation with the unfortunate Papua New Guinean, Yali), "Who have so much cargo" and those who don't, were set in motion long ago, just beyond the effective reach of his sympathetic reader. His argument is a kind of Greek tragedy with the gods played by the inescapable logic of evolutionary biology. According to Diamond, unknown and unnamed geographic forces proffered selective advantages over the centuries to unwitting but select "Eurasian" populations. Diamond's dialogue with his primitive prototype Yali, could be summarized as follows: "You see, Yali, if your ancestors had come from *here* in the northern hemisphere instead of *there* in the southern hemisphere, you might have found yourself on the other end of our equation of inequality. ... Were it not for geography, *you* might be explaining *my* unfortunate fate to *me*.

For Diamond, guns and steel were just technologies that happened to fall into the hands of one's collective ancestors. And, just to make things fair, they only *marginally* benefited Westerners over their Indigenous foes in the New World because the *real* conquest was accomplished by other forces floating free in the cosmic lottery – submicroscopic pathogens. Diamond's grand narrative cleverly rejects the racism and naked triumphalism of our not so distant forebears and embraces a nouveau-democratic narrative that speaks to the logical sensibilities and sympathies of modern readers: Colonization was an accident. Immunities to disease conferred a biological advantage, and in the contest among peoples the result was foreordained. A reader of Diamond's story, perhaps lounging in the tropics on his holidays, glances at the hired help and drifts off into a sleep made more peaceful by the notion that his fortunate fate, and indeed the fates of human societies, were settled long ago and far away.

I would feel more comfortable in my current air-conditioned perch of scorn except that I have been that reader myself, perhaps on a beach somewhere wondering about the same things. What now startles me into wakefulness is my own position as a Native American archaeologist. I have read, in courses that I have taken and now in those that I teach, the naïve and simplistic accounts of my ancestors' collective failures, for example, in the dreamtime landscape of the foremost journal in my field, *American Antiquity*. Name the tragic fable of the day, and I can find it in the ostensibly value-free and politically neutral, scientific explanations of the flagship journal of American archaeology. The cultures and histories of Indigenous peoples have been appropriated and deployed by scholars in the service of democracy, environmentalism, and gender equality since anthropology began.

It was not hard for Diamond to reach his conclusions about Chaco Canyon or the Hohokam. Any curious reader interested in learning more about these places would encounter a whole genre of academic literature devoted to the technological, environmental, and political failures of Native Americans north and south. Archaeology is the perfect source, a politically neutral data set from which social failure and contemporary marginality can be reverse-engineered. In

Diamond's work we see the logical conclusions one would reach by leafing through the last thirty-five years of archaeological literature on the U.S. Southwest. From these journals we learn that all archaeological sites, by virtue of their abandonment, represent some form of social, technological, or environmental failure. In a neo-evolutionary calculus, where adaptation insures survival (and a claim on the landscape), the Indian affirms his failure to adapt by his absence.

The connections between the archaeological record and living peoples are artfully obscured through the invention of archaeo-ethnicities such as the Anasazi, Chacoans, Athapaskans, and Hohokam-invented cultures with invisible descendents. Through a process of professional appropriation, places like Chaco Canyon became the data set of concerned scientists instead of a part of the living cosmogram of contemporary Pueblos and their neighbors. Instead, we find in *Collapse* a perfectly logical account of the shortcomings of Indigenous peoples, another origin myth of the "haves" and "have-nots" in *Guns*. Note the subtle shift (or less charitably the contradiction) between the "accident" of conquest in *Guns* and the "choice" of success or failure among Diamond's Anasazi in *Collapse*.

I wonder each time I visit the flooded golf courses and melting asphalt surrounding the Ivory Towers of the southwestern mega-universities how Indigenous peoples, who cultivated fields, rotated crops, and developed drought- and disease-resistant strains of corn for at least a thousand years in a desert, are now the *locus classicus* of willful environmental mismanagement. In *Collapse,* Diamond merely relays the well-worn tradition among many Southwestern archaeologists of explaining the abandonment of just about every archaeological site as the consequence of environmental mismanagement or warfare resulting from environmental mismanagement. It seems that before the accident of European conquest, Native Americans chose to abuse either the environment, or each other, and this set the table for conquest, colonization, poverty, and the "vanished" (or invisible) Indian.

For Diamond, following generations of archaeologists, especially the ecologically minded "processual" archaeologists of the 1960s, Indian prehistory exemplified a "tragedy of the commons" on wheels – a movable feast of miscalculation, mismanagement, and misery. Under the ostensible purpose of furthering the knowledge of human prehistory generally – where the archaeological record is viewed as a data set belonging to everyone – local, historical narratives like those of the O'Odham and the Pueblos have been generally viewed as particular, inaccurate, and above all "nonscientific." Although this situation is now changing, Native Americans have been disarticulated from both the material remains of their ancestors and the process of interpreting these remains to the public.

The result of being written out of history (and prehistory) is that the presence of 4.5 million Indians in the United States today is a complete mystery to most Americans. And how could they be led to think anything different when most of the people interpreting Native American prehistory were explaining the disappearance of a people they had never bothered to meet? Unfortunately the alienation of the O'Odham from their past is not unique. Many indigenous peoples, frustrated by the activities and scholarship of archaeologists, advocated for a greater voice in the interpretation of their histories. Passed into law in 1990, the Native American Graves Protection and Repatriation Act required archaeologists and museums to consult with Native Americans and return cultural properties and human remains to descendent communities.

It is not surprising that the main challenge posed by the NAGPRA legislation was the process of rearticulating these materials with living groups. Working with the living descendents of an archaeological landscape quickly interrupts the logical links between what archaeologists interpret as an "abandonment," the ready-made parable of "failure" and the social deaths of invented groups such as the Hohokam and Anasazi. Without such a dialogue, each archaeological site is viewed as a kind of skeleton, the corpse of an evolutionary dead end. Since archaeologists and museum curators are now required by law to consult with tribes, invisible Indians are now very visible indeed; many archaeological projects have become collaborative ventures in which ethnographic skills (and talking to living Indians) have become a central component of research.

Diamond's work has completely missed this tectonic shift in archaeology. In *Collapse* we learn that the Anasazi deforested the landscape and were "done in" by the resulting dropping water tables. Salinization, we learn, forced the Hohokam to abandon their villages. The Mogollon in the central mountains of Arizona

FIGURE 5.3 Urban sprawl of Phoenix, Arizona, that has engulfed the ancestral O'Odham site of Mesa Grande. (Source: Fish and Fish 2008, Plate 12, photograph courtesy of Adriel Heisey)

and western New Mexico exhausted their agricultural potential. All these abandonments, Diamond writes, "were ultimately due to the same fundamental challenge: people living in fragile and difficult environments, adopting solutions that were brilliantly successful and understandable 'in the short run,' but that failed or else created fatal problems in the long run, when people became confronted with external environmental changes or human-caused environmental changes that *societies without written histories and without archaeologists could not have anticipated*" (my italics).[11] According to Diamond, without archaeologists, Native Peoples not only lacked any notion of memory or concept of sustainability but were also unable to realize that they lived in a marginal environment. Their "failures," according to Diamond, should serve as a warning to more enlightened peoples – people with technological know-how, written histories, and archaeologists. These are the same people who have managed to turn the center of the Hohokam homeland into the sprawling, asphalt-covered and polluted capital city of Arizona. The region is supported by massive irrigation projects that have made the Gila River and the mighty Colorado completely disappear miles inland from their former outlets. Failure, apparently, is in the eyes of the beholder.

A LESSON IN DRIVE-BY ARCHAEOLOGY: URBAN DEFORESTATION AMONG THE CHACO ANASAZI

Jared Diamond ignores critical basic facts about the history of Chaco Canyon (in north central New Mexico) in order to cast Chaco (and the Pueblos) as models of urban and social failure. Tooling through the arid landscape of northern New Mexico, Diamond marvels at the Anasazi ability to build an advanced city in such a wasteland – a wasteland that he fails to recognize as the present homeland of nineteen contemporary Pueblo reservations. One has to wonder how Diamond was able to ignore the large permanent signs located at the entrance to every Great House in Chaco Canyon, reminding visitors that Chaco continues to serve as a sacred landscape to contemporary Native Peoples. Because he did not speak to any living Puebloan (apparently there was no "Yali" with whom he might converse), his assessments of environmental mismanagement and "the collapse and disappearance of the Chacoans" is based upon a very narrow selection of archaeological books and articles, namely, those in which environmental mismanagement is foregrounded and Pueblo interpretations of the region are largely ignored. Just as he does with the Hohokam, Diamond misrepresents the significance, the function, and the history of what was (and still is) an important center of Pueblo ritual and history. Naturally, Diamond was rightly alarmed as he left the modern urban sprawl of Albuquerque, the endless tracts of homes and strip malls, the evidence of overgrazing, erosion, and arroyo cutting, and the depressing sight of the Rio Grande, which is dry for much of the year due to the relentless groundwater pumping for urban and agricultural purposes. Meanwhile, the modern Pueblos retain their

FIGURE 5.4 National Park Service sign at the entrance to Chaco Canyon that informs visitors that Chaco is a sacred landscape. (Photo by Greg Jennings)

exceptional knowledge of agricultural planning for both good and drought years, that is, production that is not for maximum yield and profit but for sustainability.

Archaeology, of course, is the way we can investigate the human past. Over a century, excellent (and some regrettable) archaeological investigations have taken place at Chaco Canyon. These investigations directly contradict the facts as presented by Diamond. To summarize, Chaco represented the florescence of an unprecedented social movement within the Pueblo world. The evidence is embodied in a collection of large pueblo-like buildings called Great Houses, some with hundreds of rooms, along a small river in the center of an arid basin in northwest New Mexico. In *Collapse*, Diamond argues that Chaco Canyon was an oasis in which agricultural production (especially of corn) was first adopted and later intensified over a period of six hundred years (600–1200 C.E.). Gradually the population expanded beyond the carrying capacity of the land, the region was deforested by large construction projects, and the resulting erosion cut channels that lowered the water table. When the environment changed (and

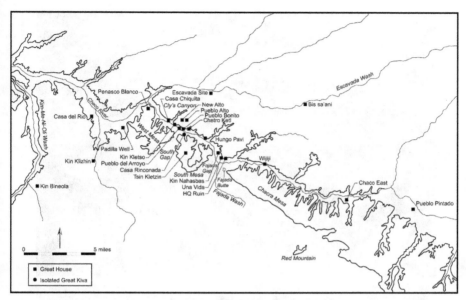

FIGURE 5.5 Distribution of Great Houses and Kivas within Chaco Canyon. (Courtesy of National Park Service, Chaco Canyon , NM)

there was an extended drought between 1125–1150 C.E.), the social system "collapsed" into a period of incessant warfare, extreme violence, and cannibalism. This scenario, however, is incomplete when it is not wrong.

First, Chaco was occupied much earlier than 600 C.E. (Atlatl Cave has been dated to 1000 B.C.E.) by small-scale, mobile groups who experimented with agriculture. Permanent villages dating to 400 C.E. are found at Shabik'eschee Village and Penasco Blanco, and there is every reason to believe that others may be similarly located.[12] Second, although environmental stresses play a part in every agricultural society, the people at Chaco lived literally for centuries in a landscape where extended droughts occurred with great regularity.[13] There were approximately *twenty* periods of drought between 650 and 1225 C.E. in which the canyon remained occupied; construction events at Great Houses span several of these periods of drought. According to Diamond, to support a rapidly expanding population, a large forest in the canyon was cleared in order to construct these large apartment and religious structures (Great Houses and Great Kivas). Deforestation

FIGURE 5.6 Architectural complexes of Chaco Canyon: Great Houses of (a) Pueblo Bonito and (b) Kin Kletso and (c) a Great Kiva within Pueblo Bonito. (Photos by Greg Jennings)

led to erosion, entrenchment (or arroyo cutting), the lowering of the water table, and the disappearance of the Chaco River.

However, there was never a forest in the canyon. Packrat middens (which contain ancient pollen) in the valley reveal a climate and ecology almost exactly like that which exists today.[14] So where did the estimated 200,000 trees that were cut down to supply building materials come from? The same place where the cycles of drought are documented, 75 kilometers to the west in the Chuska Mountains. As far as arroyo cutting is concerned, geologist Eric Force has identified several periods of aggradation (deposition of sediments) and entrenchment (erosion of water channels) at Chaco.[15] Although construction

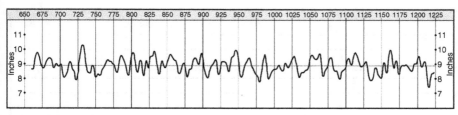

FIGURE 5.7 Rainfall trends from Chaco Region. (After Lekson 2006: 393)

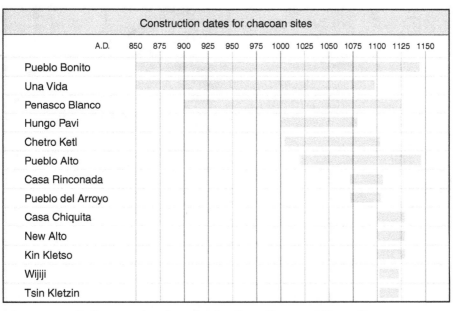

FIGURE 5.8 Construction dates for the Great Houses of Chaco Canyon.

events coincide *loosely* with the deposition of sediments, it is unknown whether drought or water diversion (and farming) led to sedimentation. Neither do major entrenchment events coincide with the abandonment of the Canyon in the 1300s. We do know that the water table at Chaco fell in the late 1800s with the introduction of cattle and that since the early 1900s a large arroyo has been cut along the course of the Chaco River. The original inhabitants of the Canyon caused none of these current changes.

The idea that Chacoans recklessly expanded farming in the valley in order to feed large populations is similarly a fiction. Temperature extremes at Chaco range from −38 to 102 degrees Fahrenheit. To

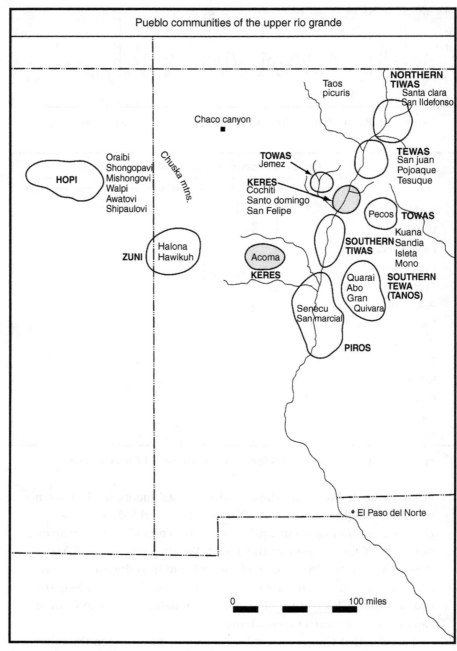

FIGURE 5.9 Chaco Canyon in relation to Chuska Mountains and contemporary pueblos (language groups indicated in boldface, ancestral and contemporary pueblo locales in regular font).

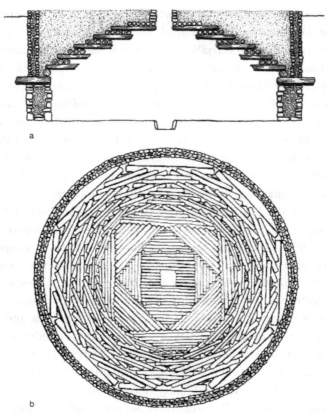

FIGURE 5.10 Schematic diagrams of wooden beam construction used for roofing structures at Chaco Canyon: (a) side view, (b) top view. (Courtesy of National Park Service, Chaco Canyon, NM)

cultivate corn, modern Pueblo farmers require 120 frost-free days.[16] In the canyon today the average is less than 100 days, making stable agricultural production impossible. So where did the food come from? It was brought in periodically – probably during pilgrimages to the ritual center that was Chaco. Corn and wood (construction materials) collected from Chaco have helped debunk the notion that the canyon was ever used as the source of building materials *or* food. Water leaves isotopic signatures (ratios of [strontium] Sr^{87}/Sr^{86}) in plants that are particular to specific geographic contexts.[17] Throughout the Chaco sequence, corn gathered from middens (garbage dumps) and wood have isotopic signatures similar to plants grown far away in the Chuska Mountains (75 kilometers to the west) or the San Juan River floodplain, 90 kilometers to the north. Corn and other food supported a very small year-round population. Early investigators were puzzled by the low numbers of burials and human remains within any of the Great Houses in the canyon. After over a century of excavations, only 350 burials have been discovered at a site that was occupied for about eight centuries (400–1300 C.E.). As for evidence of warfare, violence, and social conflict, only a very small percentage of the burials show evidence of perimortem violence, and there is no burial evidence supporting large-scale warfare at any time in the Canyon's history.[18] Finally, only a small number of rooms at Chaco have fire pits or hearths, a normal indicator of year-round occupation.

So what was Chaco? Most likely Chaco was a multiethnic ritual center where ideas, as well as some food, were exchanged. Many of the Chacoan structures appear to have been built as arenas and for ceremonies and demonstrations of sacred knowledge.[19] Current interpretations of Chaco suggest that the network of precisely oriented roads extending hundreds of kilometers throughout the San Juan Basin directed people into the canyon for festivals and ritual performances. The "end" of the Chaco system coincides with the establishment of new Pueblo settlements throughout the region, descendents of Chacoans. One important difference between contemporary Pueblos and the Chaco system is the notion that ritual centralization was socially dangerous. Secrecy and the compartmentalization of ritual knowledge (even within Pueblo communities) may have developed in response to what happened at Chaco. Diamond ignores this story, which is as interesting and significant (certainly to modern people) as the existence of Chaco itself. The relationship between social change and ideology appears to have played a significant role in the history of Chaco. Ideology is central to many of the most dramatic changes in Western civilization. There is every reason to believe that these types of changes were at least as transformative among Native Americans as they were to Europeans.

CREATING AN IDEOLOGY OF CONQUEST: CHRISTIANITY AND THE PUEBLO REVOLT OF 1680

It is significant that Diamond makes reference to the Pueblo Revolt of 1680 as a historically recorded instance of extended drought, a model for the end of Anasazi settlement at Chaco Canyon, which, as Diamond writes, the Europeans did observe. However, the archaeology of the Pueblo Revolt of 1680 tells little about the natural environment. Rather, it speaks significantly about the importance of ideology in European colonization, the responses of Indigenous peoples to social violence, and the meaning of abandonments from the perspectives of the Pueblos themselves. The revolt provides an important counternarrative of survival and helps address the most salient question for Native Peoples: How is it that we are still here?

From my own perspective, a more appropriate troika of destruction would be "lawyers, gods, and money." First and foremost, I reject the notion that any military conquest, however rapid, immediately or totally transforms any society. Conquests are continuously reformulated and reiterated through time. As we have seen recently in the news from the Middle East, conquests demand maintenance. But the maintenance and motives of conquests require ideologies and philosophies that allow one group to imagine itself as the naturally or divinely ordained instruments of progress and change. The philosophical justifications of subordination are not only the most fundamental element of conquests, they are also the most interesting.

What greater irony could one image than the manner in which Christianity, which begins as a small sectarian cult that rejected materialism and embraced a radical egalitarian philosophy, is yoked violently to the arms and economic ambitions of the Spanish state? In Spain and its colonies, Christianity was militarized through the character of Santiago Matamoros (St. James the Moor killer), a mythical brother of Christ. Between 1540 and 1600 the Pueblos endured eight successive waves of violent raids from Spanish colonists, culminating in the first permanent European settlement in the United States, Santa Fe. Santa Fe in Spain was the name of the city from which Christian warriors launched a siege against Grenada, the final Moorish kingdom to fall in the *Reconquista* of Spain. Colonial New Mexico was imagined as and became a historical projection of the Spanish *Reconquista*. When battling the Pueblos, the Spanish warriors invoked the name of Santiago and referred to Pueblo kivas as "mosques."

Justifications for the use of violence as a tool of conversion and enforcement can be traced to the theologian Augustine in the fifth century. In a series of letters to the pope, he advocated the use of force as a means of subjugating a rival Christian sect, known as the Donatists, in North Africa. Borrowing from the gospels, Augustine cites three words uttered by Jesus to his disciples: "Feed my sheep." Using this single sentence, Augustine reasoned that, for the sake of salvation, all of the earth's peoples can and should be compelled to join at the table of the lord. Thus begins nearly one thousand years of legal, morally justified warfare between Christian peoples, heretics, heathens, and idolaters.

Without this legal and theological justification, the fledgling nations of early modern Europe lacked the moral authority to interfere in the lives of peoples who were geographically separated from, and therefore could not have yet heard, the word of Christ. Conquest was far from accidental or simply a product of geography, but was accomplished under the rule of law and the philosophical underpinnings of that law, an actively constructed rationale for conquest and subjugation.

In the early Spanish *entradas* into New Mexico, a lengthy document outlining the relationship between Jesus and Peter, Peter and the popes and the soldiers of Spain was read (in Spanish and Latin) to Native Peoples as a formal requirement before military engagement. Those who resisted after its recital deserved to be conquered. Resisting the Spanish was equated with resisting Christ, and Pueblo prisoners were killed according to the rules of dealing with unbelievers – they were to be burned. Colonial violence was not a matter of passion, but a technical discipline, routinized by a bureaucracy and upheld by the rule of law.

In my work on the archaeology of the postcontact period in New Mexico I have found a very different set of responses by the Pueblos to the phenomenon of colonization than is characterized in Diamond's work. Many of the abandonments that occurred during the contact period did not result from disease, but from a desire to use mobility as a means of establishing social segregation. After sixty years of violent raids along Spain's colonial northern frontier, the Pueblos and their neighbors repeatedly used mobility as a social strategy in order to remove themselves from the social, religious, and economic coercion of Spaniards. To maintain social distance, the Pueblos created geographic distance. Until very recently few postcontact period

Indigenous sites (other than missions) have been systematically explored or documented. Now we can see that during the Revolt of 1680, when Pueblo people attacked missions and Spanish villages, several new communities were constructed on mesas or deep within the forests of the Jemez Mountains.

The existence of these sites require archaeologists, not just Jared Diamond, to rethink the meaning of abandonment. Rather than regarding abandoned sites as the corpses of a dead society, a more appropriate metaphor is that of a shell. The living organism creates it, inhabits it, and then moves from it only to construct a new home and preserve the life inside somewhere else. Abandonment, like mobility, is a social strategy and not evidence of a social failure or "collapse." One interpretation suggests continuity and creates a space for the survival of indigenous peoples, the other effectively writes Indians out of the present and alienates them from the material remains and communities of their ancestors.

As for the causes of the Revolt of 1680, human agency and ideology were at the heart of the conflict, not disease, drought, or weaponry. In the years following the permanent colonial settlement in Santa Fe in 1600, Pueblo peoples were required to work in the textile factories and fields of secular officials, but officials did not overtly interfere with Pueblo religious life. When a new regime of Christian missionaries and officials arrived from Mexico in 1650, they increased taxation from a per household rate to a per capita rate, forbade the practice of ancient Pueblo ceremonies that ensured the survival of the Pueblos, and arrested the religious leaders. Within a decade the Pueblos revolted, and Spaniards were expelled from the Pueblo world and forced to negotiate with and accommodate Pueblo religious practices.

The Spanish legal system as well as the infrastructure and the fragile economy of New Spain were all human constructs, not accidents. No story about Chaco, the O'Odham, or the Pueblo Revolt can be told without referring to ideology, culture, and history. The passage of laws such as the Desert Land Act and the failure of democratic institutions to protect the rights of small minorities such as the O'Odham are social artifacts of Manifest Destiny. The importance of Chaco as a pilgrimage site and the role of Christian evangelism as a justification for military conquest and colonization each emphasize the importance of ideology and history in shaping the trajectories of human societies.

CONCLUSION

And so we return to my original proposition. If we shift our questions 180 degrees and ask if there are narratives that explain not the invisibility and disappearance or marginality but the survival of Indigenous Peoples, we are led to an entirely different set of answers and explanations. Assuming that Indians are still here (as I am forced to do), I am asked to perform a mythic reversal. If, after reading Diamond, we are led to think that conquest was driven by invisible forces, that the table was set (and colonization is justified) by the mismanagement of the environment by prehistoric peoples of North America, we have participated and consumed the most noxious and potent agent of conquest, the narrative itself.

My criticisms are not simply of Jared Diamond himself, but of those who explain global inequalities and poverty among the have-nots – who have no cargo – as inevitable and portray have-nots as powerless victims of impersonal forces. As a reader, I cannot be held responsible for military encounters 500 years ago. But as an archaeologist I am responsible for understanding how the work I create can take on a life of its own and be interpreted as a collective explanation for Indigenous "failures" – failures that seem to justify colonization and the replacement and removal of Indian Peoples.

Diamond's tidy explanation of conquest and global poverty is not only factually incorrect; it gives us the sense that its origins lie somewhere out there, beyond the agency of the reader. The implication is that if conquests were situated long ago, somewhere else, then we are powerless over their contemporary manifestations. Conquests are never instantaneous, transformative, or all encompassing. They are enacted, reenacted, and rewritten for each succeeding generation. In this sense Diamond's narrative of disappearance and marginalization is one of conquest's most potent instruments.

Notes

*   I am a Native American archaeologist (Yuman/Choctaw) and an assistant professor of anthropology at Stanford University. I graduated from the University of California at Santa Barbara (1993) and Harvard University (M.A., 1995, Ph.D., 2001). I have conducted fieldwork at Chacoan outlier sites near Zuñi, New Mexico, and have worked for the O'Odham (Pima)

Nation in Arizona investigating Hohokam villages. Currently I work with Pueblo People of New Mexico.

My research interests include Native American history, culture, and the emerging field of Indigenous Archaeology. I specialize in the archaeology of early colonial and contact periods in the American Southwest with a special interest in the archaeology of the Pueblo Revolt of 1680. My forthcoming book *The Pueblo Revolt and the Mythology of Conquest: An Indigenous Archaeology of Contact* (2009) will be published by the University of California Press.

1. United States Office of Indian Affairs 1869: 208–209.
2. Diamond 1997; 2005.
3. Dobyns 1989: 23.
4. Robinson 1979: 38.
5. United States Office of Indian Affairs 1870: 117; 1885: 3–4.
6. Dobyns 1978; Rea 1983.
7. Dobyns 1989: 59; United States Office of Indian Affairs 1893: 121, 216.
8. Adolph Bandelier was a notable exception. Bandelier lamented the disconnect he observed in memoirs and letters to his colleagues. Bandelier et al. 1977: 142; Hodge 1893: 323–330; Fewkes 1912.
9. There are important issues surrounding this translation. The term *hohokam* was originally a common noun referring to things and objects that have been discarded. The O'Odham now understand that it has come to refer to an ancestral group, and they use this "incorrect" translation. Linguistic evidence actually suggests that the material culture archaeologists characterize as "Hohokam" is actually the remains of multiethnic communities. Other tribes in the area, such as the Papago, Maricopa, and Yuma, are likely also among the descendents of the Hohokam (Shaul and Hill 1998: 375–396).
10. Gladwin 1965: 5–18; Gladwin 1937; Haury 1976: 357; Woosley and Ravesloot 1993: 224–230; Doelle 1981: 445; Doyel 1991: 231–278; Cordell and Gumerman 1989: 19–63.
11. Diamond 2005: 155.
12. Elliott 1986; Lekson 2006: 71.
13. Huckleberry 2007: 466.
14. Hall 1988: 582; Mathien 1986: 2005.
15. Force et al. 2002.
16. Vivian 1990: 22.
17. Benson et al. 2003: 111–113; Reynolds et al. 2005.
18. Lekson 2002: 607–624. Although Lekson finds evidence for violence in the Northern San Juan Basin with Chacoan Outliers, the links between these actions and the abandonment of Chaco remain unclear. Similarly, what many archaeologists view as evidence for social violence or cannibalism can be accounted for by behaviors linked to witchcraft among the Pueblos (Darling 1998: 732–752; Dongoske et al. 2000: 179–190; Walker 2001: 573–596).
19. Mills 2002.

Bibliography

Bandelier, Adolph Francis Alphonse and Herman Frederick Carlel Ten Kat. 1977. *An Outline of the Documentary History of the Zuni Tribe.* New York: AMS Press.

Benson, Larry, Linda Cordell, Kirk Vincent, Howard Taylor, John Stein, G. Lang Farmer, and Kiyoto Futa. 2003. "Ancient Maize from Chacoan Great Houses: Where Was It Grown?" *Proceedings of the National Academy of Sciences* **100**:13, 111–13, 1115.

Cordell, Linda S. and George J. Gummerman. 1989. *Dynamics of Southwest Prehistory.* Washington, DC: Smithsonian Institution Press.

Darling, J. Andrew. 1998. "Mass Inhumation and the Execution of Witches in the American Southwest." *American Anthropologist* **100**:732–752.

Diamond, Jared M. 1997. *Guns, Germs, and Steel: The Fates of Human Societies.* New York: W. W. Norton.

Diamond, Jared M. 2005 *Collapse: How Societies Choose to Fail or Succeed.* New York: Viking.

Dobyns, Henry. 1978. *Who Killed the Gila?* Tucson: University of Arizona Press.

Dobyns, Henry. 1989 *The Pima-Maricopa.* New York: Chelsea House.

Doelle, William H. 1981. "The Gila Pima in the Seventeenth Century," in *The Protohistoric Period in the North American Southwest, AD 1450–1700.* Edited by D. Wilcox and B. Masse, pp. 57–70. Anthropological Research Papers 24. Tempe: Arizona State University.

Dongoske, Kurt E., Debra L. Martin, and T. J. Ferguson. 2000. "Critique of the Claim of Cannibalism at Cowboy Wash." *American Antiquity* **65**:179–190.

Doyel, David E. 1991. "Hohokam Cultural Evolution in the Phoenix Basin," in *Exploring the Hohokam: Prehistoric Desert Peoples of the American Southwest.* Edited by G. J. Gummerman, pp. 231–278. Albuquerque: University of New Mexico Press.

Elliott, Michael. 1986. *Atlatl Cave and the Late Archiac Period in Chaco Canyon, New Mexico.* Albuquerque: University of New Mexico Press.

Fewkes, Jesse Walter. 1912. *Casa Grande, Arizona.* Bureau of American Ethnology, Annual Report 28, pt. 1. Washington, DC: Smithsonian Institution.

Fish, Suzanne K. and Paul Fish. 2008. *The Hohokam Millennium.* Santa Fe, NM: School of Advance Research Press.

Force, Eric R., Jeffrey S. Dean, and Gary Funkhauser. 2002. *Relation of "Bonito" Paleo-Channels and Base-Level Variations to Anasazi Occupation, Chaco, Canyon, New Mexico.* Tucson: Arizona State Museum, University of Arizona.

Gladwin, Harold S. 1937. *Excavations at Snaketown.* Medallion Papers 25. Globe, AZ: Privately printed for Gila Pueblo.

Gladwin, Harold S. 1965. *Excavations at Snaketown: Material Culture.* Tucson: Reprinted for the Arizona State Museum by the University of Arizona Press.

Hall, Stephen A. 1988. "Prehistoric Vegetation and Environment at Chaco Canyon." *American Antiquity* **53**:582–592.

Haury, Emil. 1976. *The Hohokam Desert Farmers and Craftsmen: Excavations at Snaketown, 1964–1965.* Tucson: University of Arizona Press.

Hodge, F. W. 1893. "Prehistoric Irrigation in Arizona." *American Anthropologist* 6:323–330.

Huckleberry, G. 2007. "Environmental Change and Human Adaptation in the Ancient American Southwest." *The Kiva* 72:466–469.

Lekson, Stephen H. 2002. "War in the Southwest, War in the World." *American Antiquity* 67:607–624.

Lekson, Stephen H. Editor. 2006. *The Archaeology of Chaco Canyon: An Eleventh-Century Pueblo Regional Center.* Santa Fe, NM: School of American Research Press.

Mathien, Frances Joan. 1986. *Environment and Subsistence of Chaco Canyon, New Mexico.* Albuquerque, NM: National Park Service, U.S. Dept. of the Interior.

Mathien, Frances Joan. 2005. *Culture and Ecology of Chaco Canyon and the San Juan Basin.* Santa Fe, NM: National Park Service.

Mills, Barbara J. 2002. "Recent Research on Chaco: Changing Views on Economy, Ritual, and Society." *Journal of Archaeological Research* 10:65–117.

Rea, Amadeo M. 1983. *Once a River: Bird Life and Habitat Changes on the Middle Gila.* Tucson: University of Arizona Press.

Reynolds, Amanda C., Julio L. Betancourt, Jay Quade, Jonathan Patchett, Jeffrey S. Dean, and John Stein. 2005. "87Sr/86Sr Sourcing of Ponderosa Pine Used in Anasazi Great House Construction at Chaco Canyon, New Mexico." *Journal of Archaeological Science* 32:1061–1075.

Robinson, Michael C. 1979. *Water for the West: The Bureau of Reclamation, 1902–1977.* Chicago: Public Works Historical Society.

Shaul, David Leedom and Jane H. Hill. 1998. "Tepimans, Yumans, and Other Hohokam." *American Antiquity* 63:375–396.

United States Office of Indian Affairs. 1869, 1870, 1877, 1885, 1888, 1893. *Annual Report of the Commissioner of Indian Affairs to the Secretary of the Interior.* Washington, DC: Government Printing Office.

Vivian, R. Gwinn. 1990. *The Chacoan Prehistory of the San Juan Basin.* San Diego, CA: Academic Press.

Walker, Phillip L. 2001. "A Bioarchaeological Perspective on the History of Violence." *Annual Review of Anthropology* 30:573–596.

Woosley, Anne I. and John C. Ravesloot. Editors. 1993. *Culture and Contact: Charles C. Di Peso's Gran Chichimeca.* Albuquerque: University of New Mexico Press.

6

Bellicose Rulers and Climatological Peril?

Retrofitting Twenty-First-Century Woes on Eighth-Century Maya Society

Patricia A. McAnany and
Tomás Gallareta Negrón[*]

In 2007, movie producer/director Mel Gibson "treated" audiences to a spectacularly inaccurate portrayal of ancient Maya civilization. Called *Apocalypto*, the movie depicted Maya rulers and priests as blood-thirsty savages and Maya farmers as hunters and gatherers; a Spanish galleon drifting somewhere off the coast of the Yucatán Peninsula seemed the only salvation available to the Comanche and Yaqui actor Rudy Youngblood and his brave young wife and two children.[1] Why does it matter that ancestral Maya society was depicted in such an unflattering fashion? Who cares that the killing fields through which Youngblood stumbled are hauntingly similar to the places where Maya men, women, and children were exhumed from mass graves created during the Guatemalan Maya genocide of the 1980s?[2] Gibson makes movies that are entertaining and action packed; he does not claim that his movies are historically accurate, only that they portray the universality of human emotions – in this case fear of apocalypse or the total destruction of society. While he is correct that humans are fascinated by the cyclic nature of what historians and archaeologists call *civilization* – the extreme centralization of power and people into cities, the construction of colossal monumental architecture, and the invention and spread of a written script – inevitably cities contract, power is loosened, monumental architecture falls into disrepair, and written languages die. Does this mean that the leaders behind these impressive achievements failed, or did they just change in response to a changing world? This is not an easy question for historians and archaeologists. Many different opinions exist regarding the meaning and significance of societal change.

The dramatic and visible changes that occurred in ancestral Maya society during the eighth and ninth centuries invite social theorists (and lately Hollywood movie producers) to speculate about the causes of profound societal transformation. Political and environmental concerns that exist in our world today, and leaders who are unresponsive to pressing social and economic issues as well as impending climatic change, often assume a prominent place in our interpretations of the past. But how can we know if such speculation hits close to or falls short of the mark? Archaeologists try to know the past by examining various different lines of evidence. If ideas about why or how a society changed are correct, then we should be able to collect pertinent evidence from more than one source. For instance, if a society collapsed because of a drought, then we should find not only abandoned settlements but also evidence of both malnourishment in human remains and land desertification, which might be detected in deep core samples of lakes. If multiple lines of evidence don't point in the same direction, then it is likely that the conclusion is not correct.

For instance, according to Jared Diamond's popular book *Collapse: How Societies Choose to Fail or Succeed,*[3] the root causes behind the alleged eighth-to-ninth-century Maya "collapse" can be found with rulers – divine kings – who subjected their constituents to ceaseless cycles of warfare while ignoring signs of societal distress *and* climatological trends that compromised the livelihood of food producers. Does this explanation, which seems to be an apt description of U.S. society during the first decade of the twenty-first century, indicate an uncanny similarity between the past and present, or an attempt to retrofit the past on to the present? As archaeologists who have studied the remains of ancestral Maya society collectively for over four decades, we hope that knowledge of past societies will resonate in the present and inform the future, but the intersection of our knowledge of the past with our current societal problems is a critical and delicate juncture that requires careful navigation. Popular as well as academic accounts provided by Gibson, Diamond, and others can sensationalize and *decontextualize* the past. Based on a narrow range of sources, they develop simplistic historical narratives that – while

FIGURE 6.1 Maya region showing archaeological sites mentioned in text and prominent descendant populations (name of Mayan language groups indicated in capital letters). (Illustration by Josh Feola)

quite easily digested – overlook the extraordinary resilience of past societies. By glossing over significant evidence that contradicts the scenario of eighth-century Maya doom and by imputing personality traits such as passivity to Maya rulers, popular writers tell a story that is problematic scientifically and a dangerous narrative that labels the ancestors of contemporary Maya people as those who chose to craft a failed state. We challenge the accuracy of this reading of the political and demographic transformations that swept across the Maya region in the 125 years between 800 and 925 C.E. We present here an alternative perspective on Classic Maya social change by critically reviewing the lines of evidence upon which many collapse scenarios are based:

1) Escalating warfare
2) Out-of-control population growth
3) Environmental degradation
4) Drought
5) Effectiveness of divine rulership and
6) Changes in spheres of trade and influence.

Often considered the archetypal example of societal collapse and environmental catastrophe, ancestral Maya society provides a mirror for our contemporary gaze into the past. In light of this high profile, we believe that it is critically important to examine the data carefully. In every respect the ancestors of seven million contemporary Mayan-speaking people of southern México and Central America were a phenomenal American success story, and their deep history deserves to be examined with great concern for consistency and the goodness-of-fit between our ideas about the past and trends displayed by the evidence that we systematically collect from the field.

ESCALATING WARFARE?

Since the 1980s Maya epigraphers have made great strides in deciphering the hieroglyphic script of ancestral Maya society.[4] One of the most prolific literate peoples of pre-Columbian America, Maya scribes of the first millennium C.E. carved and painted hundreds, if not thousands, of texts in stone, plaster, and fan-fold codices, and on pottery and wall murals. Most were dedicatory in intent.[5] Maya script is called logo-syllabic rather than alphabetic because some glyphs stood for whole words while others represented consonant-vowel syllables, such as *la*, *ba*, or *ka*. The syllabic elements were compounded and drawn calligraphically to form beautiful hieroglyphic strings that were read left-to-right, often as two-column text. The names of some of the

Maya rulers introduced in this discussion are phonetic translations of sequences of Maya glyphs. The earliest known Maya hieroglyphs were painted and inscribed during the Preclassic period, around 300 B.C.E., and Maya literacy continued through the sixteenth-century Spanish incursions, at which point conquistadors and missionaries report on the confiscation and burning of countless Maya fan-fold codex-style books. Currently only four codices are known to exist. The bulk of known hieroglyphic texts – carved in stone and painted on pottery – date to a 250-year period from 600 to 850 C.E., otherwise known to archaeologists as the Late Classic period.

Late Classic Maya hieroglyphic texts contain many references to martial events and captive taking, such as the extraordinary account of a ruler of Quirigua (an ancestral Maya capital located on the Motagua River in Guatemala) called K'ahk' Tiliw Chan Yoaat (Sky Smoking Tapir), who in 738 C.E. captured and beheaded the ruler of nearby Copán (in Honduras), who bore the regal name of Waxaklajuun Ub'aah K'awiil (He of the Eighteen God Images).[6] This account is unusual for two reasons: (1) Quirigua had been a vassal polity of Copán but clearly was forcibly making a bid for autonomy and (2) as the illustrated glyphic inscription indicates, the captured ruler was executed. Increasingly, it appears that rulers captured during martial conflict were held for tribute ransom, and some eventually were returned to their home kingdom.[7] Such strategies of martial conflict are analogous to later medieval European warfare and rarely were conclusive militarily, although they could be devastating economically for the polity from whom a ruler had been captured. Unlike modern warfare in which political leaders as well as military generals rarely participate in actual combat, Maya rulers participated in martial combat, took captives, and were taken captive in what was essentially hand-to-hand combat. Later, Spanish accounts of military conflicts with indigenous peoples of the Maya and Aztec worlds describe the intimate nature of conflict and the emphasis on captive taking, rather than killing, among non-Spanish warriors. One can imagine that Maya rulers did not initiate martial conflict against another kingdom unless victory seemed probable since there was great personal investment in the conflict on the part of the ruler. Of course, at any point in time a ruler could be forced into a defensive military engagement by a martial attack.

FIGURE 6.2 Stela J, showing K'ahk' Tiliw Chan Yoaat (Sky Smoking Tapir), ruler of a political capital now called Quirigua (located in Guatemala). As described in the two-column hieroglyphic text of Stela J (on right), in 738 C.E. the Quirigua ruler captured and beheaded the ruler of the nearby kingdom of Copán. (After Looper 2000: 103–104; courtesy of Matthew G. Looper)

Did this type of conflict spiral out of control and bring down the congeries of participating Maya kingdoms? Many point to a purported increase in martial accounts within Late Classic hieroglyphic texts as evidence to support an ignoble end to bellicose Maya rulers and their constituents. But, in all honesty, the Late Classic corpus is simply more extensive and more completely deciphered than Early Classic texts or the more recent Postclassic script. True, there are more accounts of warfare in Late Classic texts, but they exist alongside more accounts of every category of royal activity. For instance,

FIGURE 6.3 Stela 24 from Naranjo, Guatemala, showing Lady Wak Chanil Ajaw (Lady Six Sky). (Adapted by Josh Feola)

many more statements of royal marriages are found in Late Classic texts, including an account of the daughter of a ruler of a dynastic center called Dos Pilas who in 682 c.e. married into the enervated royal line of a site called Naranjo. Her name is not fully deciphered; she is known as Lady Wak Chanil Ajaw (Lady Six Sky). We hear no one suggesting that an increase in arranged marriages brought down Maya society. But, in fact, warfare and marriage are two related strategies for territorial expansion and strategic alliance.

Certainly, we need a long-term index of the frequency and impact of Late Classic warfare in relation to what came before and after before we can invoke it as cause for the end of the Classic period. Unlike the warrior aristocracy that emerged in Bronze Age northern

Europe – attested in the weaponry buried with warriors – very few Late Classic Maya rulers were buried with weapons, even though we know that they did participate in battles. Instead, they might be shown holding a spear as on Stela 2 from Aguateca, Guatemala, or described hieroglyphically as "he of the many captives," as on Piedras Negras Stela 12; but these depictions are political statements. In 2003 George W. Bush posed for photographs wearing a military flight suit on the deck of an aircraft carrier after U.S. and allied troops captured Baghdad. The tragically apocryphal text banner that accompanied President Bush dressed as a warrior proclaimed "Mission Accomplished." But we would never suggest that George Bush was an air force fighter pilot; rather, he was a political leader who represented the triumph of U.S. military might over a despotic ruler. The message of symbolic representation is not always transparent.

If warfare during Late Classic Maya times was as frequent as it was during Medieval European times, then one might expect to find the ruins of fortifications and moat-and-ditch systems and the remains of houses clustered inside such defensive fortifications. There is some evidence of such features, including a moat around the central core of monumental architecture at Becan, a low ditch-and-berm feature defining the border of parts of the venerable old capital of Tikal, and evidence for the dismantling of the core architecture of Dos Pilas in an attempt to build a defensive wall that clearly postdated the primary use of the site.[8] Also, archaeologists have found human bone of elite and possibly royal individuals unceremoniously deposited – that is, not in tomb interments – at sites such as Yaxuná, Cancuen, Colha, and Hershey.[9] Frankly, it is not clear whether these human remains can be attributed to the killing of royal families – just as the ruling Romanov family was executed during the Russian revolution – or whether the bones came from despoiled ancestor shrines. Often stone stelae of rulers are found smashed or literally defaced, such as at Dzibilchaltún, which suggests violent change in local ruling dynasties. Within societies in which bones and imagery of ancestors carry a potent political charge, ancestor tombs and images can become targets of martial conquest. Either execution of a royal family or despoiling a royal ancestor shrine would have been rooted in hostilities. The main point is that martial conflict indeed did exist in Late Classic Maya society, and humans were

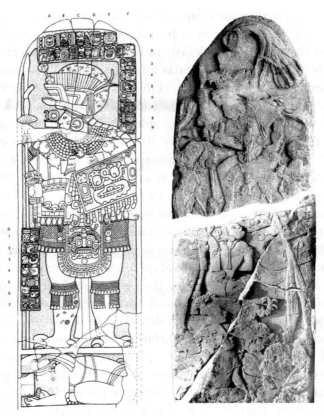

FIGURE 6.4 Martial aspects of rulers: (left) Stela 2 from Aguateca, Guatemala, showing a ruler holding a spear; (right) Stela 12, Piedras Negras, showing a ruler seated above a sea of captives and containing a hieroglyphic text that describes him as "he of the many captives." (Stela 2 after Graham 1967; Stela 12 after Maler 1970–1976, both courtesy of Peabody Museum, Harvard University)

treated in ways that today we would characterize as a human rights abuse. In this respect ancestral Maya were no different from ancestral Europeans or Asians. Throughout the Late Classic, however, the bulk of the population of Maya farmers lived dispersed throughout the countryside and only occasionally congregated into the large cities. The extent to which the lives of rural Classic Maya farming families were imperiled by interdynastic conflict remains an unanswered question.

OUT-OF-CONTROL POPULATION GROWTH AND
ENVIRONMENTAL DEGRADATION?

While a graduate student at the University of New Mexico, the senior author participated in her first Maya archaeology project at a place called Pulltrouser Swamp in Belize. Her assignment was to walk the terrain on the southeastern side of the swamp and to map all the mounds that she encountered. Small earthen mounds (around a meter in height) were considered "house mounds" – actually, low platforms upon which perishable structures of pole and thatch had been constructed long ago (knowing just how long ago required excavation, which came after survey and mapping). Higher and longer mounds might be the remains of a palace complex, which often were composed of stone houses with vaulted roofs also built of stone. Conical mounds, often quite tall, with small apices were considered shrines or pyramids, depending on their height. Not surprisingly, wherever there was high ground around the perimeter of Pulltrouser Swamp, there were house mounds with a few shrines built on tall pyramidal platforms as well. When tested with an excavation unit, most mounds revealed evidence of Late Classic construction and occupation, often with underlying and earlier construction units as well. The swamp itself had undergone significant modification in the form of island fields that had been created by digging canals and building up land surfaces to create a suitable surface for planting crops.[10] Suddenly it became apparent that both high, dry lands as well as wetlands had been profoundly modified during the 2,000 years that Maya people had lived and farmed around this site that we came to call K'axob (fallowed fields).[11] Because K'axob is not part of a large city or dynastic center but rather a hinterland or rural settlement with almost 2,000 years of occupation,[12] it provides an excellent example of the fact that, by Late Classic times, there was extensive – if dispersed – settlement throughout the Maya Lowlands.

Archaeologists have generated population estimates for the Maya Lowlands by counting the number of structures per square kilometer and multiplying that count by an assumed population size per mound (generally about five persons) and then subtracting a fraction of the total for noncontemporary occupancy and nonresidential use. Since, upon excavation, many mounds are found to contain a final Late

FIGURE 6.5 Large Classic period house platform at the Sibun valley site of Cedar Bank, Belize. (Photo by P. A. McAnany)

FIGURE 6.6 Canal and adjacent planting surfaces from landscape modification of wetlands 1,000–2,000 years ago at Maya site of K'axob, Belize. (Photo by P. A. McAnany)

Classic construction unit, this procedure for estimating population size – although only an estimate with many sources of error – is fairly straightforward for the Late Classic but becomes increasingly difficult for earlier time periods, especially at places in which little excavation (which allows ground-truthing of estimates) has been conducted. Nonetheless, this procedure has yielded population estimates as high as 150 persons per square kilometer.[13] In 1998 the U.S. Census Bureau reported a population density of 2,858 persons per square kilometer (7,400 per square mile) for Los Angeles, California, considerably higher than in the Late Classic Maya lowlands. Industrial-era urban population densities are much higher than those that existed in the political capitals of nonindustrial states; the term *high population growth* must be considered within its historical context.

Some students of Maya archaeology have written of this expansive settlement as indicative of runaway population growth that resulted in severe and irrevocable environmental degradation.[14] Often said to have supported the highest populations on record for a nonindustrial tropical environment, the Maya Lowlands produced food at peak productivity during Late Classic times, and that undoubtedly entailed significant landscape modification, such as the reclaimed wetlands described above. But recent studies of landscape modification, soils, and pollen cores by physical geographers Nicholas Dunning and Timothy Beach indicate that the predominant agricultural features of the Late Classic are those of conservation – terrace walls to control soil erosion, check dams to funnel water across dry slopes, and so forth.[15] In other words, Maya farmers of the Late Classic seem to have been doing all that they could to prevent land degradation and promote soil retention and fertility. So population growth does not necessarily lead to land degradation, although a large population of farmers inevitably will make a profound impact on their environment even under a sustainable regime of land use such as appeared to exist for 2,000 years in the Maya region.

Although tropical studies of pollen are hampered by the fact that tropical tree species tend to produce very little pollen (tropical trees are pollinated by insects rather than wind), the pollen found in lake and wetland cores does indicate that Late Classic forest cover was much diminished.[16] Just as the first pilgrims to the United States deforested New England for firewood and timber and to create fields and pastures, so Maya farmers diminished the forests of southern Mexico and upper Central America, beginning around 2,000 years before the Common Era. And like New England, where certain tree stands were preserved for construction materials and firewood, so the Late Classic Maya Lowlands appears to have been composed of a mosaic of forest, fields, and wetlands, so that some refer to the contemporary tropical forests of the Maya region as a "feral forest" that has been altered in favor of economic species such as mahogany, cacao (chocolate), and many fruit trees.[17]

Consider that the United States is a bit over 200 years of age, yet we have transformed and often desecrated a landscape that stretches "from sea to shining sea." For ancestral Maya society, archaeologists have documented a 2,000-year history of management of a complex environmental mosaic.[18] We would refer to that as "how a society chose to succeed" rather than the reverse. In fact, recent landscape analyses indicate that if Maya farmers in fact responded to an environmental crisis, it happened much earlier, around 100–200 C.E., when massive changes in land use resulted in the transformation of interior lakes into wetlands. By the Late Classic period, there seems to have been in place a resilient conservation ethic regarding soil and water management in this heterogeneous tropical landscape.

DID DROUGHT CAUSE THE ABANDONMENT OF MAYA CITIES?

In the documentary film *An Inconvenient Truth,* Al Gore – with the assistance of many charts and diagrams – drove home the message that societies of the twentieth and twenty-first centuries have achieved the ability to create global climatic change that may not be reversible. The key question here, as with all societies, is whether or not our global "village" is sufficiently resilient to adapt to a changing climate or to adopt changes that will halt or reverse permanent climatic change. Because climatic change – especially torrential rain or not enough rain – can be devastating to sedentary societies dependent on agriculture and/or stock raising for their food (which includes virtually all civilizations past and present), it provides a convenient and all-encompassing prime mover that can be invoked to explain social and political change. Without sufficient stores of food and the

United Nations to distribute food flown in from the other side of the world, societies might not have the resilience to survive a sustained drought of several years.

So, when all else fails to explain why societal change occurred, historians and archaeologists often turn to climatic change.[19] Droughts, as the ultimate *deus ex machina*, can be devastating events, as we know from recent droughts in Africa and from eighteenth-century accounts of the Chilam Balam – Yucatec historical and mythic accounts written in Mayan prose using a European alphabet. Immediately before the sixteenth-century arrival of Spaniards, the highland Aztecs faced several devastating droughts, but a drought never caused the collapse of the Aztec empire: it took ambitious Spanish warriors allied with disgruntled and coerced members of the Triple Alliance to do that. Based on deep lake cores from the Caribbean region, researchers have documented a shift to a regionally drier climate induced by changes in the El Niño–Southern Oscillation (ENSO) tropical air mass during the eighth century. Cores drilled into lakes in the Maya lowlands by paleo-ecologists D. Hodell, J. Curtis, and M. Brenner have yielded evidence of a drying trend in limited parts of the Maya region but the evidence is not widespread; nevertheless, the idea remains popular among physical scientists.[20] Analysis of the Usumacinta watershed by J. Gunn and W. Folan concluded that this drainage (located in the western part of the Maya region) was not affected by the ENSO oscillation.[21] Logically, if an alleged drought occurred at 760 C.E. and destabilized the Lowland Maya world, then its effects should have been global across the lowlands – with massive starvation and the downfall of divine rulers in quick succession. Instead, the large political capitals on the edges of the Maya world that sat astride a permanent water source – Copán, Quirigua, Piedras Negras, and Yaxchilan – were some of the earliest to stop constructing new buildings and carving sculpture with hieroglyphs and long-count dates. Archaeologists interpret this cessation as a weakening of dynastic power and an inability to command a large labor force or to sponsor sculptors and calligraphers. In contrast, dynastic seats such as Tikal, Calakmul, and Caracol that are located in the interior of the Lowlands – where there are no rivers and water is seasonally in short supply – survived longer.[22] In the northern Puuc hills – where there is no water source

FIGURE 6.7 Palace of Labna constructed during the Late-Terminal Classic period when a drought supposedly plagued the Maya Lowlands. (Photo by T. Gallareta N.)

other than rainwater stored in cisterns and *aguadas* – an ambitious phase of monumental construction, requiring huge amounts of water for mixing plaster and mortar, was undertaken around 760 c.e., and there is no evidence of drought.[23] So the pattern is complex and abandonment of dynastic centers protracted over 125 years. Change occurred and dynasties fell, but the cities most vulnerable to drought exhibit a pattern of resilience – at least for a while. It is thus unlikely that drought was a prime mover of societal change.

ARE DIVINE RULERS TO BLAME?

In most of today's world, political leaders are elected. They may come from an elite class, but they are chosen through a system of popular vote and generally hold office for a prescribed period of time. Maya rulers, on the other hand, were born to a class of royalty and, once enthroned, generally ruled until their death. Often, but not always, the eldest son might rule after the death of his father. Well before the Late Classic period, scribes began to refer to Maya rulers as *kuh'ul ajaw* (holy or divine lord), and so it seems that Maya rulers invoked a divine and sacred charter that underwrote and legitimized their right to rule. Certainly there are many stelae (stone monoliths with sculpture and hieroglyphic texts) that depict rulers dressed in the guise of a Maya god and performing a public ritual. Anthropologist Clifford Geertz among others has characterized kings who take on the trappings of divinity as well as elaborate and symbol-laden costuming as

FIGURE 6.8 Jasaw Chan K'awiil I, divine ruler of Tikal from 682 to 734 C.E. (Courtesy of Terry Rutledge)

human ideograms of society.[24] This type of iconic kingship draws heavily on the poetics of cosmic structures, and the well-being of a realm is indicated by the elaboration of kingly ritual performance and the monumentality within which such performance is situated. This compares well with Maya divine rulership, the ritual dress worn by Maya rulers, and the soaring temples and ornate palace structures that formed the backdrop for their kingly performances.

As many have written, divine kingship is a double-edged sword: it carries great privilege and unlimited power but also demands that a ruler deliver munificence to their people as would a god. A string of military defeats or seasonal droughts can do much to damage the credibility of a divine ruler, who must shoulder the blame for such misfortune. Just as there are good and bad elected leaders, there would have been good and not-so-good Maya rulers. From all indications, Late Classic times – with a large population to feed, possible cyclical droughts, and conflictive martial activity – would have been a challenging time in which to rule. Did Late Classic Maya rulers govern sagely, or did they bury their heads in sands of passivity as society collapsed around them? In *Collapse*, Diamond draws a direct parallel between Late Classic rulers and twenty-first-century CEOs and asserts that both were and are far too preoccupied with short-term personal gain. Perhaps this point of comparison is not too far off the mark, but how do we know? Just because rulers were heavily vested in ritual performance and participated in martial conflict with neighboring kingdoms does not mean that they were ineffectual rulers who were not concerned with the fertility of the lands within their kingdom and the well-being of their people. The green *quetzal* feathers that adorned the headdresses and backracks worn by Maya rulers symbolized fertility – a direct reference to the vitality of fresh corn plants. Statecraft by divine rule does not predict an inability of rulers to respond to crises. Some would argue this point, which seems a specious argument predicated upon the notion that democratic structures of governance are the only ones truly capable of solving social problems. Immediate and effective use of the Spanish judicial system during early Colonial times by Maya people suggests that some type of preexisting representational governance existed in the Maya region.[25] If divine rulership is to be blamed for the changes that occurred at the end of the Classic period, then surely we must also point a finger at the English monarchy as a primary cause for the sun setting over the British empire. Perhaps, like the British example, larger social processes need to be addressed in order to properly contextualize change within the microcosm that was Late Classic Maya society.

Although the English monarchy figuratively still rules Britain, the great dynasties that ruled over the ancestral cities of the southern Maya Lowlands appear to have dissolved at the end of the Classic period. The type of statecraft practiced during the Postclassic period (and described by Spaniards) indeed was extremely hierarchical with a sector of ruling nobility and the principle of inherited rule still widely practiced. But monumental construction projects had been scaled back (Tulum and Mayapan are perfect examples of reduced investment in colossal architecture), hieroglyphic script appears to have been restricted to paper bark codices rather than sculpted on large stelae that contained naturalistic images of rulers, and rulers did not carry the *kuh'ul ajaw* (holy or divine lord) title. In Yucatec Mayan, rulers were called *halach winik* (true men). There is no denying that a political crisis of some sort was responsible for the demise of divine rulers and the abandonment of their dynastic centers that once housed tens of thousands of people.[26] They were rendered irrelevant, became a flashpoint of resistance, or the basis of their moral authority undermined by a combination of natural and cultural factors. In summary, divine rulers proved not to be resilient to the changing milieu in which they found themselves. Some of these changing circumstances have already been discussed, but there is one final arena – that of economic change – that has yet to be considered.

SHIFTS IN SPHERES OF TRADE AND INFLUENCE?

During the nineteenth century, U.S. towns located astride railroad lines boomed as tracks were laid across the continent. Now, as passenger travel and cargo shipment via rails recede in importance, towns are abandoned or struggle to remain vital to commercial activity. Strategic positioning along trade and transportation routes provides opportunities and so always has been appealing to people, just as businesses today tend to cluster around airline hubs. How is this relevant to the past?

Over three decades ago, archaeologists such as Wyllys Andrews, Jeremy Sabloff, and William Rathje suggested that the term "Maya collapse" might be a matter of perspective.[27] Although Maya rulers of the Postclassic period clearly scaled back on investment in monumental architecture and there was a draw down of population in the southern part of the lowlands, Postclassic society was vibrant, particularly in reference to mercantile activity.[28] Postclassic sites, such as coastal Tulum, tended to be located strategically, near the coast or a major waterway in order to take advantage of canoe navigation, which allowed faster travel and the transport of larger cargo loads. Obviously canoe travel also was important during the Classic period, but many of the major dynastic seats – such as Tikal and Calakmul – were landlocked and supplied via trains of porters carrying goods in backracks or tumplines.

FIGURE 6.9 Tulum, scaled-back Late Postclassic monumental architecture rediscovered in the nineteenth century by Stephens and Catherwood. (After nineteenth-century watercolor by Frederick Catherwood)

As population levels decreased in the southern Lowlands, there was a corresponding rise in the number of people residing in the northern part of the Yucatán Peninsula, which is more coastal in orientation as it is bounded on the west and north by the Gulf of Mexico and on the east by the Caribbean Sea.

The engagement of elites with commercial activities is more apparent during the Postclassic period than during the preceding Classic period; clearly, priorities had shifted and new opportunities appeared. What Sabloff and Rathje did not realize decades ago is that the shift actually occurred earlier and was well underway by the ninth century.[29] Arguably this transformation can be seen at Late-Terminal Classic sites in which the entanglement of ritual practice with mercantile activities was materialized in circular shrine architecture. New architectural forms often accompany new economic arrangements. Just think of the rise of "ATM architecture" – those small, stand-alone buildings from which cash is dispensed – that signaled the transformational computerization of the banking industry. In the Sibun River valley of Belize where the senior author and her research team have been conducting archaeological fieldwork, a series of circular

FIGURE 6.10 Portion of an excavated circular shrine, Late to Terminal Classic period, Sibun Valley, Belize. (Photo by Kimberly Berry, courtesy of Xibun Archaeological Research Project)

FIGURE 6.11 Fruiting cacao trees growing in the Sibun Valley of Belize. (Photo by P. A. McAnany)

shrines dating to the ninth century have been found along the course of the river in a valley that today contains cacao groves, the essential ingredient of chocolate.[30] Why are these shrines significant, and why do archaeologists link them with mercantile activities?

Most Late Classic architecture is rectangular in plan, but in northern Yucatán at the Late-Terminal Classic capitals of both Chichén Itzá and Uxmal, large circular shrines were built during the Late Classic period. Thought by many to be linked to the highland Mexican wind deity, Ehecatl, or the highland feathered serpent, Quetzalcoatl,[31] the circular form seems to represent a hybrid of older Maya ritual practices with those from farther afield. The presence of more than a dozen diminutive circular shrines located on strategic waterways as well as coastal locations (such as Ambergris Cay, Belize) along the Caribbean seaboard hints at the mercantile activities that likely were associated with ritual practices performed at these shrines. Chichén Itzá, in particular, is argued to have controlled an imperial realm with a seaport at Isla Cerritos amid the northern Yucatec salt beds. The large scale of its sphere of influence may be suggested by the architectural mimicry of circular shrines that occurred in the far hinterlands. This new hybrid form of religious architecture and the ritual and economic practices that were associated with it were contemporary with the time of troubles for the venerable old dynasties and were spatially adjacent to dynastic centers. Such economic and religious innovation could not have strengthened and likely directly challenged dynastic rule and established modes for acquiring items that were iconic of dynastic authority. Late Classic pictorial art on pottery and walls indicates that rulers were closely involved with acquiring goods such as cacao, cotton cloth, jadeite, *Spondylus* shell, and quetzal feathers that often were imported from long distances.

As we learn more about Late-Terminal Classic Maya society and try to understand the changes that took place, we are finding that political factors cannot be divorced from economic change. Climatic stress could have heightened the impact of these transformations, but many aspects of ancestral Maya society – agricultural and ritual practices, traditions, and languages – exhibited a robustness that defies the term collapse. During the Postclassic period, rulers reinvented themselves in a manner that afforded the best advantage in the context of an increasingly commercialized, pan-Mesoamerican world (from north-central Mexico to western Honduras) knit together by shared ritual practices.[32] Divine rulership gave way to new forms of statecraft that explicitly included mercantilism and participation in polyethnic spheres of activity. Significantly, a monolingual hieroglyphic text was considerably less effective in this newly invented pan-Mesoamerican world.

A CONCLUDING QUERY: DO SOCIETIES FAIL OR JUST CHANGE?

Bruce Springsteen, bard and songwriter, is famous for writing lyrics about the social and economic changes that have transpired in his home state of New Jersey. In one particularly haunting riff of *My Hometown*, he sings of the closed factories and his unemployed friends and relatives and adds that "they [the manufacturing plants] ain't coming back." In fact, the eastern half of the United States increasingly is a landscape of abandoned or transformed factories, and U.S. society is poised in the middle of a profound social and economic upheaval as well-paid manufacturing jobs for a middle-class populace with rudimentary education disappear overseas. Will the United States exhibit the necessary resilience to change – in this case, toward greater investment in education to equip a populace with more sophisticated skills to stay competitive in the fields of science, technology, and medicine – or will the United States become a nation that exports nothing but entertainment (an industry that enriches only a small percentage of the population)? The jury is still out on this question, but for now, at least, the U.S. political system seems stable and capable of weathering such profound change. Will this continue to be the case, even if the effects of global warming intensify and our relationship with our material world also changes dramatically?

In hindsight, it is clear that the challenges posed to Late Classic Maya rulers could not be weathered without significant political and economic change. It is doubtful that the challenges were strictly climatic, although a role for cycles of drought as a destabilizing factor in times of political and economic stress should not be dismissed. Equally clear is the fact that Maya society – politically, economically, and socially – survived and thrived during Postclassic times, albeit in

FIGURE 6.12 Q'eqchi' and Mopan Maya schoolchildren, Toledo District, Belize. (Photo by P. A. McAnany)

a transformed state. Does this change represent success or failure? Neither really, although the seven million Maya descendants who are alive today speak directly to the resilience of Maya societies.

Finally, why is Western society so intrigued by the ancestors of contemporary Maya people and so willing to label one of their societal transformations a "failure"? Is it the presence of colossal ruins and remnants of carved-stone hieroglyphic texts that stand amid tropical forests, the romantic notion of failure amid splendor? Perhaps Classic Maya royalty invite the gaze of contemporary people by virtue of the fact that they left behind so many engaging images of themselves. One literally can gaze into the face of the past and, in doing so, connect – or *seem* to connect – in a way that is more difficult with ancient societies that were not so vested in naturalistic representation of the human body. But before we begin to compare eighth-century Maya rulers to twenty-first-century CEOs, we should consider whether the transformations that marked the end of divine rulership qualify as the apocalyptic collapse that some writers and

FIGURE 6.13 Classic Maya royal female figurine housed in the Museo Nacional de Antropología, Mexico City. (After Schele 1997; photo courtesy of Jorge Pérez de Lara)

movie producers want to suggest. Certainly, total systemic failure makes for a more dramatic plot-line, but with a descendent community of several million people, it is hardly an accurate assessment and is even denigrating to descendants who read that their ancestors supposedly "died out" by the tenth century and that they are not related to the Classic Maya who built the cities – now in ruins – on which a mega-million dollar tourist industry has been built. The past can inform us and often guide us toward a better future, but the mirror of ancient Maya society should not be refracted in hopes of inducing change in the contemporary world, no matter how badly change might be needed.

FIGURE 6.14 Cristina Coc, Director, Julian Cho Society, Toledo District, Belize. (Photo by Shoshaunna Parks)

CRISTINA COC: LIFE AND STRUGGLES OF AN INDIGENOUS MAYA LEADER

"I, Cristina Coc, am a Q'eqchi' Maya from Punta Gorda, Toledo District, Belize.

I am co-spokesperson of the Maya Leaders Alliance and currently Executive Director of the Julian Cho Society, a Maya advocacy group formed in 2005. I hold a Bachelor of Science degree in Chemistry and Biology from the University of Minnesota, Duluth, in the United States of America." So began an affidavit filed in the Supreme Court of Belize in 2007 by a consortium of indigenous Maya peoples of southern Belize who sought legal recourse to defend Maya traditional land rights and to force the government of Belize to recognize Maya land rights and to stop granting leases to international logging and oil-exploration companies who damage lands, don't consult with local residents, and don't offer compensation for damage to property (http://www.law.arizona.edu/Depts/IPLP/advocacy/maya_belize). On

October 18, 2007, indigenous people throughout the world whose land rights often are under siege won a major victory. The Supreme Court of Belize decided in favor of the rights of Toledo Maya people.

As a Q'eqchi' Maya child growing up in the Toledo District of Belize – which is 80 percent Mayan – Cristina Coc was influenced by her brother-in-law, Julian Cho, who fought for land rights, social justice, and dignity for Maya people. After his untimely death, Cristina left Belize to complete her college education in the United States, but she carried with her memories of his struggles and ultimate sacrifice. In 2005 she founded an indigenous rights organization named in honor of her brother-in-law, the Julian Cho Society. As current director of the society and one of a small number of female indigenous leaders, Cristina Coc works to promote not only indigenous land rights but also the physical and cultural survival of Maya people, who can teach all of us important lessons in societal resilience.

Notes

* *Patricia A. McAnany:* One day about thirty years ago in the dolphin lab at Kewalo Basin, Hawai'i, Sam Gon asked me if I would like to join a group of student scientists who were submitting a grant proposal to the National Science Foundation. I was an anthropology undergraduate, spending a year at the University of Hawai'i. I would be responsible for conducting an archaeological survey of the chosen study area. I had been drawn to anthropology because of its broad perspective on religious practice, and this was an invitation I could not refuse. I prepped for our field season by doing archival research on native Hawai'ian land claims and still remember the excitement I felt as I discovered new things about traditional farming and fishing before the nineteenth-century Euro-American land grab.

In the following years I discovered Maya archaeology and have pursued a career of research and teaching at Boston University and the University of North Carolina, Chapel Hill. My book *Living with the Ancestors: Kinship and Kingship in Ancient Maya Society* (1995) resumed my early interests in religion, and my edited volume, *K'axob: Ritual, Work, and Family in an Ancient Maya Village* (2004), reflects my interests in land use and everyday life.

I have come to appreciate that interpreting the past – evaluating and writing a narrative about archaeological evidence, whether from Polynesia, Yucatán, or elsewhere – holds great challenges and daunting responsibilities, the latter particularly in respect to descendant communities. My career has been one of continual engagement with the evolving challenges and responsibilities of archaeology.

Tomás Gallareta Negrón: I am an archaeologist with the Centro Yucatán del Instituto Nacional de Antropologia y Historia in Mexico. Born in Yucatán, I developed a curiosity about Maya ruins and pursued my Licenciatura at Universidad Autónoma de Yucatán and postgraduate education in archaeology at Tulane University.

I have conducted archaeological research in the northern Maya Lowlands at over fifty sites and collaborated on the archaeological atlas of the sites of Yucatán. I have provided both university-based classroom instruction and field training for international and Yucatecan students.

I am especially interested in the archaeology of residential units from small houses to palaces and in landscape utilization in the past and its implications for present sustainability. I helped establish a 1,650 hectare archaeological and environmental preserve surrounding the Late Classic Puuc Maya site of Kiuic. In conjunction with the preserve, I work to promote the conservation of archaeological and biological resources and innovative educational and economic projects with the communities surrounding the preserve. I have been instrumental in the development of an educational cultural heritage puppet film for Yucatecan children, working with the Maya Area Cultural Heritage Initiative. Currently, I am co-director of the Bolonchen Region Archaeological Project, surveying a strip of nine square kilometers between the sites of Labna and Kiuic in Yucatán, México.

1. For further information regarding inaccuracies and deleterious cultural impact of *Apocalypto*, see Callahan 2007; Freidel 2007; Lohse 2007.

2. Maya genocide of the 1980s was implemented by the Guatemalan state in response to a perceived threat of the spread of communism and guerrilla insurgencies among the majority and impoverished Maya ethnic population. For in-depth accounts and personal narratives, see Carmack 1988; Manz 2004; Menchú 1984; Sanford 2003.

3. See Diamond 2005.

4. Popular and scholarly accounts of the decipherment of Maya hieroglyphic texts include Coe 1992; Coe and Van Stone 2001; Houston et al. 2001.

5. Stuart 1998: 374 discusses the primacy of dedication texts in Maya inscriptions.

6. Martin and Grube 2008 provide the most recent synthesis of hieroglyphic evidence bearing on the political and social lives of Classic Maya royalty. For an in-depth view of Classic Maya royal courts, see Miller and Martin 2004.

7. More information on tribute ransom can be found in Houston et al. 2006; McAnany 2009.

8. For a review of evidence of defensive features at Classic Maya capitals, see Webster 2002.

9. Nonfunerary deposits of human bone bearing signature features of Classic period eliteness are reported for Yaxuná in Freidel and Suhler 1998; Cancuen in Gugliotta 2007; Hershey site in Harrison-Buck et al. 2007; and Colha in Massey and Steele 1997.

10. The extensive literature on the transformation of Maya wetlands includes Turner and Harrison 1983 on Pulltrouser Swamp; Dunning et al. 2002; Pohl 1990; Pohl et al. 1996.

11. Profound and early management of wetland land scapes at K'axob is discussed in Berry and McAnany 2007.

12. The Formative or Preclassic settlement of K'axob is presented in McAnany 2004.

13. Population estimates for Late Classic society are presented and discussed in detail in Culbert and Rice 1990.

14. The agricultural degradation/deforestation model is presented by Wingard 1996 and Rue 1987 and advocated particularly by Webster 2002: 251–259, all in reference to Copán, Honduras.

15. Beach et al. 2006; Dunning and Beach 2000.

16. Jones 1994 presents pollen evidence for a trend of diminished forest cover beginning 2000 B.C.E. Several archaeologists point out that the Late Classic landscape could not have been completely denuded of forest because high-canopy faunal species – such as tapir – occur in Late Classic archaeological midden contexts (Emery 2004: 94; White et al. 2004: 158; Wright 2006: 200).

17. Evidence of the "manmade tropical forest" of the Maya lowlands is presented by Campbell et al. 2006; Gomez-Pompa et al. 1987; Nations and Nigh 1980.

18. For more information on the mosaic concept of ancestral Maya land use, see Fedick 1996; Dunning and Beach 2000: 191.

19. Gill 2000 and Gill et al. 2007 attempt to link eighth- and ninth-century Lowland Maya societal changes to recurrent cycles of drought.

20. Climate change, core data, and Maya political cycles are causally linked in Haug et al. 2003 and Hodell et al. 1995, 2000, 2001.

21. Gunn and Folan 2000.

22. Scarborough 2003 finds evidence of ingenious water reservoir systems at some interior capitals, while Lucero 2006 emphasizes the centripetal pull of water-storage systems during the dry season.

23. See Gallareta N. 2000 on the lack of evidence for drought in the Puuc region.

24. See Geertz 1980 on Balinese kingship, and earlier Kantorowicz 1957 on Christian-based medieval kingship in Europe.

25. Restall 1997 documents Maya use of the Spanish legal system during early Colonial times.

26. For detailed discussion of the nature of this 150-year political crisis, see Freidel and Shaw 2000; Marcus 1993; Webster 2002; Yoffee 1991.

27. Andrews 1973; Sabloff and Rathje 1975.
28. Vibrant Postclassic populations are documented in the southeastern Maya Lowlands (Feldman 2000), around Laguna Petén Itzá (Rice and Rice 2005), in Belize (Chase 1986; Chase and Chase 2006; Graham et al. 1989; Masson 2000, 2003; Pendergast 1993), and in northern Yucatán (Kepecs 2005; Masson et al. 2006 among others).
29. Ringle et al. 1998 present a strong case for placing the onset of this new ideology in the Late-Terminal Classic period.
30. For more on cacao and the Sibun Valley project, see Harrison-Buck et al. 2007; McAnany and Murata 2006, 2007; McAnany et al. 2002.
31. Taube 2000 explores the symbolism of wind, feathered serpent deities, and circular architecture in Mesoamerica and the American Southwest; see also McAnany 2007.
32. Smith and Berdan 2003 provide a comprehensive overview of Postclassic society.

Bibliography

Andrews, E.W., IV. 1973. "The Development of Maya Civilization after the Abandonment of the Southern Cities," in *The Classic Maya Collapse*. Edited by T. P. Culbert, pp. 243–265. Albuquerque: University of New Mexico Press.

Beach, T., N. Dunning, S. Luzzadder-Beach, D.E. Cook, and J.C. Lohse. 2006. "Impacts of the Ancient Maya on Soils and Soil Erosion in the Central Maya Lowlands." *Catena* **65**:166–178.

Berry, K. and P.A. McAnany. 2007. "Reckoning with the Wetlands and Their Role in Ancient Maya Society," in *The Political Economy of Ancient Mesoamerica: Transformations during the Formative and Classic Periods*. Edited by V.L. Scarborough and J.E. Clark, pp. 149–162. Albuquerque: University of New Mexico Press.

Callahan, R. 2007. "Apocalypto in Cobá." *Anthropological News* **48**:28–29.

Campbell, D.G., A. Ford, K.S. Lowell, J. Walker, J.K. Lake, C. Ocampo-Raeder, A. Townesmith, and M. Balick. 2006. "The Feral Forests of the Eastern Petén," in *Time and Complexity in Historical Ecology: Studies in the Neotropical Lowlands*. Edited by W. Balée and C.L. Erickson, pp. 21–55. New York: Columbia University Press.

Carmack, R. M. 1988. *Harvest of Violence: The Maya Indians and the Guatemalan Crisis*. Norman: University of Oklahoma Press.

Chase, D. Z. 1986. "Social and Political Organization in the Land of Milk and Honey: Correlating the Archaeology and Ethnohistory of the Postclassic Lowland Maya," in *Late Lowland Maya Civilization: Classic to Postclassic*. Edited by J.A. Sabloff and E.W. Andrews V, pp. 347–377. Albuquerque: University of New Mexico Press.

Chase, D. Z. and A.F. Chase. 2006. "Framing the Maya Collapse: Continuity, Discontinuity, Method, and Practice in the Classic to Postclassic Southern Maya Lowlands," in *After Collapse: The Regeneration of Complex Societies*.

Edited by G. M. Schwartz and J. J. Nichols, pp. 168–187. Tucson: University of Arizona Press.

Coe, M. D. 1992. *Breaking the Maya Code.* New York: Thames and Hudson.

Coe, M. D. and M. Van Stone. 2001. *Reading the Maya Glyphs.* London: Thames & Hudson.

Culbert, T. P. and D. S. Rice. Editors. 1990. *Precolumbian Population History in the Maya Lowlands.* Albuquerque: University of New Mexico Press.

Diamond, J. 2005. *Collapse: How Societies Choose to Fail or Succeed.* New York: Viking.

Dunning, N. and T. Beach. 2000. "Stability and Instability in Prehispanic Maya Landscapes," in *Imperfect Balance: Landscape Transformations in the Pre-Columbian Americas.* Edited by D. L. Lentz, pp. 179–202. New York: Columbia University Press.

Dunning, N., S. Luzzadder-Beach, T. Beach, J. G. Jones, V. L. Scarborough, and T. P. Culbert. 2002. "Arising from the *Bajos:* The Evolution of a Neotropical Landscape and the Rise of Maya Civilization." *Annals of the Association of American Geographers* 92:267–283.

Emery, K. F. 2004. "Environments of the Maya Collapse: A Zooarchaeological Perspective from the Petexbatún," in *Maya Zooarchaeology: New Directions in Method and Theory.* Edited by K. F. Emery, pp. 81–95. Los Angeles: Cotsen Institute of Archaeology, UCLA.

Fedick, S. E. Editor. 1996. *The Managed Mosaic: Ancient Maya Agriculture and Resource Use.* Salt Lake City: University of Utah Press.

Feldman, L. H. 2000. *Lost Shores, Forgotten Peoples: Spanish Exploration of the South East Maya Lowlands.* Durham, NC: Duke University Press.

Freidel, D. A. 2007. "Betraying the Maya: Who Does the Violence in *Apocalypto* Really Hurt?" *Archaeology* **May/June:**36–41.

Freidel, D. A. and J. Shaw. 2000. "The Lowland Maya Civilization: Historical Consciousness and Environment," in *The Way the Wind Blows: Climate, History, and Human Action.* Edited by R. J. McIntosh, J. A. Tainter, and S. K. McIntosh, pp. 271–300. New York: Columbia University Press.

Freidel, D. A. and C. Suhler. 1998. "Life and Death in a Maya War Zone." *Archaeology* **51:**28–34.

Gallareta Negrón, T. 2000. "Sequía y Colapso de la Ciudades Mayas del Puuc." *I'INAJ* **11:**13–21.

Geertz, C. 1980. *Negara: The Theatre State in Nineteenth-Century Bali.* Princeton, NJ: Princeton University Press.

Gill, R. B. 2000. *The Great Maya Droughts: Water, Life, and Death.* Albuquerque: University of New Mexico Press.

Gill, R. B., P. A. Mayewski, J. Nyberg, G. H. Haug, and L. C. Peterson. 2007. "Drought and the Maya Collapse." *Ancient Mesoamerica* **18:**283–302.

Gomez-Pompa, A., J. Salvador Flores, and V. Sosa. 1987. "The 'Pet Kot': A Man-Made Tropical Forest of the Maya." *Interciencia* **12:**10–15.

Graham, E., D. M. Pendergast, and G. D. Jones. 1989. "On the Fringes of Conquest: Maya-Spanish Contact in Colonial Belize." *Science* **246:**1254–1259.

Graham, I. 1967. *Archaeological Explorations in El Peten, Guatemala.* New Orleans: Middle American Research Institute, Tulane University.

Gugliotta, G. 2007. "The Maya Glory and Ruin." *National Geographic* **212**(2):68–110.

Gunn, J. D. and W. J. Folan. 2000. "Three Rivers: Subregional Variations in Earth System Impacts in the Southwestern Maya Lowlands (Candelaria, Usumacinta, and Champotón Watersheds)," in *The Way the Wind Blows: Climate, History, and Human Action.* Edited by R. J. McIntosh, J. A. Tainter, and S. K. McIntosh, pp. 223–270. New York: Columbia University Press.

Harrison-Buck, E., P. A. McAnany, and R. Storey. 2007. "Empowered and Disempowered during the Late to Terminal Classic Transition: Maya Burial and Termination Rituals in the Sibun Valley, Belize," in *New Perspectives on Human Sacrifice and Ritual Body Treatments in Ancient Maya Society.* Edited by V. Tiesler and A. Cucina, pp. 74–101. New York: Springer Science+Business Media.

Haug, G. H., D. Günther, L. C. Peterson, D. M. Sigman, K. A. Hughen, and B. Aeschlimann. 2003. "Climate and the Collapse of Maya Civilization." *Science* **299** (5613):1731–1735.

Hodell, D. A., M. Brenner, and J. H. Curtis. 2000. "Climate Change in the North American Tropics and Subtropics since the Last Ice Age," in *Imperfect Balance: Landscape Transformations in the Precolumbian Americas.* Edited by D. L. Lentz, pp. 13–38. New York: Columbia University Press.

Hodell, D. A., M. Brenner, J. H. Curtis, and T. P. Guilderson. 2001. "Solar Forcing of Drought Frequency in the Maya Lowlands." *Science* **292**:1367–1370.

Hodell, D. A., J. H. Curtis, and M. Brenner. 1995. "Possible Role of Climate in the Collapse of Classic Maya Civilization." *Nature* **375**:391–375.

Houston, S. D., O. Chinchilla Mazariegos, and D. Stuart. Editors. 2001. *The Decipherment of Ancient Maya Writing.* Norman: University of Oklahoma Press.

Houston, S. D., D. Stuart, and K. Taube. 2006. *The Memory of Bones: Body, Being, and Experience Among the Classic Maya.* Austin: University of Texas Press.

Jones, J. G. 1994. "Pollen Evidence for Early Settlement and Agriculture in Northern Belize." *Palynology* **18**:205–211.

Kantorowicz, E. H. 1957. *The King's Two Bodies; A Study in Mediaeval Political Theology.* Princeton, NJ: Princeton University Press.

Kepecs, S. 2005. "Mayas, Spaniards, and Salt: World Systems Shifts in Sixteenth-Century Yucatán," in *The Postclassic to Spanish-Era Transition in Mesoamerica: Archaeological Perspectives.* Edited by S. Kepecs and R. T. Alexander, pp. 117–137. Albuquerque: University of New Mexico.

Lohse, J. C. 2007. "Apocalypto." *SAA Archaeological Record* **7**(3):3.

Looper, M. G. 2003. *Lightning Warrior: Maya Art and Kingship at Quirigua.* Austin: University of Texas Press.

Lucero, L. J. 2006. "Agricultural Intensification, Water, and Political Power in the Southern Maya Lowlands," in *Agricultural Strategies.* Edited by

J. Marcus and C. Stanish, pp. 281–205. Los Angeles: Cotsen Institute of Archaeology, UCLA.

Maler, T. 1970–1976. *Researches in the Central Portion of the Usumatsintla Valley: Report of Explorations for the Museum, 1898–1900.* 2 vols. New York: Kraus Reprint of the 1901–1903 ed. published by the Peabody Museum, Cambridge, MA, as vol. 2 of the Memoirs of the Peabody Museum of American Archaeology and Ethnology, Harvard University.

Manz, B. 2004. *Paradise in Ashes: A Guatemalan Journey of Courage, Terror, and Hope.* Berkeley: University of California Press.

Marcus, J. 1993. "Ancient Maya Political Organization," in *Lowland Maya Civilization in the Eighth Century A.D.* Edited by J.A. Sabloff and J.S. Henderson, pp. 111–183. Washington, DC: Dumbarton Oaks Research Library and Collection.

Martin, S. and N. Grube. 2008. *Chronicle of the Maya Kings and Queens: Deciphering the Dynasties of the Ancient Maya.* London: Thames & Hudson.

Massey, V.K. and D.G. Steele. 1997. "A Maya Skull Pit from the Terminal Classic Period, Colha, Belize," in *Bones of the Maya: Studies of Ancient Skeletons.* Edited by S.L. Whittington and D.M. Reed, pp. 62–77. Washington, DC: Smithsonian Institution Press.

Masson, M.A. 2000. *In the Realm of Nachan Kan: Postclassic Maya Archaeology at Laguna de On, Belize.* Boulder: University Press of Colorado.

Masson, M.A. 2003. "Economic Patterns in Northern Belize," in *The Postclassic Mesoamerican World.* Edited by M.E. Smith and F.F. Berdan, pp. 269–281. Salt Lake City: University of Utah Press.

Masson, M.A., T.S. Hare, and C. Peraza Lope. 2006. "Postclassic Maya Society Regenerated at Mayapán," in *After Collapse: The Regeneration of Complex Societies.* Edited by G.M. Schwartz and J.J. Nichols, pp. 188–207. Tucson: University of Arizona Press.

McAnany, P.A. Editor. 2004. *K'axob: Ritual, Work and Family in an Ancient Maya Village.* Los Angeles: Monumenta Archaeologica 22, Cotsen Institute of Archaeology at UCLA.

McAnany, P.A. 2007. "Culture Heroes and Feathered Serpents: The Contribution of Gordon R. Willey to the Study of Ideology," in *Gordon R. Willey and American Archaeology: Contemporary Perspectives.* Edited by J.A. Sabloff and W.L. Fash, pp. 209–231. Norman: University of Oklahoma Press.

McAnany, P.A. 2009. *Ancestral Maya Economies in Archaeological Perspective.* Cambridge: Cambridge University Press.

McAnany, P.A. and S. Murata. 2006. "From Chocolate Pots to Maya Gold: Belizean Cacao Farmers through the Ages," in *Chocolate in Mesoamerica: a Cultural History of Cacao.* Edited by C. McNeil, pp. 429–450. Gainesville: University of Florida Press.

McAnany, P.A. and S. Murata. 2007. "America's First Connoisseurs of Chocolate." *Food and Foodways* 15:7–30.

McAnany, P.A., B.S. Thomas, S. Morandi, P.A. Peterson, and E. Harrison. 2002. "Praise the Ahaw and Pass the Kakaw: Xibun Maya and the Political

Economy of Cacao," in *Ancient Maya Political Economies.* Edited by M.A. Masson and D.A. Freidel, pp. 123–139. Walnut Creek, CA: Altamira Press.

Menchú, R. 1984. *I, Rigoberta Menchú: An Indian Woman in Guatemala.* London: Verso.

Miller, M. and S. Martin. 2004. *Courtly Art of the Ancient Maya.* San Francisco: Fine Arts Museum of San Francisco and Thames & Hudson.

Nations, J. D. and R.B. Nigh. 1980. "The Evolutionary Potential of Lacandon Maya Sustained-Yield Tropical Forest Agriculture." *Journal of Anthropological Research* 36:1–30.

Pendergast, D. M. 1993. "Worlds in Collision: The Maya/Spanish Encounter in Sixteenth and Seventeenth Century Belize." *Proceedings of the British Academy* 81:105–143.

Pohl, M. D. Editor. 1990. *Ancient Maya Wetland Agriculture: Excavations on Albion Island, Northern Belize.* Boulder: Westview Press.

Pohl, M. D., K. O. Pope, J. G. Jones, J. S. Jacob, D. R. Piperno, S. D. de France, D.L. Lentz, J.A. Gifford, M.E. Danforth, and J.K. Josserand. 1996. "Early Agriculture in the Maya Lowlands." *Latin American Antiquity* 7: 355–372.

Restall, M. 1997. *The Maya World: Yucatec Culture and Society, 1550–1850.* Stanford, CA: Stanford University Press.

Rice, D.S. and P.M. Rice. 2005. "Sixteenth- and Seventeenth-Century Maya Political Geography in Central Petén, Guatemala," in *The Postclassic to Spanish-Era Transition in Mesoamerica: Archaeological Perspectives.* Edited by S. Kepecs and R.T. Alexander, pp. 139–160. Albuquerque: University of New Mexico Press.

Ringle, W.M., T. Gallareta Negrón, and G.J. Bey III. 1998. "The Return of Quetzalcoatl: Evidence for the Spread of a World Religion during the Epiclassic Period." *Ancient Mesoamerica* 9:183–232.

Rue, D. J. 1987. "Early Agriculture and Early Postclassic Maya Occupation in Western Honduras." *Nature* 326:285–286.

Sabloff, J. A. and W.L. Rathje. 1975. "The Rise of a Maya Merchant Class." *Scientific American* 233:72–82.

Sanford, V. 2003. *Buried Secrets: Truth and Human Rights in Guatemala.* New York: Palgrave Macmillan.

Scarborough, V. L. 2003. *The Flow of Power: Ancient Water Systems and Landscapes.* Santa Fe, NM: SAR Press.

Schele, L. 1997. *Hidden Faces of the Maya.* Photography by Jorge Pérez de Lara. Impetus Comunicación S.A de C.V. Singapore: Toppan Printing.

Smith, M.E. and F.F. Berdan. Editors. 2003. *The Postclassic Mesoamerican World.* Salt Lake City: University of Utah Press.

Stuart, D. 1998. "'The Fire Enters His House': Architecture and Ritual in Classic Maya Texts," in *Function and Meaning in Classic Maya Architecture.* Edited by S.D. Houston, pp. 373–425. Washington, DC: Dumbarton Oaks Research Library and Collection.

Taube, K. 2000. "The Breadth of Life: The Symbolism of Wind in Mesoamerica and the American Southwest," in *The Road to Aztlan: Art from a Mythic*

Homeland. Edited by V. M. Fields and V. Zamudio-Taylor, pp. 102–123. Los Angeles: Los Angeles County Museum of Art.

Turner, B. L. I. and P. D. Harrison. Editors. 1983. *Pulltrouser Swamp: Ancient Maya Habitat, Agriculture, and Settlement in Northern Belize.* Austin: University of Texas Press.

Webster, D. 2002. *The Fall of the Ancient Maya: Solving the Mystery of the Maya Collapse.* London: Thames & Hudson.

White, C. D., M. D. Pohl, H. P. Schwarcz, and F. J. Longstaffe. 2004. "Feast, Field, and Forest: Deer and Dog Diets at Lagartero, Tikal, and Copán," in *Maya Zooarchaeology: New Directions in Method and Theory.* Edited by K. F. Emery, pp. 1412–158. Los Angeles: Cotsen Institute of Archaeology, UCLA.

Wingard, J. D. 1996. "Interactions between Demographic Processes and Soil Resources in the Copa'n Valley, Honduras," in *The Managed Mosaic: Ancient Maya Agriculture and Resource Use.* Edited by S. E. Fedick, pp. 207–235. Salt Lake City: University of Utah Press.

Wright, L. E. 2006. *Diet, Health, and Status among the Pasión Maya: A Reappraisal of the Collapse.* Vanderbilt Institute of Mesoamerican Archaeology Series, Vol. 2. Nashville, TN: Vanderbilt University Press.

Yoffee, N. 1991. "Maya Elite Interaction: through a Glass, Sideways," in *Classic Maya Political History: Hieroglyphic and Archaeological Evidence.* Edited by T. P. Culbert, pp. 285–310. Cambridge: Cambridge University Press.

7

Collapse in Ancient Mesopotamia

What Happened, What Didn't

Norman Yoffee[*]

Jared Diamond makes only three claims about Mesopotamia in his book *Collapse: How Societies Choose to Fail or Succeed:*

1. "Some other famous collapses of prehistoric civilizations ... appear to coincide with peaks of ... drought cycles, such as the collapse of the world's first empire (the Akkadian Empire of Mesopotamia) around 2170 B.C."
2. "Salinization ... contributed to the decline of the world's oldest civilizations, those of Mesopotamia." (Salinization is the build-up of salts in soils, eventually to toxic levels for plants such as wheat and barley. It is caused by lack of proper drainage in irrigated fields and by a high water table.)
3. "There was no way for the first colonists of Australia and Mangareva to perceive that problem of soil nutrient exhaustion – nor for farmers in areas with salt deep in the ground (like eastern Montana and parts of Australia and Mesopotamia) to perceive incipient salinization."[1]

INTRODUCTION – PART ONE

These three comments may seem a poor excuse for a chapter on Mesopotamia and collapse that is critical of Diamond. Readers may think, oh, here's a picky Mesopotamia specialist who spends his time pouring over clay tablets in cuneiform script, puzzling out the details of marriages, divorces, adoptions, sales and rentals of land, court decisions about contested inheritances, and reading someone else's mail from 4,000 years ago telling us that Professor Diamond, who sees the Big Picture, missed a few things when he wrote about Mesopotamia. But Diamond has done more than offer a cartoon view of Mesopotamia. (In fact, I'm quite fond of the *Cartoon History of the Universe*, which is filled with data).[2] Diamond's view of collapse, and not only in Mesopotamia, is not only ill-informed, but it contradicts some of his own most interesting messages. Precisely because we know so much about the lives of Mesopotamians – how they had to cope with decisions of their leaders and how their leaders came to be leaders – we can give excellent accounts of the "choices and fates" of people in the remote past.

In addition to reading original texts about how Mesopotamians lived their lives, I have also pondered questions almost as large as Diamond's: how and why did various governments and dynasties and cities in Mesopotamia, the world's first civilization, fall and regenerate? And I have also thought about the ways in which collapse in Mesopotamia was like and unlike other collapses of ancient states. In 1998 George Cowgill, a scholar of the urban metropolis of Teotihuacan in Mexico, and I published the proceedings of a conference in which experts on Mesopotamia, the Maya, China, Rome, and other places explored the collapse of ancient states and civilizations.[3] Our book is the second source cited by Diamond in his section "Further Readings" in *Collapse*.

Let me anticipate my conclusion: if collapse, in Diamond's words, is "a dramatic decrease in human population and/or political/economic/social complexity, over a considerable area, for an extended time,"[4] we can't find any such collapse in Mesopotamia or, indeed, anywhere else among ancient states! (This is also the view of Joseph Tainter, whose own work on the "collapse of complex systems" is the first source cited by Diamond.)[5]

But didn't salinization cause the end of Mesopotamian civilization, as Diamond says? (No, it didn't – see later in this chapter. And Mesopotamian farmers were not too stupid to understand their environments and how their farming practices affected them.) Diamond didn't need to spend much time in Mesopotamia because he thinks that environmental mismanagement and catastrophes were the cause of collapse everywhere! He says all of the following cultures and societies collapsed because of environmental mismanagement: the

California Channel Islands, Cahokia in southern Illinois, and Mound Builder societies (all in the eastern United States), the Moche and Tiwanaku in South America, Mycenaean Greece, the Fertile Crescent (in West Asia), Great Zimbabwe (in East Africa), the Indus civilization (of South Asia), and the Khmer (of Southeast Asia)![6] But, as other chapters in this volume show, and many other studies demonstrate, there is no evidence of environmental mismanagement and collapse in any of these cases that Diamond so casually lists.

To be sure, Diamond qualifies his declarations that environmental reasons "may have played a role" in these transformations. He also declares that "It would be absurd to claim that environmental damage must be a factor in all collapses: the collapse of the Soviet Union is a modern counter-example, and the destruction of Carthage by Rome in 146 B.C. is an ancient one." Perhaps we can paraphrase Diamond as saying that in *most* instances of the collapse of ancient civilizations environmental mismanagement is the prime suspect. And this is why collapse in the past "offers a rich data base from which we can learn ... [about what might] eventually befall our own wealthy society."[7]

Although most archaeologists do believe, along with Diamond, that we *can* learn from the past, we do not think that the past was the same as the present in key aspects.[8] We are all certainly alarmed that environmental mismanagement in the present is a clear and evident danger to life on earth. What we can learn from the past is thus the more striking: *ancient kings and governments, which did not ruin their environments on a massive scale and didn't have the power to do so, are no models for the present.* Rather, the present situation is dire precisely because there is no clear precedent for global environmental mismanagement.

But there are other lessons from the past, and we can study them for more than academic interest. Although Diamond declared that we can't understand why the Soviet Union collapsed by looking at the past, it is just the kind of collapse of an enormous empire that we *can* compare with what happened, for example, in the Assyrian empire in Mesopotamia.

INTRODUCTION – PART TWO

It is astonishing to read popular accounts about the "collapse" of ancient Mesopotamia, the birthplace of the world's first cities and states and the first written language – as if Mesopotamia came to an

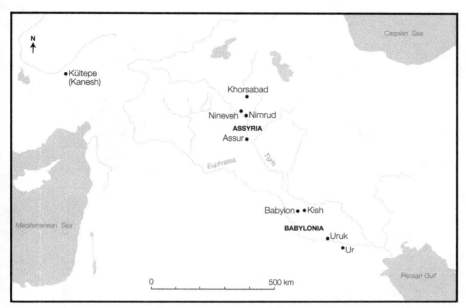

FIGURE 7.1 Map of ancient Mesopotamia showing Assyria, Babylonia, and sites mentioned in this chapter. (Illustration by Elisabeth Paymal)

TABLE 7.1. *Dates of Mesopotamian Civilization (all dates B.C.E.)*

ca. 3200	City of Uruk, tens of thousands of people, first written texts in cuneiform script
2350–2200	Dynasty of Sargon of Akkade
2100–2000	Third Dynasty of Ur
1795–1750	Hammurabi of Babylon
604–562	Chaldean dynasty of Babylonia including Nebuchadnezzar (II), who destroyed the Temple of the Judeans in Jerusalem in 586 B.C.E.
539	Conquest of Mesopotamia by Cyrus the Great of Persia
331	Conquest of Persia by Alexander the Great

abrupt and calamitous end. The first texts, written in Mesopotamian cuneiform script, appeared more than 5,000 years ago in the world's first city, Uruk. Then Uruk flourished, though not without its ups and downs, for more than 3,000 years, through the empires of Sargon of Akkade, the kings of Ur, Hammurabi and Nebuchadnezzar of Babylon, and the conquests of Cyrus the Great of Persia and Alexander the Great of Greece.

FIGURE 7.2 Mesopotamian tablets in cuneiform script: (a) early tablet, ca. 3200 B.C.E.; (b) tablet and envelope, legal case concerning land ownership at Nuzi, ca. 1400 B.C.E.; (c) fragments of Gilgamesh epic, ca. 700 B.C.; and (d) prism from Palace of Sargon II, 721–705 B.C.E. (Courtesy of Oriental Institute, University of Chicago)

Of course, there were various "collapses" of Mesopotamian states, as kings and dynasties fell or were conquered by other kings. For a short period the city of Uruk itself was abandoned, after which it was reoccupied. You can certainly read, as Diamond has done, mainly in older history books, that these collapses of dynasties were the result of Mesopotamian kings having mismanaged their environments. And there are a few new stories about how climate changes in neighboring regions forced people to leave their villages in Syria and invade Mesopotamian cities. Neither of these explanations is correct.

FIGURE 7.3 Art and architecture of Neo-Assyrian empire: (a) winged bull
protective figure; (b) reconstruction of the palace of Sargon II at Khorsabad.
(Courtesy of Oriental Institute, University of Chicago)

Studies of Mesopotamian written tablets (which exist in the hundreds of thousands) and new research in Mesopotamian archaeology reveal substantial political instability in Mesopotamian states.
Instances of internal struggle among various social and economic
groups in Mesopotamian cities and states have been identified, especially in the ethnolinguistic mix that characterized Mesopotamian
civilization. Furthermore, we can demonstrate how arrogant decisions by mighty leaders led to overextension and the fall of their
states.[9] If one "rule" of political stability/instability can be risked,
it is that the more centralized the government, the larger the
bureaucracy, and the larger the army in a state, the less stable is the

government and the more drastic and comprehensive is the fall of the state.

I now consider some collapses – and there were several – in the history of the northern part of Mesopotamia, which is called Assyria. In the last years of the seventh century B.C.E., the Assyrian empire, the largest and most militaristic in Mesopotamian history, was defeated, and Assyrian palaces, grandiose art, and libraries and learning disappeared from history. Disappeared, that is, until Assyria was resurrected by archaeologists in middle of the nineteenth century. Assyria now lives again, not only in museums and classes but also in the hearts and minds of people today who call themselves Assyrians. I shall tell a bit of their story later in this chapter.

BACKGROUND AND CONTEXT OF STATES IN ASSYRIA

To understand the rise and fall of Assyria in Mesopotamia, I first provide a bird's eye view of Mesopotamian archaeology and history. Mesopotamian cities evolved extremely rapidly. In 4000 B.C.E. there was hardly any site larger than a modest village in either north or south Mesopotamia. These sites had at most a population of a few hundred. By 3000 B.C.E. we find extremely large cities, including Uruk, which had an estimated population in the tens of thousands.[10] In south Mesopotamia the countryside was divided into about a dozen independent city-states. In central Mesopotamia, in which there were fewer cities, Kish ruled over its region and occasionally over the rival cities to the south. To the north lay Assyria, the political systems of which we know little before about 2000 B.C.E.

The southern city-states, which battled each other for power and autonomy, were brought together decisively by Sargon of Akkade; Akkade is the name of the capital city he founded. Although its location isn't known, Akkade must have been near Kish because Sargon began his career as an official in service to the ruler of Kish. His conquest of the southern city-states lasted through the reign of his grandson, Naram-Sin, but the state and empire began to fall apart thereafter. This was hardly unexpected because the formerly independent city-states attempted to break away from the rule of Akkade whenever one of its kings died and a new and untried king was being inaugurated. Naram-Sin, who led ambitious military campaigns far outside Mesopotamia, paid less attention to problems of internal governance and was remembered in some (but not all) literary texts as cursed by the gods for his actions.

After a century or so of anarchy – a time described by a Sumerian text as "who was king, who was not king?" – kings from the city of Ur managed to conquer the southern Mesopotamian cities and institute a new territorial state. This dynasty lasted only a century, from about 2100 to 2000 B.C.E., and the enormous and unproductive bureaucracy of the state, along with its increasingly unsuccessful military adventures, was effectively resisted as Mesopotamian cities again were able to assert their cherished independence.

Now, Mesopotamian scribes provided explanations for these collapses, mainly as punishments by the gods for the misbehavior of human rulers or in some cases as the result of divine whim and hence unknowable by humans. The agents of the gods were usually barbarians, foreigners who came from the mountains between modern Iraq and Iran. Older history books dutifully explained political change in Mesopotamia as a result of barbarian invasions. A few modern historians and archaeologists, generally unbelievers in the will of the Mesopotamian gods, have argued that climate change at the end of the third millennium B.C.E. caused some ancient Syrians (called Amorites) to migrate southeastward into Mesopotamia and to bring down the ruling house of Ur. Evidence for this climate change is mainly seen in a layer of sterile soil, interpreted as a time of aridity, and in the abandonment of some sites in Syria at this time.

This explanation, however, doesn't consider that neighboring regions in Syria were not abandoned. Furthermore, the texts from the period of Ur's rule show that many Amorites were peaceful inhabitants of southern Mesopotamia, some of them holding high offices in the realm of the Ur kings.[11] Finally, previous claims that the rulers of Ur overcultivated their landholdings and caused salinization in the land, which led to collapse, have been refuted by newer research.[12] Indeed, at the capital of Ur life for most citizens went on much as before after one ruling dynasty was toppled, and, after a short time, a new dynasty came into power.[13]

Similar stories of short-lived rulers and territorial states can be told, such as of the state ruled by Hammurabi of Babylon. This state took shape in the last few years of Hammurabi's rule and lasted only until the tenth year of his successor. Hammurabi's famous law code, which has in fact nothing to do with how cases were decided in Babylonia, was mainly intended to justify Hammurabi's conquest of the independent city-states who were to supposed to prosper under the tyrant's self-proclaimed perfectly just rule.[14]

So far, I have told several very short stories about the middle and south of Mesopotamia. The northern part of Mesopotamia, Assyria, has a different history, and it is to this I now turn.

STATES AND SOCIAL TRANSFORMATIONS IN ASSYRIA

If Assyria in the third millennium B.C.E. – the time of rival city-states in the south, the empire of Sargon and his successors, and the short-lived reign of the kings of Ur – is little known, the region is well documented after 2000 B.C.E. The chronology of Assyria can be broken down into three periods:

Old Assyrian period (ca. 1920–1780): time of merchant colonies
Middle Assyrian period (ca. 1450–1000): birth of an Assyrian expansionist state
Neo-Assyrian period (ca. 1000–612): the Assyrian empire.

Situated in a dry-farming area and thus not dependent on irrigation for agricultural productivity, which was the case in the south, Assyria was not a land of many cities until the Neo-Assyrian period, when new capitals were built. The Assyrian dialect of Akkadian was not greatly different from the Babylonian dialect of southern Mesopotamia. One might say that Assyria and Babylonia were more or less equal partners in what we call "Mesopotamia." In fact, there was no word for "Mesopotamia" in Akkadian. "Mesopotamia," meaning "the Land between the Two Rivers" in Greek, is what the classical Greeks called the area between the Tigris and Euphrates.[15]

The Old Assyrian Period

Ironically, the Old Assyrian documents for the most part do not come from Assyria itself, but from a colony of Assyrian merchants called Kanesh located in the heart of Anatolia (Asiatic Turkey), 470 miles northwest of the city of Assur, the capital of Assyria in this period.

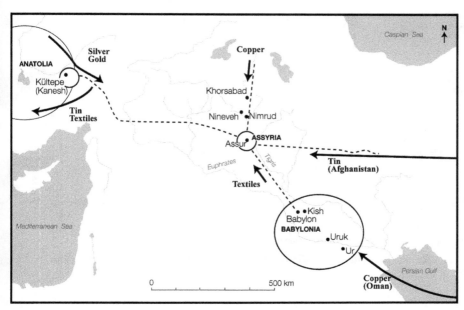

FIGURE 7.4 Extent of Old Assyrian trade network. (Drawn by Elisabeth Paymal)

During the Old Assyrian period Assyrian family firms moved goods from where they were plentiful to where they were scarce and made huge profits from their ability to market these goods.

Assyrian merchants got gold and silver from Anatolia, which they bought with tin and luxurious textiles that they transported from Assyria. Assyrian merchants negotiated long-term business contracts to amass the capital needed to buy the tin and textiles, and the Assyrian kings and state made it their business to keep trade routes open by campaigning selectively and by negotiating treaties with polities. But for the most part it was left to Assyrian merchants to bring goods via donkey caravans to Anatolia; they paid bribes to highwaymen and taxes to the local princes in Anatolia, where they had founded their colonies. These were colonies in the absence of colonialism, since Kanesh and other settlements of various sizes were under the control of Anatolian palaces and royalty.

Although there were kings, administrators, and armies in Assyria, there were also councils of "great and small" men and a "city hall" that shared power with the crown in Assyria and its bureaucracy. The

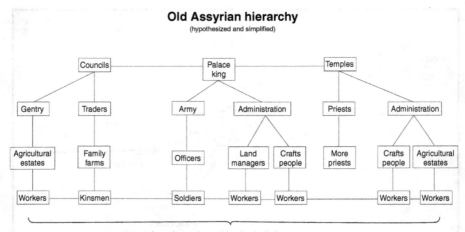

FIGURE 7.5 Schematization of Old Assyrian hierarchy. (Drawn by Elisabeth Paymal)

elite consisted of eminent traders and landowners. Figure 7.5, which to an extent is necessarily hypothetical, depicts the social and political hierarchy of Assyrian society in the Old Assyrian period.

The diagram shows three interrelated hierarchical branches. In the center there is the government, consisting of the army, the bureaucracy, and the land and workers under the governmental administration. On the right it depicts the temple estates, with priests and administrators. In Mesopotamia temples owned property in order to feed and clothe the gods. The Mesopotamian word for temple is "house of the god," and the god's "house" (or, better, the god's household estate) included those who ministered to him (or her), performing ceremonies, as well as administrators and workers who produced and prepared food and rich garments for the god. The gods (and there were many of them) needed large estates and many dependents for their households. When the (statue of the) god finished consuming the meal prepared for him (or her) and, dressed in fine raiment, departed the ritual meal chamber, the leftovers were given to priests and workers.[16]

In the third branch of this hierarchy, on the left side of the diagram, is shown the councils, consisting of traders and gentry, their kinsmen, and their villages. The councils enjoyed real power in Assur (and in the Assyrian colonies in Anatolia). Lawsuits were decided in councils, payments by merchants to the council were set, and in Anatolia taxes were collected to be given to the local rulers who suffered the Assyrian colonies to exist in their midst.

Note especially in this diagram that the workers in villages, soldiers, and laborers on all the agricultural estates were Assyrians. Toward the end of the Old Assyrian period, about 1820 B.C.E., Shamshi-Adad, a usurper king, originally from the Middle Euphrates area, conquered Assur and incorporated it in his realm. This conquest, to be sure, affected events in Assyria, leading to increased centralization of royal power, but it did not in itself explain the demise of the Assyrian merchant colony system and the end of the Old Assyrian period.

The short-lived empire of Shamshi-Adad, essentially the later years of his life, was resisted in various quarters, not least by people in his Middle Euphrates homeland and the city of Mari. On the empire's demise the Old Assyrian trading system also disappeared. For all its immense prosperity, the mercantile arrangements were extremely fragile. The Old Assyrian colonies and the political economy in Assyria itself were dependent on the relatively unrestricted passage of traders over long distances. This was relatively easy because both Babylonia to the south and Anatolia in the north didn't contain powerful territorial states. City-states and local princes in Babylonia contested for power both in their own cities and in their regions. In the eighteenth century B.C.E., however, Hammurabi unified the south, and a new people in Anatolia, whom we know later as Hittites, disrupted local political systems. When constraints were apparently imposed on the movement of goods by the rise of strong centralized governments in Anatolia and Babylonia, trade from the south, east, and north, into and out of Assyria was brought to a halt.

When the artificial state imposed by Shamshi-Adad collapsed after his death, the Old Assyrian political and economic system seems to have been reduced essentially to the rural countryside that was its original base. If we look at the diagram, it was essentially only the governmental system that collapsed soon after the reign of Shamshi-Adad. The association of local elites, now without the traders but still consisting of traditional Assyrian gentry and workers, survived, and so did, as far as we can tell, the temples and their landholdings.

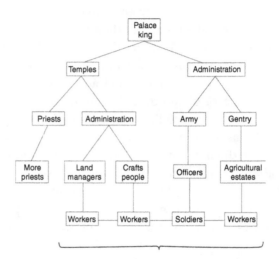

Middle Assyrian hierarchy
(hypothesized and simplified)

FIGURE 7.6 Schematization of Middle Assyrian hierarchy. (Drawn by Elisabeth Paymal)

The Middle Assyrian Period

From the end of the Old Assyrian period, about 1750 B.C.E., for 300 years we know practically nothing about Assyria. No texts are known from this period, which as a result is called a dark age; only later lists of kings and chronicles reflect something of an oral tradition that remembered – and constructed – a line of monarchs that may or may not have existed during this time. In the fourteenth century, however, Assyria experienced a political renaissance substantially in response to new states and military campaigns that impinged on its borders. To combat these enemies, which included the Kassite state in Babylonia to the south, the neighboring state of Mitanni to the west, and the Hittites in Anatolia to the north, Middle Assyrian kings began to centralize their power and create an effective military resistance that soon turned into an expansionist army.

The structure of this newly centralized state in Assyria is depicted in Figure 7.6. Comparing this with the diagram of the Old Assyrian empire, you can see that the councils of the Old Assyrian period that shared power with the king and the palace establishment have disappeared. In fact, the centralizing program of the Middle Assyrian kings was intended to displace the traditional powers of the Assyrian nobility.

However, the nobility was far from toothless and contested their subordination in the administration of the Middle Assyrian state. When an Assyrian king named Tukulti-Ninurta built a new capital across the Tigris River from the venerable capital, Assur, which he named Dur-Tukulti-Ninurta, "Fort Tukulti-Ninurta," to house his new administration and distance his rule from the old-line elites, Assyrian nobles assassinated him. They justified their actions in part because Tukulti-Ninurta had committed the sacrilege, in their eyes, of sacking Babylon and Babylonia, the cultural heartland of Mesopotamian civilization.[17] Other Assyrians, however, were proud that Assyria was not only strong enough to defend itself against the likes of an aggressive Babylonian foreign policy but also to take the battle into Babylonia itself. There's a moral here: ancient states, like more recent ones, were characterized by factions, parties, and politicians. Any attempt to reduce ancient states to vague and undifferentiated "societies" (as in "how societies choose to fail or succeed") disregards the very pulse of the past.

In our diagram of the Middle Assyrian state and society, we may note how Middle Assyrian kings, again in contrast to the Old Assyrian system, attempted to streamline and simplify the administration of the land, bringing the army, temples, gentry, and local villagers under their direct control. Although royal power was resisted by the Assyrian nobility, this power of the kings grew in this period. Whereas events around 1200 B.C.E. in which regional warfare, piracy, and movements of foreign and displaced peoples disrupted the plans of the Assyrian kings, the process of centralization in Assyria soon resumed and continued into the first millennium B.C.E.

The Neo-Assyrian Period

Neo-Assyrian kings, beginning in earnest in the early ninth century B.C.E., transformed the army into an expeditionary force, one that was enormous, professionalized, and battle-toughened. The army began to campaign yearly, to the north into Anatolia, east into Iran, and west to Syria and the Levantine coast. The highpoint of the Neo-Assyrian expansion was shortly after 700 B.C.E., when Assyrian hegemony extended to the Mediterranean coast, Egypt, Babylonia, and southern Iran. Readers of the Old Testament will know that the "Ten Lost Tribes of Israel" got lost because their king unwisely did not pay tribute to Assyrian kings in the 720s, and the Assyrian army swept through Israel and deported thousands of Israelites into the Assyrian homeland and its various provinces.

The highpoint of the Assyrian empire,[18] however, was short lived, and conquered territories soon won their freedom. The Assyrian army became bogged down in adventures to the north, where they met tough enemies in mountainous regions, and in the south, where they became enmeshed in a Mesopotamian civil war. Finally, at a time when internal succession to the Assyrian throne sowed confusion in Assyria, Medes from Iran, Babylonians from the south, and various northern enemies all invaded Assyria between 614 and 610 B.C.E. and destroyed the Assyrian capitals. With the exception of a few outposts and individuals named in later Babylonian documents, the existence of both an Assyrian political system and most Assyrian social and cultural institutions vanished.

Why did the Assyrian state collapse, and more importantly, why did it not regenerate – as had so many other defeated and "collapsed" Mesopotamian states? One salient reason was the policy of the Assyrian kings themselves. In Figure 7.7 we can see some of the policies of extreme centralization that Assyrian kings pursued, including the construction of new capitals and the promotion of generals into offices close to the king.

In the terms of those who study the formal properties of systems, the three upper levels of the hierarchy were closely coupled horizontally, while the vertical bonds connecting the upper levels to the lower ones were increasingly loosely coupled. That is, the close interconnections of the place, the army, and the elites, who no longer owed their status to their place in the traditional Assyrian kinship system and landholding traditions, but whose rank and power derived solely from their state offices, made the top levels of the system "disarticulated" and vulnerable to being wholly erased. It was not simply the government that disappeared, as in the Old Assyrian period, but the upper three levels of Assyrian society as well (in this hierarchical rendering).

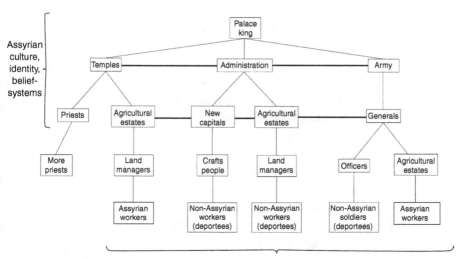

FIGURE 7.7 Schematization of Neo-Assyrian hierarchy. (Drawn by Elisabeth Paymal)

But the lower levels of the Neo-Assyrian hierarchy were changed even more profoundly than the upper levels. Beginning in the Middle Assyrian period, but increasing at an enormous rate in the Neo-Assyrian times, kings deported conquered peoples – like the Ten Lost Tribes of Israel – into the new and old imperial cities, where they worked constructing magnificent palaces and works of art. Deported peoples were also moved into the countryside as agricultural workers and canal laborers. Indeed, much of the countryside was in the hands of generals who were rewarded by the king for their military successes. Workers on these newly created estates were not Assyrians and did not speak Assyrian (but overwhelmingly spoke Aramaic, the main language of Syria/Palestine/Israel). These workers knew little and presumably cared less about Assyrian culture and history.

These laborers – to use again the terminology of our diagram above – were strongly coupled horizontally, kinsmen, and cultural neighbors – but only loosely connected vertically to the upper levels of the Assyrian hierarchy. Normally, in Mesopotamian collapses, when the top level of the hierarchy was removed, it would be rebuilt, as it were, by the lower sections of the system (as the Assyrian state was rebuilt after the Old Assyrian period). This was simply not possible in the Neo-Assyrian case, because the inhabitants of villages were increasingly not Assyrian in ethnicity, religion, or language and had little interest in reconstructing anything that was "Assyrian."

Since I've noted that Assyria and Babylonia were both parts of what we call Mesopotamia, and Assyrian and Babylonian were dialects of what we call the Akkadian language (first written under Sargon of Akkade), it is interesting to examine the relations between Assyria and Babylonia during the period when Assyria collapsed.

One interesting cultural aspect of the Neo-Assyrian policies of political centralization was the so-called cultural struggle or Babylonian problem of the Neo-Assyrian kings. The Assyrian royalty regarded Babylonia as the heartland of Mesopotamian culture (as I've noted in characterizing the adventures of Tukulti-Ninurta in the Middle Assyrian period). Even as they felt that Mesopotamian literature and ritual needed to be imported from the Babylonian south, they saw Babylonia as chaotic and even decadent.

When a rebellion broke out in Babylonia – which was governed in the last century of Assyria's power by Assyrian puppets – against the Assyrian king, Sennacherib, and the king sacked Babylonia, this was regarded in some parts of Assyria as an act of impiety. Indeed, after Sennacherib was assassinated, his son Esarhaddon repented his father's deed. Thereafter, the two sons of Esarhaddon divided their rule, one in Assyria and one in Babylonia. Perhaps unsurprisingly the Babylonian king (who was an Assyrian) rebelled against his brother in Assyria, and after a four-year civil war, Assyria conquered the south. However, this long war cost Assyria in soldiers and in lost tribute that would have been brought in by the campaigns of the Assyrian army. The civil war was a Pyrrhic victory for the Assyrians, who, in their weakened state, soon succumbed to the superior forces of their enemies.

Assyria without the State

Figure 7.8 shows why the Assyrian state was not rebuilt after the defeat of its king and army in the latter years of the seventh century B.C.E.

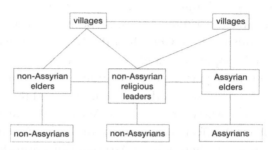

FIGURE 7.8 Schematization of Assyria without the state. (Drawn by Elisabeth Paymal)

The removal of the horizontally connected top layers of the Neo-Assyrian hierarchy did not proceed to a level of landed gentry and Assyrian nobility (as in the Old Assyrian case), since these traditional local elites had been systematically removed by Assyrian kings in their drive to establish a centralized government and an enormously large army. The successes of the army propped up the state, and the officers essentially replaced the traditional gentry of the countryside.

In that countryside and in the royal capitals lived mostly non-Assyrian workers, who, as I've noted, had little connection to Assyrian culture or even the Assyrian language. They had been deported from the west into Assyria, and after the fall of the Mesopotamian capitals, many still inhabited the ruined cities, although most lived in the countryside.

Although the Assyrian kings were defeated by foreigners, it was only the Assyrians themselves who could have destroyed the very qualities that made Assyria Assyria. Gibbon famously described the fall of the Roman empire as the "triumph of barbarism and religion." When we depict the collapse of Assyria, it is the disappearance of the religion, culture, and language of the Assyrians, which had lasted for hundreds of years, that is most significant and that explains why Assyria did not rise again. Gibbon would have understood this perfectly. People continued to live in Assyria, and remnants of the most ancient city in the land, Nineveh, are cited in a variety of sources, but Assyria was gone.

THE FATE OF ASSYRIA AND THE CHOICES OF ASSYRIANS

Today, Assyrians still walk among us. They live in the Middle East, Europe, and the United States. Although they are Nestorian Christians, members of the Church of the East, they trace their origin to ancient Mesopotamia, and this connection with the ancient Assyrians is a crucial part of their identities. The language of their liturgy is Neo-Aramaic, that is, the modern version of the language of many of the people who were brought to Assyria from the west. Some Aramaic speakers in effect became Assyrians because their ancestors lived in Assyria when there was an Assyrian state, and they were in Assyria when the Assyrian state was no more.

If the beliefs and language of modern Assyrians have little in common with those of the ancient Assyrians, modern Assyrians' self-identification as Assyrians should not be denigrated. Indeed, pride in ancient Assyria and a desire to learn about Assyria can be traced in considerable measure to the nineteenth-century archaeological excavations in northern Iraq that disclosed the palaces, temples, artifacts, and written documents of Assyrian civilization. Today's Assyrians rightly claim an attachment to the most ancient history of Iraq. Perhaps as interesting as any story that can be told about the collapse of Assyria is an account of the rebirth of Assyria in the lives and imaginations of these modern Assyrians.

MODERN ASSYRIANS

Early Christians, in the first few centuries c.e., debated the nature of Christ's divinity and humanity and the oneness of his person. Five patriarchates, in Rome, Constantinople, Alexandria, Antioch, and Jerusalem, became administratively independent with a chief bishop or patriarch at the head of each. The debates were not only theological, but also concerned ecclesiastical politics, nationalism, and cultural factors. From the various ecumenical councils that took place in the fourth and fifth centuries c.e., a Nestorian Church – so named because it refused to excommunicate Nestorius, a defender of the "Dyophysite" view that Jesus was both human and the embodiment of the *logos* (Word of God) – became independent of Constantinople. For centuries this Church, whose liturgy was in Syriac, a medieval dialect of Aramaic, was known as the Nestorian Church (especially by Europeans and Arabs) and the (Old) Church of the East. These terms were in use through the nineteenth century.

In the seventeenth century a schism in the Nestorian Church/Church of the East occurred as a group converted from the Nestorian Church to Roman Catholicism. They called themselves the Chaldean Church, since the center of this church was in present-day Iraq, often called "Chaldea" in premodern times. Their leader is the Patriarch of Babylon (or Babylonia), probably because modern Baghdad was then thought to be ancient Babylon or near it (the latter is the case). The liturgical language of the Chaldean Church was also a dialect of Syriac, which was often called Chaldean. The term Chaldean, known from the Hebrew Bible and in the writings of Greek and Arabic historians, referred to the area we now call Iraq.

In the mid-nineteenth century, British and French excavators working in northern Iraq discovered the ruins of the Neo-Assyrian capitals, their palaces, monumental art, and written tablets. As these excavations continued and especially as the tablets were deciphered and shed light on the periods previously known only from the Hebrew Bible, Christians in the area, many of whom worked for the European excavators, began to adopt the name "Assyrian" for themselves and to assert their connections with the most ancient past of their land, more ancient than the majority Arab Muslims.

In the course of the last 150 years, many of these Iraqi Christians emigrated to Europe and the United States (and other countries). In 1976 the Nestorian Church/Old Church of the East officially renamed itself the Assyrian Church of the

FIGURE 7.9 A modern Assyrian ceremony, August 7 (Assyrian Martyrs Day), 2008, Chicago.

East. Its bishop (catholicos) now lives in San Francisco. Although most professional historians of Mesopotamia, Assyriologists, are not impressed by these claims to descent from ancient peoples of Mesopotamia, a case can be made that many Assyrians and Chaldeans were precisely those deported to Assyria and Babylonia by kings who had conquered Syria and the eastern lands of the Mediterranean or those who had migrated from those lands into Mesopotamia's rich cities.

A modern Assyrian, Dr. Norman Solhkhah, writes: "I designed the Assyrian Martyrs Monument ... to honor my father and brother, as well as other Assyrians who were killed simply for being Assyrian." Perhaps extraction of genetic material from ancient cemeteries and comparison with modern people could shed light on these connections. In any case, ethnic and cultural affiliations are always, to an extent, matters of choice and acceptance by members of social groups. People construct, again to an extent, their own pasts, deciding who are their ancestors and who aren't. (I have a friend who is part German, Polish, and Irish. He thinks of himself as at least 100 percent Irish. He spent a year in college in Dublin and throws the greatest St. Patrick's Day parties. He married a Brazilian woman of Japanese descent. They have two children, one of whom has a Portuguese name (Frederico), the other an Irish one (Padraic). They report on the census tracks that they are Asian Americans.)

MODERN CHALDEANS

If scholars tend to reject modern Assyrians' and Chaldeans' claims as descendants of Mesopotamians, modern Mesopotamians are separated by religion and by country of origin, since most Chaldeans are of Iraqi descent, whereas Assyrians come from a variety of Middle Eastern countries. The two groups are not necessarily friendly. Yasmeen Hanoosh, a Chaldean born in Iraq, grew up in Detroit and has just finished her Ph.D. at the University of Michigan. In an e-mail "interview" with her, I have selected and edited some comments and used (with permission) some material from her dissertation draft.

The dispute among contemporary Chaldean and Assyrian nationalists does not revolve around the question of whether or not the ancient Assyrian and Chaldean populations survived. There is no proof that the ancient Assyrians and Chaldeans vanished after the fall of their empires in the late seventh century B.C.E. (Assyria) or late sixth century (Chaldean Babylonia). No one disputes the assumption that some indigenous people continued to live in their homelands. The survival of some versions of the Aramaic language attest to that, as does the fact that Mesopotamia continued to be populated throughout the centuries that followed the destructions of Nineveh and Babylon.

FIGURE 7.10 Sacred Heart Chaldean Catholic Church, Detroit, Michigan.

Rather, the current oppositional debates center upon discourses of history and power: was it the Chaldeans or the Assyrians who created the most powerful empire and ruled the other "ethnic" group? Which group had *first* settled the region and was the predecessor of the other group? And which group came *last*, having supplanted the other group, and preserved more accurately the language and the culture of Mesopotamia?

Amer Fatuhi, in his self-published *Chaldeans since the Early Beginning of Time*, locally promoted by many Chaldean Churches in Michigan, argues that Chaldeans are the only indigenous people of ancient Iraq, and hence its first inhabitants. Assyrian Edward Odisho, professor at Northeastern Illinois University, writes that "Assyria was literally resurrected" during the Parthian period (ca. 129 B.C.E.–224 C.E.) and Assyrians rebuilt Assyria.

These debates impact the lives of tens of thousands of Assyrians and Chaldeans in Southeast Michigan and can result in conflict among teenage gangs. This is an ironic, modern commentary to a conflict that has its roots in ancient times when Assyrians and Babylonians often fought one another.

Teaching courses on Mesopotamian history and archaeology at the University of Michigan is quite different than for teachers in other universities who do not have Assyrians and Chaldeans in their classes. Archaeologists and historians may rightly consider ourselves stewards of the past, who calmly and rationally try to understand the past. However, we must also acknowledge that our work not only creates that past, literally bringing it to the modern world, but also has helped create the present of people for whom the past is part of their present, and not just of academic interest.

Main sources on Assyrians and Chaldeans are John Joseph, *The Modern Assyrians of the Middle East* (Leiden: Brill, 2000), and Wilhelm Baum and Dietmar Winkler, *The Church of the East: A Concise History* (London: Routledge, 2003). See also Antonio Sagona, *The Heritage of Eastern Turkey* (Melbourne: Macmillan Art, 2006), and Simo Parpola, www.nineveh.com/parpola_eng.pdf.

CONCLUSION

I hope that this rather long account of "collapse" in the Assyrian part of Mesopotamia has not been too full of strange names of people and places. I also hope that my diagrams, which have necessarily simplified the structure of life in Assyria, have helped readers understand the changes in social and political structure in Assyria over about 1,500 years.

My story has included normal citizens as well as political leaders, how they lived, and how they participated in the creation and re-creation of their history and culture. This story is, as you can see, much different than Diamond's version of collapse, which leaves people out, except for vaguely identifying certain elites as the actors who ruined their own environments or were helpless victims of a train of climatic circumstances, such as Diamond's favorite calamities, drought, and salinization.[19]

In Assyria we can see how councils of elders and entrepreneurial traders were gradually eliminated by powerful kings, how traditional lands were given to generals and high-ranking bureaucrats, and how imperial successes led to the incorporation in the empire of people, like the "Lost Tribes," who had nothing in common with their rulers.

This study of Assyria and ancient Mesopotamia *does*, I submit, have some lessons for us modern observers of our own world. Ill-considered foreign military adventures by a state with vast but still limited resources and with leaders who paid progressively less attention to the internal problems of their own state sound all too modern. But the lessons from the past do not lead to straightforward recipes for policy, and those who think learning from the past should work in that way haven't really learned anything at all.

Archaeologists and ancient historians do not often have the luxury of knowing and saying exactly what happened in the past. However, we are very good at saying precisely what didn't happen. Ancient pyramids were *not* built by astronauts from other planets, and ancient states like Assyria did *not* collapse because their leaders mismanaged their environments. Also, just when you might think that an ancient civilization is dead and gone, you find that the past can be conjured up, in our case, by archaeologists and historians, and resonate in important ways with people who find their roots in that past. One lesson we may learn about the transformations of ancient civilizations, as we see in Assyria, is that, in an important sense, they didn't collapse at all.

Notes

*   In my scholarly career I have tacked between the fields of Mesopotamian studies and anthropology. I studied anthropology (which includes archaeology) as an undergraduate at Northwestern University and participated in an undergraduate field school in archaeology in north-central Arizona. I then studied Mesopotamian languages, history, and archaeology at Yale University. After getting my Ph.D., I taught for twenty-one years in the Department of Anthropology at the University of Arizona. I then moved to the University of Michigan to chair the Department of Near Eastern Studies and to hold a joint appointment in the Museum of Anthropology and the Department of Anthropology.

     My publications are divided between texts and articles on Mesopotamian social and economic institutions and studies of social evolutionary theory. I have written on "collapse" in Mesopotamia (*The Economic Role of the Crown in the Old Babylonian Period,* 1977) and, in the framework of an edited volume (with G. L. Cowgill), *The Collapse of Ancient States and Civilizations* (1988). Not unlike Jared Diamond, I have ventured a global perspective on ancient history and archaeology, *Myths of the Archaic State: Evolution of the Earliest Cities, States, and Civilizations* (2005).

1. Diamond 2005: 174, 48, and 424, respectively.
2. Gonick 1990.
3. Yoffee and Cowgill 1988.
4. Diamond 2005: 3.
5. Tainter 1988. See also Tainter 2006.
6. For the lists of areas Diamond says collapsed, see pp. 3 and 545–547. Although Diamond says (p. 11) that he doesn't "know of any case in which a society's collapse can be attributed solely to environmental change," he makes it clear that such engineered disasters to the environment are the most important factors by far in the collapse of societies. He doesn't spend much time on any other factors.
7. Diamond 2005: 3.
8. Diamond also sees differences between the past and present, such as in technology and globalization. There are more differences between ancient and modern states than these.
9. The best textbook on Mesopotamian history is Van De Mieroop 2007. A recent assessment of climate change, abandonment, and migrations brought about by climate change is the conclusion to Kuzucuoğlu and Marro 2007.
10. For plans of prehistoric sites and of the first city, see chapter 3 of Yoffee 2005. For a discussion of Uruk, see Liverani 2006. Newest research at Tell Brak in Syria has revealed a large town site in northern Mesopotamia at about 4000 B.C.E.
11. The latest word on Amorites is Michalowski forthcoming.
12. The idea that salt and silt problems caused the end of the Ur III dynasty (so called because it is the third dynasty in Ur in the "Sumerian King List") can be dated to Jacobsen and Adams 1958. Powell 1985 refuted this.
13. For life in Ur after the fall of the Ur's dynasty, ca. 2000, see Van De Mieroop 1992.
14. For a discussion of Hammurabi's law code, see chapter 5 of Yoffee 2005. There are two new books on Hammurabi: Charpin 2003 and Van De Mieroop 2005.
15. See Finkelstein 1963. A convenient summary of Old Assyrian trade is Veenhof 1995. Larsen 1977, a path-breaking book, still inspires.
16. The concept and phrase "the care and feeding of the gods" is from Oppenheim 1964.
17. The best exposition on the major source about Tukulti-Ninurta's deeds is Machinist 1976.

18. For an extensive bibliography on the Assyrian empire and directions to further bibliographies, see the syllabus to my course, "Ancient Mesopotamia," which can be found on my web site, sitemaker.umich. edu/nyoffee, under courses. Interested readers can find up-to-date literature on Mesopotamian history in the syllabus.

19. Adams 1981 reports that salinization did occur in Mesopotamia in the following circumstances. When Persian dynasties (called Sasanians) ruled Mesopotamia in the mid-first millennium C.E. and then Islamic caliphates were in power in their new capital of Baghdad in the later first millennium C.E., rulers of truly unprecedented centralized states constructed enormous canals from the Tigris to the Euphrates and demanded ever more resources from the fertile lands in south Mesopotamia for their own political goals. Eventually farmers in the south, who understood their own environments well, were forced to give up practices of fallowing every other year. The water table and its salt component rose, and the land became unproductive. None of this characterizes what happened in ancient Mesopotamia.

Bibliography

Adams, R. McC. 1981. *Heartland of Cities*. Chicago: University of Chicago Press.

Charpin, D. 2003. *Hammu-rabi de Babylone*. Paris: Presses universitaires de France.

Diamond, J. 2005. *Collapse: How Societies Choose to Fail or Succeed*. New York: Viking.

Finkelstein, J.J. 1963. "Mesopotamia." *Journal of Near Eastern Studies* **21**:73–92.

Gonick, L. 1990. *The River Realms*, vol. 3 of *The Cartoon History of the Universe*. New York: Doubleday.

Jacobsen, T. and R. McC. Adams. 1958. "Salt and Silt in Ancient Mesopotamian Agriculture." *Science* **128**:1251–1258.

Kuzucuoğlu, C. and C. Marro. Editors. 2007. "Northern Syria and Upper Mesopotamia at the End of the Third Millennium B.C.," in *Société humaines et changement climatique à la fin du troisième millénaire: une crise a-t-elle eu lieu en haute Mésopotamie?*, pp. 583–590. Paris: De Brocard.

Larsen, M. T. 1977. *The Old Assyrian City-State and Its Colonies*. Copenhagen: Akademisk Vorlag.

Liverani, M. 2006. *Uruk: The First City*. Translated by M. Van De Mieroop and Z. Bahrani. London: Equinox.

Machinist, P. 1976. "Literature as Politics: Tukulti-Ninurta and the Bible." *Catholic Biblical Quarterly* **38**:455–482.

Michalowski, P. Forthcoming. *Gender and Sites of Contestation in Epistolary Discourse: The Correspondence of the Kings of Ur*. Winona Lake, IN: Eisenbrauns.

Oppenheim, A.L. 1964. *Ancient Mesopotamia: Portrait of a Dead Civilization.* Chicago: University of Chicago Press.

Powell, M. 1985. "Salt, Silt, and Yields in Sumerian Agriculture: A Critique of the Theory of Progressive Salinization." *Zeitschrift für Assyriologie* **75**:7–38.

Tainter, J. 1988. *The Collapse of Complex Societies.* Cambridge: Cambridge University Press.

Tainter, J. 2006. "Archaeology of Overshoot and Collapse." *Annual Review of Anthropology* **35**:59–74.

Van De Mieroop, M. 1992. *Society and Enterprise in Old Babylonian Ur.* Berlin: Reimer.

Van De Mieroop, M. 2005. *King Hammurabi.* Oxford: Blackwell.

Van De Mieroop, M. 2007. *A History of the Ancient Near East.* 2nd ed. Oxford: Blackwell.

Veenhof, K. 1995. "Kanesh: An Old Assyrian Colony in Anatolia," in *Civilizations of the Ancient Near East.* Edited by J. Sasson et al., pp. 859–872. New York: Scribner's.

Yoffee, N. 2005. *Myths of the Archaic State: Evolution of the Earliest Cities, States, and Civilizations.* Cambridge: Cambridge University Press.

Yoffee, N. and G.L. Cowgill. Editors. 1988. *The Collapse of Ancient States and Civilizations.* Tucson: University of Arizona Press.

PART III

SOCIETIES IN THE AFTERMATH OF EMPIRE

8

Advanced Andeans and Backward Europeans

Structure and Agency in the Collapse of the Inca Empire

David Cahill[*]

Within a few decades after 1492, the Spaniards conquered much of the two American continents: all of Mesoamerica, most of South America except Brazil (Portugal's booty) and a few splinter territories, most of the Caribbean islands, and around one-third of the present territory of the United States of America. It was a stunning, sweeping success, unrivaled by any empire before or since. The conquerors held that the military conquest and subjugation of indigenous Americans was justified (theologically and legally) by the need to enlighten, religiously and intellectually, the benighted creatures of God who peopled the New World, its First Nations. In the classic narrative of the conquest, the conquered Amerindians were so backward that they stood paralyzed when confronted with more highly developed humans.[1] Ian Steele argues that "European invasions of North America were not automatically a disastrous parade of irresistible disease, alluring consumerism, and overwhelming martial superiority."[2] By and large, this was also true of the invasions of Mesoamerica and the Andes. The conquest of the Americas was a long-drawn-out process that lasted for centuries in some regions. By extension, short-term events and campaigns could shatter kingdoms and ruling classes, but the erosion of indigenous resistance was much longer in coming. In the Andes guns and steel were effective in the short term; but it was the subsequent virgin-soil diseases that underlay the long-term conquest. However, the Spaniards faced considerable opposition in both the short and the long terms. Native resistance took many forms, including armed conflict, impromptu riots, use of

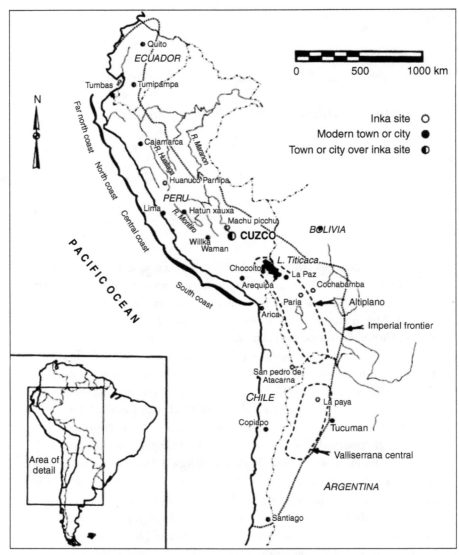

FIGURE 8.1 Map of Tahuantinsuyu. (Source: D'Altroy 2001: 202, reproduced by permission of Cambridge University Press)

the conquerors' legal system to seek judicial redress of grievances, and more generalized passive resistance. These were the "weapons of the weak" by which colonized peoples carried on a struggle against colonial powers in the long interregnums between sporadic protest riots and the rare, large-scale anticolonial rebellions.[3]

Most of the accounts of the conquest of the Incas, contemporary as well as modern, have a derring-do quality usually associated with boys' adventure stories. Above all, modern accounts derive from the self-laudatory, self-justifying accounts of the conquistadors, with Incan or other native Andean voices notable by their absence – in effect, silenced.[4] Historians long ago rejected that interpretation as simplistic, but it is nevertheless often encoded in written and televisual, popular accounts of the conquest, in either crude or sophisticated variants. Mel Gibson's apocalyptic cinematic vision *Apocalypto* is merely the most recent version of crude conquest. By contrast, Jared Diamond's account of the conquest of the Incas is a sophisticated, if brief, interpretation of the same recurring vision of the victors: the conquered as backward, saved from their own Dark Age only by Bible-bearing vectors of "civilization." Not all this press is bad: most accounts underscore Francisco Pizarro's perfidy versus the Inca's honor and respect for the European as well as Andean rites of engagement, for all that Atahuallpa appears to have devised a "secret agenda" by which the newcomers would be lulled into a sense of security, to be struck down once their guard was down.

Finding the best vantage point from which to view a historical event is tricky. Josef Stalin, perhaps thinking of his posthumous press, compared historians to archive rats. A French archive rat, Emmanuel Le Roy Ladurie, divided historians into two types: truffle hunters and parachutists. The former grub for facts, finding the smallest detail but not seeing the contours of the surrounding landscape; the latter view events from high above, seeing the big picture but none of the details. In his portrayal of the conquest, Diamond is neither: he notices few details, and his landscape is a blur. Indeed, it is difficult for any historian of the conquest to see the landscape clearly and even to apprehend the facts. The conquerors who first set eyes on the Inca Atahuallpa at the town of Cajamarca left a few scrappily written testimonies, but none of the quality of the splendid account of the conquest of Mexico by Bernal Díaz del Castillo, who fought side by side with Hernán Cortés in the conquest of Tenochtitlan.[5] Nor are there many documents of the conquest to be found in the archives; the rats go hungry. The historical archaeology of the conquest of Peru, especially of the Cajamarca event, is almost nonexistent; lab rats have rescued little from the rubble. There is therefore plenty of scope for the historical imagination in the events at Cajamarca – a literary license that some find hard to resist.

JARED DIAMOND CONQUERS THE INCAS

The remarkable success of Diamond's *Guns, Germs, and Steel* in both the public domain and within academe is little short of unique. The sales of most "general audience" books tend to be largely confined to the enquiring general reader, but Diamond's "bestsellerdom" across the academic-public divide has few nonfiction parallels that embrace the fields of archaeology, anthropology, and history, to say nothing of paleontology, physiology, biology, ecology, and other academic fields.[6] Diamond's magnum opus is taught in colleges and universities across many disciplines. It is well written, engaging, even absorbing; whatever its demerits, it is a wonderful guide on how to write for a range of audiences, without ever really (despite the many broad-brush generalizations) "dumbing down." Moreover, he takes great pains to distance himself from the primitive–civilized dichotomy and especially its reductio ad absurdum, the crude and innately racist, genetic difference model of human trajectory. Clearly, though, a book with such a chronological and thematic range lays itself open to criticism on many grounds. To approach an understanding of the Incas and their conquest by the Spaniards by way of a critique of Diamond may seem unfair, and even tendentious; after all, he is merely recounting one cameo of a complex civilization and a process of cultural encounter that endured for several years, and his portrayal of the event by no means represents the entirety of his views on either the Incas or their subjugation.[7] Nonetheless, Diamond lays great emphasis on just one event, as encapsulating the essence of the colonial encounter in the Andes, which provides a splendid point of departure for an understanding of the Incas, the conquistadors, and the clash of cultures. This essay dwells exclusively on this episode from historically documented times: the fateful meeting between conquistador Francisco Pizarro and the Inca Atahuallpa on November 16, 1532, at the Peruvian highlands town of Cajamarca. This epochal encounter was a classic "creative event" (*événement matrice*), that is, an event "which destroys traditional structures and replaces them with new ones."[8] This moment of high drama captivated the imagination of European observers even in the sixteenth century.

The Narrative of Cajamarca

The meeting between Inca emperor and chief conquistador was, for Diamond, emblematic of the colonial encounter, or at least made to serve as such. As he himself observed, such stellar events have deep historical roots. Diamond's emphasis on the *longue durée* process is almost Braudellian, in which almost imperceptible structures, changing at glacial speed, provide the foundation for conjunctural movements (such as the Spanish conquest of the Americas) in which events – be they "creative" or prosaic – ride like flecks of foam atop the waves (in Braudel's metaphor), which themselves are only the surface manifestations ("conjunctures") of the deep sea ("structure") and its inexorably powerful currents.[9] In Diamond's bird's-eye depiction, then, Cajamarca was an ephemeral moment of the conquest era but also its metaphor. It encoded all the familiar generic facets of colonial conquest as seen by Europeans: the mutual incomprehension and marveling at the mirror-image alterities; the chasm between New World and Old World epistemologies, "true" rational knowledge against heathen superstition; clever Castilian against dullard Inca; true believers versus the unevangelized barbarians, at best seen as promising neophytes; asymmetrical technology manifest in the flash of steel and thrust of lance against bronze close-combat weapons, slingshot, and cotton armor and buckler; European initiative against the kind of unquestioning obeisance associated with "oriental despotism." In sum, the early colonial chroniclers of this event, followed faithfully by Diamond, portray a binary of resourcefulness opposed to political paralysis in the respective kingship vacuums – there was no Spanish monarch or viceroy to direct the conquistadors' tactics at Cajamarca, but there was an Inca who was just emerging from a protracted civil war and had yet to establish his imperial legitimacy. Above all, there was the spectacle of the Inca being handed the Word of God inscribed in the Bible, reading nothing, hearing nothing, and casting it to the ground. To Spanish ways of thinking, the Inca's emphatic rejection of the Word ipso facto constituted moral and legal justification for conquest and colonization.[10] Taking this as their cue, the conquistadors immediately fell upon the Inca's retinue

FIGURE 8.2 Portrait of Alonso Chiguan Inca, ca. 1740–1750. (Source: Wuffarden 2005: 219, reproduced by permission of Banco de Crédito, Lima)

with their swords, in their bloodlust perpetrating the first of several massacres to come.

This is one of Diamond's pet themes: writing, who's got it and who hasn't. Except that this is not really a problem of literacy or bookishness but rather one of language. Atahuallpa is *told* what the book contains. Conquest is therefore in part a function of spoken Spanish as against spoken Quechua: in Diamond's account, the conquistadors won because they spoke not Quechua but Spanish or Castilian, the result of thousands of years of Iberian linguistic versatility, creativity, and hybridity – the cross-pollination stemming from the incursions of Phoenicians, Romans, Latin Christians, Goths, Visigoths, Moors, and other civilization-bearing human vectors. What did the Incas have to show for thousands of years of hermetic development? They produced the imperial lingua franca that was Quechua, infused variously with Aymara, Puquina, and Uru and that absorbed many regional languages (e.g., Moche) and dialects of the central and northern marches of their empire, and possibly also a special court language allegedly spoken by the Inca nobility in Cuzco. Still, Quechua was the lingua franca of an entire, vast empire, no mean feat for an ostensibly underpowered civilization. Even in present-day Spain, the Spanish (Castilian) language coexists with other vibrantly flourishing languages (Basque and Catalan above all, but also Asturian and Galician) as well as an array of distinct regional dialects. In the sixteenth century, the Incas had made greater progress toward an integrated imperial language than the Spaniards, who had also to engage with the widely spoken (and written) Arabic of southern Spain. Put another way, the Incas were linguistically more integrated than the Spaniards.

Debates and explanations concerning the comparative development of Western and non-Western countries often turn on dichotomies: "between 'us' (the civilized, advanced, logical-empirical people) and 'them' (the primitive, mythic people)." The savage-civilized opposition has strongly pejorative colonialist roots, while its more positive Enlightenment construction has distinguished avatars, from Rousseau to Lévi-Strauss. Lévy-Bruhl's "primitive savage" provides the more unwieldy (and perhaps sinister) logical versus prelogical interpretation. Diamond strives to avoid such crude tropes, but his fondness for an explanatory model contrasting the asymmetrical development of literate and nonliterate societies pervades *Guns, Germs, and Steel.* This stark contrast has, of course, many supporters among social scientists, most notably Jack Goody, an eminent historical anthropologist, who vigorously advocates writing as the key difference between "us" and "them" while rejecting cultural relativism ("sentimental egalitarianism") as such:

Relativism, in its extreme form, is saying that the people in Africa are the same as the Chinese, the Japanese and so on. Well, if they are the same, why are their achievements not the same? So the notion that arose in recent years that all human societies are the same goes against cultural history, I think, because it's not possible to equate the achievements of people without writing to those of peoples with writing. We have to take into account the fact that societies that do not have what I call the technology of the intellect are not able to build up knowledge in the same way as the ones that have. Of course, they have knowledge systems about nature but they cannot achieve the same as the societies that have books, encyclopedias, dictionaries and all that sort of thing.[11]

Diamond's views on writing thus belong to a significant anthropological genealogy. Even if Goody's concept of the "technology of the intellect" were to be accepted, it would have to be admitted that it is not a very useful descriptor, and that there is a very wide liminal territory indeed between "civilized" and "noncivilized." For it to be at all useful heuristically, comparative development needs to be plotted along a continuum: few societies are located at the extreme points of a continuum or a notional bell curve representing human achievement. The trope of "literate" versus "nonliterate" is not appropriate invariably in the case of the conquest of the Americas. It collapses entirely when applied to Mesoamerica with its sophisticated Mixtec and Maya writing systems.[12] It was presumably for this reason that Diamond chose the Atahuallpa-Pizarro encounter as emblematic of the Spanish conquest of the Americas rather than the equally fateful Cortés-Moctezuma meeting, when the conquistador captured the Aztec emperor and thereby provided an exemplary case study (there were others) of how to capture an empire with a relatively small number of allies. This was, like the events at Cajamarca, a gross simplification and thus distortion of complex historical reality.

What, then, of the "nonliterate Incas"? Recent focus on the encoded Andean *quipu* (a knotted-cord recording device) indicates a very high level of communicative sophistication, of great complexity, and one closely attuned to the requirements of running a vast empire that, for all that it had Quechua as a lingua franca, nevertheless housed numerous languages and dialects. As such, it served as a kind of "digital computer" at the imperial or macrolevel, but its local usage may have had a greater potential for specificity, for instance, when arrangements – of the length, thickness, color of threads, kind of knots and their type of twist, and even pendants – refer to land usage or field maps or collective property, by collapsing a rectangular area into a linear representation. However, some chroniclers suggested that the *quipu* could encode narratives, songs, and historical annals. Whether the *quipu* could represent a kind of writing is doubtful, but in any case it would have been a kind of writing that did not correspond to speech. A basic form of the *quipu* is still used today, for example, that used by herders to keep tally of community flocks. As for the grand primordial *quipus* of the Inca empire, a few still exist, but fragmentary knowledge of its functions, variables, and operating subtleties is still preserved in at least one modern village, its *quipu* being an icon in important community rituals.[13]

Clearly, on present evidence, and despite being unlettered, the Incas had established a communications system that was manifestly sufficient to build and maintain a great empire. What is certain is that their record-keeping faculties were fully up to the task of successfully administering and running the empire that stretched from present-day southern Colombia down into much of what are now Argentina and Chile. Hearts and minds were quite another matter, and the Incan failure to win, forge, or maintain ties of loyalty was its principal imperial flaw. However, this was also true of Spain, then as now; regionalism remains the central fault line of the modern Spanish state, of which ETA separatism (and terrorism) is just one example. In the early sixteenth century, the unified kingdoms of Castile and Aragon included numerous territories that had, in living memory, been Moorish principalities (*taifas*), while Portugal was incorporated into Spain in 1580, only to regain its freedom in 1640.[14] In Incan Peru as in Aztec Mexico, no component state or province of the empire was capable of attempting, or willing to attempt, to regain its lost sovereignty. The arrival of the Spanish interlopers suddenly made independence from imperial rule a practical possibility. Accordingly, it was not a small band of gallant conquistadors who conquered the Incas and Aztecs, but an alliance consisting of a core of militarily trained Spaniards together with breakaway, populous states that sought independence from tyrannical overlords.

Such disunity or lack of integration is a flaw characteristic of all imperial hegemonies, and of many states. Regional rivalries and divided loyalties are a perennial of Spanish history. The relative superiority of systems of communication is often most telling in politics and warfare, its "extension by other means." The Castilian monopoly of maritime technology delivered the conquistadors to the Andes, rather than Andeans invading the Iberian peninsula – this technological edge lending support to Diamond's views – but once ashore, they were to confront a vastly superior Incan control of communications. This comprised a vast network of highway(s) and transverse linking roads from Quito down into Chile and Argentina; the supply and "post" *tambo* stations; archipelago and transplant populations (*mitmaqkuna*) for nonlocal provisioning and logistics; and finally a numerous corps of postilions (*chasquis*) whose relays knitted the disparate parts together.[15] This system serendipitously facilitated conquest, not least in speeding the arrival in Cuzco of the conquistadors' indigenous allies from the northern and central Andes.

THE INCAN INFRASTRUCTURE OF SPANISH SETTLEMENT

There can be no successful conquest without successful colonization. Serial military victories followed by a shaky hegemony represent only ephemeral conquest. It is the long term that counts, and in this respect the Spaniards were most fortunate. Spanish settlement in the Andes came easily, once the initial travails of conquest were over. It was made easy by the sophisticated Incan and earlier Andean state infrastructure that was already in place, especially in the Inca heartland. The major axis of colonial prosperity was the "royal road" (*camino real*) that joined Lima, Potosí, Buenos Aires, and intermediate centers, and that followed the Incan road system for much of its distance. Similarly, irrigation canals (many still in use) also linked ecological zones, bringing highland waters to the arid coast, greatly enhancing productive capacity. This was a remarkable achievement that was an indispensable pillar of Andean civilization, because only 4 percent of Peru is at all arable, and no more than 2 percent is under cultivation at any one time.[16] This immense canal system was constructed over many centuries by pre-Inca states, and then further elaborated by the Incas, most notably in building the great agricultural terraces in the arable valleys of the "inner heartland" of the Inca empire. Earlier polities, especially in the Lake Titicaca region, had also constructed terracing as well as raised-field agricultural works. The large cities of Cuzco, Chan Chan, and Huánuco Pampa were complemented by settlements at regular intervals along the coast and in the sierra. Settlement nucleation was already well advanced by the time the Spaniards set foot on Andean soil. The eastern tropical lowlands of the hostile "Antis" were mainly uncolonized, Incan presence there signaled only by a few fortresses that were sometimes ritual complexes: Choquequirao and Machu Picchu are the best-known examples.

Diamond elides not only detail but also a sense of the long-term historical trajectory of Andean polities. Incan settlement patterns had deep roots in pre-Incan states and cultures, most obviously in the case of the Moche, Chimu, Tiahuanaco, and Huari foundations. Yet settlement initiatives long predated the growth of autochthonous states and imperial expansion in the Andes. The so-called archipelago system that conjoined the three ecological niches of coast, highlands, and tropical lowlands depended on communities establishing either temporary or permanent settlements with a view to capturing a supply of products in short supply in the "home" area.[17] The success of these *mitmaqkuna* settlements depended on the forbearance of already existing communities; however, these groups usually had a reciprocal interest in establishing their own far-flung settlements, and for the same ends. This small-scale settlement tradition was, in effect, the embryo of later Incan settlement endeavors. Successive Inca emperors implemented large schemes that involved the translocation of whole populations from one end of their empire to the other. These forced marches were arranged with military precision and under military control. They facilitated imperial reorganization and, above all, served to secure newly conquered polities. This was social engineering on a massive scale: for instance, under Huayna Capac, the Cochabamba region in what is now Bolivia was emptied of its original inhabitants, who were replaced with a cognate population from the north.[18] Manpower was highly controlled under the Incas, with *corvée* labor deployed in agriculture and public works. A highly organized labor force that was tightly controlled at local, regional, and imperial levels presented the early Spaniards with a marvelous opportunity. The early settlers were looking for riches: the great fortunes of the Andes derived from agriculture and silver mining, and these were dependent on a large, well-organized labor force, either free or heavily subsidized. Previous Andean overlords had done the European newcomers a great favor.

To a great degree, then, the early Spanish settlers in some areas of the Andes merely adapted elaborate preconquest infrastructure

FIGURE 8.3 Parish of San Cristóbal. The Corpus of Santa Ana series, ca. 1675–1680. (Source: Cummins et al. 2005: 327, reproduced by permission of Banco de Crédito, Lima)

and labor arrangements.[19] In spite of all that has been written about the epic and rapid Spanish conquest of Peru, the descent line of Inca kings – either puppet captives or insurgents in mountain fastnesses – continued until 1572. Famously, the conquistadors were aided by disaffected polities eager for liberation from Inca suzerainty. After the initial conquest years (to ca. 1531–1536), the principal impediment to stable settlement was the civil war between the several factions of the conquistadors, and between the Pizarro faction and vice-regal forces.

THE MATHEMATICAL EMPIRE

Far from being a rudimentary polity, the Incan capital, the Incan heartland, and the empire of the four quarters ("Tahuantinsuyu") were of an astonishing geometric and arithmetical complexity. This contrasted with the somewhat undeveloped Iberian political organization. Spain (the Crowns of Castile and Aragon) was a congeries of ill-defined regions, newly conquered territories: the 800-year-long *reconquista* from the North African Moors ended only in 1492, such that when Columbus stumbled on the "New World" that year, large

FIGURE 8.4 Marriage of Captain Martín de Loyola with Beatriz Ñusta, ca. 1675–1690, Church of La Compañia. (Source: Wuffarden 2005: 190, reproduced by permission of Banco de Crédito, Lima)

swathes of southern Spain were at least as much African as European. Spanish cities and towns based their politics on Medieval rights charters (*fueros*), several overlapping and thus confusing judicial jurisdictions, a few royal councils (*consejos*), an intricately ordered aristocracy in which powerful lords mixed with poor but titled tenantry, atop an estate system (nobility, clergy, and the unarmigerous and unblessed lower orders) held together by a network of variously inequitable feudal relationships. Politically, Spain was a mess, whereas Inca Peru was a model of good government, albeit of a tyrannical kind. (There were no early modern democracies; the only pre-modern republics were the fractious Italian city-states.) The conquistadors, far from representing a superior political system, went to the Americas partly

FIGURE 8.5 Portrait of unidentified colonial Inca Ñusta, ca. 1730–1750.
(Source: Wuffarden 2005: 2190, reproduced by permission of Banco de
Crédito, Lima)

to escape the social inequities and crushing rural poverty so typical
of regions such as Extremadura, La Mancha, and large swatches of
Castile itself. Famously, many leading conquistadors, Cortés and the
Pizarros among them, came from Extremadura, the direst regional
economy.[20] By contrast, and however harsh an El Niño year, the Inca's
subjects always had enough to eat, a roof over their head and, when of
age, a plot of land to till. Imperial and secondary or local storehouses
(*ccolcas*) and well-stocked way stations (*tambos, tampus*) were guarantees against famine years;[21] unlike, for example, those that devastated
(and still do) the postconquest communities of southern Peru in El
Niño years. Few Spaniards of the early modern era could count on

anything like those Incan blessings: even as late as the 1790s, Spain's population declined markedly attendant on a succession of famines. In such matters at least, Incan administration was vastly superior to successive Spanish state bureaucracies, and Inca emperors displayed more foresight than Habsburg and Bourbon monarchs.

The impressive infrastructure of the Incan empire was in part an outgrowth of earlier advanced Andean polities, not least in its unbroken urban tradition: Chan Chan, like its northern counterparts Teotihuacan and Tenochtitlan, was an enormous city, whereas Cuzco was an urban complex that represented the zenith of Andean architectonic achievement.[22] When in 1950 Cuzco suffered probably the worst earthquake in its history, the Spanish masonry collapsed but the Incan framework suffered scarcely at all. The Incan infrastructure of roads, administrative centers, and storehouses was made possible by, and was a reflection of, its advanced political organization that partly defined and was defined by social, military, fiscal, labor, and ritual organization. Apart from the elaborate highway plus intersecting roads, the infrastructure of production embraced agricultural and pastoral verticality or cultivation across several different ecological tiers defined principally by altitude.

There is abundant evidence that the absence of writing did not exclude a high level of conceptual thinking in Incan imperial organization and, by the same token, in the pre-Incan societies that it superseded, but that had developed most of the social and organizational foundations on which Tahuantinsuyu was constructed. The Ceque system still impresses with its all-embracing complexity that integrated newly conquered (by the Incas) subject populations into the greater empire: a mandala- or spoke-pattern of forty-one lines radiating out from Cuzco's Coricancha or Temple of the Sun, along each of which were strung, at least notionally, eight natural shrines or holy places (*huacas*).[23] The entire Ceque system, as indeed the religious, social, and military organization of the developing empire, was based on a highly accurate calendar. This calendar, the subject of much debate because of the scarce, often conflicting evidence of the Spanish chroniclers, probably served as both a solar and lunar calendar. Many early writers agreed that it comprised twelve months of thirty days, perhaps ordered over eleven ritual months. While this calendar owed much to many centuries of pre-Incan Andean civilization, its principal architect was, according to some traditions, the great reforming emperor Pachacutec Yupanqui, probably in the late fifteenth century.

The Ceque system informed, and was informed by, Incan ideologies of power and social, economic, political, military, and ritual organization. This was overlaid by the four great divisions (*suyus*) of the empire and infused with the traditional Andean system of oppositions and complementarity. Here were the moieties and dual political offices (*kurakazgos*), from provincial lords down to village headmen and (in some areas) headwomen, although in a few areas local political control was organized on a tripartite model (most notably the old Lupaqa kingdom based on Lake Titicaca). Suggestions have been made that *ceques* may have existed in other realms of the empire (e.g., Machaca, in present-day Bolivia). Native chronicler Felipe Guaman Poma de Ayala notes that the Incas intended to reorganize the principal nodes of the empire on the Cuzco model – the so-called New Cuzcos. This suggests that the *ceque* system would have been universalized had Pizarro's destructive forces not arrived at that precise moment in time. As if imperial organization were not elaborate enough, the Incas were progressively reorganizing their conquered realms into decimal units, from high provinces of 40,000 tributary households down to hamlets of ten households, with the traditional Andean office-holding hierarchy being systematically locked into the new systemic logic.[24]

In essence, then, the Incan empire that the Spaniards encountered after 1531 was an immensely sophisticated, layered, and hierarchical polity, in comparison to which European political organization was crude and unwieldy, save for ecclesiastical organization, which, however, did not always obey pragmatic political criteria. Were we to use (anachronistically!) the modern terminology of First World and Third World to describe Habsburg Spain and the Inca empire of the sixteenth century, then in many respects the Inca polity approximated First World development whereas Spain would look more like a Third World country.

RULING THE ANDEAN KINGDOMS

Divide and conquer is the conventional ploy of imperial powers bent on conquest, indeed a metaphor for conquest. Famously, it was the leitmotif of the Spanish conquest of the Americas. Beyond the immediate conquest campaigns, and their sequel in the imposition of imperial rule and the wider colonization process – the military, administrative, fiscal, judicial, civic, and ecclesiastical frameworks of colonialism – the trope of divide and conquer may be extended to embrace some three centuries of colonial rule (1492–1830) in Spanish America. The sixteenth-century neo-Inca insurgencies and related chiliastic uprisings gave way to a century in which anti-imperial sentiment, such as it was, appears to have been almost entirely dormant. Two decades of turmoil occasioned by the conquest finally spent itself, giving way to the reform program of Viceroy Francisco de Toledo (1569–1581) that established the definitive colonial system in the Andes. It was not until 1780 that Spanish hegemony was threatened by anticolonial mass Andean rebellion.

To focus unduly on colonial resistance movements rather obscures the circumstance that by far the greater part of the three centuries of colonial rule was peaceful. Although much effort has been expended on the institutions, social arrangements, and economic life in the colonial Andes, little attention has been directed to the key question of how and why peace was maintained for so long in such an inequitable colonial system. There was never a time when the causes of discontent were lacking; indeed, those selfsame grievances that underlay the open, violent protest of the late colonial era had for the most part always existed. The obverse of the question as to why rebellion was mainly confined to the late eighteenth century is that of how and why the colonial settlement endured for so long unchallenged. Rebellion and protest were exceptions to the rule.

A tiered structure of indigenous officeholders provided the bedrock for both the consolidation of the immediate conquest era and the subsequent three centuries of Spanish hegemony in the Andes. These officials were heirs to the complex, hierarchical Incan bureaucracy. We know from the chronicler Guaman Poma that in the preconquest era there had been a wide variety of petty officials at village level, a sophisticated division of labor that was collapsed into a handful of offices soon after the conquest. In the colonial Andes, these sorted into four groups: the several tiers of the "chieftain" office of *kuraka*, also called *cacique*; the village municipal authorities (e.g., *alcalde*, *regidor*, and *alguacil*); ecclesiastical minor officials, confraternity, and ritual sponsors (*cantor, fiscal, mayordomo, prioste,* and *alférez*); with, finally, the comparatively patrician officeholders representing the surviving Inca nobility of Cuzco, erstwhile capital of the Inca empire, and a few scattered indigenous nobles elsewhere in the viceroyalty. These indigenous governmental offices dovetailed into comparable Hispanic institutions and the overarching governmental *cum* bureaucratic colonial system. Military conquest was necessarily a short-term phenomenon. Spain could not afford a large military presence in its American possessions; a few crack regiments would have to suffice. Political control of the conquered Andean territories depended on controlling the numerous indigenous peoples. In the long term, conquest and colonialism therefore depended utterly on maintaining the loyalty of native Andean officeholders. Had they deserted en masse, colonialism might well have been stopped in its tracks.

Any study of Andean office holding is, then, a study in collaborationism. However, indigenous elites were for the most part not betrayers of their peoples, but rather intermediaries or brokers mediating between the colonial state and the communities they ruled or for which they were otherwise responsible. Colonial archives abound with detailed accounts of exploitative *kurakas/caciques,* yet such illicit behavior is usually all of a piece with the preconquest modus operandi of these local authorities: privileged access to communal resources; marshaling a labor *corvée* from willing or unwilling communities; extraction of taxes in kind or in cash; using such resources to buy allies within and outside of a community; controlling the flow and distribution of scarce produce or sumptuary goods; using force to compel loyalty or just subservience; preeminence in village justice and policing; insertion in religious and sacerdotal networks; mediating with overlords from provincial ruler to even the Inca lords themselves – all these functions were features of the exercise of many *kurakazgos* before 1532. Colonial *kurakas,* great and small, had to straddle two worlds.

CHIEFDOMS AND CADRES UNDER THE INCAS

Diamond overlooks entirely not only the crucial support from non-Incan native allies, but also the overwhelming degree to which any government, Andean or Spanish, depended on a functioning tier of local, regional, and interregional ruling cadres. The hierarchy of chiefdoms embraced powerful ethnic lords (*señores*) as well as humble village officials, all subsumed within the one colonial category of *kuraka* or *cacique*. This generic designation is warranted for all, because they depended on each other and to a large extent developed from one another – a chieftain magnified several times over, like a set of Russian dolls that fit snugly within one another. The most vivid and perhaps the best metaphor for the structure of the Andean chiefdoms is Karen Spalding's image of a "nested tier."[25] This almost perfectly describes the hierarchy of Incan imperial officials ordered in terms of the Incan decimal scheme of imperial administration, and remains a useful shorthand characterization of the several tiers of indigenous governance in the colonial era.

Moreover, as we know from the northern chiefdoms, the famous Incan decimal organization and related impositions on the Inca's subject peoples were often tentative and gradual in their implementation. It was often one step forward and two steps back, such that when the Spaniards arrived, the notional decimal system was either absent or incomplete in the northern marches.[26] The empire of Tahuantinsuyu frayed and unraveled at its edges. The decimal system was superimposed on a vast network of traditional (i.e., pre-Inca) chiefdoms, which continued functioning and operated simultaneously with the somewhat artificial decimal organization. There was considerable integration of these two parallel ruling structures, but it was always clear where precedence lay. Local autonomy was wholly subordinated to the imperatives of the empire. It was precisely resentment at this erosion of autonomy that spurred local polities (*etnias*) to cast their lot with the conquistadores. The Spanish incursion represented an opportunity for a recovery of autonomy in partnership with a powerful ally, which, to all appearances, seemed only interested in booty. In any case, anyone was better than the Incas. Insurgent Andean provinces could always settle accounts later with the newcomers, should they prove recalcitrant. From a native Andean viewpoint, the quarrelsome conquistadores, who were riven by internecine disputes embracing even civil war, were dispensable allies, right from the first moment of contact. It was a gross miscalculation. They couldn't have been more wrong: the Spanish defeat of the Incas presaged the end of the great native lords themselves.

BROKERS AND SOCIAL CLIMBERS:
THE EARLY CONQUEST ERA

In a reprise of the conquest of Mexico, Pizarro's host descended on
Peru to an enthusiastic welcome from some among the subordinate
polities of the Incan empire. The *pax incaica* was an agony for small
kingdoms, for kingdoms they were. Chiefdoms such as the Chimu,
Huanca, and Chincha had been wealthy kingdoms or "feudal"
domains (*reinos, etnias, señoríos*) – the early Spanish chroniclers coined
these designations – before their subjugation to Inca rule. The Chimu
had even consolidated their own empire, which the emergent Incas
of the fourteenth century may have sought to emulate as a model for
their own, greater empire. The glory of autonomy was in some cases
a living memory, such that tribute in kind, labor, and army levies,
and the imposition of Incan satraps and bureaucrats, served only to
underscore what had been lost. Once the Spaniards' aggressive intent
became apparent, however, the possibility of alleviation or liberation
from the reach of Cuzco and its attendant burdens was immediately
grasped by the Inca's forced "allies," most of whom reluctantly provided levies for the Incan armies. Disgruntled Andean polities now
offered martial and logistical support to the Spanish cause, invalu-
able and perhaps indispensable help in the inhospitable terrain that
the conquistadores had to negotiate along the route to Cuzco. As in
Mexico, allies counted.

Their desertion to European ranks correspondingly weakened the
Incan defenses, not least because they understood Incan warfare from
the inside. When the Spaniards laid siege to Cuzco, they were able to
count on the support of several Andean *etnias,* such as the Cañaris
from Ecuador – many of whom were already resident in Cuzco – the
Chachapoyas from the tropical lowlands of the northeastern Peru,
and the numerous Huanca from the central sierra. Famously, the
Spaniards had arrived in the midst of a war of succession to the Incan
throne, between the Cuzco- and Quito-centered pretenders, sons of
the emperor Huayna Capac. The pretender from Quito, Atahuallpa,
had like his father forged strong links with the Cañaris, such that
they came to comprise the Inca's bodyguard. Yet, at the last moment,
they turned, and became the allies of the new invaders.

The three centuries of collaboration by the several levels of
Andean chieftains in the Spanish colonial project throw into stark

relief the long-run degeneration of the *kurakazgo* or *cacicazgo*. The great *kurakas*, the *señores* who had ruled over vast domains, had been conquered by the Incas and incorporated into Tahuantinsuyu, just as the Incas, at the outset of their imperial march, had earlier crushed the smaller, independent warrior chieftains (*sinchis*) in the south. Those once great lords, whom the Çapa Inca had permitted to remain as provincial suzerains, still exercised power albeit in a kind of dominion status, at the point when the conquistadores made their landfall. Availing themselves of the possibility presented by the Spaniards to liberate their polities from Incan hegemony, a number of them willingly provided martial and logistical assistance that was vital to the eventual conquest. For a time, the provincial lords and their "kingdoms" believed themselves free, but only until such time as the conquerors began to set the parameters of colonial domination. The lords had drastically miscalculated in assuming that their martial and logistical support for the Spaniards would result in greater freedom or even full liberation. For a time some of them flourished, but they soon emulated the sad fate of other great lords whose hold on their provinces had quickly disintegrated, not least because their subjects were quick to realize that the new overlords would insist on direct rule, rather than on the maintenance of a loose alliance with the *señores naturales*.[27]

MAKING SENSE OF CONQUEST

The stark ethnocentric contrast of the clever Spaniards versus indigenous dullards who "didn't know what hit them" is a colonial trope that pervades many narrative accounts of the Spanish conquest, not just of the Andean realms, but of the Americas generally. That classic narrative encodes a message that the military conquest and subjugation of indigenous Americans was justified, at least in part, by the need to enlighten intellectually and religiously such benighted creatures of God, so backward that they stood paralyzed when confronted with superior beings, their belated (and not always futile) counterattacks on conquest society notwithstanding. Diamond rejects out of hand any racial explanations for cultural and technological difference, and this is part of the charm of his book. However, the emphasis on literate versus nonliterate societies nevertheless retains a certain flavor of superior versus lesser cultures.

This is necessarily heightened by the fact that Diamond's vignette of the Cajamarca encounter is extracted almost entirely from its monumental context that was the vast, many-layered, and efficiently functioning Inca empire, fortuitously rent asunder by a war of succession raging even as the conquistadors embarked at Tumbés in northern Peru. For historians, context is all, the sine qua non of interpretation and explanation. Diamond's account of the Cajamarca meeting is of a historical episode locked in amber, entirely divorced from the historical trajectory of Andean civilization, or from the astonishing achievements of Incan imperial organization. The arrival of the Spaniards was at first little more than a novel sidebar to that civil war, at first perhaps a mere distraction to the Inca adversaries. Of itself, the Incan civil war lent encouragement to subjugated Andean polities to break free of Incan sovereignty. The centrifugal or balkanizing tendencies within the Inca empire were crucial to Spanish success. In effect, the conquistadors were adopted by their native Andean allies. Even as late as 1570 the Spanish state in the Andes had not entirely subjugated the Inca heartland, where a parallel Inca court ostensibly ruled in the fastnesses of Vilcabamba. The principal reason this alternative Inca state collapsed had less to do with Spanish military might and superior technology than with an internecine rift within the Incan court, for all that the Vilcabamba polity undoubtedly would have collapsed eventually. As ever, divisions within the ruling elite proved decisive in the short term.

Long-run Spanish success in conquering and settling Peru and other Andean possessions rested heavily on the collaboration of native Andean elites, who provided free or thinly subsidized labor for the mines, haciendas, and textile manufactories. Had such collaboration ceased, colonialism in the Andes would have entered a phase of acute crisis. That it failed to do so was a function of a complex constellation of factors, such as the self-interest of those elites, their lack of solidarity with their indigenous charges, and ethnic and racial divisions. When native Andeans did rebel en masse in 1780–1781 – led by an Incan descendent who allegedly spoke Latin – they were defeated not just by a few Spaniards and many creoles, but by armies marshalled by a majority of native (mainly Incan) elites and an army composed overwhelmingly of indigenous foot soldiers.[28] Native elites such as Cuzco's large Inca nobility supported the Spanish Crown because they were now dependent for their standing, authority, and often incomes on the Crown's backing. The great Andean rebellion of 1780–1781 was, then, something of a reprise of the conquest itself. The guns and steel had been decisive only in a handful of battles of the 1530s; most Spanish victories were won on Spain's behalf by their numerous native Andean allies using traditional Andean weaponry. In late colonial Peru even the descendants of the Inca emperors collaborated with the Spaniards against native Andean insurgency. Indeed, by 1780 many Inca nobles were partly Spanish: the conquest ushered in miscegenation.[29] After 1532 Peru was less a land divided between Spaniards and Indians: many people were both, as Figures 8.3 to 8.6 show. Transculturation produced a new, mainstream colonial culture in which native elites participated fully as landowners, merchants, college students, and clergy. In the long run, the creation of this colonial culture arguably did as much to pacify native elites – the only potential counterinsurgent leaders – as did Spain's small standing army.

GERMS ON VIRGIN SOIL

If guns and steel are easily recognizable in conquest accounts, the impact of germs was less visible and by nature insidious. Native Americans simply had no immunity to European diseases, which found a "virgin soil" in which they would proliferate and in which they were extraordinarily virulent. In the long term, epidemics laid waste whole populations, especially in the nucleated polities of the coastal valleys that offered optimal conditions for the nurturing and spread of bacteria and viruses. Germs also cut a swathe through highland populations, though demographic recovery there came sooner. Be that as it may, indigenous population numbers did not recover until the eighteenth century, in contrast to Mexico, where indigenous populations had recovered by the early sixteenth century despite epidemic-driven demographic decline having been even more devastating than in the Andes. In both Mexico and the Andes, the invasion of germs had run its course by 1600, or at least swept aside European and native Andean alike.[30]

There is scant evidence that European disease affected the course or outcome of the wars of conquest in the 1530s. Why this should be so, given the well-known, immediate impact of virgin-soil epidemics, is a puzzle, but may have to do with a reluctance of the conquistador chronicles to ascribe their victories to causes other than their own valor and having God on their side. There is an unresolved debate as to whether smallpox was introduced into the Andean kingdoms at an early or a late date.[31] Consensus on this question is made difficult because of the fact that different terms could be used to describe just one disease, and some terms were used to describe a variety of diseases. Smallpox is a case in point: the correct term was *viruelas,* but this soon came to be used loosely for all manner of fevers. Part of the debate turns on the cause of death in Quito of Huayna Capac, the last unchallenged Inca emperor, whose sons Atahuallpa and Huascar pursued a ruinously protracted an internecine war of succession, into which the Pizarro's host stumbled when they arrived in Peru, and whose divisions greatly facilitated the Spanish conquest. Two of the earliest chroniclers claimed that Huayna Capac died from smallpox before the arrival of the Spaniards, though demographic historian Robert McCaa suggests that a native disease killed him. Were it smallpox, the disease was presumably introduced either through previous contact between natives and Spanish carriers in Mesoamerica and thence introduced by travelers or native traders to the northern Andes, or directly during Pizarro's early 1526 and 1530 expeditions along the coasts of the northern Andes. The date of the great emperor's death is likewise unclear, though ca. 1525 has been suggested. However, the first use of the word *viruelas* comes in 1549, a generation after the conquistadors marched from the coast to the highland town of Cajamarca. If Huayna Capac did indeed die of smallpox, it is strange that his northern army – he had been ruler of Quito since his father's death there – was apparently unaffected by smallpox; again, virgin-soil epidemics take root and spread quickly, above all among native populations with no immunity to European diseases. There is no mention of disease in Cajamarca in 1532. What *can* be said with confidence is that, at least once the Spaniards conquered Cuzco and founded cities, epidemics served to reinforce Spanish control of the Andes. The nature of early settlement and colonial governance often exacerbated the impact of disease; the destruction of indigenous crops by European livestock could cause hunger, and the colonial project of nucleating Andean peoples in towns created optimum conditions within which virulent diseases could wreak havoc.

THE VERDICT

As a metaphor for conquest or for relative cultural development, the Cajamarca encounter as portrayed by Diamond works only if it is abstracted from its historical and cultural context. It serves as a useful literary trope, but has no real heuristic value in that it excludes, from both description and analysis, the role of internecine divisions between Incan elites, regional and ethnic attempts to secede from the empire, and the massive help to the conquistadors provided by the advanced Incan achievements in infrastructure, communications, urban development, labor organization, and taxation systems. It overlooks the millennia-long development of Andean civilization and statehood; the Incas had been in the ascendant for little more than a century. The conquistadors had not just to conquer the Incas, but many centuries of Andean statehood, development, and culture. In failing to draw these elements into his analysis, Diamond misrepresents, perhaps unintentionally, the complexity and achievements of Incan or Andean civilization, which thus becomes a kind of "unenlightened" primitive polity unfavorably contrasted with superior European rationality. Few wars are won just by "guns and steel," but rather by military victory accompanied by morale collapse, a certain anomie. After the battle conquest is by stealth, unless the victor is prepared to maintain a large standing army indefinitely. In Peru, guns and steel were never enough, and germs did most of their work after the military conquest had become a fait accompli.

To secure victory in the long run, and once germs have ravaged populations that coevally develop antibodies to virgin-soil epidemics, colonial hegemony depends on collaborating elites in order to control and exploit indigenous underclasses. During the three centuries after Cajamarca, an Inca nobility in the old capital of Cuzco provided unconditional support for the Crown of Castile. After Cuzco was conquered in 1536, the Inca nobles became an anachronism, stripped of their reason for being. When mass revolt under the aegis of an alleged Inca noble occurred in 1780, all other Inca nobles lent their support to the royalist cause. They did so because their prestige and social standing now depended entirely on the Crown's recognizing them as nobles. If they were powerless, they still retained a certain glamour when they dressed up in royal Incan livery on great public

FIGURE 8.6 Niño Jesús de Huanca dressed as Inca. Cuzco, first half of the eighteenth century. (Private collection, Buenos Aires. Photograph by Héctor Schenone. Source: Estenssoro Fuchs 2005: 139; reproduced by permission of Ramón Mujica Pinilla, Lima)

occasions. Without large-scale collaboration, colonialism collapses, and conquest comes finally to its end station. Diamond's charming sketch of the Cajamarca encounter and the moral it points for understanding comparative cultures and civilizations is, in the final analysis, made possible only by his elision of the achievements of many centuries of Andean civilization, his excising the crucial role of the conquistadors' native allies, and his overlooking the indispensability for any sort of government of the ruling cadres of first Incan, and then colonial Peru.

Notes

* I am professor of modern history at the University of New South Wales, Sydney, Australia. I've also taught at the University of Liverpool (U.K.), the University of Bielefeld (Germany), and Macquarie University (Sydney), and in 2007 I was visiting professor at the École des Hautes Études en Sciences Sociales, Paris.

  With undergraduate academic interests in the history of First Nations peoples and the expansion of early modern Europe after 1492, and having family ties in Lima, Peru, and having backpacked in the Peruvian and Bolivian highlands, I gravitated to study of the Spanish encounter with native Andean societies. Australia's relative proximity to Peru was a happy coincidence: their shores are separated only by the Pacific Ocean, what one historian has termed "The Spanish Lake."

  Research into the colonial encounter in the Andes remains my default research field, although I make frequent forays into related themes such as Incan history, Bourbon Spain, and the Latin American independence movements. Among my recent publications are *From Rebellion to Emancipation in the Andes: Soundings from Southern Peru, 1750–1830* (2002); *Habsburg Peru: Images, Imagination and Memory* (2000), coauthored with Peter Bradley; and *New World, First Nations: Native Peoples of Mesoamerica and the Andes under Colonial Rule* (2006), coedited with Blanca Tovías.

  In 2003 I was awarded the Conference on Latin American History Prize. I am currently finalizing a biography of the Inca José Gabriel Túpac Amaru, the Inca noble who led the mass Great Andean Rebellion of 1780, and researching new projects on the Church in the Independence era as well as the ethnohistory of Southern Peru and Bolivia.

1. This is just one of the popular misconceptions about the Spanish conquest of the Americas: see Matthew Restall's indispensable book *Seven Myths of the Spanish Conquest* 2003; Restall also critiques portrayals of the Cajamarca episode, including that of Diamond's *Guns, Germs, and Steel* 1997. Diamond's *Collapse: How Societies Choose to Fail or Succeed* 2005 contains nothing on Cajamarca but erroneously states that "in five battles in which respectively 169, 80, 30, 110, and 40 Spaniards slaughtered armies of thousands to tens of thousands of Incas, with not a single Spaniard killed and only a few injured" (p. 252). This accepts at face value Spanish boasting and overlooks entirely the contribution of native armies allied with the conquerors; it also underestimates Spanish casualties (not least Juan Pizarro, youngest of the Pizarro brothers, who perished at the siege of Cuzco). The best account of the Spanish conquest of the Andes remains John Hemming's classic narrative *The Conquest of the Incas* 1970.

2. Steele 1994: 110.

3. Scott 1985.

4. Many of the chronicles are available in English translation. Especially revealing are the two native Andean chronicles: Huamán Poma 1978 and Steele 2005. Most accessible is the elegant narrative of Garcilaso de La Vega 2006, written by a "royal mestizo," the son of a conquistador and

an Inca princess, daughter of Huayna Capac. Another great narrative of the conquest is Cieza de León 1998. Cieza was inspired to go to Peru after he witnessed in Seville the gold treasures that were ostensibly the ransom for the captive Atahuallpa; Pizarro took the gold and killed the Inca. Cieza arrived in Peru after the conquest of Cuzco and fought (for the Crown) against the upstart army of Gonzalo Pizarro in 1548. See also the first-hand account by Pizarro 1921.

5. Díaz del Castillo 1963.

6. Some obvious exceptions are Brian Fagan's generalist books on archaeology and climate, and Noam Chomsky's "political" books.

7. In his comments on the symposium papers at the 2006 American Anthropological Association conference held at San Jose, California, Parker Shipton III observed that all of the contributors to the symposium had concentrated on the perceived shortcomings, rather than the positive benefits, of Diamond's books – like Shakespeare's Marc Anthony, they came to bury him, not to praise him.

8. Burke 1992: 234, citing historian Emmanuel Le Roy Ladurie.

9. This tripartite structure–conjuncture–event model structures the masterwork of Braudel 1972, associated with the influential (French) *Annales* School of History, for which see Burke 1990.

10. This was the famous Requirement (*Requerimiento*), which had to be read to indigenous peoples immediately before their surrender or forceful subjugation, and by which the King of Spain announced that any blood spilled as a result of refusal to surrender would be, legally and morally, entirely the fault of the recalcitrant natives: see Seed 1995: 70–73, 87–89. For the Cajamarca episode, see Seed 1991: 7–32.

11. Pallares-Burke 2002: 23, from an extensive interview with Jack Goody at pp. 1–29. See also Goody 2006, a denunciation of the ethnocentric bias of much Western historical writing on non-Western cultures, and its associated appropriation ("theft") of non-Western achievements.

12. Marcus 1992.

13. See especially Salomon 2004; Urton 2003; and the important collection by Quilter and Urton 2002.

14. On Medieval and Islamic Spain, the Christian reconquest (*reconquista*) of the Moorish kingdoms, and the complexities of early Spanish state formation, see MacKay 1977; Harvey 1990.

15. See Hyslop 1984.

16. Robinson 1971.

17. Wilson 1999: chap. 8.

18. Wachtel 1982: 199–235.

19. Lockhart 1994 discusses the early settlement of Peru.

20. Lockhart 1972 gives biographies of the conquistadors who witnessed the capture of the Atahuallpa and participated in the subsequent slaughter of the Inca's retinue and soldiers.

21. LeVine 1992.

22. Von Hagen and Morris 1998.

23. Zuidema 1964; Bauer 1998.
24. Julien 1988.
25. Spalding 1984: 216–238 discusses the upper strata of indigenous elites and office holders. See also Ramírez 1987.
26. Salomon 1986.
27. See Wachtel 1977: 109–135 for an important exception: Francisco Chilche, who built himself a new constituency under the Spaniards. Francisco de Toledo, Viceroy of Peru, put an end to Chilche's influence around 1570.
28. There is an immense bibliography on eighteenth-century Andean rebellions. The best introduction to the (José Gabriel) Túpac Amaru rebellion of 1780–1782 is Walker 1999: chap. 2. See also Thomson 2002; Robins 2002.
29. On the colonial Inca nobles, see Bradley and Cahill 2000; Cahill 2006; Garrett 2005.
30. The best overview is Cook 1998. See also Crosby 1986; McNeill 1976.
31. Robert McCaa and Noble David Cook are the principal protagonists: see McCaa and Nimlos 2004.

Bibliography

Bauer, Brian S. 1998. *The Sacred Landscape of the Inca: The Cusco Ceque System.* Austin: University of Texas Press.

Bradley, Peter and David Cahill. 2000. *Habsburg Peru: Images, Imagination and Memory.* Liverpool: Liverpool University Press.

Braudel, Fernand. 1972 [1949]. *The Mediterranean and the Mediterranean World in the Age of Philip II.* Translated by Siân Reynolds. New York: Harper & Row.

Burke, Peter. 1990. *The French Historical Revolution: The Annales School, 1929–89.* Stanford, CA: Stanford University Press.

Burke, Peter. 1992. "History of Events and the Revival of Narrative," in *New Perspectives on Historical Writing.* Edited by Peter Burke, pp. 233–248. Cambridge: Polity Press.

Cahill, David. 2006. "A Liminal Nobility: The Incas in the Middle Ground of Late Colonial Peru," in *New World, First Nations: Native Peoples of Mesoamerica and the Andes under Colonial Rule.* Edited by David Cahill and Blanca Tovías, pp. 169–195. Brighton: Sussex Academic Press.

Cieza de León, Pedro de. 1998. *The Discovery and Conquest of Peru: Chronicles of the New World Encounter.* Edited and translated by Alexandra Parma Cook and Noble David Cook. Durham, NC: Duke University Press.

Cook, Noble David. 1998. *Born to Die: Disease and New World Conquest, 1492–1650.* Cambridge: Cambridge University Press.

Crosby, Alfred W. 1986. *Ecological Imperialism: The Biological Expansion of Europe, 900–1900.* Cambridge: Cambridge University Press.

Cummins, Thomas, Gabriela Ramos, Elena Phipps, Juan Carlos Estenssoro, Luis Eduardo Wuffarden, and Natalia Majluf. Editors. 2005. *Los Incas, Reyes del Perú.* Lima: Banco de Crédito.

D'Altroy, Terence N. 2001. "Politics, Resources, and Blood in the Inka Empire," in *Empires: Perspectives from Archaeology and History*. Edited by Susan E. Alcock, Kathleen D. Morrison, and Carla M. Sinopoli, pp. 201–226. Cambridge: Cambridge University Press.

Diamond, Jared. 1997. *Guns, Germs, and Steel: The Fates of Human Societies*. New York: W. W. Norton.

Diamond, Jared. 2005. *Collapse: How Societies Choose to Fail or Succeed*. New York: Viking.

Díaz del Castillo, Bernal. 1963. *The Conquest of New Spain*. Translated by J. M. Cohen. Baltimore: Penguin Books.

Estenssoro Fuchs, Carlos. 2005. "Construyendo la memoria: la figura del inca y el reino del Perú, de la conquista a Túpac Amaru II," in *Los Incas, Reyes del Perú*. Edited by Thomas Cummins, Gabriela Ramos, Elena Phipps, Juan Carlos Estenssoro, Luis Eduardo Wuffarden, and Natalia Majluf, pp. 93–173. Lima: Banco de Crédito.

Garcilaso de La Vega, El Inca. 2006 [1609]. *Royal Commentaries of the Incas and General History of Peru*. Translated by Harold V. Livermore, abridged and edited by Karen Spalding. Indianapolis: Hackett.

Garrett, David T. 2005. *Shadows of Empire: The Indian Nobility of Cusco, 1750–1825*. Cambridge: Cambridge University Press.

Goody, Jack. 2006. *The Theft of History*. Cambridge: Cambridge University Press.

Harvey, L. P. 1990. *Islamic Spain 1250 to 1500*. Chicago: University of Chicago Press.

Hemming, John. 1970. *The Conquest of the Incas*. London: Macmillan.

Huamán Poma (Don Felipe Huamán Poma de Ayala). 1978 [1613] . *Letter to a King: A Picture-History of the Inca Civilisation*. Edited by Christopher Dilke. London: Allen and Unwin.

Hyslop, John. 1984. *The Inka Road System*. New York: Academic Press.

Julien, Catherine J. 1988. "How the Inca Decimal System Worked." *Ethnohistory* 35(3):257–279.

LeVine, Terry Y. Editor. 1992. *Inka Storage Systems*. Norman: University of Oklahoma Press.

Lockhart, James. 1972. *The Men of Cajamarca: A Social and Biographical Study of the First Conquerors of Peru*. Austin: University of Texas Press.

Lockhart, James. 1994. *Spanish Peru, 1532–1560: A Social History*. 2nd ed. Madison: University of Wisconsin Press.

MacKay, Angus. 1977. *Spain in the Middle Ages: From Frontier to Empire, 1000–1500*. London: Macmillan.

Marcus, Joyce. 1992. *Mesoamerican Writing Systems: Propaganda, Myth, and History in Four Ancient Civilizations*. Princeton, NJ: Princeton University Press.

McCaa, Robert and Aleta Nimlos. 2004. "Why Blame Smallpox? The Death of the Inca Huayna Capac and the Demographic Destruction of Tawantinsuyu (Ancient Peru)." Paper presented to the American Historical Association Annual Meeting, Washington DC, 9 January 2004. Available at http://www.hist.umn.edu/~rmccaa/aha2004/index.htm.

McNeill, William H. 1976. *Plagues and Peoples*. Garden City, NY: Anchor Press.

Pallares-Burke, Maria Lúcia G. 2002. *The New History*. Cambridge: Polity Press.

Pizarro, Pedro. 1921 [1571]. *Relation of the Discovery and Conquest of the Kingdoms of Peru*. Translated by Philip Ainsworth Means. New York: Cortes Society.

Quilter, Jeffrey and Gary Urton. Editors. 2002. *Narrative Threads: Accounting and Recounting in Andean Khipu*. Austin: University of Texas Press.

Ramírez, Susan E. 1987. "The '*Dueño De Indios*': Thoughts on the Consequences of the Shifting Bases of Power of the '*Curaca De Los Viejos Antiguos*' under the Spanish in Sixteenth-Century Peru." *Hispanic American Historical Review* **67**(4):575–610.

Restall, Matthew. 2003. *Seven Myths of the Spanish Conquest*. New York: Oxford University Press.

Robins, Nicholas A. 2002. *Genocide and Millenialism in Upper Peru: The Great Rebellion of 1780–1782*. Westport, CT: Praeger.

Robinson, David. 1971. *Peru in Four Dimensions*. Detroit: Blaine Ethridge.

Salomon, Frank. 1986. *Native Lords of Quito in the Age of the Incas: The Political Economy of North-Andean Chiefdoms*. Cambridge: Cambridge University Press.

Salomon, Frank. 2004. *The Cord Keepers: Khipus and Cultural Life in a Peruvian Village*. Durham, NC: Duke University Press.

Scott, James C. 1985. *Weapons of the Weak: Everyday Forms of Peasant Resistance*. New Haven, CT: Yale University Press.

Seed, Patricia. 1991. "'Failing to Marvel': Atahualpa's Encounter with the Word." *Latin American Research Review* **26**(1):7–32.

Seed, Patricia. 1995. *Ceremonies of Possession in Europe's Conquest of the New World, 1492–1640*. Cambridge: Cambridge University Press.

Spalding, Karen. 1984. *Huarochirí: An Andean Society under Inca and Spanish Rule*. Stanford, CA: Stanford University Press.

Steele, Ian K. 1994. *Warpaths: Invasions of North America, 1613–1765*. New York: Oxford University Press.

Steele, Ian K. 2005 [1570]. *Titu Cusi: A 16th-Century Account of the Conquest* [Don Diego de Castro Titu Cusi Yupanki]. Translated by Nicole Delia Legnani. Cambridge, MA: Harvard University Press.

Thomson, Sinclair. 2002. *We Alone Will Rule: Native Andean Politics in the Age of Insurgency*. Madison: University of Wisconsin Press.

Urton, Gary. 2003. *Signs of the Inka Khipu: Binary Coding in the Andean Knotted-String Records*. Austin: University of Texas Press.

von Hagen, Adriana and Craig Morris. 1998. *The Cities of the Ancient Andes*. London: Thames and Hudson.

Wachtel, Nathan. 1977 [1971]. *The Vision of the Vanquished: the Spanish Conquest of Peru through Indian Eyes*. Translated by Ben and Siân Reynolds. Trowbridge: Harvester Press.

Wachtel, Nathan. 1982. "The Mitimas of the Cochabamba Valley: The Colonization Policy of Huayna Capac," in *The Inca and Aztec States*,

1400–1800: Anthropology and History. Edited by George A. Collier, Renato I. Rosaldo, and John D. Wirth, pp. 199–235. New York: Academic Press.

Walker, Charles. 1999. *Smoldering Ashes: Cuzco and the Creation of Republican Peru, 1780–1840.* Durham, NC: Duke University Press.

Wilson, David J. 1999. *Indigenous South Americans of the Past and Present: An Ecological Perspective.* Boulder: Westview Press.

Wuffarden, Luis Eduardo. 2005. "La descendencia real y el 'renacimiento inca' en el virreinato," in *Los incas, reyes del Perú.* Edited by Thomas Cummins et al., pp. 175–251. Lima: Banco de Crédito.

Zuidema, R. Tom. 1964. *The Ceque System of Cuzco: The Social Organization of the Capital of the Inca.* Leiden: E. J. Brill.

9

Rwandan Genocide

Toward an Explanation in Which History and Culture Matter

Christopher C. Taylor[*]

INTRODUCTION

In April 1994 Hutu militias in Rwanda killed nearly a million people, mainly Tutsis. Why did this happen? In Jared Diamond's *Collapse: How Societies Choose to Fail or Succeed*,[1] one chapter seeks to explain the genocide in Malthusian terms. Thomas Malthus, an eighteenth-century economist and demographer, was not the first to attribute the terms "dismal science" to economics – his countryman Thomas Carlyle was – but Malthus's thinking is certainly in line with the sentiment that Carlyle expressed: the idea of perennial scarcity or deprivation. According to Malthus, while food production can increase only arithmetically, human populations increase geometrically, hence their propensity to outstrip food production sooner or later. The only correctives to an ever increasing population and the prospect of future famine are equally dismal: war and disease.[2] As a twentieth-century demonstration of Malthus's principles, Diamond cites Rwanda and the genocide of 1994. He pays particular attention to the commune of Kanama, whose population density in 1994 exceeded that of the world's most densely populated agricultural country, Bangladesh. However, Diamond pays scant attention to the political situation in Rwanda in the years leading up to the genocide; nor does the country's history and culture figure in Diamond's story.

There is just enough truth in Diamond's argument to make it superficially seductive. Indeed, Rwanda is very densely populated. Its

FIGURE 9.1 Map of Rwanda.

population density exceeds that of Japan's most populated islands, but its economy is far less diverse. Over 90 percent of its population gains its livelihood from farming. Most of Rwanda's arable land is already under cultivation, and very little other land is available to absorb a population that has been growing at an average annual rate of about 3 percent. Occasionally famines have occurred. However, even during the colonial period, which began in the mid-1890s and endured until 1962, Rwanda was described as an overpopulated country. If the conditions of overpopulation were of longstanding nature (probably a century or so), why did it take until 1994 for a genocide to occur? Of course, Rwanda's dense population and limited amount of land contributed to social tensions in the country. But it is quite another thing to find confirmation of Malthusian principles in all this. If so, one would have found widespread evidence of land-hungry peasants attacking and killing their more prosperous neighbors during the genocide. Diamond's only example is the

FIGURE 9.2 Christopher Taylor, 1984, during his first field season in Rwanda with the intricately terraced and intensively cultivated landscape of Rwanda in the background.

commune of Kanama, and it is dubious that most of the killings there constituted a struggle over limited resources. If Diamond's scenario were correct, this would have been class warfare at its starkest. But this is not what occurred.

Although social tensions due to class differences certainly existed in Rwanda before the genocide, these were not the fault lines along which the social fabric came asunder. Instead we must consider ethnic and regional politics in Rwanda, and the invasion of Rwanda from the north by deserters from the Ugandan army calling themselves the Rwandan Patriotic Front (RPF), who were by no means predominantly land-hungry peasants nor even 100 percent Tutsi. The main questions that should be answered when looking for causes of the Rwandan genocide are: why did this occur in this particular place (there are many other areas of the world characterized by dense population and land shortage), and why did it occur at this particular time, and with this particular group of people?

MY PERSONAL EXPERIENCE IN RWANDA

Before addressing the above questions, however, I would like to explain that I have lived and done anthropological fieldwork in

Rwanda on several occasions (1983–1985, 1987, 1993–1994, and 2005). Although I have always cautioned students against attempting to generalize from their personal experience, I believe that my experience in 1994 will help to elucidate the analysis of the Rwandan genocide.

On 6 April 1994 I was living in Kigali, Rwanda, and working as a behavioral research specialist for Family Health International on a project intended to combat STDs and HIV. Although I had been in Rwanda for over five months and was well aware of the deteriorating political situation, I was not at all prepared for the events that were to transpire that evening. At about 8 P.M., I received a phone call from another American, a Kigali resident whose responsibilities included contacting other Americans in times of danger. He warned me to stay at home because there were rumors that the president's plane had been shot at.

At the time I thought the threat to order was not serious, just a pretext on the part of the president's more extremist supporters to set up roadblocks and rob anyone they happened to catch in their traps. That was their usual *modus operandi,* and I had come close to getting caught in such binds more than once. Twice stones had been thrown at my car, and I had to beat a quick retreat in reverse gear. So that Wednesday evening of 6 April, I decided not to go out to a restaurant. My fiancée, Espérance (now my wife), a Rwandan Tutsi, and I retired a bit before midnight as usual. Neither of us believed that anything momentous was in the works. Then about 3:00 A.M. our house watchman came to the bedroom window and woke us up. He said, "They've just announced on the radio that the president's plane has been shot down near the airport and he is dead. Everyone is supposed to remain at home." I asked him if he preferred to stay inside the house, but he declined. We drifted back to sleep. An hour or so later we were awakened by loud noise. It was the sound of combat: small arms fire, grenades, and the booms of mortar and artillery shells. The degeneration of the situation that I had witnessed for months had come to a head.

Nine months of shaky truce between the Rwandan Government Forces (RGF) and the Rwandan Patriotic Front (RPF) had come to an end. The RGF started the attack, blaming the RPF and all Tutsis in general for the death of President Habyarimana. As part of the Arusha accords (in August 1993) the RPF had been allowed to bivouac six hundred men at the Conseil National du Développement (National Council for Development) in Remera, a Kigali suburb. Not far from the RPF encampment, the UN troop contingent had their headquarters. Shortly after Habyarimana's assassination, the RPF announced over their radio station, Radio Muhabura, that they had had nothing to do with it. They had not fired the missiles nor authorized anyone else to do so. They issued a general appeal for calm, saying that they would not take hostile action unless attacked. By early Thursday morning, however, their encampment at the CND was under heavy fire, but much of the ordinance that we heard exploding was not directed at the RPF headquarters. Hutu politicians opposed to Habyarimana and some Tutsi were being surrounded at their homes by RGF soldiers or Hutu militia members and slaughtered along with everyone in their households.

My fiancée and I remained at home for the next two days as fighting raged all around us. I moved a mattress into the house's central corridor. There were bedrooms on both sides of this corridor whose windows and doors I closed. I stood other mattresses up on their sides and propped them against both sides of the corridor to act as a buffer in the event that bullets or shrapnel might penetrate the walls. I closed all the other windows and doors in the house, opening a few of them only when noise of the fighting subsided. I brought into the corridor a radio that received two bands of commercial short wave and listened to it until its batteries went dead, then hooked it up to a 12 volt car battery until that died about a day later. It was from listening to the BBC World Service that we obtained the most accurate information about what was happening in Rwanda. All we heard on Rwandan radio was the occasional announcement that the president had been killed and that the population was to remain at home. These announcements, always the same, came about once every hour. The rest of the time local stations played classical music.

By late morning of Thursday, 7 April, we were fairly well aware of what was happening around us. Our house watchman, for example, learned from the watchman in the next house, who had learned from the watchman in the house next to his, that Liberal Party leader Landouald Ndasingwa, a Tutsi, had been murdered. He had been killed along with his Canadian wife, Hélene, their children, and his wife's aging mother. The news came as a shock; "Lando" and

Hélene were friends of mine. Both had worked for the United States Information Service during my earliest stint of fieldwork in Rwanda, and both had helped me during that time. I was deeply saddened by their deaths and shocked that it had happened just two houses away from where I lived. From the front room of our house, I could just barely see above the front wall of our enclosure and discern the heads of people walking one way or the other. Many were carrying objects and bundles on their heads: they were looters carting off Lando's and Hélene's belongings. What is to stop them from coming in here? I thought. What will they do when they see that I am living with a Tutsi? Will they rape her in front of me and then kill us both? This fear was reinforced when our watchman told us that twice soldiers had come to our gate and asked him if Belgians lived there. He had told them no, these were Americans.

Fighting subsided a little that Thursday afternoon. I went out into the yard and chatted with Belgian neighbors who lived on one side. I had never met them before, but found them to be quite friendly and pleasant. They seemed to think that the present situation would be resolved without much delay. I didn't tell them what our watchman had told me earlier, that soldiers were knocking on gates and asking if Belgians lived there. Later I would learn that Belgians, as well as the RPF and all Tutsi in general, were being blamed for the downing of Habyarimana's airplane. Two white men wearing Belgian uniforms had apparently been seen in the vicinity of where the missiles had allegedly been fired. Later on 7 April, ten Belgian soldiers who had been guarding an important Hutu opposition politician, Madame Prime Minister Agathe Uwiringiyimana, were taken prisoner by RGF forces and brutally slaughtered. In the days that followed, the UN withdrew all but a couple hundred peacekeeping forces.

Friday night, 8 April, was especially bad. The battle for Kigali between RGF and RPF soldiers was now well underway. Mortars and artillery shells must have been flying right over our heads, for behind our house an RGF camp was situated at a distance of about a quarter to a half mile. From the front porch of our house, I could make out the hillsides of Remera where the RPF battalion had their encampment. We were directly in the line of fire between these two points. This was not a comforting thought. Sleep that night came in short bits. I would nod off from sheer fatigue, only to be reawakened by the boom and tremor of a nearby explosion. Sometimes, while asleep, an especially loud explosion would cause all the muscles in my body to contract involuntarily, and I would leap from the mattress, expecting to see soldiers in front of me.

At around midnight I heard what sounded like firecrackers slowly advancing in our direction. It was small arms fire, I guessed, rifles and pistols. Every now and then the cracks and pops were punctuated by an explosion. Those must be grenades, I thought. The noises inched closer and closer, growing louder as they advanced. Soon they sounded like they were right on top of us, with every grenade explosion shaking our house. Both of us listened, clinging to the bed sheet as if it were a shield, petrified with fear. That's it, I thought, a grenade or mortar shell is going to come down right on our house, right on our heads. But the noises moved on. They must be out in the street right in front of our house, a fire fight between an RPF patrol and RGF soldiers. I followed the noise of the battle, imagining where it was going as it receded into the distance. First it moved to the left past our house and then farther down the street. Then it began to move to the area behind us, apparently heading in the direction of the RGF camp. It must have been an RPF patrol trying to attack the camp. Soon shots were being exchanged with such frequency that it was hard to distinguish one from another. "They're attacking the Rwandan Army base behind us," I said to Espérance.

The battle became furious, but about ten minutes or so later it began to move the other way. Why were they giving up so quickly, I wondered? I wanted them to overrun the RGF camp. Although I had met soldiers on both sides in the days leading up to this and considered one RGF soldier a friend, as a group I trusted the RPF more, because they were much more professional than the RGF. I was also well aware of what the RGF soldiers were up to. They were murdering innocent people in their homes and then looting their possessions. They were committing genocide. But the RPF attackers were not going to take the camp that evening; they were withdrawing and coming back the way they had come. Slowly the cracks and booms grew louder once again. Then they were on top of us a second time. This time it was worse. The RPF had rattled a hornet's nest, and the hornets were in hot pursuit. One explosion shook the house so badly that I thought for sure that it had been hit. The battle moved down the street, and gradually it dissolved into the general din of that night's shots and explosions.

On Saturday morning, 9 April, the battle continued but with less intensity. One would hear short bursts of automatic rifle fire and occasional booms from mortar and artillery. I felt confident enough to venture out of the corridor and inspect the inside of the rest of the house, thinking that I would certainly find a portion of it that had been blown away. But it was still intact, with not even a sign of shrapnel damage. I was utterly amazed. I opened the front door of the house and walked out into the yard and around the perimeter of the house. I saw nothing in my yard that looked like a crater from a mortar shell or a grenade. We had come through another night unscathed. I chatted with the neighbors. By now the car battery that had sustained our radio for at least twenty-four hours was dead. My neighbors were the only source of news, and they knew little more than I did. Occasionally a car or pickup truck would zoom down the street in front of the house. Hoping it might be the UN, I walked over to the metal gate and opened it slightly to get a better look. The cars were not those of the UN. They were those of ordinary Rwandan citizens carting off loads of cargo, motorized looters squirrelling away their booty in wholesale quantities. When will it be our turn to be looted? When will they come here? Then I heard the noise of a helicopter. As it drew closer I could read "UN" on its underside. Two Rwandan soldiers on the other side of the street also saw the helicopter and began firing their automatic rifles gleefully in its direction. The helicopter banked upward and retreated back in the same direction from which it had come. It was not going to take any risks. The two soldiers laughed uproariously.

Sometime after noon that day, I heard a loud banging on the gate. "Chris! Chris! Get your stuff together. We're being evacuated. You've got five minutes to get your stuff together." It was Chris Grundman of USAID. He was going around the neighborhood, rounding up Americans. I opened the gate, and he ran into our house. "Get a white cloth or a towel and put it on the antenna of your car." Then he saw a sheet on a bed and began tearing it apart. "Here, take this and tie it to the antenna. Drive over to the American school. You'll meet Rwandan soldiers along the way. Don't speak any Kinyarwanda to them. Hurry up, you've got five minutes. We've gotta get out of here."

Then he ran out, jumped into the car that a Rwandan appeared to be driving, and sped off.

On the drive to the school we did indeed encounter a group of Rwandan soldiers. There were four of them standing beside a green Peugot. Most likely they had looted it from someone in the neighborhood. One of them carried a translucent plastic jerry can, two-thirds full of what appeared to be gasoline. I knew it wasn't for their car; it was for setting houses on fire. Another one of them had a rifle with a grenade on the end of it that he enjoyed sticking in my face.

"Where are the arms?" he asked in broken French. "Where is money? Where you going? Where you come from? Where is your house?"

I tried to summon my composure, although I could feel the trembling in my legs. "We're being evacuated. We don't have any arms. We're supposed to go to the American school."

"Give us the weapons!"

"We don't have any weapons," I replied to the one with the grenade on his rifle. He walked around the car and stuck the rifle in Espérance's face.

He asked her questions in Kinyarwanda. Luckily for her, she remembered Chris Grundman's advice. She feigned ignorance of Kinyarwanda and would respond to the soldiers only when they asked her questions in French. Had she responded in Kinyarwanda, that would have affirmed what they already suspected from Espérance's physiognomy – that she was Tutsi. They would have killed her right then and there.

"Who are you? Where is your house?"

"I am that man's wife," she said pointing to me. "We live back there," pointing in the direction from which we had come.

Another soldier who seemed more reflective than his eager comrade, began to pose other questions. "What nationality are you?" he asked.

"I am an American," she responded in French. Luckily he didn't speak any English, for if he had tried that on her, it would have surely given her away.

"A black American?"

"Yes, a black American."

"Show me some identification."

"He has it," she said pointing to me.

"Show it," he asked me.

Luckily I still had a picture ID with me that said "Ambassade des Etats-Unis" (United States Embassy). It didn't mean that I was a diplomat or that I was an important person, nor did it say anything about Espérance. All the card meant was that as an American and indirect USAID employee, I could enter the U.S. Embassy in Kigali without a great deal of screening from the guard at the entryway. But the Rwandan soldier did not know that. To him it must have seemed that I was someone he shouldn't hassle too much.

"OK. You may go," he said as he moved to the side of our car. His colleague with the rifle grenade looked disappointed; he had wanted to do more.

At the American school we saw at least sixty people and about twenty or thirty cars. Someone told us to sign our names in a notebook that was being passed around and to indicate how much gas we had in our car. My gas gauge was almost on empty. Someone said that we should leave the car there and double up with someone who had more gas. We found an employee of Project San Francisco named Jackie, who had come by herself in a little white Suzuki. She was happy to let us ride with her.

The plan was to drive in a long convoy of cars, each bearing a paper American flag Scotch-taped to the rear window and a white towel or sheet tied to the antenna. We would drive southward from Kigali to Butare. There was no hostile action between the opposing sides along this route because virtually all RPF soldiers were concentrated in areas to the north of Kigali. Then we would continue on southward to Bujumbura, Burundi. We waited for others to show up at the American school for another hour or so. Soon, though, the noise of grenades and mortar shells began to intensify. Directly to the side of the American school, I could see a small group of Rwandan soldiers who were launching mortars in what seemed to be the vague direction of the CND. One could hear the booming thump of each shell as it was launched. I had a sinking feeling; it wouldn't take long for the RPF to determine where those mortars are coming from, and they would respond with ordinance of their own. This would place us right next to an important target. Others must have been thinking the same thing, for shortly thereafter it was decided that we should leave. The front gates of the compound swung open, and a long line of cars began filing out.

To gain access to the Butare road we had to pass through parts of the Kiyovu section of Kigali and through Kigali's large traffic circle known as the Round Point. As our cars filed through, groups of Rwandans lined the streets and watched us. Some waved and smiled. Others looked at us in a blank and slightly puzzled way. Over and over as I looked at those faces the words repeated in my head, "Après nous, le déluge." But who among us, I also thought, would choose to stay in Rwanda?

RGF soldiers who stopped us at our first roadblock hardly a half mile downhill from the Round Point seemed to be in a terrible mood. Many had bloodshot eyes either from lack of sleep or from drinking alcohol and smoking marijuana, which were both in evidence. Cases of unopened Primus beer could be seen here and there, and soldiers were sitting on the plastic crates. Soldiers paced ominously up and down the long line of cars, some carrying weapons that I had never seen in my life even at military parades. Catching sight of Espérance, one of them came over to our car and said "Muraho," the standard greeting in Kinyarwanda. She didn't respond. He came over to our window and asked us some questions in Kinyarwanda. It made me extremely nervous, but she didn't flinch. Then he asked us some questions in French. We answered his questions, and he walked away. There were several more roadblocks. Each one seemed to take an eternity. At just about every barrier, a soldier or two would come over to the car and say something to us in Kinyarwanda in the attempt to flush out Espérance as a fleeing Tutsi.

Our convoy was the first that they had had to deal with. I learned two weeks later in Nairobi that subsequent convoys had fared very badly at the hands of these soldiers. Suspected Tutsi or Hutu opposition politicians were pulled from cars and summarily executed either in front of everyone or later. One Rwandan that I met about a week later at the Nairobi airport told me that the car he had been traveling in had been fired on; one of its occupants had been killed and two others had been wounded.

At the end of what must have been a ten- or twelve-hour journey, we arrived in Bujumbura and went to an upscale, modern hotel. There all the American refugees assembled in a large conference room and listened to a representative from the U.S. Embassy. We filled out forms and then were told by a hotel employee how and where to register to get a room. All anyone could think about was sleep. The next day virtually everyone who had come with us was air-evacuated by U.S. forces to Nairobi. Espérance and I stayed behind because an Embassy official had expressed doubts about whether, as a Rwandan, Espérance would have been allowed on the flight.

Espérance and I stayed a few days longer in Bujumbura and then got a commercial flight to Nairobi. We spent the next four months in Nairobi, our ears still ringing from the events that we had just lived through in Rwanda. We would meet with former friends and acquaintances and learn of the death of others. Because of the horror of the genocide and the subsequent discrediting of those associated with it, most Rwandans, whether Tutsi or Hutu, claimed to support the RPF. Only a few did not. One among my former friends who was not an RPF supporter and who thought that elements of the Mouvement Révolutionnaire National pour le Développement et la Démocratie (MRND), the party of the assassinated president, should eventually be allowed to participate in a new Rwandan government pointed out to me that unless this was done, "ethnocracy" was likely to remain the dominant mode of governance for years to come. Once the RPF took over Rwanda, which appeared more and more likely as the civil war progressed, the Tutsi extremist contingent within it would seize control, and there would be an abusive "Tutsi-cracy" in Rwanda, where once there had been an abusive "Hutu-cracy." Things should return to the state that they were in during the 1980s, he claimed: limited Tutsi participation in politics, but full rights for Tutsi in the economic arena. At the time I dismissed my friend's ideas, although in subsequent years some of what he had predicted indeed came to pass.

In April and May only a trickle of Tutsi refugees made it to Nairobi. A few had probably gone elsewhere, to Burundi, Tanzania, or Zaire. Estimates claim that probably 80 percent of Rwanda's Tutsi did not survive the genocide.[3] Once in Kenya, Rwandan Tutsi were met with hostility from the Kenyan government. Kenyan President Daniel Arap Moi had been a close friend and ally of Habyarimana and an opponent of the RPF. As weeks and then months went by, more and more of the Rwandan refugees entering Kenya were Hutu fleeing the RPF advance. These refugees were treated much better by the Kenyan government and were even permitted to engage in international arms trade to reequip the RGF. By mid-July 1994 most of the RGF had been forced to flee to eastern Zaire, and a new government was in power in Rwanda.

BACKGROUND

In addition to the complex political situation, elements of which I have sketched through my personal experiences, both the history and culture of Rwanda have to be examined to understand what happened. Looking back about 200 years, we find that inequality had already begun to characterize relations among Rwanda's three ethnic groups: Tutsi, Hutu, and Twa. This was before any European ever set foot on Rwandan soil. At the time Tutsi were predominantly cattle herders. Despite their being a numerical minority, most members of the elite came from this group. Rwanda was ruled by a king who was Tutsi, and most of his close followers were Tutsi, although many and possibly most Tutsi were not particularly privileged, nor substantially better off than Hutu. Hutu, who were the majority of the population, gained their livelihood from cultivating the land. Some enjoyed relatively privileged positions in the society, but most were subordinate to Tutsi cattle lords, and many were impoverished. Twa, the least well-off of the three groups, were a very small minority. Originally they had lived by hunting and gathering, but as Rwanda's forests were cleared to make way for farms and pasture lands, most became potters. Many were also musicians and entertainers, and a few enjoyed privileged status among the king's retainers.

We need to recognize the failure of German, then Belgian, colonialists to address these ethnic cleaveages during the colonial period (1895–1962).[4] Although colonialists did not invent the ethnic labels, nor create the original conditions of inequality, their interference in the Rwandan social system worsened the situation. Relying on nineteenth-century ideas about human differences that were racist in nature, they believed that Tutsi were closer to white Europeans and intellectually superior to Hutu and Twa. Europeans believed that they should rule through the existing Tutsi elite and, if anything, enhance its control of the country. Social inequality for the Europeans was simply a fact of nature. It was to be expected that Tutsi should rule in Rwanda, the Europeans thought, just as it was natural for white Europeans to dominate the world. Why attempt to redress the grievances of the oppressed Hutu majority, the colonialists reasoned, when that oppression stemmed from immutable biological causes?

Later, in the years preceding Rwandan independence in 1962, mission-educated Hutu became increasingly politicized and increasingly vocal in their opposition to this system. Negative reactions to them from the Rwandan king and Tutsi traditionalists eventually led to a Hutu revolution that resulted in the overthrow of the monarchy.[5] Then, however, supporters of the new Hutu government proceeded to exact revenge. Thousands of Tutsi were killed, and tens of thousands fled to neighboring countries such as Uganda. This government, dominated by Hutu from central and southern Rwanda, continued to persecute Tutsi whenever and wherever it suited their purpose until 1973, when a northern Hutu military man, Major General Juvenal Habyarimana, seized the reins of power. He and a clique of northern Rwandan Hutu proceeded to run the country for the next two decades.

President Habyarimana brought the most extreme measures of Tutsi persecution to an end and instituted a policy of ethnic and regional equilibrium. In principle this policy seemed well intentioned. Every ethnic group and every region of Rwanda, according to its percentage of the population, was to be granted a share of state jobs and admission to institutions of higher learning. The reality, however, was much different. Hutu from northern Rwanda (Habyarimana's own region) benefitted disproportionately from the system, whereas Tutsi never received their allotted 10 percent of jobs and school placements. In addition, the Habyarimana government retained many of the previous Hutu government's policies that kept Tutsi in a state of second-class citizenship. Rwanda's national ID cards, for example, had one's ethnicity stamped on the card, and one's chances in life depended on it. If one were Tutsi, one could not serve in the national army, nor occupy a high position in government.

Rwandan Tutsi did their best to make the most of a difficult situation. Many sought employment in the private sector or with international organizations, and many, despite the obstacles arrayed against them, managed to receive secondary school or even university-level educations. In the meantime the expatriate Tutsi community grew larger with the passage of the years and dreamed of the day when it would be able to return to Rwanda. Although talks were held between the Rwandan government and some of these expatriate groups, no serious measures of repatriating exiles were ever implemented.[6]

Both exiled Tutsi and disaffected Hutu (mostly from southern Rwanda), were dissatisfied with the Habyarimana regime. In 1990 members of the Rwandan Patriotic Front, who until then had been soldiers in the Ugandan Army, decided to invade Rwanda from Uganda. Despite initial setbacks, this group (70–80 percent Tutsi, 20–30 percent Hutu) managed to wrest a favorable peace settlement from the Rwandan government in 1993. Had the latter honored its agreement, there would have been no genocide in 1994. These social, political, and historical factors were what led to the genocide of 1994 and not some Malthusian struggle over limited resources. These factors, which I have outlined here, have been addressed at length by scholars in the literature dealing with Rwanda's genocide, and there is no need to repeat all the findings.[7]

Instead, what I would like to emphasize in this chapter are the symbolic and cultural factors that served to generate the passions that were unleashed before and during the genocide. Human beings do not commit momentous crimes like genocide in a casual or offhand manner, nor can a genocide occur without preparation. Motivations have to be engendered, nurtured, and mobilized. This takes time and requires the use of mass communication (radio, television, and print media). Moreover, these media have to incite passion in an imaginative and culturally appropriate way. Messages that do not address concerns that are specific to a particular group of people fall flat and are without effect. Images and symbols have to be used that resonate with a particular people's image of itself, its shared emotional commitment to a set of values, and its shared notion of history.

In addition, events must occur that catalyze these passions and allow for their expression. Several years ago, for example, I visited an art exhibit that required stepping on the American flag in order to view a painting that was next to impossible to see otherwise. Most people craned their necks into unnatural and uncomfortable positions curious to view the painting while trying to avoid stepping on the flag. Virtually no one simply stepped on the flag. Had the exhibit been anywhere but the United States, it is clear that people would not have manifested the same degree of queasiness about disrespecting a symbol that was not their own.

In like fashion, we cannot impose our Western assumptions about other peoples' motivations. Rwandans are not necessarily motivated in the same ways by the things that motivate us. When Western onlookers assume that Rwandans possess the same motivations that we do about wealth and power, they are doing just that. Instead, what anthropologists do is to look at things from the Rwandan point of view: their values and their symbols. One way we can do this is to look at the images that were used in the popular Rwandan news magazines and that were in circulation in the years just before the genocide.[8] What we find is that the institution of sacred kingship was an important source of symbols in these media.

more widespread than Diamonds case study

KINGSHIP

Although kingship in Rwanda came to an end in 1961, it is useful to study this institution because many of the values that characterized it have continued to this day.[9] In early Rwanda collective care for the fertility of land, people, and livestock was one of the most important values held by all ethnic groups. The king's role in ensuring fertility was perceived as indispensable. Through the rituals prescribed by a complex dynastic code, the king presided over the descent of *imaana* (fertility or divine beneficence) from sky to earth. The king's capacity to accomplish this was contingent on the degree to which he successfully embodied the ideals of kingship.

Liquids – including rain, milk, honey, semen, blood, and even rivers – were important as symbols of these ideals. For example, the king was the foremost rainmaker for the kingdom and risked his throne in the case of prolonged drought. He also risked it in the case of excessive rain. The orderly flow of fertility from sky to earth involved the king's maintenance of ritual purity and the eradication of impurity. Potency invested the liquids of his body. His saliva, for example, was used in the most important procedures of divination. Special ritualists were charged with obtaining and guarding the royal saliva, then inserting it into the mouths of sacrificial bulls. Potency invested his semen, as can be seen from the numerous instances of ritual copulation in the royal ceremonies. Even when kings died their bodies continued to possess potency and to transfer it to Rwanda as a whole, for the royal tombs were located on a hill whose numerous streams coalesce to form the headwaters of the ritually important Nyabugogo River, a tributary of another ritually important river, the Nyabarongo. As the deceased kings' bodies dissolved, their *imaana* entered these rivers' waters. Potency also invested the king's blood, for he was ultimately the kingdom's sacrificial victim of last resort. In essence the king's body could be seen as the conduit through which *imaana* passed in its descent from sky to earth.

A sacrificial king, or a substitute for him, was called an *umutabazi* (liberator). He was an ambivalent and ambiguous character. Sometimes the *umutabazi* is depicted as selflessly giving his life in battle to save Rwanda. In other instances it seems as if the king was killed because he did not live up to the ideals of sacred kingship. Sometimes the *umutabazi* is a little bit of both, a bad king who is killed, then later idealized, at least by his followers.

In the two years preceding President Habyarimana's death, I believe that the path was being prepared in Rwanda's print media for a kind of "king sacrifice." At first we see hints of this in the opposition press and its portrayal of the president as a tyrannical or incompetent ruler whom the country would do well to get rid of. Later even some Hutu extremists deserted him, because they were determined to eliminate Tutsi and saw Habyarimana as an impediment to this. Rwandan journalists attacked the president in ways that constituted a radical departure from the timidity that had prevailed during the 1980s. This was due in part to democratization, supported by France and other Western powers, that occurred during the 1990s and to which Habyarimana and the MRND were forced to acquiesce. The press became free and open, but the sudden easing of restraints did not coincide with a corresponding rise in concern for journalistic standards. Innuendo, calumny, and veiled and not-so-veiled calls for assassination characterized the printed and spoken media of the time. Comparing Habyarimana in the popular political literature to a traditional sacred king was not without irony, for the president was Hutu (all former kings had been Tutsi), and much of the avowed ideology of his party, the MRND, was antimonarchist and superficially, at least, egalitarian.

In hindsight it is not difficult to perceive an equivalence between the Rwandan presidency and the country's former monarchy. When I began my first period of fieldwork in Rwanda in 1983, I quickly became aware of the "cult of personality" surrounding President Habyarimana and the autocratic nature of his reign. At the time Habyarimana was running for reelection, and MRND party faithful were very busy campaigning. There was little chance of his losing the election, though, as he was running unopposed and the MRND was the country's only authorized political party. In the 1983 elections Habyarimana asked for and was reported to have won an incredible 99 percent of the vote. For many years afterward, it seemed as if he would hold power forever.

At the time adulation of Habyarimana was virtually required of Rwandans. Almost everyone had a portrait of the president hanging on a wall at home, and many wore the MRND party button on their shirt or blouse. On Wednesday afternoons groups met to practice chants and skits celebrating the Rwandan state, its overthrow of the Tutsi monarchy, and its rejection of the *ubuhake* cattle contract signifying Hutu servitude to Tutsi, but most of all honoring the country's president, Juvénal Habyarimana. It didn't seem to bother anyone that these Wednesday afternoon get-togethers, called *animation*, took people away from their jobs and did nothing to augment the country's gross domestic product. Even songs on the radio seemed to equate Rwanda, its beauty, and relative prosperity with the person of its president.

Of course, much of this adulation was self-interested. The state, with Habyarimana at its head, was the country's primary source of patronage. Showing support for it and its leader could never hurt your career. Even in contexts in which nothing obvious was to be gained, however, many people expressed their admiration of the country's president. Some people made comments about the appropriateness of Habyarimana's name, from the verb *kubyara* (to engender) and *imaana*, which together could be translated as "It is God who gives life." Nothing could have been more appropriate in a Catholic, anti-abortion, and basically pro-natalist culture, yet very few names could have resonated so well with the more "traditional" themes of fertility, prosperity, and good luck. During most of the 1980s Rwanda was doing well economically (in comparison to neighboring states), and many Rwandans attributed this to the good stewardship of its president. The orchestrated affection for Habyarimana was part theater, certainly, but there were many Rwandans who were sincere.

Closely associating the country's fertility and prosperity with the person of the president was not the only way in which we see the lingering influence of the representations of sacred kingship. In other instances we see this influence in references to the country's rivers, the body, and violence. Sometimes the assimilation of Habyarimana to a Rwandan sacred king was explicit; at other times it was more implicit, bordering on the unwitting. In many cases the association was intended to be flattering; in other instances, it was intended to be critical. Let us look at some examples.

Rivers

One reference to Rwanda's rivers with an explicit association to sacred kingship appeared in the popular political magazine *Zirikana* on 30 January 1993, in an article written by Bonaparte Ndekezi, a party hack, entitled "Habyarimana hagati ya Mukungwa na Nyabarongo" ("Habyarimana between the Mukungwa and the Nyabarongo"). *Zirikana* supported the viewpoint of the party known as the Coalition pour la Défense de la République (Coalition for the Defense of the Republic, CDR), a party formed from Hutu extremist elements of the MRND and known for its racist views toward Tutsi. Ndekezi was well known for his extremism. The article's title refers to a river in northern Rwanda, the Mukungwa, and to central Rwanda's main river, the Nyabarongo, which in earlier times divided the Rwandan kingdom into two sacred halves.

The article can be interpreted in several ways. At one level, and this is the theme that is most strongly advanced in the article, is that Habyarimana in 1993 finds himself in trouble and with little room to maneuver politically. The article goes on to describe Habyarimana as a good leader, but if anything, a little soft on his opponents, particularly the Tutsi-dominated Rwandan Patriotic Front and the internal Hutu opposition. In other words, Habyarimana is in trouble because of his magnanimity in the face of his adversaries' treachery.

On another less explicit level one could interpret Habyrimana's
finding himself between the Mukungwa and the Nyabarongo as his
being confined within the most sacred portion of his "kingdom" –
the north, his natural constituency, that portion of Rwanda enclosed
within the confines of the Mukungwa in the north and the Nybarongo
in the center. Is the article subtly exhorting Habyarimana to be less
of a peaceful "king" and more a warrior "king"? It may carry a subtle
warning to Habyarimana: "Leave the confines of your sacred kingdom,
proceed southward, cross the Nyabarongo and wage war! Otherwise
you will lose everything." The author is referring to an earlier Rwanda,
the days of sacred kingship, and to Habyarimana as a modern-day
"sacred king." This is clear from one of the following claims: "At the
level of authority, there is no difference between him [Habyarimana]
and the former kings of traditional Rwanda, only the fact that he was
not born clutching the *imbuto* (magic seeds of fertility) in his hand."

The allusion here to traditional Rwandan sacred kingship is interesting because it was intended to flatter Habyarimana. This is ironic,
even paradoxical given its source, the Hutu extremist CDR. After all,
Rwandan Hutu were the group that overthrew the (Tutsi) monarchy
in 1961. This apparent contradiction is diminished somewhat when
we realize that the CDR was not really opposed to autocrats, dictators, or even monarchs as much as it was opposed to Tutsi and to the
RPF. What the author appears to be saying is: "Habyarimana, a Hutu
king, is every bit as worthy a king as his Tutsi forebears. His only flaw
is his reluctance to use the iron fist."

In another popular political journal, the 27 November 1992 issue
of *Umurangi,* which was closely associated with the party known as
the Mouvement Démocrate Républicain (Democratic Republican
Movement, MDR) and opposed to the MRND and CDR, Habyarimana
is pictured in proximity to the Mukungwa and about to attack
southern Rwanda with his army and militia (Fig. 9.3). *Umurangi*'s
indirect allusion to the boundaries of the sacred kingdom and to
Habyarimana is not intended to flatter. In this cartoon we see the
three major democratic opposition parties, the MDR, the Parti Social
Démocrate (Social Democratic Party, PSD), and the Parti Liberal
(Liberal Party, PL) poised close to the Nyabarongo and preparing to
fend off Habyarimana's descent into what was once the most sacred
territory of the Rwandan kingdom. To the northeast we see the RPF

Muri mirongo inani **HABYARIMANA** baramubwiye ntiyumva kandi
ibintu byari bigifite igaruriro, bimaze kuba agasitswe ati: Ndi IKINANI...

FIGURE 9.3 Political cartoon using metaphor of rivers. (From *Umurangi*,
no. 13, 27 November 1992)

delighted that southern Hutu (MDR, PSD, and PL) and northern
Hutu (MRND and CDR) are divided among themselves. At another
level the cartoon seems to be saying that Habyarimana is an illegiti-
mate pretender to the throne, a northerner, an outsider, and one
responsible for terrorist killings in the south and center.

The headline beneath the cartoon reads as follows: "In 1980 when
things could have been arranged, we told Habyarimana, but he
wouldn't listen. When things flew out of control, all he could say was:
I am *Ikinani* (the invincible)." Habyarimana (upper left) says: "We are
well dressed (i.e., in military uniforms). We are descending to the
Nyabarongo to conduct the campaign. Try to spare a few so that they
will tell the story of Ikinani's victory. But once we have crossed [i.e.,
the Nyabarongo], my children, what I haven't told you, figure out for
yourself." The RPF (upper right) responds: "What are they thinking
in Rwanda? Is it true that he wants the votes of cadavers?"

The Body and Its Violation, Adorning
the Royal Drum, Castration

The mystical power of the early monarchy was said to reside in the royal drums, particularly the one called a *Karinga.* Loss of the drum signified the king's defeat and Rwanda's takeover by an enemy. Even though the drums of Rwandan kingship have long since been relegated to museums, the term *ingoma* (drum) continues to be used to refer to a specific group or individual's political hold over a region or a group of people. In "Habyarimana hagati ya Mukungwa na Nyabarongo," the author sometimes refers to Habyarimana as the one who possesses *ingoma Nshiru,* in other words, power over the region of Nshiru in northern Rwanda.

Rarely does one find ideological consistency among the various uses of kingship symbols before Habyarimana's assassination. About eighty popular journals, each with a different point of view, arose in the period between 1990 and 1994, which is quite extraordinary for a country with a population of about seven million. Some, but not all, of these journals employed symbols of kingship, but more often, Hutu extremist journalists explicitly accused the Rwandan Patriotic Front of wanting to restore the (Tutsi) monarchy, its trappings, and its rituals. Routinely, Hutu extremist journalists referred to RPF members as "feudo-monarchists." Several of their cartoons recall the former custom of emasculating slain enemies and then using these body parts to adorn the royal drum.

In the cartoon (Fig. 9.4) from an extremist Hutu magazine, *La Medaille-Nyiramacibiri,* RPF soldiers are depicted crucifying, impaling, and castrating Melchior Ndadaye, neighboring Burundi's first democratically elected Hutu president. Elected in October 1993, he was subsequently killed by Burundian Tutsi army officers in an abortive coup attempt.

Cartoon captions
> A civilian RPF supporter: "Kill this stupid Hutu and after you cut off his genitals, hang them on our drum."
> Ndadaye: "Kill me, but you won't exterminate all the Ndadayes in Burundi."
> [Paul] Kagame (formerly RPF general, now president of Rwanda) [right side of cartoon]: "Kill him quickly. Don't you know that in

FIGURE 9.4 Assassination of Melchior Ndadaye. (From *La Medaille-Nyiramacibiri*, no. 17, p. 10, November 1993)

Byumba and Ruhengeri we did a lot of work. With women, we pulled the babies out of their wombs; with men, we dashed out their eyes."

The drum: "*Karinga* of Burundi."

In the annals of Rwandan Hutu extremism, very few images condense as much symbolic violence and in so many ways as this one. At one level we see a clear iteration of the oft-repeated charge by Hutu extremists that the RPF were "feudo-monarchists" intent on restoring kingship, the royal rituals, and the monarchy's principal emblem – the *Karinga*. Another claim is advanced by depicting Hutu victims of the RPF as Christ-like martyrs, for Ndadaye is being crucified.

FIGURE 9.5 Metaphorical Eden, political cartoon. (From *Umurangi*, no. 9, 22 June 1992)

Beneath these claims, however, a subtler message is being conveyed. By impaling Ndadaye the RPF torturers are turning his body into an obstructed conduit, and as such they are transforming his person into an inadequate, unworthy conduit for *imaana*. In former times Rwandans killed cattle thieves in this way. At another level a complex synthesis has been forged. Specifically Rwandan symbols with deep historical roots have merged with those that are the more recent product of Christian evangelization.

The imagery of castration occurs repeatedly in the popular press of the time. In another cartoon from *Umurangi* (Fig. 9.5), there is a synthesis of Christian and earlier Rwandan imagery. Here members of the MRND and CDR parties (two women and three men who correspond to real personalities from these parties) are seen accepting the severed scrotum of a defeated enemy. Two snakes, one wearing an MRND cap bearing the party insignia of a hoe crossed over a curved knife and the other wearing a hat of the CDR, are coiling up the "tree of knowledge" in the "Garden of Eden," which is labeled "the *Interahamwe* Club." In fact, Rose and Matthieu Ngirumpatse

Kwa Ba Rugotomerankaba ipfa riracyari ryose.

Ni iki bita kujya mu kwaha kw'Ikinani.

FIGURE 9.6 *Karaso* drum symbolism in political cartoon. (From *Umurangi*, no. 12, 9 November 1992)

(formerly secretary general of the MRND and now accused of war crimes before the International War Crimes Tribunal in Arusha, Tanzania) were proprietors of a popular Kigali restaurant and night spot called "Eden Garden," a noted hangout for MRND, CDR, and *Interahamwe* militia members. The snake says: "I castrated him, and he wasn't the only one." Accepting the snake's gift is Rose Ngirumpatse. The bearded man at the right says: "How can they ever defeat us!? Let's go do our rituals. You'll see."

In another cartoon, also from *Umurangi* (Fig. 9.6), CDR and MRND members are depicted enjoying a cannibal feast seated around their version of Karinga, in this case a drum named *karaso* (blood), adorned with the testicles of slain enemies. The caption reads: "Among the greedy, you can never get enough." The woman with her

FIGURE 9.7 Theme of political castration. (From *Umurangi*, no. 11, 7 October 1992)

finger pointed in the air says: "Bring me the guts of Byabagamba." The other woman says: "I won't be satisfied until I get Nsengiremye's flesh to eat." The man seated next to her replies, "I'll do anything to make you happy, dear. You shall have him."

Yet another use of the castration image appears in *Umurangi* (Fig. 9.7). Here a woman named Habimana, a close associate of Habyarimana's and head of the Rwandan Office Nationale de la Population (National Office of the Population), instructs a doctor with scissors to castrate each man standing in line. Mme. Habimana commands: "Castrate them in the name of the *umwami w'akazu* [i.e., king of the *akazu* or 'little house,' the small clique of people who were Habyarimana's closest supporters and most favored clients]. He has his aim in mind. Don't ask questions." The doctor in the picture replies, "You don't have to tell me, we eat from the same trough."

The preceding cartoons show many things, but what I think is most noteworthy is their depth of anger and their degree of symbolic aggression. In expressing this, cartoonists drew on the symbols of precolonial sacred kingship and the more recent symbols of Christianity. Whether you were a supporter of the pre-genocidal government or a critic of it, journalists in both camps used these symbolic sources to appeal to their readers' basest emotions – fear, hatred, and sadism – emotions that run rampant in most wars. It is difficult to judge how effective these journalists were in inciting violence, but they certainly contributed to an atmosphere in which it came to be seen as part of the natural order of things. Once violence is represented in the media as if it were a reasoned and justifiable defensive response to the imagined threat of aggression, real violence cannot be far away. The old child's rhyme "Sticks and stones may break my bones, but names will never hurt me" has never been true. Representational violence inevitably precedes and accompanies real violence, and ultimately people are killed.

media & its relationship to apocalypse

CONCLUSION

In this chapter I have attempted to show that we cannot simply take our Western notions about limited resources and individual struggle over these resources as a given when we try to understand something as complex as the Rwandan genocide of 1994. Instead, we must try to interpret Rwandan motivations and Rwandan thinking. One way of gaining access to this thinking is to look at Rwandan popular media and to consider what was being said and depicted in it before the genocide. One theme that I believe was important, although not always in a direct and explicit way, was the theme of Rwandan sacred kingship.

The central preoccupation of Rwandan sacred kingship was *imaana*, the Rwandan term for supreme being or, more generally, diverse forms of potency thought to invest certain people, objects, and substances and to embody fertility and prosperity. The most important human embodiment of *imaana* was the Rwandan sacred king. Understanding *imaana* requires understanding the nature of symbolism having to do with liquids and their movement, including rainfall, rivers, milk, and honey, as well as bodily fluids important in life and reproduction: blood, semen, and breast milk. According to this symbolism perturbations in fluid flows such as blockages (as in drought) or overly abundant fluid flows (as in flooding) were negative. One of the sacred king's responsibilities was to direct and control these flows. His body was *imaana*'s conduit in its descent from heaven to earth. Yet the king also ran the risk of being perceived as the one responsible for complete cessation of beneficial flows in times of crisis, in which case he might be judged to be an inadequate embodiment of *imaana* and thus a candidate for elimination. Collective remembering of such events in dynastic histories usually followed the model of *umutabazi* sacrifice, masking tragedy and making it appear as if the sovereign had died a selfless and heroic death.

Judging from the images found in the Rwandan popular media in the years before the genocide, Rwandan notions of sacred kingship have not been completely effaced by the forces of modernity and globalization. We see this in the person of President Habyarimana and in the intimations that he was to become, like some sacred kings of the past, an *umutabazi*. In the popular media depicting Habyarimana and other political leaders, we find cartoons suffused with symbolism reminiscent of Rwandan sacred kingship. We see images in which Habyarimana's exercise of power and sovereignty are defined by rivers, as if he too were subject to their constraints, as were kings in earlier eras. In other cartoons we observe depictions of the body as an agent of flowing fluids and as a conduit. We see this in cartoons showing anal impalement, castration, and imaginary adornment of the royal drum with the genitalia of slain enemies.

Most dramatically, we sense the move toward the veiled accusation that Habyarimana had become an inadequate king, for Habyarimana in many instances is portrayed as an unworthy sovereign, a bad "king," one who impedes the descent of *imaana*. Once sacrificed, however, his death became the rallying cry behind which Hutu extremists mobilized their genocide against Tutsi and Hutu moderates who were blamed for his assassination. Kings were very powerful, but also vulnerable, and occasionally they could be killed. Woe, however, to those who might bring about a king's death. They in turn could be seen as enemies of the moral order. In this way President Habyarimana conforms closely to the early image of the *umutabazi*, a sacred king who must rule appropriately and whose power is magical and traditional.

In all this we find little confirmation of Malthusian principles. Clearly Rwandans think about their leaders, their social system, and their place in this world in their own terms, not as Westerners, who try to find "scientific" reasons for cultural catastrophes.

Notes

* I am a professor of anthropology at the University of Alabama at Birmingham. I began doing fieldwork in Rwanda in 1983 as part of my dissertation research. Previously I had studied anthropology as an undergraduate at Yale and later as a graduate student at the University of Paris-X (Nanterre), where I earned a master's degree. I then continued graduate study at the University of Virginia, earning a Ph.D. in 1988. My first book, *Milk, Honey and Money* (1992), is about Rwandan traditional medicine and changes brought about by colonialism, Christian evangelization, and integration into the world capitalist system. The book was a finalist in the 1993 Herskovits competition for best book in African studies.

   I have also worked as an applied anthropologist on projects concerned with HIV/AIDS prevention. It was in this capacity that I was present in Rwanda in 1994. Unfortunately the project with which I was associated was brought to an untimely end when the president of Rwanda was assassinated on 6 April 1994. This event triggered the 1994 genocide in which close to one million Rwandan Tutsi were killed.

   In recent years I have studied matters of ethnicity, nationalism, war, and reconciliation, and in 1999 I wrote *Sacrifice as Terror*. I intend to continue fieldwork in Rwanda and to explore the reconciliation process that is underway there.

1. Diamond 2005.
2. For a good critical summary of Malthus's views on economics and over-population, see Ross 1998.
3. Chrétien 1997.
4. Linden 1977.
5. Ibid.
6. Prunier 1995. This was one of the first books to be written about the 1994 genocide and remains very useful. It covers the events that preceded and occurred during the genocide, and all the important players and their agendas are discussed.
7. Besides the book by Prunier, another book of interest was published shortly after the genocide by African Rights (Omar 1994). Researchers associated with African Rights did fieldwork in Rwanda after the genocide. This book, consisting of nineteen chapters, is long and extensive, but its table of contents is useful in leading readers to areas of specific concern. Many of the chapters have extensive accounts from people who were present in Rwanda at the time of the genocide.
8. Chrétien 1995.
9. Texts of the royal rituals in both Kinyarwanda and French form the core of d'Hertefelt and Coupez 1964. The authors add useful explanatory remarks.

Bibliography

Chrétien, J.-P. Editor. 1995. *Rwanda: les médias du génocide*. Paris: Karthala.

Chrétien, J.-P. Editor. 1997. *Le Défi de l'ethnisme: Rwanda et Burundi: 1990–1996*. Paris: Karthala.

d'Hertefelt, M. and A. Coupez. 1964. *La royauté sacrée de l'ancien Rwanda*. Tervuren, Belgium: Musée Royal de l'Afrique Centrale.

Diamond, Jared. 2005. *Collapse: How Societies Choose to Fail or Succeed*. New York: Viking.

Linden, I. 1977. *Church and Revolution in Rwanda*. Manchester: Manchester University Press.

Omar, R. Editor. 1994. *Rwanda: Death, Despair and Defiance*. London: African Rights.

Prunier, G. 1995. *The Rwanda Crisis: History of a Genocide*. New York: Columbia University Press.

Ross, E. B. 1998. *The Malthus Factor: Population, Poverty and Politics in Capitalist Development*. New York: Zed Books.

10

"Failed" States, Societal "Collapse," and Ecological "Disaster"

A Haitian Lesson on Grand Theory

Drexel G. Woodson[*]

Today's iteration of the human spectacle features complex problems, old as well as new, and more or less successful efforts to alleviate if not solve them. Warfare, civil strife, pandemics (and ordinary diseases or ailments), hunger and starvation, ignorance and miseducation, unemployment, underemployment, and perpetual debt, environmental degradation, and the tension between development and conservation immediately come to mind. When these diverse problems reach crisis proportions, they temporarily draw attention in the global media – print, spoken, and visual. Yet long-term observation and reflection show that the problems are surface phenomena, projections of a common and enduring set of underlying conditions. Humans inhabit culturally constructed, power-breached worlds, where inequalities and injustices ("traditional" or "modern") coexist with hopes, dreams, and opportunities for better ways to live, work, and play. Moreover, the livelihood systems that generate and sustain the world's highest human standards of living (work and play) degrade the physical environments on which earthly existence, human and nonhuman, depends. This casts doubt on whether those livelihood systems offer replicable, let alone sustainable, models for change.

These facets of the human spectacle place the social sciences in an ambiguous position regarding knowledge production and dissemination. On the one hand, intellectual progress in any discipline rests on the cumulative comparison, criticism, and synthesis of information assembled and interpreted by numerous individuals or teams over long time periods and in varied settings. On the other hand, researchers must simplify information to ensure its accessibility and usefulness to policymakers and the general public. Many social scientists consider fashioning grand theory the most compelling approach to comparing, synthesizing, and transmitting information about the human spectacle's complex cultural, social, political-economic, and ecological dimensions. However, preoccupation with grand theory begs more modest questions of method that contribute to intellectual progress and effective communication.[1]

Development discourse, a good example of grand theory, has dominated thought, talk, and action concerning directed change around the globe since the end of World War II. The Development Set – the bilateral or multilateral agencies, governments of nation-states, and international or national nongovernmental organizations (NGOs) – is now more tightly integrated than ever by conformity to a normative institutional discourse. This includes free markets, free and fair elections, an open society, and a participatory polity guaranteed by a state that recognizes its citizens' human rights and meets their basic needs. However, actual development programs and projects since the late 1940s have typically produced as many unforeseen or unintended consequences as anticipated or desired outcomes. Consequently, a substantial number of researchers, some policymakers, and the citizens of many nation-states are less certain about the wisdom of conventional development objectives and the feasibility of prevailing means to achieve them. "Feasibility" itself no longer denotes the mere capacity to achieve presumably reasonable, necessary, or beneficial socioeconomic objectives efficiently, but also connotes the sustainability, political as well as environmental, of directed change, along with equity for the people involved.

Aware of this shift in thinking, development professionals have devised a new classification to position the world's nation-states in today's global political-economic and sociocultural order. Gone are earlier binary oppositions between "modern" and "backward" societies or "developed" and "underdeveloped" countries or, euphemistically, LDCs ("lesser developed countries"). Now "transitional states" are distinguished from "failed states": those meeting the political-economic, ecological, social, and cultural "conditionalities" (conditions in everyday speech) for development versus those that do not. "Failed states" need and deserve humanitarian assistance instead of economic investment. "Developed states" is the normative category, encompassing states that exploit fully the relevant conditions and function satisfactorily. Yet, like earlier classifications of the world's diverse nation-states, the new one conceals as much as it reveals. It eschews careful investigation of relations between "normal," unmarked categories and "abnormal," marked ones – along with the details of culture, history, society, political economy, and ecology that must be understood to interpret such relations.[2]

Haiti is a case in point. For many professional observers and indeed Haitians of all colors (black, brown, and yellow) and of all economic classes, genders, and political beliefs, Haiti exemplifies a "failed" state, societal "collapse," and ecological "disaster." These observers portray the entire country as if it resembled the apparently forlorn children on late-night infomercials sponsored by faith-based groups soliciting contributions. "Haiti is the poorest country in the Western Hemisphere!" This simple and often-repeated cliché closes conversations (and minds), making poverty a phony all-purpose explanation for Haiti's many and many-sided problems – political-economic, social, cultural, and ecological.[3] My research on Haiti in basic and applied cultural/social anthropology since 1972 reveals a different and far more complicated story.

Jared Diamond's *Collapse: How Societies Choose to Fail or Succeed*, like his earlier work *Guns, Germs, and Steel*,[4] illustrates the ambiguous position of the social sciences. More specifically, the books disclose the limitations of presumptions about grand theory's role in promoting synthesis among social science disciplines and greater communication with general audiences. Although *Guns, Germs, and Steel* received accolades from the media and nonspecialists, Diamond seemed uncomfortable with the book's simplistic environmental determinism. In *Collapse* he attempted to rectify the excesses of determinism by investigating agency – how and why a society's leaders and followers make choices that have positive or negative environmental and socioeconomic consequences. One of his case studies is a comparison of Haiti and the Dominican Republic, the

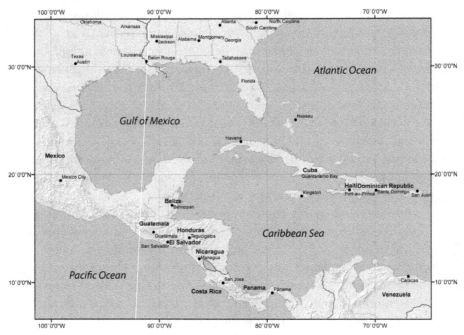

FIGURE 10.1 Caribbean region including southernmost states of the United States. (Drawn by Satoru Murata)

nation-states that share Hispaniola, the Caribbean Sea's second largest island.

Diamond bashing by social scientists who know the societies that Diamond covers better than he does is a vainglorious exercise. General readers may think that those social scientists are jealous of Diamond's fame. In any case, bashing Diamond serves no constructive purpose in an intellectual marketplace where book sales trump the quality of ideas. Instead, here I discuss Diamond's comparison of Haiti and the Dominican Republic to illustrate the pitfalls of privileging grand theory as "the" way to encompass social scientific knowledge about and understanding of some facet of the human spectacle. Doing so denies anthropologists, as well as policymakers and the general public, an opportunity to explore connections among culture, history, and ecology. Such an understanding, I contend, enhances prospects for more effective action to change the human spectacle in Haiti, the Dominican Republic, and elsewhere.

FIGURE 10.2 Haitianist at work conducting interviews during the St. Martin Patron Saint Festival in the town of Dondon (Department of the North). Author present at far left. (Photograph by Brackette F. Williams, November 1980)

AN OVERARCHING CONTEXT: ONE BLACK AMERICAN'S VIEW OF HISPANIOLA

I am a native of Philadelphia, Pennsylvania, who chose to become a Haitianist – a cultural/social anthropologist concerned with basic and applied research on people and things Haitian, present and past. My choice, at once personal and professional, required me to learn to speak, read, and write Haitian Creole as well as French, and to read Spanish. Focusing on Haiti, but taking regular, sidelong glances at other peoples and places, I use ethnography, history, and bibliography to gather, sift, and interpret information in the interest of understanding what people do, say, and think. Therefore, I view the Dominican Republic from the Haitian side of Hispaniola.[5]

During the twenty-six years since my first Haiti sojourn, research and travel for pleasure have taken me to nine of Haiti's ten administrative departments (analogues of states in the United States), but I have visited the Dominican Republic only briefly. My most recent visits were day trips during a study of rural livelihood systems in

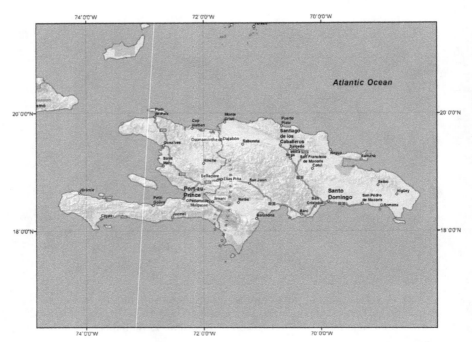

FIGURE 10.3 Island of Hispaniola showing Haiti and the Dominican Republic. (Drawn by Satoru Murata)

1996 between three pairs of Haitian and Dominican border towns: Malpasse and Jimaní, Belladère and Elias Piña, and Ouanaminthe and Dajabón. My fieldwork-based perspective on Hispaniola is thus one-sided and incomplete. Nevertheless, my Haitianocentric discussion is a corrective for the methodological disparity underlying Diamond's grand theory in *Collapse* about why Haiti differs from the Dominican Republic.

Haiti became the Western Hemisphere's second former European colony to declare independence in 1804, twenty-eight years after the United States. Haiti was also the first state in the Americas whose revolutionary political leaders were former slaves or free people of color, and who saw fit to attack slavery, colonialism, and racism simultaneously as a gambit to promote individual freedom as well as collective security and prosperity. The gambit was partially successful for four decades. However, it included a side-bet that, inside Haiti, a hierarchical cultural, social, and political-economic system, one that was

TABLE 10.1. *Hierarchical Ranking of Selected Haitian Identity Markers*

Identity-Markers	Observations
Former free person over former slave	Privileged legal status before 1804
Mulatto over Black	Implied a greater proportion of European (usually French) or African ancestral "blood"
City dweller over rural resident	Justified government policies favoring coastal urban settlements, rather than settlements in the mountains or plains of the interior
Large landowner and/or liberal professional over peasant smallholder or landless worker	Assigned greater value to property ownership and to the production of coffee and timber for export than to labor and the production of food crops – especially plantain, corn, beans, and tubers (sweet potatoes, yams, taro, or cassava) – for direct consumption and internal trade
Bilingual French/Haitian Creole-speaker over monolingual Haitian Creole-speaker	Signified that formal educational achievement trumps learning in life's school of hard knocks
Devotee of "frank" Catholicism over practitioner of Vodou, plus Catholicism	Suggested greater openness to the "civilizing effects" of Christianity
Male over female	Implied that women lack mental or physical capacities for entrepreneurial initiative and leadership outside their households, despite abundant counterevidence, including the skill of ambulatory market women and sedentary merchants

export oriented and privileged minorities, might sustain and advance political order as well as economic prosperity. Table 10.1 summarizes information about the hierarchical ranks of seven important identity markers for Haitians, without knowledge of which it is impossible to understand their country.

Outside Haiti slavery remained big business and, together with racism, the bedrock of society, economy, and politics. Before the middle of the nineteenth century, this was the case in the United States, free, but dependent on slavery and racial hierarchy privileging whites. A similar situation existed among European powers, which had predominantly free populations at home but depended on slavery and racial hierarchy privileging whites in Caribbean colonies – Spanish Cuba and Puerto Rico, British Jamaica and British Guiana, Dutch Guiana, and French Martinique and Guadeloupe. Thus, leaders of the nineteenth-century "international community" viewed Haiti as a threat to the global order of nation-states because Black slaves (mostly African-born) and emancipated Creoles (mostly Mulattos or other mixed blood/mixed race people born in the Americas) had forged a coalition to win their homeland's sovereignty.

Haiti, known to foreigners since 1830s as "the Black Republic," "the Magic Island," or "Voodoo Land," has figured prominently in both national and international narratives on race/color, poverty, superstition, political liberty, oppression, and corruption – and heroic resistance to inequality and injustice. Bad press, coupled with slipshod or tendentious social scientific research, has broadcast sagas of failure by inept, incompetent, and/or short-sighted Haitian leaders – autocrats, dictators, oligarchs, or tyrants all. Haitian efforts to improve living and working conditions for the Haitian majority have received short shrift, because they have often gone awry after brief periods of success.

Neither the significance of choice in human affairs nor lessons to be learned from investigating choice making (the process and its outcomes) is at issue here. Nevertheless, debates among anthropologists about choice-based grand theory demonstrate that, although individual actors have and make choices, their options are not always good, and they do not choose the contexts of choice making. Forces beyond individual control canalize choices (much like a canal system channels the flow of water), as do the decisions of more knowledgeable, prestigious, powerful, or determined actors, who feel no obligation to respect the interests of other men or women. Likewise, forces beyond the control of any single society, as well as policies adopted by leaders of wealthier and more powerful nation-states, restrict a society's range of options.[6]

It is misleading, therefore, to think, as Diamond suggests, that whole societies "choose" lifeways and courses of action leading to collapse or resilient adaptation. Decision-making playing fields are uneven, and powerful and wealthy segments of societies call the shots for everyone else. Likewise, given that some nation-states are wealthier and more powerful than others, the international playing field is also uneven. Ignorance of choice-making contexts, or a refusal to address them, mars Diamond's often factually accurate comparison of Haiti and the Dominican Republic.[7]

GRAND THEORY ON HISPANIOLA: "CHOICE" OF STATE FAILURE, SOCIETAL COLLAPSE, OR ENVIRONMENTAL DISASTER?

Cuba is the Caribbean region's largest and most populous island. Two nation-states share Hispaniola, the second largest island. Haiti occupies one-third of the land area (28,000 square kilometers) and its population is roughly eight million, whereas the Dominican Republic occupies the other two-thirds (49,000 square kilometers) and has a population of some seven million. Thus, although there are perhaps one million fewer Dominicans than Haitians, Haiti's population density is much higher. Culturally and racially Haiti is said to be African and French. The Haitian constitution of 1987, ratified after the fall of the dynastic dictatorship of Presidents for Life Dr. François Duvalier (1957–1971) and his son, Jean-Claude Duvalier (1971–1986), declared that the country has two official languages, French and Haitian Creole. However, Haitian (as people who find "Creole" pejorative call it) is the most widely spoken and understood of the two. The Dominican Republic is said to be Spanish, Indian, and African culturally and racially, and its official language is Spanish. For both sides of Hispaniola, these naïve characterizations privilege cultural and racial origins over processes of differential mixing, interpenetration, and transformation that reshaped origins since Christopher Columbus's "discovery" in 1492 of the island called *Ayti* by the Taino, who had lived there for several hundred years after their ancestors migrated to the Caribbean islands from South America.[8]

"One Island, Two Peoples, Two Histories: The Dominican Republic and Haiti," Diamond's chapter on Hispaniola in *Collapse*, reports these facts. Nonetheless, it displays a jarring methodological imbalance. Diamond had direct, personal contacts with "Dominican friends" but did not interact with Haitians or did not bother to mention those interactions. Although apparently more comfortable reading Spanish than French, he does not know Haitian Creole. Finally, Diamond found more sources about the Dominican Republic for his comparative objectives, and he apparently gathered information about Haiti by reading five books.[9] Diamond's choices are not bad, but they merely scratch the surface of scholarly research and debate.

Swedish development economist Mats Lundahl's magisterial *Peasants and Poverty*,[10] along with his two collections of essays on Haitian underdevelopment, provided Diamond with economic and environmental facts, contemporary and historical. Lundahl's neo-classical economic analyses emphasize two main causes of Haitian underdevelopment: the declining productivity of rural labor (i.e., pressure from a growing population relying on stagnant manual technology) after 1850, and poor government planning coupled with pervasive corruption from 1804 through the 1990s. However, ignoring the controversy surrounding Lundahl's analysis, Diamond misses illuminating critiques of conventional economic assumptions and analytical maneuvers.[11]

To his credit, Diamond relies on venerable Trinidadian Marxist C. L. R. James's *The Black Jacobins*[12] for information about the Haitian Revolution. This classic remains unmatched for its perspective on political cross-currents – global, regional, and local – that made the Revolution at once unthinkable and all too real in the nineteenth century. Once again, though, Diamond overlooks works that correct or reinterpret numerous points of fact, especially works based on research in archives that were unavailable to James seven decades ago.[13] Finally, information for Diamond's explicit comparisons of Haiti and the Dominican Republic comes chiefly from U.S. anthropologist Michele Wecker[14] and Dominican geographer Rafael Emilio Yunén.[15] One wonders how discerningly Diamond read the five books on Haiti. In any case, his exploration of Hispaniola's political, economic, and ecological histories is biased toward the Dominican side of the island.

This general methodological imbalance aside, Diamond's comparison deploys questionable descriptive and analytical maneuvers. Factual errors about historical events, cultural attributes, or socioeconomic and political processes, although numerous and alarming to specialists, need not detain us. More important is Diamond's penchant for reporting decontextualized facts and extrapolating their significance.

Diamond initially expected to find evidence for the simple and seemingly persuasive proposition that environmental damage causes societal collapse. However, he gradually came to appreciate the importance of contributing factors ("complications," he calls them) that stand between a simple cause and an equally simple effect. Consequently Diamond proposes a five-point comparative framework, linking environmental damage to climate change, hostile neighbors, friendly trade partners, and responses to environmental problems. Each point, he emphasizes, actually encompasses a set of factors. Table 10.2 shows how Hispaniola fares according to Diamond's framework.

Contextual matters (Diamond's "complications") are most interesting to me because they influence fact gathering and the interpretation of facts for all five factors, and thus require elaboration. Consider, for instance, his factors 3 and 4. Sharing an island, Haiti and the Dominican Republic have intermittently been both hostile neighbors and friendly trading partners since the seventeenth century. People and goods of all kinds moved easily across an uncertain, officially contested, and porous border between the two sides of the island, except during times of heightened political tension. Moreover, Haiti's military and civilian leaders invaded the Dominican Republic in 1822 for reasons of national security (to prevent the reestablishment of European colonial rule) and incorporated "the East" into Haitian national territory until 1844. Similarly, the United States has loomed large in the foreign relations of both Haiti and the Dominican Republic – alternately an economic or political friend and adversary – since the 1760s, when all three were still colonies.

Geographical proximity and autonomist sentiments led eighteenth-century planters and merchants in Saint-Domingue (colonial Haiti) and Santo Domingo (the colonial Dominican Republic) to seek profits from trade with Great Britain's thirteen North American colonies, "short-circuiting" triangular trade circuits for raw materials or agricultural products, manufactured goods, and slaves that

TABLE 10.2. *Hispaniola, According to Diamond's Framework for Comparing Societies: "Choosing" Failure or Success*

Contributing Factors	Haiti	The Dominican Republic
1. Environmental damage*	Extensive	More limited
2. Climate change	Unclear or incomplete information, but rising air temperatures, as well as declining and increasingly erratic rainfall, have affected both sides of Hispaniola.	
3. Hostile neighbors	The United States (including the 1915–1934 Marine Occupation, and the 1994–1995 U.S.-UN Operation Restore Democracy)	The United States (including the 1916–1930 Marine Occupation and the 1965 military intervention)
	The Dominican Republic periodically since independence in 1876 (especially during 1936–1940)	Haiti periodically since independence in 1804
	The Caribbean's European colonial powers (i.e., France, Great Britain, and Spain) intermittently ca. 1790–1915	The Caribbean's European colonial powers (i.e., France and Great Britain and Spain) intermittently ca. 1790–1915
4. Friendly trade partners	The United States, the Dominican Republic, Great Britain, France, and Germany	The United States, Haiti, Great Britain, and Central and South American nation-states
5. Responses to environmental problems	Few and inadequate (e.g., Haiti has established just three national parks)	Many more and relatively successful (e.g., the Dominican Republic has established 27 national parks)

Source: Diamond 2005: 11–15.

* Deforestation, soil erosion, loss of marine habitat, dropping water table, and/or watershed damage.

linked Europe, the Americas, and Africa. When the North American colonies won their independence in 1781, the newly independent United States became an even more attractive trading partner, and an inspiration to advocates of colonial autonomy as well as anticolonialists on both sides of Hispaniola.

The nineteenth-century "international community," dominated by European Powers that ruled New World colonies with slave-majority populations, treated independent Haiti as a pariah state. Although British, French, and U.S. firms and individuals traded with Haiti, the governments of those nation-states were slow to recognize Haitian independence officially. France did so in 1825, in exchange for a 150 million franc indemnity offsetting Saint-Domingue colonists' losses of property in land and slaves. Great Britain recognized Haitian independence in 1838. In the United States, Southern congressmen repeatedly opposed recognition to prevent the "Haitian contagion" from infecting their region's massive slave populations. The Lincoln administration recognized Haitian sovereignty in 1862, apparently a strategic move during the Civil War to resolve the United States' "[Free] Negro Problem" through overseas colonization. The first Minister Resident arrived in the Haitian capital, Port-au-Prince, the following year.

Foreign powers regularly interfered in the internal affairs of Haiti and the Dominican Republic throughout the nineteenth century to safeguard national commercial interests and to redress the grievances of diplomats or private citizens. In the United States, however, the ideology of political expansion and territorial control spawned serious talk of annexation during the administration of President Ulysses S. Grant (1868–1876) and provided a rationale for negotiations by subsequent administrations to acquire a deep-water military installation until the turn of the twentieth century. Then, just before entering World War I, the United States occupied both countries. Elected federal government officials, partnering with bankers and businessmen, invested state resources in projects to take what they considered rightful control over "backward peoples and countries" in the Caribbean region, the United States' "backyard." Spearheaded by Marine invasions, the United States' Occupation of Hispaniola lasted nineteen years: in Haiti from 1915 to 1934, and in the Dominican Republic from 1916 to 1930.[16]

BACKGROUND TO ECOLOGICAL CONTRASTS

Contextual information raises similar "complications" regarding factor 5 of Diamond's comparative framework, "responses to environmental problems." The Treaty of Ryswick in 1697 ratified a decision by the seventeenth-century French and Spanish monarchies to divide Hispaniola in a way that created contrasting physical environments and ecological challenges in the two colonies. Diplomats drew Hispaniola's boundary from north to south rather than east to west, creating French Saint-Domingue (the western third of the island) and Spanish Santo Domingo (the eastern two-thirds). Saint-Domingue included most of the island's mountains and just five of its narrowest alluvial plains, whereas Santo Domingo included few of the mountains, but the most extensive alluvial plains. One of this colonial political decision's consequences is particularly noteworthy. Hispaniola has always been vulnerable to hurricanes that originate in the Atlantic Ocean and follow northerly or southerly tracks through the Caribbean. The topography of a land mass influences wind patterns and other climatic factors that determine a hurricane's local effects. Thus, although Haiti's mountains are deforested today, they may still modify the force, hence destructiveness, of a hurricane in Haiti and the Dominican Republic.

Deforestation on the Haitian side of the border, Diamond points out, is an obvious difference between the two countries. Flying over Hispaniola, say, on the lucrative American Airlines flight from Miami to Port-au-Prince, one immediately notices that Haiti's denuded mountains contrast with the Dominican Republic's relatively lush, green plains. Reforestation efforts since the 1970s have achieved partial success in some areas of Haiti and have helped stem soil erosion and depletion in the process. Research associated with those efforts has refuted one common assumption about deforestation's causes: namely, that tenure insecurity in a minifundia system (one characterized by very small landholdings) encourages peasants to fell trees, but not to plant them in equal numbers.

Although title insecurity is widespread in the countryside (most peasant landowners do not hold legal deeds), it occurs in the shadow of tenure security (relatively steadfast control over owned, leased, and sharecropped land). Thus, another assumption loses its

FIGURE 10.4 Making boards from a tree trunk near Petite-Rivière des Bayonnais (Department of the Artibonite), November 1980. (Photograph by Drexel G. Woodson)

force: that Haitian peasants, ignorant, careless, and desperately seeking to produce a meager subsistence, choose to mine trees, along with other natural resources. Many peasants are willing to plant trees on land that they control, but the use of trees to produce charcoal and supply construction material for a primarily urban market has outpaced the supply of seedlings. In addition, given pressing income and energy needs among rural Haitians, tree cutting has overwhelmed programs promoting sustainable tree planting that might make wood a renewable resource.[17]

Since 1804 most of Haiti's central governments, allied with powerful interest groups or individuals in "polite" society, have assigned a low priority to capital investments in education, physical infrastructure, and support for productive or commercial activities. Coping with these choices by people dubbed in French *les responsables irresponsables* (irresponsible decision makers), the Haitian majority – peasants, rural artisans, and unskilled urban laborers – improvised ways to, as they say in Creole, *chache lavi* (make a living and a life).[18] For instance, peasants remained obstinately committed to own-account farming, petty commerce, and craftwork using rudimentary tools and technology. Meanwhile, the Haitian elite staunchly opposed foreign property ownership, particularly by white men. According to most foreign observers and many Haitian planners, these elements of Haitian political-economic organization hindered external capital investment that would jump-start development. Things changed during the U.S. Occupation. The Haitian Constitution of 1918, a document for which Franklin Delano Roosevelt, then Undersecretary of the Navy, claimed credit, not only removed the ban on foreign property ownership, but also settled the longstanding Haitian-Dominican border dispute.

Few scholars have systematically investigated pre-occupation business practices by foreign firms and Haitian–foreign partnerships, or the role of transnational marriages (especially between Haitian citizens and citizens of France, Germany, Great Britain, or the United States) in the inheritance and management of real estate or other property.[19] Accounts of shady financial arrangements, such as usurious foreign loans to Haitian insurgents and speculation on Haiti's national debt, outnumber studies of ordinary business operations. Nevertheless, historical studies offer tantalizing leads about foreign businessmen's deals with Haitian governments and well-connected individuals to secure supplies of exportable timber, particularly mahogany and logwood from 1804 to 1920. Did these deals canalize the environmental choices of Haitian peasants, city folk, and governments? What were the environmental consequences of intermittently heavy timber exports? Answers to such questions require additional research.

It is worthwhile in this connection to reread Columbus's description of the northern coast of *La Isla Española* during the first Voyage of Discovery in 1492.[20] The Admiral of the Ocean Seas sailed with a faulty sense of geography, and his appraisal of flora and fauna was suspect. Even so, a keen interest in the profitability of expeditions for the Spanish crown and the Christian faith led Columbus to observe people and places carefully. The Tainos' *Ayti* was indeed an island with lush primary forest, but it only appeared from the coast to be covered with trees. Dry, rocky coasts existed at the end of the fifteenth century, and primary forest cover varied in density across the island, largely a function of differential rainfall and wind patterns on a landscape featuring more mountains than plains to the west and the converse to the east, and the uneven progress of Taino slash-and-burn agriculture.

Although Diamond is correct to focus on the more recent past, it is inadequate, to say the least, to cast a comparison of responses to environmental problems by emphasizing that Dominican dictator Rafael Léonidas Trujillo (1930–1961) was fond of botanical gardens, whereas Haitian dictators François Duvalier and Jean-Claude Duvalier seemed unconcerned about trees and bushes, let alone flowers, from 1957 to 1986. Misplaced concreteness mars Diamond's discussion here. The sentiments of dictators (who are not omnipotent, even though they claim and exercise extensive powers of coercion and intimidation) pale in significance compared to the disconnect between the regular promulgation of environmental protection legislation in the Haitian capital and its inconsistent (or nonexistent) enforcement in urban or rural settlements. Moreover, as already mentioned, rural Haitians "consume" trees, not only to meet their own needs, but also to supply steadily growing urban markets with charcoal for cooking and lumber for construction. This "choice," though ecologically detrimental in the medium-to-long run, has short-term economic benefits, given that charcoal, planks, and pole wood fetch higher prices than most agricultural products.

CRITICISM OF HAITIAN AFFAIRS: SIMILAR FORMS AND CONTENTS, CONTRASTING CONTEXTS

No foreigner could be a harsher critic of Haitian affairs than Haitians themselves. However, harsh criticism may differ in its acknowledgment of links between form and substance, as well as in its contextual sensibility regarding cause-and-effect relations. Criticism by foreigners tends to be formal, large scale, and broad gauge, whereas

Haitian criticism is small scale and narrow gauge. Diamond joins a long list of foreigners in leveling formal criticisms that seek to establish probable connections between one causal factor or compound causes and a complex set of outcomes. In contrast, Haitian criticism, often sarcastic or sardonic, tends to be circumstantial, although it emphasizes cause-and-effect relations too. However, embodying intimate familiarity with certain aspects of culture, society, and politics, Haitian criticism discloses a bittersweet fondness for the homeland, *Ayiti Cheri/Ayiti Toma* (Dear Haiti/Deceptive Haiti). In other words, the local analysis of causes and effects grounds them in knowledge, implicit or explicit, of people, places, and things.[21]

A few examples, described in broad strokes, must suffice to illustrate my points about Haitian criticism.

In a French-language manuscript written two years after the U.S. Occupation ended, Haitian bibliophile, merchant, and sometime public official Edmond Mangonès meditated on the strengths and weaknesses of Haitian political consciousness associated with what he called the Haitian "ethic of strong government" from 1843 to 1888.[22] Mangonès reserved strongest criticism in his historical and social psychological investigation for Haiti's *la bourgeoisie politicienne* (the politicking elite) – a French expression designating several thousand people, Mulattos and Blacks in Port-au-Prince and the departmental capitals, for whom politics was an occupation or an avocation. Aside from perpetual presidential candidates, Mangonès's politicking elite included perpetual candidates for state ministries, high-ranking army officers, and civilian bureaucrats, along with businessmen who doubled as political brokers and fixers, low-level political hacks, and certain politically well-connected intellectuals and artists.

The conduct of these men (Mangonès overlooked women) was relentlessly self-interested and self-aggrandizing, Mangonès maintained, setting a bad example for ordinary Haitian citizens, who were saddled with endless duties to the state (or men temporarily wielding state power), but were accorded few rights or entitlements by the state. While noting that the U.S. Occupation institutionalized *la bourgeoisie politicienne* in novel, and in some regards non-Haitian, ways, Mangonès traced its roots to the initial Haitian social contract, consolidated from 1804 to 1830 and embodying the hierarchical principles that I described earlier. Mangonès's meditation and criticism might easily be dismissed as another expression of regrets by a liberal moralist and member of *la bourgeoisie politicienne* were it not for his detailed observations about Haitian historical events and processes, and the persons – not faceless populists or tyrants – who made Haitian history.

During the 1970s and 1980s, young Haitian development researchers and sociopolitical activists bemoaned what they considered the Haitian peasant's routinized lament: *Mwen pa genyen, mwen pa konnen, mwen pa kapab, se pa fòt-mwen* (I ain't got nothin', I don't know nothin', I can't do nothin', and it ain't my fault). To Haitian researchers and activists, self-styled change agents, the litany was no mere statement of facts; it implied internalization of a sense that one was powerless to combat sociocultural and political-economic ills, if not a fatalism about life. For the peasants, the statement summarized a keen perception of their own limited access to resources and curtailed choice-making authority, which were (and largely remain) the prerogatives of their superiors in Haiti's hierarchical system.

Soon after the fall of the Duvalier dictatorship in 1986, *l'état démissionnaire* (the state that resigned) became a staple conversation topic among educated Haitians fluent in French. It evolved into a cry of alarm when the difficulties of uprooting the dictatorial state to allow a democratic one to flourish became clear. Repressive rule under successive military governments from 1986 to 1990 signaled the state's weakness regarding nearly every function except control of forces of coercion. The 29 September 1991 army coup against President Jean-Bertrand Aristide, who was democratically elected under universal suffrage and by a wide margin in 1990, quashed burgeoning hopes for peaceful, progressive improvement of living and working conditions. After the U.S./UN Multilateral Force restored President Aristide to power in 1994, and President René Garcia Préval succeeded him after another democratic election in 1995, hope resurfaced. However, the state still appeared weak, unwilling or unable to lead and inspire progressive change.

To U.S. ears, one Haitian assessment of the situation in 1995 sounds obscene. During a conversation with a demure elderly woman from Port-au-Prince's Mulatto elite in 1995, I asked about the results of post-Duvalier socioeconomic and political transformations, and whether conditions had improved five months after exiled President

Jean-Bertrand Aristide's return to Haiti. She said bluntly, *"Peyi-a fòkop nèt"* (The country is completely fucked up).[23] This woman had experienced the transition to the Duvalier dictatorship during 1957–1964, the *dechoukaj* (uprooting) that attempted to dislodge it after 1986, and the populist-led transition from dictatorship to democracy during 1990–1995. Although the last transition was incomplete, she found fault with it. In her view there was less political freedom and economic opportunity for people of her class and color category than had existed under the Duvalier dictatorship and less personal security for Haitians of any class or color category. Moreover, Port-au-Prince's physical environment had sharply deteriorated. Once a clean city, in her recollection, it was now *sal* (filthy and nasty) – odiferous trash and garbage was piled high on every street corner in wealthy and poor neighborhoods alike. No one in the state or private sectors seemed willing or able to set things right.

A decade later *peyi-a fòkop nèt* remains an assessment muttered by many Haitians of all color categories and classes. They point to the fragmentation of the populist movement and the destruction of the progressive coalition that brought President Jean-Bertrand Aristide to power in 1990. Equally important in their view is Aristide's forced exile on 28 February 2004, a year before the end of his second term – the work of a peaceful coalition of opposition groups and an armed insurrection by former Aristide supporters, seconded by the governments of the United States, France, and Canada.[24] *Peyi-a fòkop nèt* still seemed appropriate for the next two years as selected Prime Minister Gérard Latortue's transitional government talked better plans for change than it implemented. Haitians expressed cautious optimism about security conditions as well as promising economic and environmental initiatives during 2006–2007, President Préval's first year of a second term. Since then, however, the world's poorest nation-states have suffered the most noxious effects of what the development professionals call "a perfect storm," ambiguous because it benefits some nation-states (or interest groups) while harming others. The storm encompasses rising oil costs; increased food consumption (and more specifically meat eating) in India and China, the world's two largest and fastest-growing economies; the allocation of larger proportions of food harvests to produce bio-fuels; the longstanding bane of droughts, floods, and pestilence, exacerbated by global warming – and financial speculation.

At this writing, therefore, Haitians once again appear unwilling to revise the *fòkop nèt* assessment, because of the rapidly escalating cost of living, especially the prices of imported fuel and food. Protests and food riots in Les Cayes (the largest city in the south) as well as in Port-au-Prince and its upscale suburb Pétionville forced President Préval to accept his prime minister's resignation and form a new government. Perhaps this is a small sign of Haitian political maturity, a kind of democracy between free and fair elections. Haitian citizens may now be ready to hold Haitian leaders responsible for choices that have negative effects. Will the citizenry sustain its vigilance long enough to demand choices of efficient, effective, and equitable responses to Haiti's economic, social, and environmental problems? *Nap suiv*, as Haitians say – "We're watchin' and keepin' tabs."

BEGINNING AGAIN: WHY METHODOLOGY MATTERS AS MUCH AS GRAND THEORY

On 19 October 1997, I spent an afternoon and evening with Albert Mangonès at his self-designed "tropical house" in Martissant, a Port-au-Prince suburb. As usual, our conversation switched from Haitian Creole to French or English and back, depending on the topic. When Albert's "Le Christ" came up, he explained that the sculpture's four pieces of mahogany instructed him how to work, rather than allowing him to give his artistic vision and skill free reign. Unfortunately, Albert continued, the French priest who commissioned the sculpture fled François Duvalier's repression, and his successor at the Catholic church disliked the sculpture, which Albert eventually retrieved. Genuine understanding, we concluded from the story, only emerges when abstract knowledge confronts concrete circumstances.

"Context" is surely among the most cavalierly defined concepts and overused words in anthropology. One need only recall hearing or reading about "context of the situation."

"Failed" state, societal "collapse," and ecological "disaster" may be serviceable concepts for grand theory as well as catchy terms for media coverage. Are they useful for understanding Haiti's compound crisis, its many and many-sided problems? No, if one considers failure, collapse, and disaster fixed and incontrovertible end points. No, if one contends that Haitians, leaders and followers, "chose" crisis and problems. No,

FIGURE 10.5 Haitian trees are not just for charcoal, boards, and poles. Albert Mangonès (1917–2002) standing next to his sculpture "Le Christ" (ca. 1960), at his home in Martissant, a Port-au-Prince suburb, 19 October 1997. (Photograph by Drexel G. Woodson.) While carving the figure from a single mahogany tree trunk, Mangonès explained, the material gave him directions rather than allowing him to impose his ideas on it; however, the church that had commissioned the statue rejected it.

if the concepts and terms are deemed self-explanatory and treated as rationales for inaction or for humanitarian assistance as the only form that action may take. But yes, if the concepts and terms prompt careful, methodologically sound investigation of Haitian realities, present and past. In Haiti, as elsewhere, these realities include how the facts about one nation-state are forged in the crucible of struggles, within that nation-state and in its relations with other nation-states, over the proper uses of power to achieve and sustain prosperity.

Perhaps my chapter can contribute to a renewal of detailed comparative research on, and heated though largely constructive debates about, the two sides of Hispaniola. Haitian and Dominican intellectuals (assisted by foreign colleagues) initiated the research and the debates following the U.S. Occupations, but both have waned or become one-sided in recent decades. Haitians and Dominicans jointly inherited *Ayti*, the Taino land that, since 1492, has undergone transformations wrought by Spanish and French colonialism, the Haitian Revolution and the diverse outcomes of statecraft as well as popular action in independent Haiti, Dominican independence and the equally diverse outcomes of statecraft and popular action there, along with the policies of foreign governments and private firms. Sound comparison of the two nation-states entails bringing contextual sensibility to bear on brute facts. Haitians and Dominicans still struggle to benefit from those transformations and overcome their impediments.

ACKNOWLEDGMENTS

This essay is dedicated to Haitian architect and artist Albert Mangonès (1917–2002), whose statue *Le Marron Inconnu* (1966), honoring the Haitian Revolution's unknown rebel slaves, was selected by the United Nations in 1989 as the image for a stamp commemorating the Universal Declaration of the Rights of Man. As Director-General of L'Institut pour la Sauvegarde du Patrimoine National (ISPAN) from 1979 to 1991, Albert used funding from UNESCO and the Organization of American States for successful ISPAN projects to study and reconstruct the Citadel, the Sans Souci Palace, and the Ramiers Site, historical monuments to Haitian independence that are now centerpieces of the Citadel National Park.

I thank Patricia A. McAnany and Norman Yoffee for inviting me to participate in the Amerind Foundation Advanced Seminar "Choices and Fates of Human Societies: An Anthropological and Environmental Reader," held in Dragoon, Arizona, 9–14 October 2007, along with Amerind Director John Ware and his staff for their hospitality. I am grateful to all of the participants for stimulating commentary or conversation that prompted revisions of this essay. However, I owe special debts of gratitude to discussant Frederick Errington for pointed anthropological criticism, to John McNeil for saving me from embarrassing errors of historical fact, and to Yoffee for "light editing" that tightened my argument. Likewise, Frédéric Mangonès corrected certain facts in my account of his father's statue "Le Christ." Aside from authorizing my use of a photograph, Brackette F. Williams helped me think about connections (and disjunctions) among grand theory, methodology, and communication as they relate to choice making, its contexts, and outcomes. I might wish to blame these colleagues for factual mistakes, errant interpretations, and infelicities of writing style, but they reflect my choices.

Notes

* Experiences at home, in public schools, and on the streets of Philadelphia sparked my interest in history and individual psychology during the 1960s, when demands for Black Power replaced agitation for civil rights, and attitudes toward the Vietnam War progressed from indifference through support to opposition. My parents, teachers, and Baptist minister Leon H. Sullivan, along with street-wise storytellers, taught me about differences of race/ethnicity, nationality, class, sex (today's gender), religion, and language, emphasizing their roles in struggles for and over freedom, wealth, and dignity.

    I took degrees in cultural/social anthropology at Yale University (B.A., 1973) and the University of Chicago (M.A., 1978; Ph.D., 1990). Working with scholar-teachers at those institutions, I became a Caribbeanist, and, focusing on Haiti, I learned how to combine ethnography, historiography, and bibliography to study connections, in the present and the past, among culture, language, society, and political economy. I also learned to view basic and applied anthropology as two sides of a coin. Anthropological knowledge and understanding of the human spectacle are inherently valuable, but they are also useful for trying to change it.

    Since the 1970s my work has zigzagged between theoretical and methodological issues and the practical problems of development, to improve the conditions under which people live, work, and play. For me, research projects – in Haiti, other Caribbean countries, the United States, or elsewhere – reiterate that anthropological knowledge and understanding are necessary but not sufficient conditions for changing the human spectacle, because power limits their usefulness.

1. I speak of social science disciplines individually, thinking of the one I know best: cultural/social anthropology, basic and applied. Interdisciplinary fields (better dubbed "multidisciplinary" given actual research practices) face compound challenges of internal comparison and synthesis and external communication.

2. Arturo Escobar (1995) and the volume edited by Mark Hobart (1993) appraise development discourse, projects, and programs.

3. I have discussed this cliché as an obstacle to communication about rural Haitian livelihood systems and food security (Woodson 1997) and about poverty, a complex phenomenon that must be unpacked descriptively and analytically to formulate and interpret "indicators," development discourse's main symbols of sociocultural, agroecological, and economic conditions and processes (Woodson 2007b).

4. Diamond 2005, 1997.

5. The University of Arizona's Bureau of Applied Research in Anthropology (BARA), where I work, designed and supervised three diagnostic baseline studies of livelihood security throughout rural Haiti in the mid-1990s (BARA 1996a, 1996b, 1997). The baseline series aimed to improve the information infrastructure for efforts to enhance household food security by the United States Agency for International Development (USAID) and its cooperating NGO Sponsors of the Food for Peace Program. Two brief accounts of my anthropological research in Haiti during 1972–1980 are available, one in English (Woodson 1990: ii-xviii, xvii–xl) and one in Haitian Creole (Woodson 2007a:103–105).

6. Barth (1981a, 1981b), Asad (1970, 1972), and Paine (1974) offer interested readers a sense of the anthropological debate about the roles of choice making and choices in human affairs.

7. I draw on Michel-Rolph Trouillot's insight that the histories of peoples and countries in the Global South undermine conventional Western understandings of the hyphen in "nation-state." In Haiti, Trouillot (1990) shows, the state developed in opposition to the nation rather than as its complement, and this, he argues (Trouillot 1995), helps to explain silences and mentions in the production of Haitian history. Trouillot (2003) illuminates the pitfalls and possibilities of a historically informed anthropology of globalization. My encyclopedia article (Woodson 2008) assesses my Haitian friend and colleague's work.

8. Rouse 1992 provides an accessible discussion of archaeological evidence about the Tainos in pre-Columbian *Ayti*. Focusing on Saint-Domingue/Haiti, I explore some of these processes, which Caribbeanists broadly call "creolization" (Woodson 1994).

9. Diamond 2005: "Further Readings: Chapter 11," 548–549.

10. Lundahl 1979.

11. Lundahl (1979, 1983, 1992). In reviews of Lundahl's work, Haitian and foreign scholars have outlined the foci and range of criticism from different disciplinary vantage points. See Caprio 1982; Lowenthal 1979; Mintz 1987; Nicholls 1981; Trouillot 1980.

12. James 1963 (1938).

13. Commemorating the two-hundredth anniversaries of the French Revolution (1789), the slave revolt that initiated the Haitian Revolution (1791), and Haiti's Proclamation of Independence (1804), a mini-growth industry in scholarship revisited and revised received wisdom about events, structures, processes, and personalities during the Age of Revolutions. Geggus (2002) writes authoritatively about the Haitian Revolution and C. L. R. James's pivotal role in its historiography.

14. Wecker 1999.
15. Yunén 1985.
16. Accounts of U.S.-Haitian diplomatic relations during the nineteenth century by Logan (1941) and Montague (1940), which include the United States' relations with the Dominican Republic, remain the most instructive. Schmidt (1971) provides a detailed, comprehensive, and accessible account of the U.S. Occupation.
17. Anthropologists and agroforesters have assessed these efforts since 1950 and have conducted fresh research on their moderately encouraging results in difficult circumstances during the 1980s and 1990s. See Murray 1978, 1984, 1986, 1987; Murray and Bannister 2004; Smucker 1981; Smucker and Timyan 1995.
18. Barthélemy (1989) illuminates the principal causes and consequences of "self-regulation" in the Haitian countryside – the city- and town-dweller's "back country" or "outlands" (Haitian Creole, *andeyò;* French, *le pays en dehors*). Unless otherwise indicated, all foreign language words and expressions are in Haitian Creole, written according to the official orthography. *MOZAYIK: yon konbit literè ann Ayisyen (An Anthology in the Haitian Language)*, a collection of Haitian Creole essays on social science and humanities topics, includes a brief description of the orthography (Saven and Woudsonn 2007: 132).
19. Focusing on Haiti, Plummer (1988) has studied immigration to the Caribbean by Levantine peoples, who, often carrying U.S. passports, established footholds in local import-export sectors. Haitians call the Levantines *Arab* (Arabs) or *Siriyen* (Syrians).
20. Columbus (1987), the Admiral's log, is a good place to begin.
21. Woodson (1990: chaps. 4–6) explores "reckoning place," a microlevel (face-to-face or back-to-back) interaction process, whereby the peasants and townsfolk of a northern Haitian locality contextualize factual or interpretive statements.
22. See Mangonès (n.d.). Edmond Mangonès (1884–1967) mined his personal library for fugitive nineteenth-century documentation. The Mangonès Collection holds most major works in European languages about Haiti and the Dominican Republic from 1680 to 1967, the year that Mangonès died (Lowenthal and Woodson 1974).
23. The obscene English adjective "fucked up" entered Haitian Creole as *fòkop,* a crude and impolite (though not obscene) descriptor for a thoroughly disorganized and dysfunctional state of affairs. I cannot say with certainty whether Marines supplied the loan word during the U.S. Occupation (1915–1934) or whether it has been a lexicosemantic "remittance" from Haitian immigrants to the United States since the 1970s.
24. My encyclopedia entry about former President Jean-Bertrand Aristide (Woodson 2006) surveys his political career from 1983 to 2004, along with maneuvers by Haiti's established Haitian order and populist movement. In this regard, Dupuy (2007) emphasizes the negative role of "New World Order imperialism," the work, he argues, of the United States, the World Bank, and the International Monetary Fund. Mintz (1995), the

dean of U.S. Haitianists, considered Haiti's political crisis insuperable and recommended a UN protectorate or trusteeship.

Bibliography

Asad, Talal. 1970. *The Kababish Arabs: Power, Authority and Consent in a Nomadic Tribe.* New York: Praeger.

Asad, Talal. 1972. "Market Model, Class Structure and Consent: A Reconsideration of Swat Political Organization." *Man* (n.s.) **7**(1):71–94.

Barth, Fredrik. 1981a [1966]. "Models of Social Organization I, II, and III," in *Selected Essays of Fredrik Barth, Volume I: Process and Form in Social Life,* pp. 32–75. International Library of Anthropology. London: Routledge and Kegan Paul.

Barth, Fredrik. 1981b. "'Models' Reconsidered." In *Selected Essays of Fredrik Barth, Volume I: Process and Form in Social Life,* pp. 76–104. International Library of Anthropology. London: Routledge and Kegan Paul.

Barthélemy, Gérard. 1989. *Le pays en dehors: essai sur l'univers rural Haïtien.* Montréal: Centre International de Documentation et d'Information Haïtienne; Port-au-Prince: Henri Deschamps.

Bureau of Applied Research in Anthropology (BARA). 1996a. *A Baseline Study of Livelihood Security in Northwest Haiti.* M. Baro, Principal Investigator. Final draft, April. Port-au-Prince: CARE/Haiti, and Tucson: BARA, University of Arizona.

Bureau of Applied Research in Anthropology (BARA). 1996b. *A Baseline Study of Livelihood Security in the Southern Peninsula of Haiti.* Prepared for Catholic Relief Services (CRS)/Haiti and the Interim Food Security Information System (iFSIS). D. G. Woodson and M. Baro, Principal Investigators. Final draft, April. Port-au-Prince: CRS/Haiti, and Tucson: BARA, University of Arizona.

Bureau of Applied Research in Anthropology (BARA). 1997. *A Baseline Study of Livelihood Security in the Departments of the Artibonite, Center, North, Northeast and West, Republic of Haiti.* Prepared for the Adventist Development and Relief Agency (ADRA)/Haiti and the Interim Food Security Information System (iFSIS). D. G. Woodson and M. Baro, Principal Investigators. Final draft, May. Port-au-Prince: ADRA/Haiti, and Tucson: BARA, University of Arizona.

Caprio, Giovanni. 1982. [Compte-rendu de] Mats Lundahl, *Les Paysans et la pauvreté, une étude sur Haïti* [1979]. *Conjonction: Revue Franco-Haïtienne,* No. 152 [page numbers missing].

Columbus, Christopher. 1987. *The Log of Christopher Columbus.* Translated by Robert H. Fuson. Camden, ME: International Marine Publishing.

Diamond, Jared. 1997. *Guns, Germs, and Steel.* New York: W. W. Norton.

Diamond, Jared. 2005. *Collapse: How Societies Choose to Fail or Succeed.* New York: Viking.

Dupuy, Alex. 2007. *The Prophet and Power: Jean-Bertrand Aristide, the International Community, and Haiti.* Critical Currents in Latin American Perspectives Series [No. 4]. Lanham, MD: Rowman and Littlefield.

Escobar, Arturo. 1995. *Encountering Development: The Making and Unmaking of the Third World*. Princeton, NJ: Princeton University Press.

Fatton, Robert, Jr. 2002. *Haiti's Predatory Republic: The Unending Transition to Democracy*. Boulder: Lynne Rienner Publishers.

Geggus, David. 2002. *Haitian Revolutionary Studies*. Bloomington: Indiana University Press.

Hobart, Mark. Editor. 1993. *An Anthropological Critique of Development: The Growth of Ignorance*. London: Routledge.

James, C.L.R. 1963 [1938]. *The Black Jacobins: Toussaint L'Ouverture and the San Domingo Revolution*. 2nd rev. ed., with an appendix, "From Toussaint L'Ouverture to Fidel Castro" [1962], by the author. New York: Vintage.

Logan, Rayford W. 1941. *The Diplomatic Relations of the United States with Haiti, 1776–1891*. Chapel Hill: University of North Carolina Press.

Lowenthal, Ira P. 1979. Review of Mats Lundahl, *Peasants and Poverty: A Study of Haiti*. *Revista/Review* [1979]. *Interamericana* **9**(3):500–503.

Lowenthal, Ira P. and Drexel G. Woodson. Editors. 1974. *Catalogue de la Collection Mangonès, Pétionville, Haïti*. ARP Occasional Papers 2. New Haven, CT: Antilles Research Program, Yale University.

Lundahl, Mats. 1979. *Peasants and Poverty: A Study of Haiti*. London: Croom Helm.

Lundahl, Mats. 1983. *The Haitian Economy: Man, Land and Markets*. New York: St. Martin's Press.

Lundahl, Mats. 1992. *Politics or Markets? Essays on Haitian Underdevelopment*. London: Routledge.

Mangonès, Edmond. n.d. *Aspects of History and Psychology: The Ethic of "Strong Government" in Haiti, 1843–1888/Pages d'histoire et de psychologie: l'ethique de nos gouvernements forts, by Edmond Mangonès*. Annotated, translated, and edited, with a critical introduction by D. G. Woodson. In progress.

Mintz, Sidney W. 1987. Review of Mats Lundahl, *The Haitian Economy: Man, Land and Markets* [1983]. *Nieuwe West-Indische Gids/New West Indian Guide* **61**(1&2):55–59.

Mintz, Sidney W. 1995. "Can Haiti Change?" *Foreign Affairs* **74**(1):73–86.

Montague, Ludwell Lee. 1940. *Haiti and the United States, 1714–1938*. Durham, NC: Duke University Press.

Murray, Gerald F. 1978. *Terraces, Trees and the Haitian Peasant: An Assessment of Twenty-Five Years of Erosion Control in Rural Haiti*. Port-au-Prince, Haiti: U.S. Agency for International Development.

Murray, Gerald F. 1984. "The Wood Tree as a Peasant Cash-Crop: An Anthropological Strategy for the Domestication of Energy," in *Haiti – Today and Tomorrow: An Interdisciplinary Study*. Edited by C.R. Foster and A. Valdman, pp. 141–160. Lanham, MD: University Press of America.

Murray, Gerald F. 1986. "Seeing the Forest While Planting the Trees: An Anthropological Approach to Agroforestry in Rural Haiti" (with "Addendum: Agroforestry Update," by Glenn R. Smucker), in *Politics, Projects, and People: Institutional Development in Haiti*. Edited by D.W. Brinkerhoff and J.-C. Garcia-Zamor, pp. 193–226. New York: Praeger.

Murray, Gerald F. 1987. "The Domestication of Wood in Haiti: A Case Study in Applied Anthropology," in *Anthropological Praxis: Translating Knowledge into Action*. Edited by R. Wulff and S. Fiske pp. 223–242. Boulder: Westview Press.

Murray, Gerald F., and Michael E. Bannister. 2004. "Peasants, Agroforesters, and Anthropologists: A 20-Year Venture in Income-Generating Trees and Hedgerows in Haiti: New Vistas in Agroforestry." *Agroforestry Systems* **61**(1):383–397.

Nicholls, David. 1981. Review of Mats Lundahl, *Peasants and Poverty: A Study of Haiti* [1979]. *Journal of Development Studies* **17**(2):248–249.

Paine, Robert. 1974. *Second Thoughts about Barth's "Models."* Royal Anthropological Institute Occasional Paper No. 32. London: Royal Anthropological Institute of Great Britain and Ireland.

Plummer, Brenda Gayle. 1988. *Haiti and the Great Powers, 1902–1915*. Baton Rouge: Louisiana State University Press.

Rouse, Irving. 1992. *The Tainos: Rise and Decline of the People Who Greeted Columbus*. New Haven, CT: Yale University Press.

Saven, Woje E. and Dreksèl G. Woudsonn (kowòdonnatè) [Savain, Roger E., and Drexel G. Woodson]. Editors. 2007. *MOZAYIK: yon konbit literè ann Ayisyen (An Anthology in the Haitian Language)*. Kolèksyon Language EXPERIENCE, Inc. West Conshohocken, PA: INFINITY Publishing.

Schmidt, Hans. 1971. *The United States Occupation of Haiti, 1915–1934*. New Brunswick, NJ: Rutgers University Press.

Smucker, Glenn R. 1981. *Trees and Charcoal in Haitian Peasant Economy: A Feasibility Study of Reforestation*. January. Port-au-Prince: USAID Mission.

Smucker, Glenn R. and Joel C. Timyan. 1995. *Impact of Tree Planting in Haiti: 1982–1995*. Prepared for the USAID Haiti Productive Land Use Systems Project. April. Auburn, GA: Southeast Consortium for International Development, Auburn University.

Trouillot, Michel-Rolph. 1980. Review of Mats Lundahl, *Peasants and Poverty: A Study of Haiti* [1979]. *Journal of Peasant Studies* **8**(1):112–116.

Trouillot, Michel-Rolph. 1990. *Haiti, State against Nation: The Origins and Legacy of Duvalierism*. New York: Monthly Review Press.

Trouillot, Michel-Rolph. 1995. *Silencing the Past: Power and the Production of History*. Boston: Beacon Press.

Trouillot, Michel-Rolph. 2003. *Global Transformations: Anthropology and the Modern World*. New York: Palgrave Macmillan.

Wecker, Michele. 1999. *Why the Cocks Fight: Dominicans, Haitians, and the Struggle for Hispaniola*. New York: Hill and Wang.

Woodson, Drexel G. 1990. *"Tout mounn sé mounn, men tout mounn pa menm:* Microlevel Sociocultural Aspects of Land Tenure in a Northern Haitian Locality." Ph.D. diss., University of Chicago.

Woodson, Drexel G. 1994. "Which Beginning Should Be Hindmost? Surrealism in Appropriations of Facts about Haitian 'Contact Culture.'" Unpublished paper.

Woodson, Drexel G. 1997. *"Lamanjay,* Food Security, *Sécurité Alimentaire:* A Lesson in Communication from BARA's Mixed-Methods Approach to Baseline Research in Haiti, 1994–1996." *Culture & Agriculture* **19**(3): 108–212.

Woodson, Drexel G. 2006. "Aristide, Jean-Bertrand," in *Encyclopedia of Africa-American Culture and History: The Black Experience in the Americas.* 2nd ed. Edited by Colin Palmer, pp. 133–138. New York: Macmillan Reference USA.

Woodson, Drexel G. 2007a. "Kontre zo nan gran chemen, sonje vyann te kouvri li: koudjè antwopolojik sou kèk lèt yon blan nwa voye bay Ayisyen natifnatal, 1980–1983," in *MOZAYIK: yon konbit literè ann Ayisyen (An Anthology in the Haitian Language).* Kowòdonne pa Woje E. Saven ak Drèksèl G. Woudsonn, pp. 103–108. Kolèksyon Language EXPERIENCE, Inc. West Conshohocken, PA: INFINITY Publishing.Com. [Article title: "If You See a Bone on the Main Road, Remember That It Once Had Meat: An Anthropological Perspective on a Few Letters from a Black Foreigner to Haitians, 1980–1983." Volume title: *Mosaic: A Literary Work-Party (An Anthology in the Haitian Language).* Edited by Roger E. Savain and Drexel G. Woodson.]

Woodson, Drexel G. 2007b. "What Do Indicators Indicate? Reflections on the Trials and Tribulations of Using Food Aid to Promote Development in Haiti," in *Anthropology Put to Work.* Edited by Les W. Field and Richard G. Fox, pp. 129–147. Wenner-Gren International Symposium Series. Oxford: Berg.

Woodson, Drexel G. 2008. "Trouillot, Michel-Rolph," in *International Encyclopedia of the Social Sciences.* 2nd ed. Edited by William A. Darity, vol. 8, pp. 457–458. Detroit: Macmillan Reference USA.

Yunén, Rafael Emilio. 1985. *La isla como es.* Santiago, Dominican Republic: Universidad Católica Madre y Maestra.

11

The Power of the Past

Environment, Aborigines, Archaeology, and a Sustainable Australian Society

Tim Murray[*]

The fates of both indigenous and settler Australians loom large in both of Jared Diamond's books *Guns, Germs, and Steel* and *Collapse,* either as victims of Eurasian "civilization" transplanted to Australia, or as potential victims of a twenty-first-century form of the "ecocide" that Diamond considers to be the prime cause of the collapse of civilizations. This is big history at its most dramatic, the meaning of history divined from its grand sweep since the end of the last glacial maximum, with the lessons for us all to learn identified and forcefully expounded. This is history in which the fates of Aboriginal societies in Australia were either sealed by the arrival of Europeans, or by a combination of isolation and invasion (in the case of Tasmania). As the descendant of settler Australians and one who studies the long-term and recent history of Aboriginal Australians, I believe that Diamond fails to grasp the significance the roles Aboriginal people have come to play in contemporary Australia, roles that are crucial for the development of a sustainable society in my country.

The importance of sustainable ecologies (and the societies in which they are embedded) is widely understood in Australia, but sustainable societies are created from more than compacts about greenhouse gas reductions and the development of regimes of sustainable resource exploitation. Sustainable societies also require members to enter an open and honest discourse about their histories, not just those of the mainstream, but also those "hidden" histories of the marginalized and oppressed. Particularly vital in Australia is the ways in which indigenous and settler populations identify and deal with the consequences of the conquest and appropriation of Aboriginal Australia, a process that began slightly over 200 years ago. The fates of Aboriginal societies since the invasion of Australia in the late eighteenth century may be of little concern to Diamond (indeed, they barely rate a mention in *Collapse*), but they are a matter of prime importance to contemporary Australians, whatever their ethnicity, and whenever they have arrived in the country.

In this chapter I discuss some of the roles that archaeology and history have come to play in the complex process of dealing with the consequences of history, indeed, of considering the fates of indigenous societies in contemporary Australia. Significantly, there is no single story here, more a multitude of interactions and negotiations that occur at all scales – local, regional, national, and global. The human history of the continent has been mobilized by both indigenous and nonindigenous Australians to support separatist, integrationist, and multicultural agendas. I will exemplify this using the example of Tasmania. The bulk of what I have to say turns on a simple question: If the answer to Yali's question in *Guns, Germs, and Steel* ("Why is it that you white people developed so much cargo and brought it to New Guinea, but we black people had so little cargo of our own?") is, according to Diamond, something like "It's mostly explained by the extent to which ecology constrains human creativity," then what is the point of exploring the archaeology and history of Australia, either before or after occupation by Europeans? Is there anything else worth knowing about the *human* history of Australia? And, if so, who is this knowledge for? I argue that a knowledge and understanding of the past is a prerequisite for building a sustainable future.

Central to my approach in this chapter is the contrast between the abstract and crypto-scientific "big history" questions asked by Diamond (through Yali) and the much more direct and very important "small history" questions, such as What led to the destruction of traditional Tasmanian Aboriginal society? How have indigenous communities survived and maintained Aboriginality in a society seemingly totally dominated by non-Aboriginal culture? Here the focus switches from interesting discussions of the constraints of ecology and opportunity to a different, human scale: How can history be mobilized for the creation of a more just society in Australia?

Obviously these explorations are highly charged politically. History, archaeology, and heritage have consequences for us now and into the future.

ARCHAEOLOGY AND THE CREATION OF
HERITAGE IN AUSTRALIA

In Australia archaeology is playing a significant role in the recon-figuration of national polities in the late twentieth and early twenty-first centuries, providing the material elements of *both* ancient and modern cultural identities. In Australia identity politics plays out in a number of fields of public discourse, including "Republicanism," "Multiculturalism," and "Relationships with Asia," but the discussion that has had the most impact on cultural heritage (and on the moral legitimacy of the nation) is that of reconciliation with Aboriginal and Torres Strait Islander peoples, the indigenous inhabitants of the con-tinent. This discussion is made more significant when we recognize that this is both a discourse and a process without end. On the sur-face it makes good sense to be clear about process and outcomes, but this clarity is illusory because it tends to ignore the fact that although the pattern of the mutual destinies of Aboriginal and non-Aboriginal Australia might be changed, our mutuality will continue. Of course, not everyone (even archaeologists) agree about mutuality, with some preferring a notion of separate identities free from the appropria-tions of colonialism. In this view the descendants of white settlers create new identities "stolen" from the identities and histories of indigenous people.[1] For me this is an unnecessarily negative inter-pretation of cultural exchange that portrays indigenous people as only passive victims of a "culture grab," rather than as active players appropriating cultural elements as diverse as art, music, dance, sport, and literature from nonindigenous Australians.

The growing recognition that a shared past, present, and future exists within the process of reconciliation has resulted in a pro-found shift in the popular understanding and appreciation of Aboriginal Australia. One of the most tangible signs of that inter-est is that Australian governments (both state and federal) have introduced legislation protecting Aboriginal heritage. The history of heritage legislation in Australia is still in its infancy and remains a highly contested field, but it is possible to make some worthwhile generalizations about it.[2]

The first round of state legislation occurred between 1965 and 1975, but apart from the Australian Heritage Commission Act of 1975, effective federal legislation in this area had to wait until 1984. Aboriginal sites and contexts were protected before colonial European ones, and we still search for convincing explanations for why this happened and what the difference in timing might mean for the relative significance of the two types of cultural heritage for Australia.[3]

Until the 1960s archaeology was focused on fundamentally anti-quarian pursuits, such as collecting material culture such as tools, baskets, and utensils, but there was a long-standing interest in unraveling the pre-European history of Australia. However, analysis of this way of "possessing" Australia has rarely progressed beyond the observation that there was a big gulf separating such "stamp collecting" from serious (although amateur) explorations into continental archaeology undertaken between 1930s and the 1960s by Fred McCarthy, Norman Tindale, or D. S. Davidson.[4]

Generations of energetic antiquarians such as Robert Etheridge could not persuade governments to preserve archaeological sites in Australia. Indeed, when legislation was first proposed in the states of South Australia and New South Wales in the mid-1960s, the activities of amateurs and collectors were seen as being one of the great *threats* to the integrity of archaeological sites. With the exception of people like Fred McCarthy, many antiquarians simply separated the "Aborigine from the artifact."[5] They regarded artifacts as the relics of societies either now passed from the earth, or well and truly on their way to extinction or assimilation. Although many investigators were keen to understand traditional methods for manufacturing material culture such as stone tools, it is clear that these studies were not presented as contributions to Aboriginal history, but to something much more abstract. Artifacts were, rather, seen as steps toward the solution of a puzzle of the antiquity and origins of Aboriginal people. This was a game played by, and for the benefit of, non-Aboriginal people either as part of the great imperial project of writing the history of human evolution or as part of a more ambiguous process of "understanding the history of the country."[6]

The theme of this early legislation was the preservation of "relics" rather than the "heritage" of living societies. When we search for explanations for the sudden significance of such relics, the records of parliamentary debates reveal politicians speaking of "nation" and "heritage." Politicians also celebrated archaeological discoveries as playing their role in an awakening interest in Aboriginal people, who were to achieve full rights of Australian citizenship only in 1967 and were beginning to occupy a cultural space somewhere between extinction and multiculturalism. Parliamentarians were happy to embrace the idea that "relics" were to become important in the definition of national "self."[7]

By the end of the 1970s a "national heritage" had been described and defined by non-Aboriginal people in a way that essentially reflected a separation of a scientific past from an Aboriginal present. This "colonization of the past" was more than just the state assuming legal control of physical relics, it was an appropriation of the entire human history of the continent into the heritage of Australia, an appropriation that endorsed the science of archaeology as the vehicle through which the meanings of that heritage would become manifest. At the end of this period, the Australian Heritage Commission could speak confidently of a "National Estate," the preservation of which was a collective responsibility.[8]

But this notion of a National Heritage, based on the appropriation of the "relics" of Aboriginal Australia, has been remarkably short lived. During the last twenty-five years Aboriginal organizations around the country have successfully fought to gain control over what had previously been understood as "relics" and have now been publicly redefined as "Aboriginal heritage," thus putting the interests of a living culture ahead of a scientific interest in one that was passed or passing. Much of the conflict was directed by indigenous people toward archaeologists and the heritage organizations run by state and federal bodies. These peoples stressed that the legislation of the 1960s and early 1970s might have ensured the conservation of archaeological sites, but it also excluded the owners of the heritage from its management.

As a result of this intense political action all state and federal governments have either produced new legislation or have radically changed the way they administer existing acts. In each case a central question has been the moral legitimacy of the state to pass legislation on matters related to the heritage of indigenous groups, which might specifically limit their rights of control, or to argue for the legitimacy of other rights and interests in such heritage. Today making policy about indigenous heritage in Australia is firmly based on the notion that it should be an expression of the interests of Aboriginal people.[9]

Whereas these significant changes have made it possible for Aboriginal people to regain control over heritage, governments and Aboriginal organizations also have to manage a non-Aboriginal interest in the human history of Australia, which retains much of the original focus on sites and artifacts. Government and nongovernment organizations have also struggled to find ways that allow non-Aboriginal people to make meanings about and to confer values on these things, be they "relics" or "cultural heritage," if only to ensure that heritage can survive into the future. This has proved to be difficult because it is self-evident that such heritage policies (if they are to be successful) cannot simply be an expression of the interests of Aboriginal people, given that the society that presents the greatest threat to that heritage, and that has to live with and make sense of such policies, is predominantly non-Aboriginal.[10]

To be effective, policies concerned with the management of indigenous heritage cannot only arise from the interests of indigenous people, but must also engage the perspectives and interests of the broader society in which such policies are expected to be effective. In this sense effective policies have to be meaningful to Aboriginal *and* non-Aboriginal people, an increasingly tall order if policy is developed on the assumption that the interests of Aboriginal and non-Aboriginal society cannot be coincident, and that they should be kept hermetically sealed one from the other. It is also made more difficult when ways of establishing the cultural significance of Aboriginal heritage for non-Aboriginal people (such as archaeological study) are marginalized as "colonialist" or denigrated as being slightly more subtle attempts at appropriating Aboriginal Australia into a manufactured Australian identity.[11]

In Australia governments have rightly sought to correct gross imbalances in the administration of Aboriginal heritage by recognizing the paramount importance of an Aboriginal interest in Aboriginal heritage, and by parlaying that recognition into an increasing control of that heritage by Aboriginal people. This empowerment of Aboriginal people, which is commonly expressed as an ownership of that heritage, has led to a lessening of freedoms for archaeologists and to much greater regulation of archaeological activity by governments and Aboriginal heritage organizations.

After more than two decades of this regime, instances of effective collaboration between archaeologists and Aboriginal communities are common, if not as frequently celebrated in the literature as the inevitable conflicts.[12] Reconciliation does not (and should not) require that the places, contexts, and artifacts that together make up the heritage of Aboriginal Australia must have the same meanings and values for everybody. It should also not require that only one strategy for establishing the meanings of places or things be mandated, be it the views of Aboriginal people, "scientists," adherents of postcolonialist perspectives, or New Age crystal gazers. What reconciliation should mean is that all Australians come to value the cultural heritage of Aboriginal and non-Aboriginal Australia so that it can be conserved for future generations and become an active principle in the process of experiencing, describing, and understanding Aboriginal and non-Aboriginal Australia as they continue to unfold. In this way heritage can be transformed into cultural capital that can play a vital role in creating a just and sustainable society in the country. This is a goal far beyond the horizons either of *Guns, Germs, and Steel,* or *Collapse.* The fact that indigenous societies survived in Australia, and that their fates have become so inextricably linked with the futures of nonindigenous Australians, makes their near invisibility in *Collapse* all the more surprising.

There was history in Australia before the arrival of Europeans, and much more to the heritage and archaeology of Aboriginal Australia than the limited role assigned by Diamond of 40,000 years of "noble savages" keeping economies in balance with continental ecologies. Although conveniently ignored by Diamond, there is every possibility that human beings were an active principle in the extinction of megafauna in Australia.[13] There is also ample evidence of cultural diversity and change over a long continental history that did not cease with invasion in the late eighteenth century. Coming to grips with this history is a vital part of the story of modern Australia.

FIGURE 11.1 Pleistocene archaeological sites in greater Australia (Sahul).

SURVIVAL, "HIDDEN" HISTORY, AND CHANGING
THE FOCUS OF ARCHAEOLOGY IN AUSTRALIA

Until recently, for most Australian archaeologists research into the archaeology of Aboriginal Australia has focused on the very earliest periods of colonization and settlement, from about 45,000 to 10,000 before present[14] – a result of a desire to establish continental chronology and to contribute to answering some of the "big" questions of global prehistory. However, over the past twenty years the focus has begun to change from a concern with "deeper" prehistory to the archaeology of Aboriginal people since 1788, when the English began to colonize Australia. There are many reasons for this change of focus, but for me the crucial explanation flows from the requirements of heritage legislation (which I have just discussed). Chief among these is the need for archaeologists to gain the informed consent of communities in order to conduct archaeological research (and the fact that the vast bulk of that research is undertaken in heritage or "applied" settings) has fostered the evolution of collaborative research projects that serve a broader range of interests (both indigenous and archaeological).[15]

Two of the most important indigenous interests are in the revival and maintenance of traditional culture and community, and (directly connected to the first) regaining ownership of lands appropriated by the government at the time of colonization. Legislation has made it clear that archaeological data from remote antiquity in Australia are not considered to be of much use in defining tribal or clan affiliations from the distant past. For more recent times information derived from ethnography and ethnohistories is thought to be much more useful.

It is increasingly common for indigenous communities to regard the period immediately before European colonization, and the roughly 200 years of dispossession and occupation that followed, to be of the greatest cultural, hence political, significance. Over the last decade the historical archaeology of Aboriginal Australia (or contact archaeology as it is more commonly known) has sought to reconstruct the trajectories of Aboriginal societies from "prehistory" to history and to dissolve the artificial divide between the two. Here the content and form of history matters very much indeed, and the goal is to write original histories with very little assistance from written historical sources.[16]

Another significant issue has to do with how archaeologists can identify the forces that changed indigenous societies over the last 200 years, helping us toward a better understanding of the *way* things changed. Significantly, archaeological research allows us to chart the active roles played by indigenous societies since colonization. Here we can demonstrate that indigenous societies were not

just passive receptors of alien cultures, but are actively combating
the effects of exotic diseases and subsequent population collapse,
and developing strategies in an attempt to ensure social and cultural
survival.

An indigenous interest in "contact" archaeology revolves around
the need to comprehend the experience of dispossession and cultural
survival. For Aboriginal people, exploring a historical archaeology
of Aboriginal life over the past 200 years can enhance understanding about the histories of separation and sharing that are so much a
feature of community life, while at the same time they provide a rich
store of information from which such communities can renegotiate
or reshape their identities within modern Australian society.

FIGURE 11.2 Archaeologist Mark Grist. (Courtesy of Mark Grist)

MARK DUGAY GRIST[17]

"For me archaeology has immense significance in writing the
recent history of indigenous Australia. When linked with oral histories, archaeology has the capacity to teach us something new,

or (because of the impact of colonization) something that our people might not have known." (Interview, 31 January 2008)

"What I have tried to express is the need for our people to have the basic toolbox (both mentally and physically) to ensure our involvement in heritage management for the future. How and where Aboriginal oral history and cultural practices enhance the archaeology and cultural heritage management within Australia is a matter for each individual Aboriginal community. Science should be seen and used as a tool to enhance Aboriginal people's lives and not seen as something that is still strongly related to colonialism." (Dugay-Grist 2006: 378).

The creation of new archaeological perspectives on the history of Aboriginal Australia also takes into account the impact of a widespread desire for reconciliation between black and white Australians, but it has had a price. Significantly the cultural landscapes of reconciliation created through this research are the product of a series of revelations (profoundly shocking to many) of contact with Europeans and its consequences.[18] The cultural landscapes of reconciliation often flow from the difficult and confronting process of making the invisible – a product of ignorance, fear, or a desire to suppress or forget – visible, and of discovering how much of the history of such landscapes is shared among their populations. Nowhere in Australia is this more apparent than in Tasmania, where stories of frontier violence and wholesale extirpation can now link with the product of thirty years of archaeological research to produce an account that has real political significance in contemporary Australia. Here issues of heritage, of the importance of the local story over the global "big" picture, come to the fore, allowing us to "see" the Tasmanians as something more than the product of 10,000 years of isolation (which began when sea waters rose at the end of Pleistocene about 10,000 years ago). It also reinforces the point that postcolonial societies can be divided about the meaning of history and the ways in which it can be used to change societies.

WHAT CAUSED THE DESTRUCTION OF TRADITIONAL TASMANIAN ABORIGINAL SOCIETY?

Beginning in the early 1990s and gathering much greater momentum after the election of a conservative government in 1996, the nature of the settlement of Australia by the British became the subject of intense national debate. Was it a generally humane appropriation of essentially virgin lands by colonists seeking a better life, or was it something less noble, less praiseworthy? Up to this point the national story had been one of courage, will to win, innovation, and egalitarianism, but it came to be understood that this worked only if you managed not to mention the original owners of the land and what had happened to them in the 200 years since first settlement.[19] Aboriginal history was born in the late 1960s, and in the thirty years that followed, research unfolded a complex and troubling story that is widely understood to have bolstered moves toward granting self-determination and land rights to indigenous groups. Although there was widespread public approval of attempts to seek reconciliation with indigenous Australians, some historians and politicians on the Right firmly believed that their opponents had, to all intents and purposes, fabricated evidence of conflict on the frontier, and subsequent transgressions of the rights and liberties of Aboriginal people. Chief among these is Keith Windshuttle, whose *The Fabrication of Aboriginal History* was published in 2002. The back cover blurb states its purpose loud and clear. His intention was to reappraise: "The now widely accepted story about conflict between colonists and Aborigines in Australian history.... Windshuttle concludes that much of their case is poorly founded, other parts are seriously mistaken, and some of it is outright fabrication.... the author finds the British colonization of Australia was the least violent of all Europe's encounters with the New World."

Fabrication is a work of historical revision, seeking to undermine the accounts of life on the frontier (and afterwards) that have driven much of the drive toward reconciliation. It is an attempt to counter what is called "black armband history" and to restore national pride in the achievements of European pioneers. *Fabrication* is an excellent example of why the archaeology of Aboriginal Australia is a site of cultural and political debate.[20]

In *Fabrication* Windschuttle writes about the history of Van Diemen's Land (the original name of Tasmania) between 1803 and 1847 and makes several claims about traditional Tasmanian Aboriginal society that he regards as being supported by available archaeological and ethno-historical evidence. Most memorably when summarizing the fate of the Tasmanians, he writes:

> They had survived for millennia, it is true, but it seems clear that this owed more to good fortune than to good management. The 'slow strangulation of the mind' was true not only of their technical abilities but also of their social relationships. Hence it was not surprising that when the British arrived, this small, precarious society quickly collapsed under the dual weight of the susceptibility of its members to disease and the abuse and neglect of its women.[21]

In essence the destruction of traditional society was the fault of the Tasmanians themselves, not the British: "the real tragedy of the Aborigines was not British colonization per se but that their society was, on the one hand, so internally dysfunctional and, on the other, so incompatible with the looming presence of the rest of the world."[22]

Archaeological and historical research conducted over the last thirty years allows us to evaluate Windschuttle's account of traditional Tasmanian society (particularly such aspects as population size, the treatment of women, the incidence of warfare, and technology) and to reflect on why he seemed so keen to effectively blame the Tasmanians for their own fate. For Windshuttle, Tasmanian society before the arrival of the Europeans was internally maladapted, precariously balanced, and dysfunctional.

Tasmanian archaeological data do not support his claim that this was a society poised on the brink of extinction because of the consequences of long-term isolation (incidentally an argument in part supported by Diamond in *Guns, Germs, and Steel*). Windschuttle's account is based on a very partial and narrow understanding of the results of more than thirty years of archaeological research into the history of Tasmanian Aboriginal society.[23] For these reasons

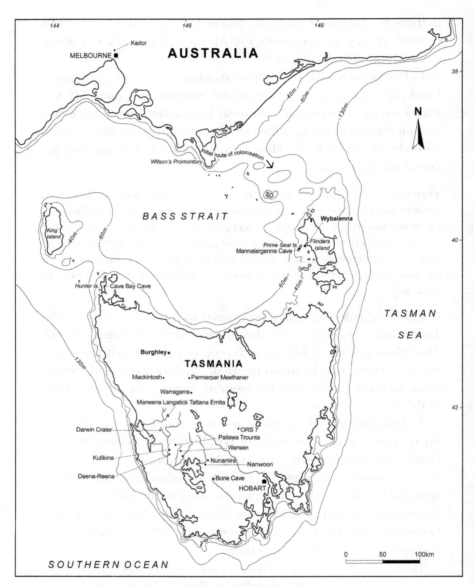

FIGURE 11.3 Key archaeological sites of Tasmania.

the implication that his "counter-history" in some way or another mitigates the culpability of European dispossession as the primary cause of the destruction of traditional Tasmanian society should be firmly rejected.

THE LAST TASMANIAN[24]

In 1978 Tom Haydon produced a documentary film, *The Last Tasmanian,* that skillfully integrated archaeological and historical information to present a history of Tasmanian Aborigines from earliest times until the vicious conflicts with white settlers during the early nineteenth century. Haydon (along with Rhys Jones and Jim Allen, two archaeologists who appeared in the film) did not shrink from describing those conflicts as genocide, but *The Last Tasmanian* gained its greatest notoriety from two highly contentious assertions: first, that the death of the woman Truganini marked the extinction of the Tasmanian aboriginal people, and second, that Tasmanian Aboriginal society was doomed to extinction *before* the arrival of Europeans. Given that there was a substantial population in Tasmania identifying themselves as Aboriginal (they were the descendants of unions between Aboriginal and European men and women), Haydon's claims for extinction were hotly disputed and seen to support opposition to land rights for those people. But it was the claim of there being strong archaeological evidence that traditional Aboriginal society had been suffering the effects of cultural isolation since the separation of Tasmania from the mainland of Australia that created the most conflict.

The arguments and counterarguments about estimates of the pre-European population of Tasmania, the reliability of early explorers' accounts of relations between men and women in traditional society, and the "regressive" nature of Tasmanian technology are very technical and detailed, but it is worth observing that the commonly held view that the Tasmanians were suffering cultural regression as the result of 10,000 years of isolation from Australia (because of rising sea levels that created the island of Tasmania) is highly debatable. Of course, archaeological data are often equivocal and require the use of inferential reasoning to be developed to the point where they may count critically as historical or anthropological evidence. However, this does not mean that they must be either inherently insecure or mute.

Fortunately our stock of both archaeological and historical evidence about the first forty-five years of European occupation of Tasmania further strengthens the argument against regression, which was a provocative idea about the consequences of isolation that had flowed from early research in the 1970s. These ideas have now been comprehensively refuted or at the very least seriously questioned. There is clear evidence that during this period Aboriginal people rapidly adopted new animals (dogs) and material culture (guns and blankets), sometimes modifying them to traditional uses (glass for tools and rust as a substitute for red ochre, which was used in ritual). Clearly the descendants of those who had coped with an Ice Age and the separation of Tasmania from Sahul (the prehistoric land mass including Australia and New Guinea) had not lost their desire (or indeed their capacity) to cope with change. The picture that is slowly emerging from recent archaeological research is one of cultural dynamism and adaptation. Sadly this was cut short by belief of the colonists that the Tasmanians were subhuman, a belief that led to policies of genocide that brought traditional society in Tasmania to the brink of extinction.

THE SITE OF BURGHLEY

Much work remains to be done in gathering evidence of the impact of colonialism on the indigenous Tasmanians, but sites such as Burghley, a partially excavated stratified site in the northwest, demonstrates the potential of archaeology to contribute to our understanding of the Aboriginal experience of contact, while at the same time emphasizing the resilience and adaptability of traditional Tasmanian society and culture.

Located between the Medway and Leven Rivers and established in 1825 as one of the sheep stations established in northwest Tasmania by the Van Diemen's Land Company (VDLC), Burghley was excavated in the early 1990s.[25] During the excavation an assemblage of Aboriginal artifacts was recovered – among which were items, such as flaked glass tools, clearly dating to the postcontact period. The history of the VDLC has been discussed in detail by others,[26] but it should be noted that it was then common practice in the Australian colonies that sheep would be extensively grazed under the care of shepherds, who lived for long periods at "stations" (ranches) such as Burghley.

During the ten or so years that Burghley was occupied, relations between the men living there and the Aboriginal population of the region were anything but friendly, again a state of relations that is widely acknowledged.[27] Violence began almost as soon as the Company arrived in the region as they rapidly placed their settlements and sheep runs on Aboriginal hunting grounds, made use of native paths and roads, and generally disrupted the movements of Aboriginal people through the area.

By 1835 George Augustus Robinson, the person employed by the Van Diemen's Land government to facilitate the removal of all Aboriginal people from Tasmania, was reporting successful completion of his task.[28] However, the VDLC continued to report attacks on their stations, and in November 1836 Robinson sent out one of his sons to round up the stragglers, for whom a £50 reward had been offered.[29] The party encountered a family of six near Cradle Mountain but could not convince them to make the trip back to Launceston.[30] Until recently it was thought that from 1835 onwards these people were the only free Tasmanians left on the island, and those most likely to have been responsible for continuing attacks on Company servants.[31] The family, a middle-aged man, Lanna (John Lanna), and woman, Nabunya/Nabrunga, two young men aged between eighteen and twenty, Banna/Manney (Barnaby Rudge) and Pleti, and three children under ten, Albert (Charley), William, and Francis (Frank), were captured in 1842 and sent to Flinders Island off the coast of Tasmania.[32]

When the site of Burghley was relocated the only surface evidence remaining was a pile of collapsed rocks indicating the position of a chimney. Two seasons of excavation uncovered a total of 145 square meters of materials. Initial excavation focused around the collapsed chimney butt and attempted to delineate the boundaries of the associated hut structure. At the end of excavation the outlines of a hut measuring ten by four meters, a stone chimney and hearth with flagstones, a cobbled outside area where it was thought that a doorway

FIGURE 11.4 Excavated remains of house at Burghley, Tasmania. (Courtesy of author)

had been located, another cobbled area further from the house that led into a drain structure, and a dump zone had been revealed.

During the excavation it became apparent that the hut had burnt down – probably when the chimney caught fire. Although the flaked glass implements identified at the site are clearly the result of a post-contact Aboriginal presence, it also became apparent that much of the Aboriginal flaked stone assemblage overlay this destruction layer and therefore also dated to the postcontact period. Aboriginal arti-facts were located in the uppermost deposits and also found lying on the cobble surface near the doorway, indicating that they were deposited before destruction of the hut.[33]

It is clear from the historical records that Aboriginal and European people did not coexist at Burghley. At no time during the station's period of European occupation would it have been left unattended, so there would not have been opportunities for Aboriginal people to make sporadic use of the site in the absence of Company servants. Any postcontact Aboriginal occupation of the site must have occurred after the Company abandoned it in the late 1830s – probably around 1836 or 1837. The family group captured in 1842 is the most likely candidate for occupying the colonial encampment.

Burghley offers a unique opportunity to investigate the Aboriginal experience of contact through the archaeological record. It also provides the basis of a secure and detailed archaeological refutation of Windschuttle's claims concerning the nature of traditional Tasmanian society. However, the analysis of the recovered assemblage by Williamson indicates that the Aboriginal occupants of the hut were adapting European goods such as bottle glass, ceramics, and musket flints to produce traditional implements such as points and scrapers. Williamson's analysis of the Burghley stone and glass assemblages has opened a window into the Tasmanian experience of contact with Europeans.[34] At the very least it provides a significant body of site-specific evidence to weigh against the accounts of settlers, explorers, or conciliators such as Robinson.

Windschuttle's attempt to ignore such strong contradictory evidence speaks to the power of long-held notions of the cultural poverty of traditional Tasmanian indigenous society, notions adopted by Diamond from the work of Rhys Jones. But it also relates to an unwillingness to confront the realities of the European settlement of Australia that, as I have already remarked, can be profoundly shocking. True reconciliation between black and white Australia can flow only from a frank acknowledgement of that history – its good as well as its bad bits, and there is every reason to believe that through research, criticism, and debate, progress can be made, and we can reach a clearer understanding of the richness and strength of Tasmanian society and the impact of dispossession on it.[35] But above all we need to be clear that there is no evidence that Aboriginal society in Tasmania was on the brink of extinction before the European invasion. Indeed, both the proximate and ultimate causes of the extinction of traditional Tasmanian Aboriginal society flowed from European settlement, and the frequently violent contest for control over land that dispossession entailed.

SETTLER "ECOCIDE"?

I have already remarked on the absence of Aboriginal Australians from Jared Diamond's *Collapse* and explained this as being the outcome of Diamond's desire to portray contemporary indigenous Australians only as the victims of colonial slaughter or as bit-part players in the pastoral and whaling industries.[36] This is in contrast to the rosier picture he paints of Aboriginal life prior to European invasion: "When that European settlement of Australia began in 1788, Australia had of course been settled for over 40,000 years by Aborigines, who had worked out successful sustainable solutions to the continent's daunting environmental problems."[37]

Leaving aside the fact that this assertion is based on circular logic (how would we know whether such "solutions" were "worked out" or happened by chance, or indeed whether an archaeological record comprised of tiny and random samples of over 40,000 years of human history allows us to assess claims about choice); it sits oddly with Diamond's explanation for the extinction of Australian megafauna during the early phases of human occupation. In *Guns, Germs, and Steel*, Diamond concluded that the "most likely" cause was human action, "both directly (by being killed for food) and indirectly (as the result of fires and habitat modification caused by humans)."[38] Was this an "unsustainable" solution that was incorrectly "worked out" by ancestral Aborigines, presumably because they did not have enough information about the ecology of the megafauna? Diamond's account glosses over the fierce debates about whether megafauna were all made extinct early, allowing readers to assume falsely that after early bloodletting the descendants of these early settlers decided to live sustainably in Australia. But this also contrasts with another of his conclusions: "Those extinctions eliminated all the large wild animals that might otherwise have been candidates for domestication, and left native Australians and New Guineans without a single native domestic animal."[39] Are we to assume that sustainable solutions incorporating the domestication of animals (if not plants) in Australia may have developed if the early slaughter had not occurred?

It is not entirely clear what Diamond is searching for here, but it may well have more to do with his desire to strengthen a contrast between the "sustainable Eden" of hunter-gatherer Australia with the consequences of settler colonialism for the broader environment of the continent. Here the tale is one of near unrelenting horror, of a poor environment made poorer by introduced agricultural practices, of wholesale "mining" of both renewable and nonrenewable resources to the point where the Australian economy (and by extension Australian society) may well become unsustainable. Diamond paints a picture of an Australia enmired in British culture, teetering on the brink of destruction, literally consuming its future.[40] For Diamond, Australia is exemplary:

Australia illustrates in extreme form the exponentially accelerating horse race, in which the world now finds itself....On the one hand, the development of environmental problems in Australia, as in the whole world, is accelerating exponentially. On the other hand, the development of public environmental concern, and of private and governmental countermeasures, is also accelerating exponentially. Which horse will win the race?[41]

Diamond powerfully creates a sense of crisis, if only to support an argument that the best thing Australia could do for itself, and the world, is to get rid of its cattle and to "voluntarily phase out much of its agricultural enterprise."[42] But how much of the claimed "facts" of Diamond's analysis can be confirmed, and are there accounts of the immediate past and future of the continent alternative to those Diamond presents? It is significant to note that the chapter "Mining" Australia "contains no data, no tables or figures showing past or current trends with respect to particular indicators, and Diamond makes no reference to particular studies."[43] This makes for compelling reading, but it is bad science.

A close reading of "Mining" Australia reveals a highly colored interpretation, which has been created to serve clear political ends. Here we need to be very careful. An attack on the factual basis of Diamond's arguments does not necessarily imply complete disagreement with his message that all societies should strive to achieve sustainability and to rein in consumption that requires us to overuse nonrenewable resources. Diamond's discussion of the impact of mining nonrenewable resources such as coal, uranium, and iron ore has much merit, especially when we consider the impact of coal burning on the emission of greenhouse gases.

Indeed, many of the points made in *Collapse* about the possibility of Australian "ecocide" were already made in the 1970s and have been a spur to action since. But in his arguments concerning the "mining" of renewable resources such as water and soil fertility, Diamond's zeal to rid Australia of agriculture, and to conserve remaining forests, water, and fishing grounds, leads him to excess. Diamond regards low crop yields (and low soil fertility) as supporting his arguments for phasing out agriculture in Australia.

These Draconian recommendations about the future of Australia do not constitute a practical basis for action by Australians. For example, Australian rice and cotton farmers produce yields of double the world average. Australia exports sugar and, directly contrary to Diamond's assertion, it exports almost three times the quantity of citrus it imports.[44] Again, it is worth stressing that these facts do not in anyway justify using scarce water to grow crops such as rice and cotton in Australia. Turning to soil fertility we find that Australian farmers have been using manure and other fertilizers since the eighteenth century (as have farmers everywhere) and that developments in tillage technologies have dramatically reduced soil degradation. Salinization of soils is not only understood but regarded as a major challenge that is being met.

Much the same story applies to his observations about forestry, fisheries, the future of the Great Barrier Reef, and climate change in Australia. Notwithstanding Diamond's carefully cultivated sense of impending doom, Australian governments (and farmers, fishers, and foresters) are acutely aware of the challenges posed by sustainability and by climate change. Much has been done by choice that has not involved anything like the radical solutions (such as the end of agriculture on the continent) proposed by Diamond. The situation in Australia does not involve a choice between extremes (unsustainable levels of production and consumption versus drastic reductions) because *neither* option provides a basis for social sustainability. It is interesting that Diamond does not advocate the cessation of intensive irrigation and fertilization practices in the Imperial Valley of California, his home state.

The simple point here is that (to follow Diamond himself) good choices must be based on good information, and Diamond has provided very little with respect to Australia. Indeed, it would be an act of the grossest folly if Australians were to choose such a course of action when much less radical, but no less effective, means of improving sustainability are already available. Of course, much remains to be done, and there is still a very long way to go persuading governments and the people who elect them to take a longer-term view of the issues involved. However, huge steps have been taken in raising consciousness of the challenges posed by sustainability. But surely the recognition of the need for change and for the development of policies that emphasize sustainability and the understanding that the fate of the planet is a global rather than simply a national or regional concern demonstrates the power of knowledge and understanding as the best bases for making choices. Perhaps it is in this way, as an exemplar of a sustainable future, rather than as a participant in Diamond's horse race to extinction, that Australia might serve as a beacon to the rest of the world.

But this is still to see sustainability in a simplistic way. If we broaden our focus to consider the creation of sustainable societies that foster innovation, clear-sighted inquiry, and a commitment to social justice, then we have the chance to imagine different kinds of communities. In Australia one of the major outcomes of the reconciliation process between Aboriginal and settler Australians has been the recognition of a deep Aboriginal interest in land both as a symbol of identity as well as a resource for sustaining societies through economic and cultural action. Here the recognition of the rich human history of Australia, and the understanding that sustainable communities cannot be created by marginalizing and excluding nonmainstream interests, articulates powerfully with the drive to develop sustainable land use practices.

For the last decade Australian governments at all levels have begun to create policies that explicitly recognize that the values placed on land, culture, and heritage by Aboriginal people are vital resources in the battle against salinity, the exhaustion of soils, and the destruction of forests.[45] In this way, far from being written out of the picture as victims of the grand sweep of "big" history, the "small" history of Australia over the past 200 years has played out in a way in which Aboriginal people have come to play key roles in developing a sustainable future for Australia.

CONCLUSION

In this chapter I have stressed how archaeology and history have been and continue to be mobilized to ensure a reconciliation between black and white Australia. This is a complex and politically sensitive process. It is also dynamic, especially in terms of the ways in which identities (both Aboriginal and non-Aboriginal) are created from the raw materials of historical data and contemporary experience. One of the most significant aspects of such dynamism is the sense in which societies and identities have changed, will continue to change, and are open to influences from both the past and the present. Aboriginal societies were not completely destroyed as a result of the European invasion of the continent. Indeed, the survival of indigenous Australians, the richness of their cultures, and the diversity of their experiences over the last 200 years have become indispensable components in the cultural and social makeup of contemporary Australia. I have also discussed the importance of recognizing the vital role that Aboriginal communities can play in managing land in Australia, thereby supporting attempts to develop both ecologically and culturally sustainable land use practices in mining, forestry, and agriculture. In this sense the process of reconciliation has begun to develop in ways not originally envisaged when it was begun some fifty years ago.

A curiosity about the past, a desire to understand the histories of the places we inhabit, and a search for meaning in human history are things to treasure. They are also resources for building better societies. That there is diversity and difference does not imply chaos and disorder. Indeed, understanding the genesis and histories of such perspectives might help people to come to grip with the idea that, although their interests may not be coincident, they have a greater interest in terms of ensuring some form of global (as well as local) conversation that everyone can participate in.

ACKNOWLEDGMENTS

I thank Mark Grist and Norman Yoffee for valuable input, Tricia McAnany for her great patience, and Susan Bridekirk for editorial assistance. Rudy Frank and Wei Ming of the Archaeology Program at La Trobe produced the maps.

Notes

* I am a professor of archaeology and head of the School of Historical and European Studies at La Trobe University, Melbourne, Australia. I have also taught archaeology in Beijing and in several European universities. I have published thirty books, among the most recent *Keeping Up with the Macnamaras* (2005), a case study in the archaeology of nineteenth-century immigration to Australia, and a single-volume history of archaeology, *Milestones in Archaeology* (2007).

My current field research is focused on two major projects – The Origins of the Tongan Maritime Empire, which explores the immediate precontact archaeology of this Pacific island kingdom, and Building Transnational Archaeologies of the Modern World 1750–1950, which compares domestic assemblages from sites in Melbourne, Sydney, and London to write new social histories of migrant populations.

I was raised in outback Australia and have worked on the archaeology of indigenous Australia with members of local Aboriginal communities in Tasmania and elsewhere in Australia. The core of my approach to the complex issues that arise in this kind of archaeology are discussed in my edited book, *The Archaeology of Contact in Settler Societies* (2004).

1. See especially McNiven and Russell 2005.
2. For example, Boer and Wiffen 2005; Chanock and Simpson 1996; Davis 2007; Langton 1994; Murray 1996a; Meyers and Field 1998; Smith 2004.
3. Some examples of this inquiry are, e.g., Colley 2003; DuCros 2002; Murray 1992, 1998; McNiven and Russell 2005.
4. A notable exception to histories such as White and O'Connell 1982 and Horton 1991 is that of Griffiths 1996, which has fostered a rethinking of the history of antiquarianism in Australian archaeology and anthropology.
5. Specht 1993.
6. These matters are usefully discussed in Ireland 1996, 2002, and Murray 1992.
7. See, e.g., Elder 2007.
8. See, e.g., Purdie 1997.
9. Colley 2003; McNiven and Russell 2005; Murray 1992, 1996a, 1996b, 1996c; and Smith 2004 canvass a range of opinions on this aspect of heritage history.
10. Murray 1993a, 1996d.
11. DuCros 2002; Colley 2003; McNiven and Russell 2005; Smith 2004.
12. There is a considerable literature devoted to the impact of changing relations between archaeologists and indigenous people in Australia. There have been conflicts, most notably related to Tasmania, which have been used to advance both separatist and postcolonial agendas; see Colley 2003; DuCros 2002; McNiven and Russell 2005; and Smith 2004 for both inaccurate and one-sided accounts. For alternative images see Murray 1996b, 1996c; Murray and Allen 1995. More positive accounts of collaborations exist, see, e.g., Davidson et al. 1995.
13. The causes of the extinction of the giant fauna (megaufauna) of Australia have been hotly debated since the nineteenth century, when the first specimens came to light. Crucial elements of debate are the timing of extinctions – did all megafauna become extinct at the same time everywhere in Australia? – and agents – was it human over-predation or climate change, or a combination of the two? Useful discussions of the issues (in Australia and elsewhere are Barnosky et al. 2004; Johnson 2002; O'Connell and Allen 2004; Trueman et al. 2005.

14. bp = before the present, which has been established by scientific convention as 1950.
15. See Murray 2004a for examples.
16. See Murray 2004b and Silliman 2005 for reviews of the extensive literature in this field.
17. Mark is an Aboriginal man from the Werigia, Nyeri Nyeri, and Wamba Wamba peoples of northwest Victoria, Australia. He has an honours degree from the Australian National University and is Manager of State-wide Heritage Programs and Heritage Services, Aboriginal Affairs Victoria. Interviewed 31 January 2008.
18. Murray 2004a.
19. Over the last decade there has been significant debate in Australian society about the nature and purpose of Australian history. These debates have come to be known as the "history wars" and revolved around the ways in which the history of black and white relations in Australia should be written. Flashpoints have been arguments about the reality of massacres on the frontier and the actions of state governments in removing Aboriginal children from their families (especially during the twentieth century) creating what have become known as the "stolen generations." Useful surveys of the debates include Atwood and Foster 2003; Macintyre and Clark 2003.
20. A version of this discussion appears in Murray and Williamson 2003.
21. Windschuttle 2002: 386.
22. Ibid.
23. Derived mostly from Jones 1977.
24. The great controversy sparked by *The Last Tasmanian* can be explored by reference to Onsman 2004 and O'Regan 1984.
25. Murray 1993b.
26. For the history of the VDL Company see Meston 1958; Lennox 1990; and Murray 1993b.
27. Lennox 1990; McFarlane 2002; Murray 1993b; Plomley 1966: 196, 1992.
28. Plomley 1966: 926.
29. Davies 1973: 153.
30. Plomley 1966: 926.
31. McFarlane 2002.
32. Murray 1993b.
33. Ibid.: 509.
34. Williamson 2002.
35. After many years of debate and advocacy, on 13 February 2008, the Labour government of Kevin Rudd issued a formal apology in the Federal Parliament to the "stolen generations" of Australia. For further information see http://www.dfat.gov.au/indigenous_background/index.html.
36. Diamond 2005: 389–390.
37. Ibid.: 389.
38. Diamond 1997: 44.

39. Ibid.
40. Flannery 1994.
41. Diamond 2005: 415–416.
42. Ibid.: 415.
43. Marohasy 2005: 457.
44. See, e.g., ibid.: 459.
45. See, e.g., Australian Heritage Commission 2002; Department of Primary Industries 2006; English and Gay 2005; Parks Victoria 2005.

Bibliography

Atwood, B. and S. G. Foster. Editors. 2003. *Frontier Conflict: The Australian Experience.* Canberra: National Museum of Australia.

Australian Heritage Commission. 2002. *Ask First: A Guide to Respecting Indigenous Heritage Places and Values.* Canberra: Australian Heritage Commission.

Barnosky, A. D., P. L. Koch, R. S. Feranec, S. Wing, and A. B. Shabel. 2004. "Assessing the Causes of Late Pleistocene Extinctions on the Continents." *Science* **306**(5693):70–75.

Boer, B. and G. Wiffen. 2005. *Heritage Law in Australia.* South Melbourne: Oxford University Press.

Chanock, M. and C. Simpson. 1996. *Law and Cultural Heritage.* Bundoora, Victoria: La Trobe University Press.

Colley, S. 2003. *Uncovering Australia: Archaeology, Indigenous People and the Public.* Crows Nest, N.S.W.: Allen & Unwin.

Davidson, I., C. Lovell-Jones, and R. Bancroft. Editors. 1995. *Archaeologists and Aborigines Working Together.* Armidale, N.S.W.: University of New England Press.

Davies, D. 1973. *The Last of the Tasmanians.* London: Frederick Muller.

Davis, M. B. 2007. *Writing Heritage: The Depiction of Indigenous Heritage in European-Australian Writings.* Kew, Victoria: Australian Scholarly Publishing.

Department of Primary Industries. 2006. *Keerna – Indigenous Partnership Framework. Strengthening Indigenous Opportunities in Primary Industries.* Melbourne: Department of Primary Industries.

Diamond, J. 1997. *Guns, Germs, and Steel.* New York: W. W. Norton.

Diamond, J. 2005. *Collapse. How Societies Choose to Fail or Succeed.* New York: Viking.

DuCros, H. 2002. *Much More than Stones and Bones: Australian Archaeology in the Late Twentieth Century.* Carlton, Victoria: Melbourne University Press.

Dugay-Grist, M. 2006. "Shaking the Pillars," in *Archaeology of Oceania: Australia and the Pacific Islands.* Edited by I. Lilley, pp. 367–379. Oxford: Blackwell.

Elder, C. 2007. *Being Australian: Narratives of National Identity.* Crows Nest, N.S.W.: Allen & Unwin.

English, A. and L. Gay. 2005. *Living Land Living Culture: Aboriginal Heritage and Salinity.* Hurstville, N.S.W.: Department of Environment and Conservation (NSW).

Flannery, T. 1997. *The Future Eaters: An Ecological History of the Australian Lands and People*. Sydney: New Holland Publishers.

Griffiths, T. 1996. *Hunters and Collectors: The Antiquarian Imagination in Australia*. Cambridge: Cambridge University Press.

Horton, D. 1991. *Recovering the Tracks: The Story of Australian Archaeology*. Canberra: Aboriginal Studies Press.

Ireland, T. 1995. "Excavating National Identity," in *SITES. Nailing the Debate: Interpretation in Museums*. Edited by S. Hunt and J. Lydon, pp. 85–106. Sydney: Historic Houses Trust of NSW.

Ireland, T. 2002. "Giving Value to the Australian Historic Past: Historical Archaeology, Heritage and Nationalism." *Australasian Historical Archaeology* **20**:15–25.

Johnson, C. N. 2002. "Determinants of Loss of Mammal Species during the Late Quaternary 'Megafauna' Extinctions: Life History and Ecology, but Not Body Size." *Proceedings of the Royal Society* **269**(1506):2221–2227.

Jones, R. 1977. "The Tasmanian Paradox," in *Stone Tools as Cultural Markers*. Edited by R. V. S. Wright, pp. 189–204. Canberra: Australian Institute of Aboriginal Studies Press.

Langton, M. 1994. *Valuing Cultures: Recognizing Indigenous Cultures as a Valued Part of Australian Heritage*. Canberra: Council for Aboriginal Reconciliation, Australian Government Publishing Service.

Lennox, G. 1990. "The Van Diemen's Land Company and the Tasmanian Aborigines: A Reappraisal." *Papers and Proceedings of the Tasmanian Historical Research Association* **37**:165–208.

Macintyre, S. and A. Clark. 2003. *The History Wars*. Carlton, Victoria: Melbourne University Press.

Marohasy, J. 2005. "Australia's Environment Undergoing Renewal, Not Collapse." *Energy and Environment* **16**:457–480.

McFarlane, I. 2002. "Aboriginal Society in North West Tasmania: Dispossession and Genocide." Unpublished doctoral dissertation, University of Tasmania.

McNiven, I. J. and L. Russell. 2005. *Appropriated Pasts: Indigenous Peoples and the Colonial Culture of Archaeology*. Lanham, MD: AltaMira Press.

Meston, A. 1958. "The Van Diemen's Land Company 1825–1842." *Records of the Queen Victoria Museum*, New Series Number 9.

Murray, T. 1992. "The Discourse of Australian Prehistoric Archaeology," in *Power, Knowledge, and Aborigines*. Edited by B. Attwood pp. 1–19. Melbourne: Special Journal of Australian Studies, La Trobe University Press.

Murray, T. 1993a. "Communication and the Importance of Disciplinary Communities: Who Owns the Past?" in *Archaeological Theory: Who Sets the Agenda?* Edited by N. Yoffee and A. Sherratt, pp. 105–116. Cambridge: Cambridge University Press.

Murray, T. 1993b. "The Childhood of William Lanne: Contact Archaeology and Aboriginality in Tasmania." *Antiquity* **67**:504–519.

Murray, T. 1996a. "Mabo and Re-creating the Heritage of Australia." *Working Papers in Australian Studies*. London: Sir Robert Menzies Centre for Australian Studies.

Murray, T. 1996b. "Towards a Post-Mabo Archaeology of Australia," in *In the Age of Mabo*. Edited by B. Attwood, pp. 73–87. Sydney: Allen and Unwin.

Murray, T. 1996c. "Archaeologists, Heritage Bureaucrats, Aboriginal Organisations, and the Conduct of Tasmanian Archaeology," in *Proceedings of the 1995 Australian Archaeological Association Annual Conference*. Edited by S. Ulm, I. Lilley, and A. Ross, pp. 311–322. University of Queensland: Aboriginal and Torres Strait Islander Studies Unit.

Murray, T. 1996d. "Contact Archaeology: Shared Histories? Shared Identities?" in *SITES. Nailing the Debate: Interpretation in Museums*. Edited by S. Hunt and J. Lydon, pp. 199–213. Sydney: Historic Houses Trust of NSW.

Murray, T. 1998. "Introduction: The Changing Contexts of the Archaeology of Aboriginal Australia," in *The Archaeology of Aboriginal Australia*. Edited by T. Murray, pp. 1–6. Sydney: Allen and Unwin.

Murray, T. 2004a. "In the Footsteps of George Dutton: Developing a Contact Archaeology of Australia," in *The Archaeology of Contact in Settler Societies*. Edited by T. Murray, pp. 200–225. Cambridge: Cambridge University Press.

Murray, T. 2004b. "The Archaeology of Contact in Settler Societies: An Introduction," in *The Archaeology of Contact in Settler Societies*. Edited by T. Murray, pp. 1–18. Cambridge: Cambridge University Press.

Murray, T. and J. Allen. 1993. "The Forced Repatriation of Cultural Properties to Tasmania" (with Jim Allen). *Antiquity* **69**:871–874.

Murray, T. and C. Williamson. 2003. "Archaeology and History," in *Whitewash: On the Fabrication of Aboriginal History*. Edited by R. Manne, pp. 311–333. Melbourne: Black Ink Press.

Myers, G. A. and A. Field. Editors. 1998. *Identity, Land and Culture in the Era of Native Title: Selected Essays from the 1996 Seminar Series of the National Native Title Tribunal*. Perth, WA: National Native Title Tribunal.

O'Connell, J. and J. Allen. 2003. "Dating the Colonization of Sahul (Pleistocene Australia-New Guinea): A Review of Recent Research." *Journal of Archaeological Science* **31**(6):835–853.

Onsman, A. 2004. "Truganini's Funeral." *Island* **96**. Available at http://www.islandmag.com/96/article.html.

O'Regan, T. 1984. "Documentary in Controversy: the Last Tasmanian." Available at http://wwwmcc.murdoch.edu.au/ReadingRoom/film/Tasmanian.html.

Parks Victoria. 2005. *Indigenous Partnership Strategy and Action Plan*. Melbourne: Parks Victoria.

Plomley, N.J.B. 1966. *Friendly Mission*. Hobart: Tasmanian Historical Research Association.

Plomley, N.J.B. 1992. *The Aboriginal/Settler Clash in Van Diemen's Land 1803–1831*. Queen Victoria Museum and Art Gallery, Launceston, Occasional Paper No. 6.

Purdie, R.W. 1997. *The Register of the National Estate: Who, What, Where?* Canberra: Department of the Environment.

Silliman, S. 2005. "2005 Culture Contact or Colonialism? Challenges in the Archaeology of Native North America." *American Antiquity* **70**(1):55–74.

Smith, L. J. 2004. *Archaeological Theory and the Politics of Cultural Heritage.* New York: Routledge.

Specht, J. Editor. 1993. *F. D. McCarthy, Commemorative Papers (Archaeology, Anthropology, Rock Art).* Sydney: South Australian Museum.

Trueman, C. N. G., J. H. Field, J. Dortch, B. Charles, and S. Wroe. 2005. "Prolonged Coexistence of Humans and Megafauna in Pleistocene Australia." *Proceedings of the National Academy of Sciences of the United States of America* **102**(23):8381–8385.

White, J. P. and J. O'Connell. 1982. *A Prehistory of Australia, New Guinea and Sahul.* Sydney: Academic Press.

Williamson, C. 2002. "A History of Aboriginal Tasmania: 3500 BP to AD 1842." Unpublished doctoral dissertation, La Trobe University.

Windschuttle, K. 2002. *The Fabrication of Aboriginal History.* Paddington, NSW: Macleay Press.

12

Excusing the Haves and Blaming the Have-Nots in the Telling of History

Frederick Errington and Deborah Gewertz[*]

We admit to being chauvinists of anthropology. We respect our discipline because of what it demands as well as what it can provide. In effect, anthropology insists that to understand people in other places and in different times – to understand what they want and seek – we must often scrutinize our own understandings, our own (often early) responses and appraisals. Anthropology urges us – and helps us – to examine our own taken-for-granted ideas about why and how people act: our ideas about human nature, about the causes and objectives of human action, about the ways people intend one thing to follow from another, about how and why people engage in collective action. We must recognize that not everyone in the world has the same objectives as (many) contemporary Americans, wanting and seeking the same sorts of things as we do. This is to say, we must be aware of historical and cultural context. We must recognize that our own desires and lives, like the desires and lives of others elsewhere, are historically and culturally constructed. To think about such things, which is to say, to think not only about how differently located others think and live, but also about how we think and live, can be a sobering, if not a daunting, experience. However, working hard – taking care – to get such matters relatively right can be very much worth doing, both intellectually liberating and politically significant.

In this chapter we would like to illustrate why examining our taken-for-granted explanations is both intellectually liberating and politically significant. To this end, we take as our topic the ways in which a famous biologist, Jared Diamond, has sought to explain human history in his two major and widely read books, *Guns, Germs, and Steel,* which won the Pulitzer Prize, and *Collapse,* which has been less generally praised, but praised nonetheless.[1] From our anthropological perspective, these books, while in many ways impressive and compelling, are problematic. We should make it clear at the outset that we discuss Diamond's books because they have become such popular and influential examples of a more general trend in the telling of history. This is a trend that, in basing history on what appear to be commonsense (Western) suppositions, makes complex political processes into simple, inevitable laws – laws that absolve (those Diamond calls) the "haves" from any real responsibility for oppressing (and creating) the "have nots." It is a history that may justify expansionism as an expression of legitimate self-interest. It is a history that, for example, allows many of us to celebrate Thanksgiving without pondering much about why Native Americans have significantly less to be thankful for. It is a history that links manifest destiny at home to shock and awe policies abroad. And it is a history that may serve to render the "have-nots" into a bunch of left-behind losers who resent (if not hate) the "haves" out of envy.

ON PAPUA NEW GUINEA: DESIRE WITHIN
A COLONIAL CONTEXT

In *Guns, Germs, and Steel,* Jared Diamond begins by addressing a plaintive question posed by a local political leader he encountered on a Papua New Guinea beach in the early 1970s. Yali, active as a so-called cargo-cultist in the region around Madang, asked Diamond, "Why is it that you white people developed so much cargo [items of Western manufacture] and brought it to New Guinea, but we black people had little cargo of our own?"[2] Diamond answers this question by presenting the seemingly inevitable and inexorable unfolding of global patterns. These patterns, he believes, are the result of the geographical differences that allowed certain people to have the power of guns, germs, and steel on their side, power that they would (apparently) always use to maximal effect in the domination of others. It has been the use of this power – a power that stems from the luck-of-the-environmental draw – that Diamond argues has accounted for "history's haves and have-nots."[3]

Diamond assumes that Yali was upset primarily because he wanted more "cargo" – more Western stuff. But we are not so sure.[4] In fact, we think it important to step back from a likely first response that "of course" Yali would value Western things and to wonder what he – as a "have-not" – might have actually sought. We also think it important to ask why, living as he did during the mid-twentieth century, was Yali unable to get whatever it was that he wanted from the "haves" – mostly Australian colonists. After all, he had long lived among these colonists and had served them with great distinction during World War II.

We never met Yali. Consequently we do not know for sure what he meant in his question to Diamond. However, we have made numerous research trips to Papua New Guinea (beginning in 1968 for Fred and 1973 for Deborah) and do know something of what other Papua New Guineans (including some who did know Yali) were asking for – and about – at the time. And, as well, we do know something of the way many anthropologists working in New Guinea (and elsewhere) have explained why people desire one thing or another. Below we convey these anthropological ideas about desire before we return to a consideration of Yali's question: of what he might have wanted and why he could not get it.

Most anthropologists argue that what people want tends to be socially constructed. In particular, they have found that what people ask for is shaped by their history and in turn shapes their history. This is to say, what people want is formed in the context of narratives: stories they are told and tell about the way the world works or might work, stories about what human beings might plausibly hope for.

Anthropologist Marilyn Strathern, in a famous paper titled "The Decomposition of an Event," illustrates well such a social construction of desire in discussing those who were first contacted in the 1930s by Australian explorers in the Highlands of Papua New Guinea's interior.[5] The Australians assumed that these Papua New Guineans were impressed with their complex technology – for example, guns and steel. Yet, in Strathern's view, possession of this novel technology initially marked these explorers as spirits, and, from the perspectives of Papua New Guinea Highlanders, the appearance of spirits among the living was extraordinary but ultimately not very consequential. Spirits, after all, would likely disappear without affecting social interactions

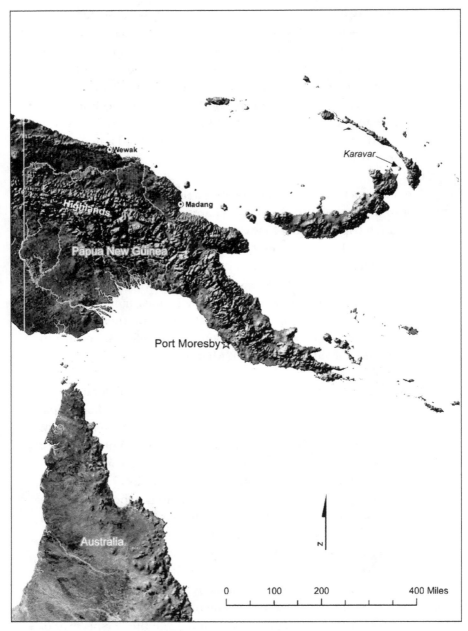

FIGURE 12.1 Papua New Guinea.

very much. Only when Highlanders discovered that these Australians both had large quantities of pearl shells and wished to transact with them did the Australians become plausibly human. Pearl shells, traded up from the coast, were for a long time central in the Highland exchanges through which marriages were contracted, compensation for death or injury was paid, and alliances were effected within and between groups. In other words, only when the Australians showed that they apparently valued what the Highlanders already valued and desired did the Highlanders regard them as interesting and socially significant. Only then could the Highlanders fit these otherwise strange and fundamentally peripheral beings into their own narratives (again, stories people tell about the way the world works or might work) as full human beings: as they became persons with whom they could, and would want to, interact. Only at this point did these whites appear to enter history – Highlands style – as people who were and would continue to be social players. This is to say, that the way Highlanders understood what was happening around them and the way that they reacted to what happened depended, in significant part, on their expectations for the future – expectations shaped by local conventions, by the stories they told about the past, present, and future.

To be sure, Yali's people, who lived along the coast of Papua New Guinea, had a much longer history of European contact. (Some coastal peoples engaged extensively with Europeans since the latter part of the nineteenth century.) Yali, himself, had especially extensive contact with Europeans. He served as a policeman in New Guinea's colonial administration before World War II and as a member of the Allied Intelligence Service during the war. There is a photograph taken in 1944 in the Australian War Memorial archives commemorating his military service, in which Yali is inside the *Dace,* an American submarine, together with other members of his company of intelligence-gathering "Coastwatchers." In advance of a major Allied landing, Yali's group of twelve – seven Europeans, one Indonesian translator, and four Papua New Guineans – was sent to Hollandia, then Dutch New Guinea, on a hazardous mission to gather strategic information. In the picture Yali and the other men are posed next to their weapons in obviously cramped, machinery-packed quarters. After the war, as a distinguished veteran, Yali

FIGURE 12.2 Sergeant Yali and his comrades on the World War II submarine *Dace*. Yali is second from left in the front row. (Permission to publish negative PO1090.001 granted by the Australian War Memorial)

embarked on a controversial political career, one that kept him in extensive contact with Europeans.

Yet, like the Highlanders Strathern describes, Yali's life and aspirations followed a largely Papua New Guinean historical narrative. In outline, this historical narrative focuses less on the material attributes of things themselves than on the social uses to which things are put. Things have value because they can be used in transactions to establish relationships of recognition and respect. Things are more like gifts than commodities, establishing qualitative relationships between the people exchanging them rather than quantitative ones between the items exchanged.[6] The major point of these transactions, thus, is to establish relationships of obligation, alliance, and friendship rather than to get "good deals." Therefore, when Highlanders desired pearl shells, and they did desire them with a passionate intensity, it was not for the sake of the shells alone. Indeed, many anthropologists have made a similar point about coastal Papua New Guineans – that men there acquired coveted shells (including the famous "kula" valuables) so as to be able to give them away at a later time.

Because the Highlanders were relatively inexperienced in European ways, they apparently thought that the explorers were generous in offering them the coveted pearl shells that affirmed their fundamental worth. In contrast, the coastal peoples long before learned that the colonists were stingy, offering them only meager wages that denied a common humanity – a common humanness. Moreover, exacerbating raw feelings was local recognition that whites had real and intrusive power. Certainly colonial administrators sought to bring many aspects of native life under their discipline, and they could certainly punish those who, by flouting their directives, challenged their power. Indeed, Yali was to spend nearly six years in jail during the 1950s for his recalcitrance.

Yali and many other Papua New Guineans became preoccupied with the reluctance, if not refusal, of many whites to recognize their full humanness – to make blacks and whites equal players in the same history. In their efforts to establish the transactions, the exchanges, on which the elusive equality would be based, many Papua New Guineans sought, often through magical and ritual means, the European things – the "cargo" – that whites so evidently valued. Without denying that some European possessions – matches and steel tools among them – may have had immediate appeal, it would be an error to believe that it was the things alone that interested them. Rather, with these things, they hoped to become interesting and socially significant (exchange-worthy) to the Europeans. In an important book about "cargo cults," *Road Belong Cargo*, anthropologist Peter Lawrence, who knew Yali well, says as much in his definition of such cargo cults:

[Such a cult] is based on the natives' belief that European goods (cargo) – ships, aircraft, trade articles, and military equipment – are not man-made but have to be obtained from a non-human or divine source. It expresses the followers' dissatisfaction with their status in colonial society, which is to be improved imminently or eventually by the acquisition of new wealth. It has, therefore, a disruptive influence and is regarded by the ... Australian Administration ... as one of the [its] most serious problems.[7]

Deeply resenting their inferiority in colonial society, coastal Papua New Guineans sought for decades to improve their status by gaining access to cargo. During Fred's early Papua New Guinea research on the island of Karavar (in 1968 and 1972), local people remained preoccupied with gaining long-denied respect from Europeans. In discussing their contemporary cargo activities (which focused on learning how to place an order such that a small payment would elicit a shipload of manufactured items), they described a history of their efforts to compel Europeans to recognize mutual humanness. In particular, they referred to the "dog movement," a series of meetings they held during the 1930s. The question addressed with perplexity and anger at these meetings was why the Europeans persisted in treating them with contempt – driving them away, telling them to get out, as if they were unwelcome dogs. Through obtaining cargo, they sought to win European respect by having that which Europeans so obviously valued.[8]

Over a considerable period of time, Papua New Guineans frequently sought to acquire and master the ritual techniques by which Europeans accessed cargo. Influenced by Yali or other cargo-cult leaders, they tried a combination of recalcitrance and ritual experimentation. They interrupted and transformed normal routines: they refused to pay taxes, repudiated the directions of colonial administrators, established alternative governments, wrested theological control from missionaries, and mobilized villages, if not whole regions, in fervent invocation and prophesy. As Lawrence makes clear in his definition of cargo cults, Papua New Guineans, in their choice of such means, often became interesting and socially significant in ways the Europeans considered undesirable – in ways that provoked greater exercise of European power and made recognition of mutual equality even less likely.

Thus, we think that Diamond misunderstands what many Papua New Guineans desired when he explains the background to Yali's question (about the differences between white and black people). In Diamond's words: "whites had arrived, imposed centralized government, and brought material goods whose value New Guineans instantly recognized, ranging from steel axes, matches, and medicines to clothing, soft drinks, and umbrellas. In New Guinea all these goods were referred to collectively as 'cargo.'"[9] Because Diamond misunderstands that Yali really was asking less about cargo per se than about colonial relationships between white and black people, he describes the introduction of centralized government as almost parenthetical to the indisputable fact that whites and their goods had arrived. Hence, he presents local resentment as directed not at the nature and use of concerted colonial power so much as at the differential access to goods.

Perhaps consistent with Diamond's focus on cargo per se is his use of the word "goods." To call things "goods" means that they are inherently desirable – instantly recognizable as worth acquiring. Yet, as we know from advertising, many things become desirable only when they are defined repeatedly as such. Moreover, in defining cargo as goods, Diamond implies that local people will do whatever it takes to get such things. This kind of account suggests that, in their desire for these goods, local people are the agents of their own domination.[10] (Another example would be of the Native Americans who, ostensibly, wanted beads so badly that they were willing to trade Manhattan Island for just a few dollars worth of them. Although they may have liked beads, they never thought that they were selling their land for them since land was not, in their view, alienable as a commodity. Their probable intent was to establish an exchange relationship with the Dutch colonists.) Such a goods-centered rendition of history, we think, serves to displace attention from the nature of colonial power relationships. These relationships are not vested in the "nature of things." They are not inevitable because of the instantly recognized value of manufactured items – even granting that some items might be quite useful. Instead, colonial relationships are imposed, often to the resentment and resistance of local people.

That Papua New Guineans such as Yali wanted cargo, less because they recognized its inherent value, and more because they desired to transform the colonial relations of inequality between whites and blacks, was echoed in many Papua New Guineans' narratives. These narratives elaborated a sense of being ill appreciated and ill used. These stories often presented Papua New Guineans and Europeans as sharing a prior history of social obligations. They were, in effect, arguments designed to demonstrate European immorality in denying this history and in behaving in ways that were inappropriately, almost inhumanly, asocial. As Lawrence demonstrates in his analysis of cargo cults, Papua New Guineans often understood and represented this prior history in a range of changing forms. For Yali and others of his region, this history of social obligation was conveyed through myths, Christian beliefs, and accounts of wartime service.

For instance, some of these stories focused on a mythic brother who, after teaching cargo secrets to Europeans abroad, was prevented by Europeans from returning to instruct his brother remaining at home. Some, on Christian beliefs about the kinship of blacks and whites as descendants of the same original parents. And some, on the wartime actions of Papua New Guineans who jeopardized their own safety by saving Australians from death and capture. All of these stories were told as proof that Australians should recognize them as equals. This history of social obligation, in all its variations, showed that for reasons of fairness, kinship, and/or alliance, Papua New Guineans not only were worthy recipients of such recognition, but also were owed this recognition and the transformed future that would follow.

We are, thus, arguing that Yali and other Papua New Guineans were preoccupied with "cargo" for reasons less obvious than might be initially thought – for reasons more related to their "common sense" than to ours. As anthropologists, to repeat a point we made at the beginning of this chapter, we are suspicious of particular kinds of interpretations that are "too easy" – too readily consonant with a familiar cultural view of how the world works. We feel a disciplinary imperative to probe more deeply. Certainly, as anthropologists, we need to be mindful of ethnographic context – and (for example) to work hard to see things from the perspectives of Papua New Guineans. At the same time, we need to be mindful of the mind-set we bring to any particular ethnographic context: we have to work hard to be clear about our own taken-for-granted assumptions. It is in this latter regard that we fault Diamond's larger argument. His interpretation of Papua New Guinea aside, we think that his broader argument about the course of human history is flawed because it does not question crucial taken-for-granted assumptions. Although we do not doubt that guns, germs, and steel were necessary to make certain historical outcomes possible, including those so upsetting to Yali, we do not have to assume that their possession was sufficient to explain these outcomes. In so assuming, Diamond conflates necessary with sufficient causes.

The perspective that there is an inevitable and inexorable course of human history rests on what seems to us to be an implicit – and unexamined – view of human nature. This is a culturally familiar view of human beings as necessarily seeking to extract maximum advantage over others: give a guy – any guy – half a chance, and he will conquer the world; give a guy a piece of appropriate metal, and he will inevitably fashion a sword to cut you down; give a guy a piece of appropriate metal, and he will inevitably fashion a chain to enslave you within the hold of a ship bound for a New World hell hole. In a way that many in the contemporary West may find seemingly self-evident – once again, in a way that does not question the way the world works – those who hold such a view suggest that people everywhere and at all times, if they had sufficient power, would necessarily use it in seeking to maximize their own advantage through the domination of others. This implicit view of a transhistorical and transcultural human nature is consistent with Diamond's argument, an argument that renders both historical context and cultural perspective as irrelevant – an argument that many contemporary anthropologists challenge.

It is the case that Yali was poor and that, as Diamond makes clear in his discussion of Pizarro's conquest, the people of the New World were brutally conquered by representatives of the Old.[11] It is also the case that those who beat up on other people have the capacity to do so. However, as anthropologist Raymond Kelly indicates in his book *Warless Societies and the Origin of War,* human beings always are capable of a range of behaviors, and they always are capable of engaging with each other and their neighbors in a range of ways.[12] They might make war, but they also might make peace. Whether they choose one or the other is powerfully affected by the particular contexts in which people live: by their historically and culturally located ideas about what is worth striving for and why.

Additionally and importantly, to argue that culture and historical context matter not only challenges a vision of history as an inevitable expression of geographic advantage and human nature, it also introduces the possibility that powerful actors (such as Pizarro), operating as they do within historical and cultural contexts, may appropriately be held accountable for some of history's outcomes. Since it has become clear to anthropologists that cultures contain multiple perspectives about alternatives and how they might be pursued and otherwise dealt with, it follows that human beings – especially the well-positioned ones – have a measure of choice about how to act. Thus, for instance, from American ideas of the worth of the individual, one can generate political perspectives as diverse as libertarianism and welfare statism: the first position holding that no individual should be interfered with or regulated; the other, that no individual should be neglected or deprived. The existence of such alternatives means that those with guns, germs, and steel may, realistically, be held accountable for the choices they make.

We find this stipulation important both in combating the kind of world history represented by *Guns, Germs, and Steel* and in constructing an aspect of Papua New Guinea's more particular one. Pizarro had the capacity and resources to behave with remarkable brutality in the New World. But the mere capacity to behave brutally does not absolve him from having done so. Likewise, Europeans had the resources to treat Yali and other Papua New Guineans with contempt. But that position should not absolve them from having done so. Such considerations, we argue, are important in rethinking – in reevaluating – historical outcomes. (Perhaps the haves may be prompted to do such rethinking by recognizing that the have-nots may already have come to their own conclusions.)

Thus, we must carefully scrutinize taken-for-granted ideas about what people want and why. Although it is difficult to think against the grain of the familiar, we must stretch our imaginations if we want to understand whose perspectives are projected at whose expense – if, to reiterate, we want to replace a history of (apparent) inevitability with one of (potential) accountability.

ON PAPUA NEW GUINEA: COPING WITHIN A POSTCOLONIAL CONTEXT

In *Collapse*, the story of why certain societies have experienced environmental disaster, Diamond shifts to a different kind of history: one that acknowledges not only the possibility, but also the importance, of choice. The subtitle to his book indeed is "how societies *choose* to fail or succeed" (emphasis ours). Moreover, in focusing on choice, such a history does potentially become less inevitable and actors, more accountable. Hence, in describing why it would be unfair to treat native peoples poorly, Diamond writes: "it's based on a moral principle, namely, that it is morally wrong for one people to dispossess, subjugate, or exterminate another people."[13]

Nonetheless, we see continuities between the arguments of both of Diamond's books. In neither does he adequately consider context to think through how goals and choices are historically and culturally shaped and constrained. Indeed, in neither book does he challenge assumptions that echo the perspectives of the powerful: those who control others, those whose choices outweigh – constrain – the choices of others. Thus, in *Guns, Germs, and Steel* he assumes that everyone will inevitably choose to dominate; in *Collapse* he assumes that everyone will have an equal capacity to choose. In effect, whereas in *Guns, Germs, and Steel* no one is held responsible for the course of history, in *Collapse* just about everyone is. And in both histories, it is, we think, the have-nots (the Yali's, so to speak) who end up with the historical raw deal when their lives and circumstances are misread. *Collapse*, in our view, exemplifies a kind of history that, in ignoring context, clouds our understanding of the processes actually affecting the world today – including the serious environmental problems it faces.

Diamond does grant in *Collapse* that "social institutions and cultural values ... affect whether the society solves (or even tries to solve) its [environmental] problems."[14] Yet, he believes that (vile dictatorships, such as that once in power in Haiti, aside) societies are free to make, and, correspondingly, responsible for making environmentally sound choices. This is the case even in the oft-cited "tragedy of the commons" wherein people do not solve an unfolding environmental problem because of selfishness, clashes of interest, or the belief that if each doesn't take a full share, another will. The result is a general depletion of resources, which might precipitate collapse. The obvious solution, from Diamond's perspective, is for people to "trust and communicate with each other" so as to realize that they "share a common future."[15] If they fail to come to this realization, they should be held responsible for having made bad choices. As we have suggested, we do think that those with power should be held responsible for the choices they make. However, we also think it is crucial to probe the contexts in which the choices of some may constrain those of others. Below we present our argument concerning the importance of such a probing with reference to one of the primary cases in *Collapse*, that of Papua New Guinea's silviculture – past and present.

The case begins in the Highland valleys some 7,000 years ago, with archaeological evidence that humans were clearing forests and draining swamps to provide land for their gardens. These agriculturally based populations expanded over the next 5,000 years or so – eventually becoming the largest and densest populations in New Guinea. And, as their numbers grew, a decrease in forest pollen and an increase in nonforest pollen indicate that they continued to clear their forests to make way for crops and to obtain timber and fuel. Then, about 1,200 years ago, a volcanic eruption deposited an enormous amount of ash in the Highlands, enhancing soil fertility and, hence, crop growth. This, in turn, likely stimulated population increase, which put additional pressure on resources. Such changes might have resulted in ecosystemic collapse had the Highlanders not somehow addressed their linked problems of population growth and deforestation.

Their solution, as shown by the pollen record, lay in silviculture, which focused on a particular and most useful tree: cultivation of *Casuarina oligodon*, indeed, proved a boon for expanding – increasingly land-short – populations. Because this tree fixes nitrogen in its root nodules, adds additional nitrogen as well as carbon to the soil through its copious leaf-fall, and is fast growing, it could decrease the fallow period necessary in garden rotations as well as provide fuel and building materials. In addition, the tree could reduce erosion when planted on steep slopes and (for reasons still unknown) diminish the depredations of the taro beetle. Diamond suggests that people "in any village could see the deforestation going on around them, could recognize the lower growth rates of their crops as gardens lost fertility after being initially cleared, and experienced the consequences of timber and fuel scarcity."[16] Concurrently Highlanders – always curious and experimental – must have noticed casuarinas growing by streams, brought them home, planted them, and observed their numerous beneficial effects. Thus, through silviculture – and other means including population control by infanticide, post-partum sexual taboos, contraception, abortion, and warfare – Highlanders were able to avoid "collapse."

For Diamond the adoption of casuarina silviculture was a type of "bottom-up problem-solving" in "ultra-democratic" societies in which decisions were "reached by means of everybody in the village

FIGURE 12.3 Casuarina trees in Papua New Guinea.

sitting down together and talking, and talking, and talking."[17] This Highlands instance becomes important to Diamond as a model for the making of environmental choices.

Before continuing with this model of decision making, we should briefly note that there are aspects of his depiction of Highlands activities that could be challenged or qualified. For instance, it has become obvious, given the work of Paula Brown and George da Buchbinder in their collection of essays *Man and Woman in the New Guinea Highlands* that decisions there were more likely made by men than by "everybody."[18] Moreover, Buchbinder, in her Ph.D. dissertation, "*Maring Microadaptation*," and William Clarke, in his book *Place and People,* have shown that environmental deterioration and poor diet have persisted in the Highlands, at least for some.[19] Finally, it seems likely that the growing of casuarina trees probably did not require much collective consultation and deliberation among Highlanders. Once someone got the idea (at least that cultivated trees could be a convenient source of wood), their propagation would be a relatively straightforward, easily emulated practice – something people could just do without much discussion to meet their own evident needs.

However, these concerns about precontact Highland ecological decision making aside, what about Diamond's basic proposition that this form of bottom-up decision making might be a model of how contemporary societies could make successful environmental choices? In thinking through the present-day relevance of this model, we must consider not just the obvious point that the context of precontact Highlands decision making no longer exists for contemporary Papua New Guineans. We must also recognize that the transformation of this context has been linked to the transformation of our own. All of us are now living in a world shaped significantly by a mutual history (what we have elsewhere called a "twisted history"), one in which haves and have-nots have emerged through mutual – although certainly asymmetrical – engagements.[20]

To think more about the relevance of a model of bottom-up decision making to environmentally consequential choices in a contemporary world of mutually engaging haves and have-nots, let us continue with Papua New Guinea silviculture in its most current manifestation – as the subject of a predatory, foreign-controlled logging industry exporting tropical timber to the haves.

We agree with Diamond's description of Papua New Guinean logging practices. International logging companies, with home offices mainly in Malaysia, lease logging rights on land still owned by local people. They often acquire logging permits through bribes to government officials or through promises to local people of money, roads, schools, and hospitals – promises on which they may make only minimal down payments. At one site we visited in the East Sepik Province near Wewak – and this proved a hardly extreme instance – the logging company had landed a barge at a remote beach (and was prepared to dynamite the reef if necessary to get on shore). From the barge rolled bulldozers that carved a logging road over which trucks and other machinery traveled to extract high-value tropical timber. Clear-cutting the ridges because they were easy to access, loggers left a broad swath littered with discarded low-value trees. Our visit was only several weeks after the company had, with no notice, concluded its operation, winding it all back into the barge, which departed for its next, to use Diamond's apt phrase, "rape-and-run" operation.[21] The adverse consequences were obvious. Animal habitats had been substantially destroyed, and adjacent streams and rivers were already becoming choked through erosion. Moreover, the logging road, which had been presented to local people as a significant infrastructural benefit, was slipping off the hillside. With the next heavy rain, it would become impassable.

And, as often happens, the cash the company did pay local people had appeared enormous to them, but would be soon gone on consumables – on food, beer, bride prices, and rapidly disintegrating motor vehicles (given the state of local roads). Yet many of those Papua New Guineans to whom we spoke looked forward to further logging in their area – albeit by a different company such as the (Malaysian) one associated with the province's most prominent politician (and the nation's current prime minister), Sir Michael Somare. Their enthusiasm for logging operations seemed comparable to that of the Ipili, another group living in the Highlands, for the mining taking place on their land. Indeed, in a paper entitled "Who Is the 'Original Affluent Society'?" Alex Golub, one of the anthropologists who has worked among the Ipili, says that they were happy about the mine on their territory – happy to have "traded their mountain for development."[22] Moreover, in "Deep Holes: Community Responses to Mining in Melanesia," Colin Filer and Martha Macintyre report that local people often continue to welcome mining on their land with eagerness.[23]

How are we to make sense of this? One perspective has it that trading one's mountain for development is an example of a bad choice – one that should be reappraised by those with the courage to do so. Diamond does lament that few Papua New Guineans at both the local and national levels would act like the small-island-dwelling Tikopians who had the "courage to eliminate their ecologically destructive pigs, even though pigs are the sole large domestic animal and a principal status symbol of Melanesian societies."[24] (For the sake of accuracy, Tikopians are not Melanesians, but Polynesians.) Or, to bring the case closer to Papua New Guinea, he laments that few would exhibit the (remarkable) courage of one Aloysius, who, we are told, braved death threats from logging companies to protect the environment.[25]

While we would not applaud such environmentally costly decisions as to trade one's forest or mountain for cash – and while we genuinely admire the likes of Aloysius – we do find the Papua New Guinean desire for money to be spent on consumables understandable in a contemporary context: a context in which worth is now constructed, not only through local, valley-wide references, but through global ones. In other words, we do find such decisions, allowing as they do the have-nots a glory day, much more than simply bad choices. In fact, to think of such decisions as simply bad choices is to obscure the conditions of such choices and, thus, to limit effective responses to them.

Concerning the conditions of choice: We must inquire what it means to hold local Papua New Guineans – again, largely have-nots – responsible for living within their ecological means in a postcolonial, market-driven, global system ostensibly based on the capacity of all to make choices. It is, of course, hard for such people to exercise effective choice in dealing with their own corrupt and powerful politicians, not to mention with voracious and sometimes murderous logging companies. And there is an additional constraint on choice because they live in a world increasingly coerced by the World Trade Organization, the World Bank, and the International Monetary Fund to operate according to ideas of "comparative advantage" – a world in which what Papua New Guineans do have to offer is (the likes of) timber and gold. Furthermore and importantly, such people often recognize that they not only lack real power, but are, as well, seen by the haves as lacking real power – seen as the have-nots. Hence, the world of the haves and have-nots is not just an outcome of a historical process that has allowed some to dominate others (with the aid of guns, germs, and steel); it is a rankling and ongoing circumstance that conditions contemporary and future choices – including seizing the momentarily redeeming possibility of having money to burn. (We have become increasingly aware of the rankling in our latest work tracing the commodity chain that brings "lamb flaps," a cheap cut of fatty sheep meat that white people tend to feed to their pets, from Australian and New Zealand pastures to Papua New Guinean pots. While Papua New Guineans enjoy their flaps – when they can afford them – they are also aware that they are enjoying what many of them call a Western "waste product.")[26]

Concerning why thinking of such momentary apotheoses – such fleeting glory days – as simply bad choices limits effective responses to them: it is interesting that Diamond does not look to Papua New Guineans to be successful in solving their contemporary environmental problems. Nor does he look for restraint from the logging companies operating there. He writes: "Depending on the circumstances, a business really may maximize its profits, at least in the short term, by damaging the environment and hurting people. That is still the case today ... for international logging companies with short-term leases on tropical rain-forest land with corrupt governmental officials and unsophisticated land owners."[27] The hope he does see returns us to a modern variant of the talk, talk, talk of precontact Highlanders – a modern variant of a bottom-up problem-solving that relies on an entity he calls "the public." It should be the public's role, he believes, "to reward businesses for behavior that the public wanted, and to make things difficult for businesses practicing behaviors that the public didn't want."[28] In relationship to logging, we in the first world, as members of the public, should, for instance, refuse to buy wood that has not been certified by the Forest Stewardship Council (FSC), an organization that guarantees that wood comes from companies subscribing to "sound and sustainable forest management."[29] We agree that such a response from members of the public would be commendable if it prevented rapacious logging practices in places such as Papua New Guinea. However, such a response would, in and of itself, leave unaddressed and, indeed, would exacerbate many of the difficult circumstances local Papua New Guineans face. As Paige West points out in her book *Conservation Is Our Government: The Politics of Ecology in Papua New Guinea,* those members of the first world public who are concerned with sustainable forestry in Papua New Guinea tend to value the contribution of diverse, tropical ecosystems to the well-being of the planet and humanity in general. They tend to see Papua New Guineans as adding to the problem they wish to overcome.[30] It is the rainforest that needs protection from Papua New Guineans – and from their willingness to sell their forests and mountains for money. Those members of the first world public who are concerned with advancing the interests – the well-being – of Papua New Guineans in particular tend to offer them charity – the "kindness of strangers" (perhaps in the form of used books, medical supplies, and disaster relief). Either way, for the public to pressure the likes of Home Depot to eschew non-FSC certified woods obviously creates some difficulties for Papua New Guineans: they are, at least often, rendered either blameworthy or needy.

The problem we see in *Collapse* is thus comparable to the one we saw in *Guns, Germs, and Steel.* Both books give the have-nots a historical raw deal because neither probes context sufficiently. Certainly, neither deals in any systematic way with the relationship between the haves and the have-nots. Whereas *Guns, Germs, and Steel* does not encourage the haves to take sufficient responsibility for the creation of the have-nots, *Collapse* does not encourage the haves to take sufficient recognition of the extent to which they benefit from the existence of the have-nots – a benefit centrally manifest in their much greater capacity to choose. For an example close to home, Barbara Ehrenreich's *Nickle and Dimed,* a wonderful account of the lives of the working poor in America, shows clearly how the enhanced choices of haves are reflected in the constrained choices of the have-nots.[31] The latter would include the minimally paid at such stores as Home Depot, whose merchandise includes FSC-certified lumber. Thus, and somewhat perversely, that some of us have the choice of spending more for FSC-certified timber is likely a function of there being have-nots.

There is no doubt that many of the issues concerning environmental degradation are extremely important to address, and Diamond is to be greatly credited for his contribution in bringing them to the world's attention. However, to address effectively both sociohistorical inequalities and environmental degradation, it is necessary to probe, to challenge, to rethink. More specifically, it is necessary to recognize – and to help others recognize – that there is a world system busily at work, and that in this system a market-based ideology is often employed to present political and economic relationships as voluntary and fair – as choices made on an even playing field. This, despite the case that choice is often delimited and the consequences of that fact obscured. To provide an example from our recent research on a Papua New Guinean sugar plantation, it is a world system in which many forces come together to threaten the viability of one of Papua New Guinea's few nonextractive industries, a plantation that provides incomes to 18,000 people. On the one hand, first world countries such as the United States still subsidize their own sugar industries. For example, sugar producers in the United States – politically influential in Louisiana and Florida – are given favorable treatment in the form of USDA price supports, publicly supported cheap irrigation water, and protection from the likes of Cuban sugar. On the other hand, third world countries such as Papua New Guinea are strongly discouraged from subsidizing or otherwise protecting their own sugar industries. For example, Papua New Guinea's government is heavily pressured by the World Bank and the World Trade Organization to eliminate all tariffs on imported sugar. These free-trade policies are strongly supported by such international corporate interests as those of Coca-Cola, which wishes to import cheap sugar for use in the soft drinks it sells to Papua New Guineans.[32]

It is a world system in which, to provide another instance, TIAA/CREF, the pension fund of most American academics, is heavily invested in the Freeport-McMoRan copper and gold mine in Indonesia's West Papua – a mine notorious for its atrocious environmental practices and human-rights violations.[33] It is a world system in which – to refer to Diamond's analysis of the genocide in Rwanda – "the country's ... [failure] to modernize, to introduce more productive crop varieties, to expand its agricultural exports, or to institute family planning"[34] are "choices" clearly related to broader political and economic processes. These processes, ones that Diamond refers to either not at all or only in passing, include a colonial history, contemporary U.S. strictures on its aid going to support effective contraception, and contemporary World Bank pressures for belt-tightening structural adjustments and for growing cash crops such as coffee (for an already glutted world market) rather than subsistence crops. (See Taylor's chapter in this volume for a fuller discussion.)

It is, in other words, a world system in which choosing to act responsibly by refusing to purchase non-FSC-certified timber is laudable, probably necessary, but certainly not sufficient.

Notes

* We are respectively professor of anthropology at Trinity College (F.E.) and professor of anthropology at Amherst College (D.G.). Singly and together, we have written about the confrontations of Melanesian people with various forms of modernity. These include *Yali's Question: Sugar, Culture, and History* (2004). We are now completing a book about the flow of fatty meat from the First World to the developing world, tentatively entitled *Cheap Meat*.

    First arriving when Papua New Guinea (PNG) was a de facto colony of Australia (in the late 1960s, for Fred, and early 1970s, for Deborah), we made many subsequent field trips over the past thirty-five or so years. These field trips led to projects about a range of subjects, many of them focused on change: traditional ritual as well as evangelical Christianity; clan organization as well as class formation; male initiation through skin cutting as well as university graduation through test taking; fish for sago barter markets as well as canned mackerel and rice-purveying trade stores.

We often wondered about the frequent movement of Papua New Guineans from their villages to urban settlements and attempted to understand why they found urban life desirable despite its only marginal feasibility – despite (as we personally observed in squatter settlements) malnutrition, if not chronic hunger.

Our interests eventually led us to write a social history of Ramu Sugar Limited, a sugar plantation that was built as part of PNG's efforts to develop its economy. As we were to discover, RSL is located in a part of PNG where the political leader, Yali, had been active. And Yali's activities not only affected the lives of people we met at RSL, but played a role in Jared Diamond's book, *Guns, Germs, and Steel* (1997). In fact, Diamond frames his book as an answer to "Yali's Question": "Why is that you white people developed so much cargo and brought it to New Guinea, but we black people had little cargo of our own." We became convinced that Diamond's answer to this question was partial, if not wrong. In this chapter, we elaborate and extend some of the reasons we have previously discussed.

1. Diamond 1997, 2005.
2. Diamond 1997: 14.
3. Ibid.: 93.
4. Some of the analysis below is drawn from Errington and Gewertz 2005.
5. Strathern 1992.
6. We draw in the analysis of goods and commodities from Gregory 1982.
7. Lawrence 1964: 1.
8. For more about the Karavaran cargo cult, see Errington 1974.
9. Diamond 1997: 14.
10. For an elaboration of this point, see Thomas 1991: 83–124.
11. Diamond 1997: 67–81.
12. Kelly 2000.
13. Diamond 2005: 10.
14. Ibid.: 15.
15. Ibid.: 429.
16. Ibid.: 285.
17. Ibid.: 284.
18. Brown and Buchbinder 1976.
19. Buchbinder 1973; Clarke 1971.
20. We first used the phrase "twisted history" in Gewertz and Errington 1991.
21. Diamond 2005: 472.
22. Golub 2006: 288.
23. Filer and Macintyre 2006.
24. Diamond 2005: 523–524.
25. Ibid.: 470–471.

26. For more about this, see Gewertz and Errington 2008.
27. Diamond 2005: 483.
28. Ibid.: 285.
29. Ibid.: 274.
30. West 2004; see also Garland 2006.
31. Ehrenreich 2001.
32. For more about this sugar plantation, see Errington and Gewertz 2005.
33. Stuart Kirsch, e-mail communication, 6 April 2007.
34. Diamond 2005: 319.

Bibliography

Brown, P. and G. Buchbinder. 1976. *Man and Woman in the New Guinea Highlands*. Washington, DC: American Anthropological Association.

Buchbinder, G. 1973. "Maring Microadaptation." Ph.D. thesis, Columbia University.

Clarke, W. 1971. *Place and People*. Berkeley: University of California Press.

Diamond, J. 1997. *Guns, Germs, and Steel*. New York: W. W. Norton.

Diamond, J. 2005. *Collapse*. New York: Viking.

Ehrenreich, B. 2001. *Nickel and Dimed*. New York: Henry Holt.

Errington, F. 1974. "Indigenous Ideas of Order, Time and Transition in a New Guinea Cargo Movement." *American Ethnologist* **1**:255–267.

Errington, F. and D. Gewertz. 2005. *Yali's Question: Sugar, Culture, and History*. Chicago: University of Chicago Press.

Filer, C. and M. Macintyre. 2006. "Deep Holes: Community Responses to Mining in Melanesia." *Contemporary Pacific* **18**:215–230.

Gewertz, D. and F. Errington. 1991. *Twisted Histories, Altered Contexts: Representing the Chambri in a World System*. Cambridge: Cambridge University Press.

Gewertz, D. and F. Errington. 2008. "Pacific Island Gastrologies: Following the Flaps." *Journal of the Royal Anthropological Institute* **14**:590–608.

Garland, E. 2006. "State of Nature: Colonial Power, Neoliberal Capital and Wildlife Management in Tanzania." Ph.D. thesis, University of Chicago.

Golub, A. 2006. "Who Is the 'Original Affluent Society'?" *Contemporary Pacific* **18**:265–289.

Gregory, C. 1982. *Gifts and Commodities*. London: Academic.

Kelly, R. 2000. *Warless Societies and the Origin of War*. Ann Arbor: University of Michigan Press.

Lawrence, P. 1964. *Road Belong Cargo*. Oxford: Oxford University Press.

Strathern, M. 1992. "The Decomposition of an Event." *Cultural Anthropology* **7**:244–254.

Thomas, N. 1991. *Entangled Objects: Exchange, Material Culture, and Colonialism in the Pacific*. Cambridge, MA: Harvard University Press.

West, P. 2004. *Conservation Is Our Government: The Politics of Ecology in Papua New Guinea*. Durham, NC: Duke University Press.

PART IV

REFLECTIONS ON SUSTAINABILITY

13

Sustainable Survival

J. R. McNeill*

DEFINITIONS, DURATIONS, AND DISPLACEMENTS

In *Collapse: How Societies Choose to Fail or Succeed,* Jared Diamond attempted to write a hopeful book about environmental and Malthusian calamities. His definition of collapse is as follows:

By collapse, I mean a drastic decrease in human population size and/or political/economic/social complexity, over a considerable area, for an extended time. The phenomenon of collapses is thus an extreme form of several milder types of decline, and it becomes arbitrary to decide how drastic the decline of society must be before it qualifies to be labeled as a collapse.[1]

This is a flexible definition, as judgment calls are required with words such as "drastic," "considerable," and "extended." A reduction in human numbers or in the complexity of human social organization, of an unspecified and arbitrary quantity, constitutes a collapse – provided it happens over a "considerable area" and for an "extended" length of time. The collapse of France in 1940 or that of the Soviet Union in 1991 is not a collapse in this sense, nor is any merely political collapse.[2] The biological and cultural elimination of indigenous Tasmanians in the nineteenth century, which Diamond writes about in *Guns, Germs, and Steel* (1997), is not a collapse either, because Tasmania quickly acquired more population and more social complexity than it ever had had before, albeit of a completely different sort, Anglo-Irish immigrants. The near-total replacement

355

of Algonquin speakers by (mainly) English colonists in southern New England ca. 1620–1720 probably would not qualify as a collapse, because human numbers and social complexity increased in that area within a century – assuming that an "extended" period of time is longer than a century. The extinction of several peoples and cultures in the long, slow expansion of China since the Han Dynasty would not qualify. Indeed, over the past 5,000 years or so, thousands of peoples and cultures have been obliterated, either biologically driven to extinction by violence and epidemics, or culturally and biologically assimilated into a larger and more powerful polity and culture. None of these were collapses, by Diamond's definition, because they did not involve drastic declines in numbers or complexity; they involved drastic cultural and political changes.

On the other hand, episodes in which cultures survived but people moved would qualify, provided either numbers or complexity declined drastically. So when the Mongols overran Baghdad in 1258, destroyed its irrigation and agricultural systems, and killed many people, driving others to emigrate, this was a collapse in Mesopotamia. Numbers and complexity did decline, although whether drastically or not is a matter of definition. The Mongols did their best to reshape the landscape to suit their preferences for steppes and ponies rather than fields and grain. When climatic patterns shifted so that people migrated away from a region and did not return for several centuries, as happened from time to time on the southern edges of the Sahara, or perhaps happened in fifteenth-century Greenland (according to Joel Berglund's interpretation), this too would be a collapse. Diamond, of course, is free to define his terms as he sees fit. I merely wish to point out some of the implications of choosing population and complexity as one's criteria, especially how arbitrary and difficult the required distinctions and judgments can be.

The Greenland Norse are a fine case for illustrating one further conundrum in the concept of collapse: duration. The Norse lasted in Greenland for roughly 450 years before failing and collapsing. This is longer than any of the "modern societies" that Diamond uses to illustrate the notion of societies choosing to fail or succeed in the modern world. Diamond's friends and neighbors in Montana (Chapter 1) are part of a society that has existed in Montana for perhaps 140 years at the most.

The other "modern societies" appear in chapters 10–13 of *Collapse*. First is Rwanda, presented as a Malthusian tragedy. The Rwandan state is not quite forty years old. Its colonial predecessor was formed roughly 100 years ago, counting both Belgian and German rule. The cohabitation of Hutu and Tutsi (in any case not firm categories) dates back perhaps 300 years, although no one can know for sure.

Next come Haiti and the Dominican Republic, the former deemed a failure and the latter a success. Together they make up the island of Hispaniola. Haiti has existed as such since 1804; the slave plantation society that preceded the independent republic took shape in the early and mid-eighteenth century. French political control, very loose at first, dates to 1697, and the first French settlers (pirates) took root around 1659. The Dominican Republic has existed as a (usually) independent state since the 1880s. Before that it was sometimes controlled by Haiti, sometimes by Spain, sometimes by France, and often by nobody at all. Diamond counts it as a modern success because its environmental problems are much less severe than those of Haiti; its environmental legislation dates back to 1901. But most of what qualifies the Dominican Republic as a success is legislation undertaken since the rise to power of Joaquín Balaguer in 1966. Balaguer enacted several conservation and forest protection laws, but whether his legacy in this respect will endure is much too early to tell.

China, Diamond's next modern case, is reckoned a failure in the making (chapter 12). Of course, China as a geopolitical entity in one form or another extends back about 3,700 years. But this is not the China with which Diamond is concerned. His story of environmental degradation and ineffective regulation is mainly from the 1980s and 1990s, with brief mentions of trends extending as far back as the 1950s. Only in passing, in connection with China's political unity, which is attributed to geographical reasons as in *Guns, Germs, and Steel* (chapter 20), does Diamond mention the country's longevity. Diamond is quite right to emphasize the environmental catastrophes of contemporary China. But can a quarter century of recent experience, divorced from the preceding thirty-five centuries, serve as the basis for conclusions about a society choosing to fail or succeed?

Last among the modern societies comes Australia (chapter 13), which is a tale of environmental woe leavened by some rays of hope for the future. Most of the story concerns recent decades, although

Diamond does reach back to the foundation of colonial Australia in 1788 and mentions the prior millennia of aboriginal occupation. But the heart of his story is at most 220 years long. He ends by saying that "[m]any readers of this book are young enough, and will live long enough, to see the outcome."[3] Thus Australia's status, as a society that chooses to fail or succeed, will reach its conclusion within 300 years of its start.

The timelines adopted in these chapters about modern societies vary in length, but none of them is as long as the time the Greenland Norse lasted. Had their society been examined on its 300th birthday (around 1280 C.E.), to take the outer limit of the Australian example, it would have been found intact and presumably therefore judged a success. Simply put, none of the cases of modern societies judged successes endured as long as the Greenland Norse, judged a failure.

Diamond also judges Tokugawa Japan a success story, because the Tokugawa Shogunate (1603–1867) found a way out of an "environmental and population crisis" after the mid-seventeenth century, the chief symptom of which was deforestation and a timber shortage. The Tokugawa managed to impose forest conservation. Ordinary Japanese found ways to lower birth rates and achieve population stability (via delayed marriage, abortion, and infanticide). And both state and society took the opportunity presented by a militarily weak population in Hokkaido, the Ainu, to expand their resource base considerably through conquest, expropriation, and near-genocide. The Japanese success came at a considerable price, to the Ainu, to young Japanese unable to marry, and to still younger Japanese who fell victim to infanticide. Indeed, if seen from the point of view of the Ainu, the whole episode might appear something other than a success. But, in any case, the success lasted only from the mid-seventeenth century to the late nineteenth century, about 200 years. By the 1890s Japanese society seemed to its leaders desperately short of resources, in need of new lands for its growing population, which put it on a course of imperial expansion into Korea, Taiwan, and soon Manchuria, China, and the Pacific. That led it into a disastrous war with the United States, during which the home islands of Japan were stripped of timber and almost all other resources in an all-out war effort. If seen from the vantage point of 1850, at roughly age 200, the Japanese experiment may seem a success (except to the Ainu), but if seen from 1900 or 1945, at age 250 or 300, it would not. Thus, in the case of Tokugawa Japan, as well as of those modern societies having (as Diamond sees it) chosen success, they have a ways to go before they will have endured as long as the Greenland Norse. The chronological vantage point, as well as the cultural one, makes all the difference in whether or not a given case may plausibly be represented as a success or failure.

I dwell on Diamond's definition and its implications because I think this explains part of the disagreements between him and some of the anthropologists writing in this volume. If a people, a language, and a culture survive, as among the Maya, the Norse, or the Anasazi, is this a collapse? To Diamond it is, because either human numbers or societal complexity declined drastically. To others it is not, because something central survived, and the people involved made a prudent adjustment to changing circumstances, in effect migrating to avoid the worst. For Diamond numbers and complexity are all; for others, especially anthropologists perhaps, cultural survival in such forms as language, religion, or foodways trumps Diamond's chosen variables. And I dwell on Diamond's timelines because for historians – at least this one – time and duration matter. Diamond's flexible timelines, by which some societies are judged successes and others failures, seem unsatisfying, in the same way that a footrace would seem pointless if different runners were awarded prizes at different distances along the course.

The Tokugawa case illustrates one further issue that clouds the notion of societies choosing to succeed or fail, that of the geographic displacement of environmental problems. Tokugawa Japan had the military power to help itself to the land and resources of Hokkaido.[4] Such frontier expansion is routine in world history and has helped many a society postpone reckoning with unsustainable ecological arrangements. It has also led to the marginalization or extirpation of thousands of peoples, cultures, and languages, many of which vanished into the mists of history, leaving no trace.

The displacement of environmental problems, of course, continues to this day, although usually in different forms. Diamond overlooks this in his quest for stories of success. At the end of the book, where Diamond includes a section specifically designed to inspire hope that humankind can choose sustainable survival, he offers the contemporary Netherlands as a society that has recognized its common interests because most of the country lies below sea level, and without cooperation among all ranks of society, the Dutch could not keep the sea at bay. Thus the Dutch minimize clashes of self-interest, cooperate politically, and have unusually high levels of environmental awareness. But the Dutch case must be understood in the context of the Dutch position in the wider world. The Dutch do not have to fight bitterly self-interested battles over land and resource use within the Netherlands because they are near the top among countries in per capita timber imports, most of it tropical hardwood from Southeast Asia. The Dutch can raise 13 million pigs and 100 million chickens in a small country by importing fodder, notably soya from Brazil. They can lead the world in the exports of cocoa products because they lead the world in cocoa imports, mainly from West Africa. Thus the Dutch do not suffer the deforestation and other environmental ills associated with the production of timber, soya, and cocoa – these are felt in Indonesia, Brazilian Amazonia, and West Africa.[5]

Judgments of success or failure, survival or collapse, are often more difficult to make than we might wish. Perspective and context matter. Can a society that survived a century be counted a success whereas one that lasted 450 years count as a failure? Can one that responds to environmental stresses by migration be judged a failure whereas one that responds by conquering neighboring lands, or enlisting resources from other continents, be judged a success?

Simplicity has its virtues, especially when trying to stir an audience to action. In *Collapse*, Diamond appears motivated by a deep concern for the environmental state of the earth. I find this prudent, appropriate, and laudable. Many environmentalists face choices between what is most intellectually rigorous (which usually involves admitting to legions of uncertainties) and what is most likely to rally people to action (which usually involves skating over uncertainties). Different authors will make different choices when confronted with this dilemma, and careful readers will be interested in them. Diamond many times acknowledges uncertainties, especially with archeological evidence. But he nevertheless has chosen to rally readers as best he can even when it leads him into intellectual difficulties.

SUSTAINED SURVIVAL

Diamond's laudable concern for the avoidance of collapse, for sustained survival, raises the question of what that might mean. To Diamond it apparently means the maintenance of levels of population and social complexity in a given place. But there are other ways to see it. One, which is of particular interest to many anthropologists, is the maintenance of a culture. In this view survival consists of the maintenance of whatever the preferred markers of a culture may be, such as language or religion. Whether a million people share this culture or only a few thousand is less important, so long as the culture survives. Whether those sharing this culture live in cities, with complex social hierarchies, or in villages, is less important. Whether those sharing this culture live where their ancestors did, or have migrated elsewhere, is less important. What is important is that the culture survives. This is also often important to bearers of a given culture, especially if they are migrants, not just to anthropologists. The indefinite survival of Chinese culture means a lot to many Chinese, whether they live in China or in California. As chapters in this book emphasize, the same is true for some cultural (and biological) descendants of the ancient Maya and Anasazi today.

Another way to look at sustained survival is through a political lens. For some people what matters most is the survival of a specific polity, rather than a culture, or certain levels of population and complexity. This is especially true in times and places where people identify, via nationalism or some other mechanism, with their state. One thousand or 3,000 years ago almost no one aside from royalty cared about the survival of a given state. But royalty and their allies went to great lengths to try to perpetuate their own states, not least by doing all within their power to encourage ethnic, tribal, nationalist, or religious identification of the population with the state. More recently broader segments of societies have identified with their states and often have made great efforts, through voluntary military service, for example, to advance the interests of their states.

The boundary between cultural survival and political survival is, of course, often permeable. Sometimes it seems that the best way to perpetuate one's preferred culture is through the perpetuation of the state that most embodies it. Many Jews presumably feel this way about Israel, Finns about Finland, and Vietnamese about Vietnam.

In the end, of course, no culture or polity lasts forever. Survival is provisional. None of the states in existence 1,500 years ago exist today. Only with the most flexible of definitions could one say that any of the cultures in existence 1,500 years ago exist today. But for most people, this does not matter. Political or cultural survival in the short term is often worth, for most people, considerable sacrifice, even if, when seen in the long run, it is all in vain.

A third way to look at sustained survival is through an ecological lens. Diamond does this himself, emphasizing environmental factors in his analyses of various collapses. But are there any enduring ecological success stories, any cases of sustainable survival that lasted longer than the Tokugawa regime or the Dominican Republic? The answer, I think, is that there are, but they are not many, and none of them are of much use as a direct example to help us resolve the problems of today.

The most enduring ecologically sustainable societies in human history have been those that did not practice agriculture. For the great majority of the human time on earth, our ancestors foraged for food and other materials they needed. They had local environmental impacts, often unhelpful from the point of view of ensuring their own survival. But because they were few in number and the earth large, they could always walk somewhere else and find more of what they needed. The key was mobility and sparse population. It was probably a demanding life in several respects, but it was ecologically sustainable.

With the emergence of agriculture, which happened several times in several places but for the first time probably around 11,000 years ago, sustainability became a potential problem. All farming is a struggle against the depletion of soil nutrients. Crops absorb nutrients; these are eaten by people or animals; then they spend shorter or longer periods of time in human or animal bodies, before returning to the soil. If these nutrients in one manner or another return to farmers' fields, then a nutrient cycle can last indefinitely. If they do not, then those fields gradually lose nutrients and over time produce less and less food – unless some intervention such as fertilizer counteracts nutrient loss. In most farming systems, some nutrients were returned to farmers' fields as manure, "night soil," or ashes, but some was lost. In systems of shifting agriculture, where farmers raise a crop for a few years and then abandon plots for a decade or more, nutrient loss is checked. But in farming systems that supplied cities, many more nutrients were lost, because they were exported, as food, to distant places and never returned as night soil or manure. In places where soils were deep and rich, the nutrient problem might safely be ignored for centuries. But not forever.

In a few important situations, farming societies overcame this fundamental nutrient problem. Perhaps the most durable, the gold-medal winner for ecological sustainability, was Egypt. For 7,500 years people have been farming in Egypt. Until 1971 they did so in an ecologically sustainable manner. The source of Egypt's success and ecological continuity is not that elites chose to succeed in recognition of their broader interests. Rather, it is, or was, the silt carried by the Nile flood. Every year, except in the worst droughts, the Nile flooded and deposited on its banks and throughout its delta a nutrient-rich silt from the volcanic highlands of Ethiopia. In effect, Ethiopia's erosion subsidized Egyptian farmers, allowing them to sidestep problems of nutrient loss and sustainability. The annual flood also carried plenty of organic matter from the wetlands of southern Sudan (the Sudd), further enriching the silt that settled on Egyptian fields. This happy situation came to an end only when the Aswan High Dam was completed in 1971, and the Nile's silt began to accumulate in the dam's reservoir instead of spreading over farmers' fields. Nowadays Egypt is one of the world's greatest importers of artificial fertilizers – and of food – and is as far from ecological sustainability as a society can be.

Between the introduction of farming in Egypt and 1971 tremendous changes took place. One political regime followed another. The culture of the earliest Egyptians disappeared under layers of Pharaonic Egyptian, Greek, Roman, Byzantine, and Arab cultures, marbled with numerous other influences. Through it all, farmers won their daily bread from the banks of the Nile by combining seed and silt with the sweat of their brows.

Southern China and Medieval Europe also developed more or less sustainable agricultural systems as long as 1,000 to 1,500 years ago. In China it involved an interlocking system of paddy rice, fish ponds, and mulberry trees (for silkworm cultivation), which kept nutrients cycling within an almost closed system. Medieval European agriculture, if not supporting cities, was also very nearly sustainable, as livestock browsed in woodlands and in "outfields" and brought their manure to "infields," thereby constantly topping up the nutrient supply. As one sixteenth-century Polish nobleman put it, "manure is worth more than a man with a doctorate."[6]

Like Egypt, these systems were ecologically successful over long periods of time, far longer than any of the successes offered by Diamond. States, rulers, and – in Europe if not in China – cultures came and went, but these farming systems endured. As in Egypt, their success did not result from wise leadership, but instead from centuries of trial and error and some favorable circumstances. This means that they cannot serve Diamond's hortatory purposes. He could scarcely offer them as hopeful examples for humankind today, even if they proved far more durable than, say, the ecological systems of the twentieth-century Dominican Republic or Tokugawa Japan.

Sustained survival can come in different forms, depending on what one most values. If it is ecological sustainability one prizes above other forms of continuity, then Egypt before 1971 deserves the highest marks. But it is well to remember Egypt was a unique case, the gift of the Nile.

THE CONTEMPORARY WORLD AND SURVIVAL

The environmental problems that bedevil the world today are, for better or for worse, vastly different from those that beset Tokugawa Japan or Easter Island. They are different in scale, as Diamond recognizes. They do not, for the most part, readily lend themselves to solution via wise decisions by enlightened leaders, because they are all complicated, and many of them derive in large measure from the energy system that has gradually come to prevail over the past 200 years: a fossil fuel energy system.

Fossil fuels function as an Ethiopian highlands for the modern world: they represent an enormous subsidy, not from a distant place, but from a distant time, the carboniferous era. They make it possible for 6.5 billion people to eat. Fossil fuels are the fertilizer of modern agriculture. They pump up groundwater and power tractors. They serve as the feedstocks for pesticides and herbicides. They make nitrogenous fertilizers practical. And they power the vehicles that move crops to kitchens. They sustain us.

But they also make us unsustainable. First and most obviously, they exist in limited supply. Predictions of the imminent exhaustion of coal and oil go back at least to the 1860s and have always proved wrong so far. But they are not fundamentally wrong. A time will come when all that is left is too difficult to extract at reasonable cost. For oil this might be ten years off or 100. For coal it will be longer. But it will come – unless we abandon fossil fuels first. Second, fossil fuels make our global society unsustainable because of climate change. Roughly three-quarters of the carbon dioxide emitted into the atmosphere derives from the combustion of fossil fuels (most of the rest comes from the burning of biomass and destruction of forests). This has been warming the earth's atmosphere for at least the last few decades, and probably the last 150 years. If we were to use fossil fuels for the next 200 years as we have used them for the last 200, we are likely to raise temperature and sea level (through thermal expansion) to levels not experienced on earth at any time in the human career, indeed, not in many millions of years.

Our ways are radically unsustainable. Diamond is right to be concerned by that. He is right to prefer hope to despair, and admirable in that he has used his fame to draw attention to issues of sustainability. But he is, as often as not, wrong in his judgments about successes and failures among societies of the past.

Notes

*   I was born and raised in Chicago and remain passionately devoted to the professional sports teams of the Windy City. I earned, or at any rate was awarded, a B.A. from Swarthmore College and a Ph.D. from Duke University. Since 1985 I have cheerfully served two masters, as a faculty member of the School of Foreign Service and History Department at Georgetown University. From 2003 until 2006 I held the Cinco Hermanos Chair in Environmental and International Affairs, until my appointment as University Professor.

I teach world history, environmental history, and international history at Georgetown and write books and direct Ph.D. students, mainly in environmental history. I live an agreeably harried existence with my triathlete wife and our four exuberant children.

My environmental history books include *The Mountains of the Mediterranean World* (1992); *Something New under the Sun: An Environmental History of the 20th-Century World* (2000); and *Epidemics and Geopolitics in the Greater Caribbean, 1600–1920* (2009).

I conduct research mainly in archives and libraries, as is true of most historians, although for the Mediterranean book I visited dozens of mountain villages. Unlike most historians, I have no real geographic specialization, and prefer – like Jared Diamond – to hunt for large patterns in the human past.

1. Diamond 2005: 3.
2. On p. 509, however, Diamond does use the word "collapse" in reference to the end of the Soviet Union.
3. Diamond 2005: 416.
4. Walker 2001.
5. Netherlands data are from the Netherlands Committee for the IUCN (World Conservation Union): http://www.nciucn.nl.
6. Gostomski 1588.

Bibliography

Diamond, Jared. 1997. *Guns, Germs, and Steel.* New York: W. W. Norton.

Diamond, Jared. 2005. *Collapse: How Societies Choose to Fail or Succeed.* New York: Viking.

Gostomski, Anzelm. 1588 [1951]. *Gospodarstwo.* Wroclaw: Wydawn Zakladu Narodowego im. Ossoli'nskich.

Walker, Brett. 2001. T*he Conquest of Ainu Lands: Ecology and Culture in Japanese Expansion, 1590–1800.* Berkeley: University of California Press.

Index

BIOGRAPHY

Lila Devi (pronounced *lee-lah day-vee*) founded Spirit-in-Nature Essences in 1977. Her love of the outdoors and an innate belief that Nature cradles an untold wealth of healing secrets inspired her, under the guidance of J. Donald Walters, to develop this line of essences. Lila's first experience in taking a Bach Flower Remedy proved so extraordinary that she began studying the few essence books available at that time. Self-training metamorphosed into experience and led to the preparation of the first batch of Spirit-in-Nature Essences.

Also a playwright, actress, poet, songwriter, and musician, Lila teaches Spirit-in-Nature Essences in the United States and abroad, combining ongoing experience, insight, humor, and music in her classes and radio and television appearances.

The Essential Flower Essence Handbook is now published in English, Italian, Japanese, Czech, and English in India. Her second book, *Flower Essences for Animals*, is available in English and Japanese. *Bradley Banana and The Jolly Good Pirate* is published in English, Italian, and German.

Lila graduated with honors from the University of Michigan with a Bachelor of Arts degree in English and psychology and a secondary education teaching certificate. Before developing Spirit-in-Nature Essences, she taught high school English and ran a group home for developmentally disabled women. *Bradley Banana and the Jolly Good Pirate* is the first of 20 hardcover children's picture books, each personifying a flower essence's uplifting quality in a thrilling adventure.

Lila lives in the Ananda communities. Her lifelong commitment is to help others find their own perfect well-being.

Timeless Books of Truth

When you're seeking a book on practical spiritual living, you want to know that it is based on an authentic tradition of timeless teachings and resonates with integrity.

This is the goal of Crystal Clarity Publishers: to offer you books of practical wisdom filled with true spiritual principles that have not only been tested through the ages but also through personal experience.

Started in 1968, Crystal Clarity is the publishing house of Ananda, a spiritual community dedicated to meditation and living by true values, (as shared by Paramhansa Yogananda, and his direct disciple Swami Kriyananda, the founder of Ananda.) The members of our staff and each of our authors live by these principles. Our work touches thousands around the world whose lives have been enriched by these universal teachings.

We publish only books that combine creative thinking, universal principles, and a timeless message. Crystal Clarity books will open doors to help you discover more fulfillment and joy by living and acting from the center of peace within you.